D0603152

A
Language-Thinking
Approach to Reading

DIAGNOSIS AND TEACHING

A Language-Thinking Approach to Reading

DIAGNOSIS AND TEACHING

Lenore H. Ringler

New York University

Carol K. Weber

York College of The City University of New York

Harcourt Brace Jovanovich, Publishers

San Diego   New York   Chicago   Washington, D.C.   Atlanta
London   Sydney   Toronto

About the cover photograph: Using written language—both
writing and reading—can be as natural for children as playing
is. They can experience the written language of others through
books, in advertising, and on television. They can even
experience *their own*—in this case by writing on the sidewalk
and reading what they themselves have written. These two
young learners express their thoughts in chalk. Although the
rain will wash away their words, this experience, among others,
helps them develop reading and writing competence.
(Photograph by Hildegard Adler, Madison, Wisconsin.)

T he time of a book is not the limited time of its writing, it is the limitless time of reading and memory. The meaning of books is in front of them and not behind them; it is in us: a book is not fixed meaning lasting forever, a revelation we have to suffer; it is a reserve of forms waiting for their future meanings. It is the "imminence of a revelation that is not yet produced" and that every one of us has to produce for himself.

Gerard Genette, 1964

Preface

Teachers in the classroom are continually making important decisions about the way children learn and how they as teachers can facilitate this learning process. We wrote this book with the conviction that educators must understand the relation of language and thinking to reading in order to be effective teachers of reading. How learners think about their world, apply information they have gained from experience, and use language all influence their interactions with reading materials.

Our purpose in writing this book was to provide prospective and practicing teachers with the information they need to be decision makers when applying a language-thinking approach to the teaching of reading. This text may be used with both undergraduate and graduate students in college and university courses. It is most appropriate for courses that focus on diagnosis and teaching of reading within classroom situations.

The first chapter offers a key to understanding how different children function in their classrooms and discusses possible contributors to reading problems. Background knowledge about the developing learner, reading theory, and language and concept development as it relates to reading instruction is found in Chapters 2 and 3. Teachers use this base of information as they create a teaching-learning environment, keeping language and thinking central to the learning process. We describe this teaching-learning environment in Chapter 4.

Following these introductory chapters, we devote the major part of the textbook to specific approaches to the teaching of reading. The approach to teaching reading developed in Chapters 5 through 13 is one in which reading is viewed as communication. In our approach, reading is considered an active process in which children interact with print to construct messages and interact with other learners and adults as they react to what they have read. Within this framework children read real materials for real purposes. The focus is on having children read about things that are meaningful to them while they are learning to read. In this context children's own writings, stories, and informational materials are the primary resources.

Diagnostic techniques are presented with the teaching chapters because we consider diagnosis and instruction inseparable. We contend that when diagnostic information indicates that children may need to learn a specific reading skill that will facilitate their ability to read real materials, the teacher will want to instruct students in specific strategies separately from customary integrated methods. When this has to occur, the teacher will always make children aware of the purpose for the skill teaching and let them know that this proficiency in skills, while facilitative of reading, is not reading.

The next section provides a brief overview of special learners—the gifted learner, the learning disabled, the bilingual learner, and the bidialectal learner—all of whom are commonly found in regular classrooms. In Chapters 14 and 15 we describe some of the characteristics of these learners and implications for classroom instruction within the framework of a language-thinking approach.

The final section of the book elaborates on the interrelatedness of reading and writing and the importance of the home in helping children develop as readers. Although we discuss these ideas throughout the book, we highlight them in Chapters 16 and 17 to reinforce their importance.

This text provides an approach to diagnosing reading problems and a framework for teaching that can be used with materials available in any classroom. Basal readers, literature series, library books, newspapers, magazines, and content area textbooks as well as students' writings are the suggested teaching materials. These materials provide the content for thinking about and reacting to what is read. Teaching children to examine their thinking, to question others, and to evaluate critically what others say and write is the foundation of all learning and is used as a paradigm for the teaching of reading throughout this text.

Writing this book has been a special experience. Our own collaboration has been an extremely close one, and we have been fortunate to have had opportunities to interact with a number of people. We wish to express our appreciation, first, to our friend and colleague Dr. Ruth S. Meyers, Council on Interracial Books for Children, who read the entire manuscript and provided us with expert advice whenever we called on her. Her perceptive criticisms and creative suggestions were invaluable. We also thank Professor M. Trika Smith-Burke, New York University, who read portions of the book and gave us helpful criticisms, and Professor Angela M. Jaggar, New York University, who graciously shared her professional library with us.

We gratefully acknowledge the cooperation of the administrators, teachers, and children of Community School Districts 4 and 27 in New York City. Their enthusiastic involvement in this project enabled us to integrate theory and practice. Feedback from the classroom guided us as we modified and refined our ideas. Our graduate and undergraduate students at New York University and York College, CUNY, also played a special role in the development of this book. We field-tested many of our ideas during class sessions, and some of our students in turn applied our work with school-age children, while others used the knowledge to further their own reading growth.

We wish to acknowledge those colleagues who reviewed the manuscript and gave us valuable criticism for revision: Richard L. Allington, SUNY at Albany; Irene J. Athey, Rutgers University; David Bloome, University of Michigan; Judy S. Richardson, Virginia Commonwealth University; and Harry Singer, University of California, Riverside. A special thank-you to Irene Athey for reading both the initial draft and the final manuscript.

Without the expertise of our editors, William Wisneski, who began the project with us and continued to support our work, and Albert Richards and Gene Carter-Lettau, who are responsible for completing the project, this book would never have come to fruition.

Finally, but most importantly, we thank our husbands, Jerry and Stan, for their confidence in our endeavors and for their patience and understanding as we worked on this book.

Lenore H. Ringler
Carol K. Weber

Contents

A Final Word   410

A FRAMEWORK FOR TEACHING

CHAPTER 1
An Introduction

CHAPTER 2
The Developing Learner and the Reading Process

CHAPTER 3
Concept and Language Development

CHAPTER 4
The Teaching-Learning Environment

1

An Introduction

Case Studies
CASE 1—LAURIE, AGE 8
CASE 2—STEVEN, AGE 7
CASE 3—CINDY, AGE 10
CASE 4—ROBERT, AGE 7½
CASE 5—MAYRA, AGE 9

Contributors to Reading Problems
EDUCATIONAL FACTORS
EMOTIONAL FACTORS
PHYSICAL FACTORS

Teaching All Children

Summary

D o you recall how you learned to read? While this question seems simple, it is often difficult to answer. For most of us reading has become such an automatic process that we are unaware of the steps we took along the way to develop this proficiency. And yet we know that reading is a complex process and that learning to read was a complex task which many different factors influenced.

For many young children learning to read occurs with such ease that it seems a simple task; a few even accomplish this task prior to entering school. For some children learning to read requires a more concentrated effort; and for a small number, learning to read is a difficult task complicated by many problems. All of these children pose challenges for the classroom teacher—their strengths, their abilities, their individualities. The way the teacher deals with these challenges forms the basis for the classroom reading program.

No wonder Seymour Sarason (1971), one of the leading mental health consultants active in the schools, emphasizes the extreme complexity of the teacher's role:

> . . . a classroom of 25 children or so is a lot of children for any one person to handle. In addition, the children vary enormously in terms of academic achievement, intellectual level, behavior, interest, likeability and maturity. . . . The strong feeling that teachers have about the complexity of their task stems from the awareness that they are expected to bring their children (if not all, most) to a certain academic level by a time criterion. (p. 152)

To succeed at this difficult task, the teacher needs to create a classroom environment that recognizes the individuality of children and to implement a program geared to their specific backgrounds and needs. An important step in meeting the diverse needs of children is getting to know them. The classroom teacher, with whom children spend most of their structured learning time, has the best opportunity to observe how they function in learning situations. All children, from those who are proficient readers to those who have reading problems, are the concern of the classroom teacher.

This chapter describes some of the children teachers find in their classrooms. In the case studies, you will see children with diverse abilities and needs, any one of whom could be in your class. A section on factors that may contribute to reading problems follows the case studies. This section highlights factors that may interfere with children's reading progress. In observing children as they interact with reading materials, teachers must keep in mind the many different influences that can affect children's reading performances.

Case Studies
The case studies describe five children specifically selected because they illustrate the wide range of children who may confront the classroom teacher. The cases describe both children who are functioning successfully

in the classroom and children whose problems require the coordinated efforts of classroom teachers and other professionals. Each case study highlights different factors that may influence children's reading development. The factors illustrate only a small sample of the many potential influences on children's performances. Also, while reading the cases, remember that factors may be present in many different combinations, which educators can expect given the complexities of the process of learning to read.

CASE 1—LAURIE, AGE 8

Laurie, an 8-year-old girl, is an alert and eager student. She has many friends both in and out of school, participates in class and school-wide activities, and can often be seen reading during her free time. Laurie entered school at the kindergarten level and was already reading picture books and simple story books. The parents confirm that Laurie spoke individual words at 8 months and was putting two words together by her first birthday. By age 2 she was speaking in simple sentences and was a demanding conversationalist. She asked many questions and insisted on getting responses during her preschool years. Her parents report that Laurie's curiosity and enthusiasm for learning could be annoying at times; however, they generally responded to her questions with patience and detail appropriate to her level of understanding.

Laurie was read to from age 1, had many simple books to look at, beginning with cloth books and books that appealed to the senses. She continued to enjoy books, including nursery rhymes, familiar stories, and books about things in her environment. She attended a story program at the local library for preschoolers and at age 3½ begin to attend a half-day nursery school program. During kindergarten Laurie's ability to read simple stories increased, and she was an active participant in informal and formal language activities. Her reading program during first and second grade was a combination of a meaning-based basal reader approach and extensive independent reading of a variety of materials.

At present, Laurie is reading materials at levels well beyond those expected of an average third grader. She is comfortable reading narratives from the fifth-grade basal reader and chooses materials of comparable difficulty for her supplementary reading. She enjoys writing and is able to react in writing to what she has read. Her oral language fluency is consistent with her other language skills, and Laurie participates with confidence in classroom discussions. Laurie has a wide range of reading interests that include mysteries, realistic fiction, and poetry. A special interest of Laurie's is meteorology. She has built a simple weather station from a kit, tracks the daily weather, and reads widely on this topic. Her interest has led her to read the weather map and related information in the daily newspapers.

Laurie is typical of those children who function effectively in the classroom and who spark the interest of other children. There are many children like Laurie who enjoy reading and can independently read materials at or above their grade level. Of course, even within this group of children individual differences in abilities and functioning exist. For the most part, however, these children continue to develop as readers with minimal difficulty.

CASE 2—STEVEN, AGE 7

Steven is a 7-year-old in the second grade who is having difficulty learning to read. Upon school entry in kindergarten Steven knew the letters of the alphabet and some sight words and enjoyed listening to stories. Toward the end of kindergarten and into the first grade, his teachers noticed that his overall curiosity had lessened, that his self-initiated verbal interactions were less frequent than they had been, and that he withdrew from the group at unpredictable times. While Steven appeared to enjoy playing with other children, he would often lose his temper—yelling, crying, or fighting with minimal provocation.

At a conference with the second-grade teacher, his mother reported that she and her husband had had serious marital problems for several years that escalated into violent episodes followed by separation. Steven witnessed a final family argument in which his father physically attacked his mother and then abruptly left the home. Legal separation and divorce proceedings followed. At this point Steven was just beginning first grade. Contact with his father during first grade was infrequent and erratic. For financial reasons Steven and his mother had to move from their own home to his grandparents' home in a different neighborhood. As a result, Steven had to change schools in the middle of first grade.

Steven's second-grade teacher was concerned about his lack of progress in learning to read and his behavior in class. The teacher referred him for a complete psychoeducational evaluation. The results of this evaluation indicated that Steven was of normal intelligence, that he had a language experiential background appropriate for his age, but that he had suffered serious trauma as a result of family problems. In the process of resolving these problems, the adults in Steven's life had significantly altered his world. He missed his home, his neighborhood, his friends, and, most importantly, his father. Channeling his energies into learning activities with so many problems and worries on his mind was difficult for Steven.

The recommendation to the classroom teacher was that Steven continue with regular classroom activities while the family received psychological counseling. The evaluator also recommended that his teacher and therapist speak periodically about Steven so they could share ideas about helping him to manage his behavior. After an initial discussion, his teacher and therapist have determined that Steven's classroom behavior and ability to learn require that he receive special encouragement to participate, and praise for attending to learning activities. He should not receive undue penalties when his feelings and thoughts about his family interfere with his functioning. Since testing has indicated that Steven is particularly interested in astronauts and space programs, the counselor has suggested that his teacher use this topic to try to spark an interest in reading.

Steven represents those children who have the potential to function effectively in the regular classroom but have emotional problems that require professional help.

CASE 3—CINDY, AGE 10

Cindy, who is just completing fourth grade, lives in a stable family environment. Her parents support her school efforts and believe they should not question decisions made by the school or teacher. Therefore, they are unaware that Cindy is developing a problem. Her fourth-grade teacher has noticed that Cindy is beginning to have difficulties in reading comprehension. Her school history indicates that she began to read in first grade. Her reading instruction placed a heavy emphasis on phonics. Cindy continued to make adequate progress in reading in the second and third grades. However, her reading achievement test score at the end of third grade showed that she was falling behind the norm for the grade.

At present Cindy's decoding skills continue to be good, and she is able to read regular classroom materials aloud with practically no pronunciation errors. Cindy volunteers to answer questions when she feels confident about answers. However, she often becomes distracted by objects and children in the room during silent reading activities. Her teacher does not understand why Cindy has so much difficulty during silent reading, and the teacher has requested that the reading specialist carry out an in-depth analysis of Cindy's reading.

The reading specialist has indicated that Cindy is at least of normal intelligence, can talk freely about familiar topics, has good oral reading skills, and can respond to questions that require her to locate specific details clearly stated in the text. Upon questioning, Cindy has told the reading specialist she enjoys reading to the class and feels good doing this. She also has reported that even though she likes to read she gets nervous, often loses her place, and mixes up ideas when she has to read silently without any help from the teacher. The reading specialist has noted that much of what Cindy has reported is accurate. Cindy has difficulty in giving the gist of a story, in seeing relations among ideas that are not directly stated, and in organizing her thoughts. These problems indicate that Cindy has trouble in comprehending what she reads although she can pronounce most of the words. Also, the reading specialist has noted that Cindy resists reading silently and asks to read everything aloud. He recommends that Cindy receive supplementary reading services while continuing to function in a regular classroom reading program that emphasizes comprehension.

Cindy is typical of those children who can manage to get by in reading activities in the early grades. This is possible because they have good decoding skills and generally have not had to read silently and participate in activities that foster thinking. Cindy, similar to some other children her age, has not developed the ability to function effectively with stories of increasing complexity and content area materials such as science and social studies texts that are part of the middle-grade curriculum. Cindy was not able to develop proficiency on her own, and her educational program did not emphasize reading as thinking. As a result, Cindy, who is about to enter fifth grade, has reading problems that appear to be primarily the result of her school experiences.

CASE 4—ROBERT, AGE 7½

Robert is in the second grade. His teacher considers him to be a pleasant, verbal child of normal ability. His overall school achievement is below what would be expected of him, and his school records indicate that he has had problems in reading since school entry. Robert has a history of excessive school absence and suffers from asthma and several allergies. His teachers have noted that when in school he often appears tired, pale, and suffers from water eyes and runny nose. Although his attendance has improved since first grade, he is still absent more frequently than his peers.

In school he is reserved, hesitant when called upon, and in general seems to lack self-confidence. He is never quite in tune with the class and the ongoing activities. Peers do not seek him out for group activities or at playtime, and he often sits at the fringe of a group activity or alone.

Robert is in the slow reading group and does try to keep up when in class. When he misses reading experiences due to absence, he approaches the reading task more hesitantly than usual upon his return. In general he does not seek information or ask questions without prompting from the teacher.

As a first step the school guidance counselor and the teacher set up a conference with Robert's parents. The goals for this conference were to set up ongoing communication with the home, to find out the extent of his physical problems, and to determine the extent of family support for Robert's school activities. His parents reported that they have always been concerned about his fragile health. They have tended to keep him at home whenever he appeared particularly tired or uncomfortable or even when he complained about not feeling well. At the conference the parents said that they would try to see that Robert comes to school more regularly and that they were willing to help him with his school work when he is absent. They also mentioned that Robert has one or two friends that he plays with in his neighborhood and that when he is not feeling well and stays home, he spends a lot of time watching television, drawing, and playing with his electric train set.

Following this conference, the guidance counselor and teacher plan to maintain communication with the home so that Robert's parents will feel comfortable in sending him to school even on those days when his allergies bother him. The teacher plans to use his ability in art and his interest in electric trains in an effort to encourage his participation in class. The teacher chooses group activities that require Robert's drawing skills and guides him to reading materials that relate to his interest in electric trains.

Robert is typical of those children who develop physical problems at a young age; family reactions, the child's reaction, and peer and teacher reactions complicate these problems and as a result affect school behavior and learning.

CASE 5—MAYRA, AGE 9

Mayra came to the United States from South America at age 6. She lives with her parents and younger siblings who all speak Spanish at home although both her parents are learning English through adult education courses. Her parents maintain the customs of their country and firmly believe that Mayra should understand her cultural heritage. Thus, Mayra has a rich experiential background but lacks many concepts specific to the English-speaking community in which she now lives. Mayra enjoys reading simple stories in both Spanish and English at home.

When Mayra began school in the middle of first grade, she was unable to speak English. Although she quickly learned to communicate in school using her second language, she still speaks primarily Spanish with family and friends. Mayra has always been an attentive and hardworking student and learned the sound-symbol correspondences of the English language in first and second grades. Her school followed a curriculum in which she had to read and write English before she was fluent in listening and speaking English. There was no provision for Mayra to have classroom learning experiences in her native language.

Now that Mayra is in the third grade, her teacher observes that her major reading problem is in the area of comprehension. There are inconsistencies in her performance. When she reads about familiar events and characters, Mayra is able to remember the story accurately and relate the behaviors of the characters to her own experiences. A problem for Mayra is that stories and materials selected for the class often include concepts and ideas not a part of her cultural background, and she has not yet shared these experiences in her adopted country. As a result she sometimes misinterprets the ideas and responds to questions with what appears to be illogical thinking.

Even in oral language activities Mayra is not always familiar with concepts being discussed. In both oral and written language activities she sometimes misses important information because she is unfamiliar with the structure of the language and its use in nonliteral ways.

The teacher confers with the supervisor responsible for language arts instruction and, based on their discussion, recognizes that Mayra's difficulties in understanding some stories may be due to a lack of familiarity with some concepts and related language. The teacher decides that learning more about Mayra's culture and interests as the basis for selecting stories within her experiential background is important. At the same time, the teacher, recognizing that Mayra may be at a disadvantage when confronted with reading materials that contain unfamiliar concepts and language, plans to assess Mayra's knowledge of important concepts prior to any group reading experience. As necessary, the teacher will plan special activities for Mayra to give her the necessary background to participate in the group.

Although Mayra's teacher is able to provide for her needs in the regular classroom setting, other bilingual children have more difficulties in reading than Mayra and need supplementary reading instruction.

Mayra is typical of those bilingual children who manage to learn English and progress adequately within the regular classroom. She is not considered fully bilingual because she is not yet able to think and speak as well in English as in Spanish. Learning for children like Mayra could have been easier if, upon school entry, the schools had offered learning experiences in the native language, and these experiences and language had provided the basis for beginning reading experiences. Further, if her early school program had emphasized comprehension in both oral language and reading, Mayra's difficulties due to cultural differences would have been obvious sooner. Mayra's parents request that for these reasons her younger siblings receive supplementary instruction in a bilingual or English as a second language program.

As these case studies show, many reasons contribute to a child's succeeding or having problems with reading. Rarely can a teacher isolate any one factor as the sole contributor to the child's functioning. Generally a number of factors work together to support or interfere with reading development. Because reading is such a complex act and because efficient reading requires the smooth interaction of so many factors, the developing reader may be vulnerable. A child can be at risk at many points along the way to becoming a proficient reader. Recognizing those factors that may contribute to the presence of a reading problem enables the teacher to work toward eliminating the contributing factors or toward adapting the educational program to maximize learning. At times the teacher must use resource persons both within and outside the school to plan and implement an educational program for a child with learning problems.

Contributors to Reading Problems

In any discussion of factors that may contribute to reading problems, remembering that factors rarely operate in isolation but operate in conjunction with each other is important. Therefore, when reading the following section, keep in mind that typically more than one factor contributes to a reading problem and frequently the interaction of several factors makes reading a difficult task for some children. And, of course, remember, too, that the presence of any of these factors does not necessarily mean that a reading problem will exist. This section will give an overview of educational, emotional, and physical factors that may contribute to reading problems.

EDUCATIONAL FACTORS

The educational experience of the child is an important but frequently overlooked factor that may contribute to reading problems. School experiences from the first day a child enters school to the first time the teacher notices a reading problem may have had an impact on the development of the problem. As a child progresses through school, administrators and teachers make any number of decisions about the child's "learning to read." Some of these decisions may be inappropriate for an individual child. These decisions depend on the philosophy and approach to teaching reading that influence the specific materials selected for reading, the amount of time allotted for reading and language-related activities, and the classroom climate as it relates to language communication. Decisions about the philosophy and approach to teaching reading should be based on sound theory. Research over the years has indicated that reading should be an active, thinking process with the emphasis on gaining information. Children bring all of their experiences, knowledge, and feelings to each reading situation. Learning to read and expanding reading proficiency should take place in a provocative, problem-solving environment using "real" reading materials. As children read stories, newspapers, magazines, and textbooks, they become aware that reading is a form of communication between a writer and a reader and that reading is thinking about and reacting to what they read.

Decisions about the allocation of time for reading and other related activities (speaking, listening, and writing) are crucial ones. That a relationship exists between time devoted to language activities and reading achievement is well-documented. The general classroom climate for the most part reflects what the teacher knows and feels about children and how they learn. A room that contains stimulating areas of general interest with abundant language-related materials and that gives children the freedom to explore the environment and express ideas encourages communication among children. This language-rich environment encourages all forms of communication: listening, speaking, reading, and writing. Reading is purposeful, exciting, and valued. Teachers as well as children read for both enjoyment and information. In contrast, an environment that inhibits the flow of ideas, is devoid of experiential materials and books, and isolates reading from other language and learning activities can only hinder the language and reading development of children.

When teachers make decisions about instruction, the question of individual differences among children arises. Teachers who view reading as encompassing many language activities and who use varied materials have built-in flexibility that allows them to adjust their teaching program to accommodate individual differences among children. Differences important to reading fall within the areas of language development, experiential background, intellectual ability, and interests. Children naturally differ in these areas, and teachers must adapt instruction to meet the learner's needs.

All children bring language to the learning situation. However, variations exist in the amount of language knowledge children have and in their ability to apply their knowledge during reading and related activities. Of particular concern are children often referred to as those having diverse language and experiential backgrounds. These children bring to the learning situation language and cultural experiences that may differ from the majority of children and/or the teacher.

A teacher who is accepting and knowedgeable about the different language backgrounds and cultural experiences of the children in the school's community can plan instruction that takes advantage of this background. At the same time, the teacher expands the child's experiences to meet the school's expectations that include the use of standard English for listening, speaking, reading, and writing.

Recognizing the range of intellectual abilities among the children in a classroom is also an important prerequisite to adapting instruction. Teachers must not use this knowledge to set limits on a child's performance, for intellectual ability alone does not determine the reading performance of any child. However, this information can be particularly useful when working with children who appear to learn at a rate slower than the norm for the class. In such cases, reading instruction, although not necessarily different, will adjust to a pace that is comfortable for these children. Also, there may be children in the class who perform at grade level yet show the potential to perform at a higher level. These children, too, need an adapted program to facilitate reading growth consistent with their intellectual ability.

Finally, teachers cannot overlook children's experiences and how they relate to reading. These early experiences are motivational, and when children pursue their interests, they lead to increased knowledge about a topic that is important in understanding what children read. If teachers do not give children choices in what they read and habitually overlook their strong interests, children may not sustain their efforts and attention in the reading task. In reading programs that include a balance of teacher-selected and student-selected reading materials and activities, children are more likely to feel that their interests and knowledge are important, to persevere at those tasks that may not be particularly motivating to them, and in the long run to become "readers."

EMOTIONAL FACTORS

Emotional problems often become apparent during the early years of learning to read. Reading, a complex and demanding activity, is one of the first major tasks of schooling. Learning to read requires motivation, effort, and sustained attention. Children bring to the reading situation feelings and thoughts about school, growing up, and conforming to the demands of family and society. Some of these feelings and thoughts may interfere with their ability to focus on the reading task.

A home environment with serious problems about the basic necessities of life—health, employment, housing, food—may produce tension, anxiety, or insecurity in the child. Family discord between parents or sibling relations or disturbing treatment of the child may also arouse such feelings. Feelings and concerns about family life are difficult for children to put aside and, therefore, are potentially negative influences on school behavior, interfering with children's ability to interact positively in learning situations.

Peers can also influence children's attitudes and behaviors. Peers' views become increasingly influential when strong support for learning is lacking at home. Children whose peers consider learning and reading as negative societal values must have a strong sense of themselves to overcome peer pressure. Unfortunately, some children who, due to any number of personal factors, conform to negative group attitudes toward learning may develop problems in reading.

Problem behaviors can also arise as a result of learning experiences. Difficulties in learning to read or negative experiences with teachers and peers during reading activities may lead to emotional problems associated with reading. The type and extent of any difficulty depends on the individual child. For example, if a child's pace in learning to read is slower than that of the majority in the class, the way in which the teacher adjusts instruction to meet the child's needs can help or hinder the child's development as a reader. In some cases, mishandling of the reading situation can lead to embarrassment, undue frustration, and the eventual development of emotional difficulties around reading and related school tasks. Even a child who is keeping up with the class can react negatively to inappropriate actions or attitudes by the teacher or other children. Sarcastic comments about a child's response to questions, discussions about his or her reading materials, or about fluency in oral reading may cause unnecessary anxiety and may even inhibit a child's future participation.

In addition to family, peer, and school factors, constitutional factors may also influence learning behaviors. Genetic, neurological, and biochemical factors or combinations of these can influence behavior. Within the developing child separating constitutional from environmental factors is not possible. The interaction of the two factors influences the way a child develops and behaves.

Symptoms of emotional problems are often apparent during reading activities. Some children may openly refuse to participate or need frequent prodding to remain involved. They may distract others by showing off or acting aggressively by teasing, hitting, having tantrums, or destroying materials. Other children may be withdrawn or timid. They may appear preoccupied and disinterested in activities. Some children may have difficulty interacting with other children or adults. Other behaviors include excessive nervousness, restlessness, hypersensitivity, or sadness. Also, noticing whether children finish tasks on their own or resist when tasks are difficult is important.

In observing a child's behavior, the teacher may have difficulty in determining if underlying emotional problems contributed to learning problems or if problems in learning precipitated problem behaviors. The important questions for teachers to keep in mind are, does the observed behavior occur frequently and does it interfere with learning? If the answers are "yes," the teacher should refer such children to specialized psychological staff for evaluation.

PHYSICAL FACTORS

The physical condition of the child may contribute to the development of a reading problem. Hearing and visual factors, general health factors, and neurological factors that may interfere with learning to read need consideration.

Hearing and Vision Problems

During regular classroom activities, so much information is available that the child in listening or looking must attend selectively and maintain this attention to make sense of the information. Difficulties in maintaining attention may lead to imperfect intake of this information, resulting in poor performance on school tasks. Problems in maintaining attention may vary. For example, some children can focus on relevant information but are distracted easily by competing sounds and images. Other children can maintain attention in the face of simultaneous stimuli but have difficulty discerning relevant from irrelevant information. Still other children have problems shifting attention from one type of stimuli to another or from one task to another.

When attention is focused, hearing and visual acuity are necessary to hear or see the incoming information clearly. In most cases, auditory and visual problems can be corrected or compensated so that they are not major learning handicaps. However, considerable individual variations exist in the functioning of children with auditory and/or visual problems. Severe problems require the combined efforts of the classroom teacher and specialists to plan and carry out instruction.

Hearing problems. Problems in hearing are related to impairment of the outer and middle ear or impairment to the inner ear and auditory nerve. Impairment of either the outer or middle ear may result in a conductive hearing loss that means the person has decreased ability to hear both high- and low-pitched tones. In conductive losses, sound is less clear due to the decreased ability to hear sounds across all frequency ranges, but sound is not distorted. Generally, most conductive losses are the result of temporary conditions that, if neglected, can result in permanent damage to the hearing system. These conditions may occur as the result of accumulated, hard earwax, the presence of a foreign object in the ear canal, the accumulation of fluid in the middle ear cavity, or an infection in the middle ear or surrounding structures. As listening and speaking are at the base of reading experiences, obviously children who have to strain to hear are at a disadvantage.

Problems in the inner ear or auditory nerve result in a sensorineural hearing loss from damage to the sensitive nerve receptors that transmit incoming sounds to the brain. These problems are usually the result of birth defects or childhood diseases. When diseases are the cause, the damage may be either temporary or permanent. The area and extent of nerve damage determine the type and severity of the hearing impairment. Sensorineural damage results in selective hearing loss where the individual may not hear only certain sounds (high or low). Damage to high frequency receptors is the most common type of sensorineural hearing loss and results in the inability to perceive the majority of consonants—such as *f, p, s,* and *t*—even when pronounced loudly. Damage to lower frequency receptors can result in the inability to perceive vowels, semivowels, and other consonants—such as *m, g, b,* and *h*. Thus, sensorineural losses involve both the loudness of sounds and the understanding or discrimination of speech and other signals. At the extreme, severe nerve damage results in little or no hearing of most sounds since limited conduction of sound to the brain occurs. For children who cannot hear specific sounds, parts of words are distorted, which results in problems in language comprehension.

Mixed hearing impairments involving both the conductive system and the sensorineural system also occur, and hearing problems can affect either one or both ears. For the classroom teacher, recognizing the problems of children with extreme hearing loss is easy. Children with mild to moderate hearing interferences are the ones who often go undiagnosed.

In many cases of hearing problems, hearing aids can help to amplify sound and thus reduce some of the strain in listening. The child with a conductive hearing loss is likely to benefit more from a hearing aid than the child with a sensorineural hearing loss because hearing aids increase loudness of sounds but do not correct built-in distortions of sounds due to nerve damage. Hearing aids, by their very nature as mechanical instruments, are limited in that they do not always reproduce sounds accurately. Also, they amplify all sounds unselectively, which may be a distraction for some children. Therefore, the teacher should remember that although hearing aids can be of considerable value, they do not restore hearing to normal.

Vision problems. Children need clear vision and should be comfortable when reading. Common interferences with vision include defects in the physical structure of one or both eyes and/or defects that affect the coordination of movements of both of their eyes. Three main types of structural defects occur in which light rays or visual images do not focus properly on the retina of the eye, falling short or long of their mark. Farsightedness, or hyperopia, is the most common problem among school-age children. When the distance from the front to the back of the eye is too short, the visual image falls behind the retina. This leads to difficulties in seeing objects up close as when reading a book. In contrast, nearsightedness, or myopia, results in blurred vision for distant objects. When the distance from the front to the back of the eye is too long, the visual image falls in front of the retina rather than on it. Children with this problem will have difficulty seeing writing on the chalkboard, while their ability to see written materials held at arm's length is usually normal. Astigmatism results in distortion or blurring of visual images when focusing on objects at near points or far points. It tends to occur when there is unevenness in the curve of the front part of the eye (the lens). As a result, the eye cannot place visual images uniformly at the same point as it receives them. This visual problem can lead to blurred or distorted vision when reading or difficulty in keeping one's place in reading. Glasses or contact lenses can correct structural errors resulting from the inability to see objects clearly at varying distances. However, corrective lenses may not necessarily result in normal vision.

Common nonstructural vision problems concern difficulties with binocular vision. Binocular vision involves the coordinated functioning of both eyes. It successfully occurs when separate images of the same object in the two eyes are fused into a single clear object. This process depends on the smooth coordinated functioning of the muscles of the eye. When the eye muscles do not coordinate, several difficulties may occur. When the eyes attempt to focus on an object, the tendency may be for one or both eyes to turn inward (esophoria), turn outward (exophoria), or move upward (hyperphoria). Since the child must use extra muscular effort to compensate for these weaknesses, the child may experience fatigue and discomfort that interferes with reading. If compensation is not successful and the reader sees blurred or double images or has problems with depth perception, reading can be frustrating and uncomfortable. When extreme interference with the coordination of the eyes occurs, an actual lack of alignment of one or both eyes (strabismus) may be present. Sometimes when this condition is not corrected, the person may not use or may suppress the vision in one eye, usually in an attempt to avoid the discomforts of uncoordinated processing.

The classroom teacher can best observe symptoms of hearing or visual problems and create an environment that will aid learners with such problems to function efficiently and effectively. Teachers should remember that different learner behaviors may indicate similar problems or that similar behaviors may indicate different problems. For example, two learners with a similar type of hearing problem may behave quite differently. One learner may frequently interrupt teachers and peers with both related and nonrelated comments, often to the annoyance of the group, while another learner may withdraw from classroom interaction by gazing out the window, attending to visual stimuli in the room, or appearing to be asleep. Although the teacher's job is to recognize that an auditory or visual problem may exist, the teacher's responsibility is not to diagnose the type or extent of the problem. When a teacher becomes aware of behaviors that may be indicative of auditory or visual problems or a child reports problems in one of these areas, the teacher makes a referral for full evaluation through the appropriate school channel and follows up the referral to be sure that proper action takes place. In the interim, the teacher's responsibility is to create a supportive classroom environment and plan for learning activities that avoid undue stress on the learner. Based on the information from the full evaluation, the teacher is in a better position to understand the learner's needs and to plan the most facilitating instructional program.

Health Problems
The child who is in poor general health, suffers from malnutrition, or has a chronic illness frequently is unable to pay appropriate attention in the learning situation. Poor general health may cause a child to become fa-

tigued easily during the school day and make concentrating on tasks that involve reading difficult. Malnutrition may also influence concentration as the child may be unduly fatigued both physically and mentally. Chronic illness generally results in excessive absence from school. A loss of instruction at crucial times, particularly in the early grades when learning to read is such an important part of the school day, may result in a frustrating learning experience when the child is in school. For those children who receive special help either at home or in school to compensate for their frequent or long absences, learning to read is generally not a problem. Some children, however, never seem to catch up, and reading for them becomes a difficult and frustrating task.

Neurological Factors

Interferences in normal brain functioning can contribute to reading problems. Neurological problems can be present at birth or can arise at any point during childhood. Some interferences are manifested in obvious physical or cognitive defects. Others are more subtle, evidenced primarily by interferences with language and reading activities. Neurological problems present at birth can result from congenital factors or difficulties during the perinatal and postnatal periods. At any point in childhood, brain injury can result from disease or accident. Sometimes children with no history of disease or brain injury show an irregular pattern of brain development with some functions developing as expected and others being delayed.

The teacher would be likely to refer a child for neurological evaluation if in addition to reading problems the child exhibited symptoms such as extreme distractibility and difficulty in paying attention, general physical restlessness, problems with gross or fine motor coordination, persistent perceptual and directional confusions, and difficulties in understanding spoken language and expressing ideas in oral and written form.

In summary, many children who have obvious disabilities do learn to read. However, disabling factors working at cross purposes can inhibit a child's learning ability.

Teaching All Children

Providing a reading program to meet the needs of all children involves many decisions on the part of the teacher. Knowledge of the educational, emotional, and physical factors just described is important for the teacher responsible for making decisions about children with reading problems. As one or more of these factors may contribute to the reading problems of some children, the teacher needs to be able to differentiate between the possible contributors and to take the appropriate steps to help alleviate the problem. The more information the teacher has about contributors and about the children in the class, the more likely the teacher is to make decisions that will foster the reading growth of each child.

As teachers learn more about their children, they will be able to resolve some situations by using classroom management techniques; they will need to refer other problems to specialists. In some cases a specialist's recommendation for intervention such as providing eyeglasses or hearing aids coupled with the appropriate physical management in the classroom can quickly resolve a problem. Still other situations may require ongoing supportive services from educational, medical, or psychological specialists coordinated with the activities of the classroom teacher. Teachers may need to adjust the environment, teaching techniques, and materials to deal with whatever problems are interfering with reading development.

In all of these situations, the teacher makes decisions about the reading program within the framework that reading is a language-thinking process. Although there are individual differences among children, the basic concepts of developing reading programs are the same for every child. Children need to understand that reading is part of the communication process and that looking for meaning in print is similar to sharing messages through listening and speaking, familiar activities to all children. From the teacher's perspective the individual child's background of experience and language form the base of the reading program. Language—thinking and communicating orally and with print—are at the heart of this program. No matter what adaptations are made for individual children, teachers maintain the language-thinking approach. This approach is appropriate for all learners. Teachers can incorporate whatever provisions are necessary to facilitate learners' participation and growth as readers without distorting the integrity of the language-thinking paradigm. Any adjustments in methodology and materials can conform with the language-thinking approach to reading.

Summary
This chapter introduces the teacher to the many types of children found in classrooms and presents several case studies. For those children who may have reading problems, the chapter discusses factors that may contribute to their problems including educational, emotional, and physical factors. The chapter concludes with a discussion of the need for a language-thinking approach to teaching reading for all children.

2

The Developing Learner and the Reading Process

T he classroom teacher, as a decision-maker, must be able to integrate knowledge about children, the reading process, and the classroom environment. The first component of teacher decision-making is knowing the child as a changing, growing organism. Many psychologists, despite their theoretical differences, view the child as moving through a series of progressive stages of development in which differentiation becomes more and more refined, flexibility increases, and knowledge accumulates. The child moves from simple to more complex levels of concept development and thinking and expands social-emotional functioning. Viewed from this perspective, the teacher must be familiar with important scholarly work in the fields of cognitive and affective development.

The second component in teacher decision-making is knowledge of the reading process and how various aspects of the process interact with one another and with the development of the child. The reading process is presently being examined by linguists, psycholinguists, and cognitive psychologists, among others. Although theorists have not yet reached a consensus as to "how we read," information is now available for educators to begin to translate theory into practice. This bridging of the gap between research and practice will expand the knowledge base of the classroom teacher. To use this knowledge flexibly, the teacher must be familiar with various viewpoints of the reading process.

The final component of teacher decision-making is the classroom environment. This environment includes teacher knowledge and ability to stimulate reading/language interactions, to select and implement appropriate teaching-learning strategies, to structure a print-rich classroom using materials prepared by the students and teacher as well as commercial materials. That is, the teacher strongly influences the classroom environment. The teacher plans and implements the reading/language program using knowledge of child development and the reading process. To facilitate the establishment of an effective reading/language environment, this chapter presents background information in the areas of child development and the reading process. Chapter Three will relate these areas to language development, and Chapter Four will discuss the teaching-learning environment.

Learner Development

The development of the mature reader depends on an interaction between the learner and the reading process, and, therefore, considering those cognitive and affective aspects of child development that interact with reading is important. Children organize their world through cognitive development; they use language and reasoning to make sense of their world. In their affective development children also learn to make sense of their world; they form feelings and beliefs about themselves and their world. Conceptualizing cognition and affect this way allows one to consider all behavior as an attempt to make sense of the world and relations with it—in order to "master the world" in ways which will accomplish the individual's goals. Perception, memory, concept development, language, attitudes, and feelings all contribute to the individual's attempts to construct meaning from experiences. Reading, too, becomes an important tool for coping with incoming information since the written symbol is such an integral part of the world around us. A developmental focus highlights that ways of responding and coping vary with age, development, and experience, incorporating both affective and cognitive factors. Since cognitive and affective development are intertwined and cannot be separated in real-life situations, it is through the ongoing interplay of these factors that children make sense of their world in changing ways.

Children bring to early life experiences unique and individual ways of responding. They have their own peculiar combinations of sensitivities and their own levels of readiness to discharge tensions and to achieve satisfaction. Children have their own rates of maturing, and even an individual child will have different rates for different functions (Cameron, 1963). These individual differences not only influence how an infant reacts to adults, but also how adults react to the infant. As the child grows, personal-social relationships expand from interactions within the family unit to include relationships with peers and significant adults in the environment. Experts accept that a basic need exists to deal competently with one's environment, which presupposes a basic need to organize the environment and learn about it. However, the fulfillment of these basic needs depends on experiences that the child has with significant people in the environment. These experiences help shape the child's personality and influence how the child will react in learning situations. The knowledge base of the child comes first from early experiences within the family and then expands with later experiences in the broader environment. The result of this personal-social growth and the store of accumulated knowledge contributes to how children feel about themselves and others and how they think about their world. This accumulation of feelings and knowledge directly influences children's perceptions of their school environment and their ability to perform in learning situations.

This performance involves adjusting to the school environment and formalized learning situations. As Cameron (1963) notes, the major stresses of school adjustment

> . . . arise from the daily separation from family, from the necessity for adapting to the peer culture and the school system, and from the increasing demands made upon the child, coming from every direction, that he master new skills, exert more and more emotional control, acquire more and more knowledge, and enter into a number of new and often conflicting social roles. . . . Life between the ages of five or six and twelve or thirteen demands a great deal. (pp. 83–84)

Children's adjustments to these stresses directly influence all aspects of school functioning. As Athey (1976) emphasizes, "Intellectual variables involved in reading do not operate in isolation but are modified by the individual's attitudinal and personality characteristics" (p. 352).

COGNITIVE FACTORS

Although cognitive and affective factors develop simultaneously and continuously influence each other throughout learner development, theorists have tended to study these factors separately.

Jean Piaget and Jerome Bruner most clearly exemplify those psychologists who have described stages of cognitive development based on their extensive observation and experimental work with children. Although they may differ in their views of the specific processes and stages that occur, they both suggest that every child passes through stages of cognitive development in the same order, although at varying rates. That is, emphasis is on the progression as it relates to the cognitive processes of learner development and not on the age of the learner. One child at a certain age may reach a particular stage of cognitive development, whereas another child of the same age may be either at a higher level or lower level of cognitive functioning. Looking at development as these theorists hypothesize helps in conceptualizing the child as a growing, changing organism.

Piagetian Theory

Piaget (1952) views the acquisition of knowledge as a gradual developmental process in which learners actively experience and organize their environment. According to Piaget, people have a biological tendency to organize and adapt their experiences in relation to their current store of information. When learners interact with their environment, they use their accumulated store of prior experiences to organize the new information, and they modify their behavior to meet increasing demands from the environment. This accumulated store of prior experiences is known as a person's "cognitive structure," made up of schemata, and defined

> . . . as coherent systems of mental operations, which allow the thinking person to arrive at concepts, to solve problems and come to conclusions (either in logic or about the real world surrounding him) without the person himself being necessarily aware of the operations he performs. (Sinclair, 1975, pp. 223–24)

In Piagetian terms, this is the process of adaptation that involves both assimilation and accommodation. Assimilation involves using structures already stored to deal with new information in the environment; accommodation involves modifying these structures so that the new information can be incorporated into the existing cognitive structures. As a result of the process of adaptation (assimilation and accommodation), new structures are continually being developed that enable the individual to make further sense of the environment. In other words, learning occurs when there is sufficient, but not excessive, conflict between new and old information. At this point structures need modification. Assimilation and accommodation are complementary processes that occur in every act. Once these processes have occurred, the individual's store of knowledge and, therefore, be-havior have been reorganized to take account of the new information. That is, learning has taken place, and the learner has achieved a new level of equilibrium.

Piaget views development as movement through four main stages using the above processes. This movement results in changes in what the learner is capable of understanding and the depth of understanding. The stages, which are described below in Piaget's own words (Piaget, 1964), illustrate the progressive nature of cognitive development:

The first is a sensory-motor, pre-verbal stage, lasting approximately the first 18 months of life. During this stage is developed the practical knowledge which constitutes the substructure of later representational knowledge. An example is the construction of the schema of the permanent object. For an infant, during the first months, an object has no permanence. When it disappears from the perceptual field it no longer exists. No attempt is made to find it again. Later, the infant will try to find it, and he will find it by localizing it spatially. Consequently, along with the construction of the permanent object there comes the construction of practical, or sensory-motor, space. There is similarly the construction of temporal succession, and of elementary sensory-motor causality. In other words, there is a series of structures which are indispensable for the structures of later representational thought.

In a second stage, we have pre-operational representation—the beginnings of language, of the symbolic function, and, therefore, of thought, or representation. But at the level of representational thought, there must now be a reconstruction of all that was developed on the sensory-motor level. That is, the sensory-motor actions are not immediately translated into operations. In fact, during all this second period of pre-operational representations, there are as yet no operations as I defined this term a moment ago. Specifically, there is as yet no conservation which is the psychological criterion of the presence of reversible operations. For example, if we pour liquid from one glass to another of a different shape, the pre-operational child will think there is more in one than in the other. In the absence of operational reversibility, there is no conservation of quantity.

In a third stage, the first operations appear, but I call these concrete operations because they operate on objects, and not yet on verbally expressed hypotheses. For example, there are the operations of classification, ordering, the construction of the idea of number, spatial and temporal operations, and all the fundamental operations of elementary logic of classes and relations, of elementary mathematics, of elementary geometry and even of elementary physics.

Finally, in the fourth stage, these operations are surpassed as the child reaches the level of what I call formal or hypothetic-deductive operations; that is, he can now reason on hypotheses, and not only on objects. He constructs new operations, operations of propositional logic, and not simply the operations of classes, relations, and numbers. He attains new structures which are on the one hand combinatorial, corresponding to what mathematicians call lattices; on the other hand, more complicated group structures. At the level of concrete operations, the operations apply within an immediate neighborhood: for instance, classification by successive inclusions. At the level of the combinatorial, however, the groups are much more mobile. (pp. 9–10)

Later, Piaget (1972) elaborated on the fourth stage, that of formal operations. He suggests that all individuals do not necessarily reach the same level of formal operations in all areas; their aptitudes and profession may in part determine the types of formal operations that they reach as well as broader aspects of socialization.

Bruner's Theory

Bruner, like Piaget, was interested in the ways in which people develop, how they interact with the environment, and how they represent their experiences. Bruner developed his ideas through ongoing controlled experiments and descriptive studies using relatively large numbers of subjects, in contrast to Piaget whose work was based predominantly on observation of a small number of children. Similar to Piaget, Bruner traces the developing child as growing in abilities to represent experiences by moving from reliance on concepts that are physically organized, to growth in the use of different perceptual sensitivities and various forms of imagery, and on to the use of different forms of symbolization, particularly language.

According to Bruner (1964, 1973), cognitive development may best be viewed as the successive development of three forms of representation. He describes three ways of interacting with the environment or knowing about something. People know through doing, through sensing, and through symbolic means, one of the most important of which is language.

Doing something or acting on something means knowing through physical contact or manipulation. Bruner calls this form of interaction "enactive representation." He emphasizes that this mode of thinking, although developed first, continues throughout life. Some things can always be better represented through physical means than through imagery or language. Bruner explains enactive representation as follows:

By enactive representation I mean a mode of representing past events through appropriate motor response. We cannot, for example, give an adequate description of familiar sidewalks or floors over which we habitually walk, nor do we have much of an image of what they are like. Yet we get about them without tripping or even looking much. Such segments of our environment—bicycle riding, tying knots, aspects of driving—get represented in our muscles, so to speak. (1964, p. 2)

Bruner used the terms "iconic representation" and "symbolic representation" for the two modes of thinking that emerge after enactive representation. In Bruner's words,

Iconic representation summarizes events by the selective organization of percepts and of images, by the spatial, temporal, and qualitative structures of the perceptual field and their transformed images. Images stand for perceptual events in the close but conventionally selective way that a picture stands for the object pictured. Finally, a symbol system represents things by design features that include remoteness and arbitrariness. A word neither points directly to its referent here and now, nor does it resemble it as a picture. The lexeme *Philadelphia* looks no more like the city so designated than does a nonsense syllable. (1964, p. 2)

According to Bruner, although action, image, and language as forms of representation emerge in that order, one representational system does not replace a subsequent system. Instead, the systems supplement each other, with each becoming interrelated and continuing throughout life.

Application to Educational Practice
Both Piaget and Bruner emphasize the active nature of learning, the influence of the environment, and the importance of experiences to enable learning to occur. Both describe growth during the preschool and school years as moving developing children from domination on immediacy and appearance to a state of being able to transcend the present and perceptual, moving to increased flexibility in thinking about their world (Bruner, 1973). Bruner's work includes direct references to educational implications of cognitive development. He sees schooling as a critical influence on the development of adequate symbolic representational systems. He sees teachers as having the opportunity to provide ongoing experiences that encourage the matching of language to actions and perceptions, necessary for higher-level thinking to develop. Piaget does not directly relate his theories to educational practice. Yet the work of both of these theorists has important implications for education.

Teachers need to be aware of the knowledge base that children have and how children think about their world. Only then can teachers provide experiences appropriate to children's cognitive functioning to help them to expand and restructure their knowledge as they work to make sense of their world. By providing an experience-rich environment in which children are encouraged to explore and relate language to experiences, the teacher facilitates children's natural inclination to learn. When teachers organize this environment around the backgrounds and needs of individual learners, they provide children with familiar yet stimulating new experiences that leave room for exploration and growth and yet are not so far removed from the children's range of understanding as to inhibit integration of the new information.

Although the teacher is the creator of the learning environment and the shaper of the experiences, for learning to occur the children themselves must act on the environment—explore, question, predict, test, confirm and disconfirm. Teachers cannot give new knowledge to a child; the child must experience, feel and integrate new knowledge into his or her cognitive system. Thus the emphasis in learning is on acting and experiencing so that children can integrate new knowledge with old knowledge and apply both to new situations.

In relating cognitive factors to reading, both specific prior learnings and more general developmental factors influence reading performance at any given time. In implementing a language-thinking approach to teaching reading, teachers must always consider the specific knowledge base and the general developmental level of the child. Teachers teach reading within the framework of how children think, what they already know about language and the reading process, as well as their knowledge of the specific content they read. As children read, they expand their knowledge of the reading process while they gain specific information about a particular topic. They use all this expanded knowledge in constructing meaning during subsequent reading experiences. Therefore, children approach each new reading experience with a changed knowledge base. This ongoing learning enables children to read increasingly more complex and abstract materials as they grow.

Influence on Reading Comprehension

Work in the area of children's literature and children's stories (Applebee, 1978; Westby, 1979; Sutherland, Monson, & Arbuthnot, 1980; Cullinan, 1981) relates the developmental levels of children to books and discusses trends in children's responses to story material. Consider the *sensorimotor stage* child who, during approximately the first two years of life, develops a wide base of nonverbal symbolic schemata by exploring the physical environment through the senses—seeing, hearing, touching, tasting. Books for this child should be congruent with these real-life exploratory experiences. Picture books that stimulate tactile, visual, and auditory experiences provide opportunities for the child to explore the environment through the senses.

As symbolic functions increase and language develops, the child moves into the *preoperational stage*, anywhere from approximately age 2 to 7. During this time the child increases in mental capacities and the ability to deal with stories. However, interactions with stories are limited in that even the late preoperational child is not yet mentally able to manipulate ideas of more than one dimension at the same time—classification, seriation, conservation, time, or space. Therefore, at this stage the child's representations of stories indicate little or no evidence of reorganizing events by superordinate categories or more general frameworks. The child is grounded in the physical; the child's retelling of stories is typically a listing of concrete actions and events that may or may not relate to each other and will vary in completeness and accuracy from child to child. The focus is on particular details of stories, events, or characters, to the neglect of more important information. The egocentrism of this preoperational child results in limited awareness of characters' feelings or motives and the communication needs of the listener as stories are being shared. This child can often identify how other people feel or what they think but the child does not yet have the mental capacity to see the world through other people's perspectives. Nor can the child separate fantasy from reality; nursery characters are real, animals talk, and inanimate objects are alive. Thus, the story telling of the preoperational child is marked by inconsistencies in information, reasoning, and conclusions. An example of a child's retelling, illustrating both the length and detail that some preoperational children are capable of, comes from the research of Applebee (1978).

Once there was the three little pigs. And they asked the man with some straws, "Can we have some straws?" says the first little pig. And he gave them some straws and he built a straw house. In came the wol–, the wolf. He puffed and he puffed and he blew the house down. And he puffed and he puffed. And when the house fell down and so three little, the second three little pig went to the man with some sticks and he said to the man, "Can I have some sticks for to build a house?" And then the man said, "Yes," says the man and he gave him some sticks. And when he builded the house up and he was, and he puffed and he puffed, and he puffed and he puffed. And he blew all the sticks all fell down. And then he went to the man with some bricks. He said, "Can I have some bricks for the house, to build a house?" "Yes," said the man, and he gave him some bricks.

So when he builded the house of bricks, the wolf came along and blew the house down but he couldn't. So one day the wolf came and said to the, to the second pig, "Shall we go to Farmer Field's house, Farmer Field's grass?" And he said, "Alright." And then he did go already but the wolf came back and he said, "Let's go to it now." And he said, "I've been to the Farm Field's house." So he said, "Let's go and go to the next field and pick some apples, there's an apple tree there. So we can pick some." So first he went to the apple tree and picked some apples. And then it was so fat and so he runned away and the apple went down the hill into the road. So the three little, the pig went into the, into the churn and he went around and he runned the wolf over. And he said, "I runned you over." Then he rolled back to the house. And then . . . so . . . then the wolf went in the chimney pot and the three little pigs put some water, some hot water in then and then he fell down into the pot, "Plop." And he lived happily ever after.
(p. 93)

Eric M., 6 yr 1 mo

As children move through the *concrete operations stage* from approximately 7–11 years of age, they become increasingly systematic in their organization of information. They master conservation and are able to reverse operations. They have increased ability to classify, to deal with concepts and their generalizations, and to use categorizations based on one set of experiences to classify other information.

Since children at this stage can hold more than one idea in mind for comparative purposes, they have increasing ability to analyze information and sequence events and, therefore, to understand story events and characters. They can analyze events from beginning to end or vice versa. Their abilities to think about the past and predict the future increase. Ordering, comparing, and categorizing also allow for their growing ability to summarize stories, a major addition and marked difference from the preoperational child's characteristic listing of story information.

With these growing mental capacities come a reduction in egocentrism and an increasing ability to put themselves in other people's shoes. They understand that a person may feel more than one feeling and their ability to judge other people's feelings, intentions, purposes, and actions increases. This growth allows developing children to identify closely with a character and assume the character's role when reading stories. They can now separate reality and fantasy in stories. Thus, they gain significantly in thinking and reasoning during the elementary years, but concrete operational children, despite all this growth, still remain rooted in the given, within the general limits of the concrete operational logic structures.

Not until the period of *formal operations* can children reason on hypotheses that go beyond the events in stories in search of "what might be" instead of "what is" (Applebee, 1978, p. 108). Thus, for concrete operational children, ordering and organizing information about events and characters in stories is still based on concrete attributes and characteristics, and they focus mainly on recreating or summarizing actions and events. An example of a child's sharing of the story *Charlotte's Web* follows. This retelling exemplifies the newly emerged summarization abilities of concrete operational children.

> I like the story *Charlotte's Web*. It tells about Charlotte, the spider, and Wilbur, a pig, who live in a barn. In the story they have many adventures. You see Wilbur is supposed to be killed. He's supposed to go to market. At the end of the story Wilbur is saved. Charlotte dies. I especially liked Charlotte.
>
> **Barbara, 9 yr 4 mo**

The emerging mental capacities of formal operations have a dramatic effect on adolescents' responses to stories. In place of the concrete operational child's concern with summarizing or recreating actions, adolescents have growing concern with analyzing the parts of a story and for forming generalizations about its meaning. They can increasingly treat a story in terms of "how it works: its mechanics, the logic of its structure, its images and symbols" (Applebee, 1978). Adolescents' increased abilities to think about complex combinations of ideas and to reflect on their own thoughts allow them to analyze critically the way characters react in stories and the way they react to stories. Adolescents can understand character's motivations and, with the introspection and return to egocentrism common to adolescence, can and will relate to stories on personal levels.

The following example illustrates how a junior high school learner at the early formal operations stage organizes her analysis of a story in terms of how it works, how she feels about it, and why.

> I don't know who wrote *Rebecca*, but I loved her style of writing. All the time while she was writing she was describing in a different way to others.

Always I wanted to see what else would happen—perhaps it was because
she used small details. I liked best the bit where she first came to
Manderly—I didn't like the mystery bit so much—because it didn't seem
so real. I didn't really enjoy the first two chapters. But on the whole I
thought it was a good book. (Applebee, 1978, p. 109)

                                                        Jill V., 13 yr 8 mo

From reviewing these developmental trends in children's responses to
stories, you can see that ongoing cognitive growth results in changes in
what learners are capable of understanding from stories and in the depth of
their understanding. As in all learning these changes are gradual—do not
appear all at once—and are built on and integrated with the learner's store
of knowledge. Although developmental processes do underlie responses
to stories, not every child will follow the developmental patterns outlined
above. Children's experiences in the home, in the school, and in the
community play a role in determining the nature of their story retelling and
reading comprehension. As with all aspects of cognitive development,
children's interactions with significant adults in their environment shape
their abilities to respond to stories and other forms of print. The dialogue
between child and adult or older child, beginning in the preschool years in
which guidance and help is received, enables the child to progress in story
retelling. This help from others provides the foundation for children to
apply their developing cognitive abilities to the world of print.

AFFECTIVE FACTORS
Affective factors as well as cognitive factors affect the way a child integrates
new information. All of the child's experiences and interpretations of these
experiences help structure the developing personality and affect the way
the child views new information. Perceptions, feelings, and beliefs about
self and environment, then, affect the way a person integrates new information. Somehow the developing child has to integrate all of these things
to construct knowledge and/or action. As we have noted, this integration
occurs over time and is influenced first by the interaction of the young child
with significant family members. Peers and teachers take an increasingly
important role as children progress through school.

   Society, too, impinges on development by imposing certain tasks as the
individual moves through the life span, first within the family and then
within the community. These societal requirements influence the child
directly and indirectly as family, peers, teachers, and others in the community attempt to mold the child to meet the demands of society as they
interpret them.

Erikson's Theory
Erikson (1963) has focused on these societal influences on personality
development. He has theorized that the healthy personality progresses
through a series of eight stages of psychosocial development, moving from
infancy to maturity, from limited to more complete mastery over the

environment. Erikson's work recognizes that society imposes certain tasks throughout the life span and that these tasks assume special significance at certain stages of development. Specifically for each stage he describes life tasks appropriate to the particular phase of development and problems that may ensue if the individual does not master these life tasks. In other words, Erikson views each stage as a crisis situation in which the developing personality must resolve tendencies that are in conflict. Through successful resolution of the conflict, so that positive tendencies predominate, the individual increases the sense of self and mastery over the environment. This "healthy balance," toward the positive side, provides a base for resolution of conflicts at later stages. Failure in a given stage tends to precipitate failure in each of the successive stages. However, it is important not to view this description too simplistically as some failures may strengthen character more than some successes. Or a failure may lead to a new strategy that in turn leads to success. Remember also that what the child perceives as success or failure is crucial. Thus, the degree of accomplishment or mastery at each particular stage is influenced by the child's prior experiences, thoughts and ongoing experiences. Since success or failure affects future behavior, the development of successful ways of dealing with the environment and the development of a positive sense of self require a history of successful school experiences and an understanding of failures so that even these "negative" experiences can help shape future behavior in a positive direction.

The stages of greatest interest to teachers are the first four stages, ranging from infancy through preadolescence. First, during infancy the major developmental crisis is *basic trust versus mistrust.* That is, the task of the child is to establish a reasonably trustful feeling toward people in the immediate environment. This "implies not only that one has learned to rely on the sameness and continuity of the outer providers, but also that one may trust oneself and the capacity of one's own organs to cope with urges. . . ." (Erikson, 1963, p. 248). Second, during the second and third years the major developmental crisis is *autonomy versus shame and doubt.* Autonomy, or a sense of independence, grows through mastery of the physical and social environment as movement and language abilities develop. At first, the child can separate from significant adults as long as there is a continuation of perceptual connection (auditory, visual, or tactile). With growth, the child will become more able to move away from significant adults, provided that the child has the security of being able to return and be positively accepted. During this phase the growing child gains the awareness that one can become separated from significant love objects and still survive. According to Erikson,

> This stage . . . becomes decisive for the ratio of love and hate, cooperation and willfulness, freedom of self-expression and its suppression. From a sense of self-control without loss of self-esteem comes a lasting sense of good will and pride. (p. 254)

In the fourth and fifth years, the child uses these expanding autonomy, locomotion, and communication skills to initiate activities and social interactions further. This third stage is called the stage of *initiative versus guilt*. Erikson notes that the healthy child

> . . . is at no time more ready to learn quickly and avidly, to become bigger in the sense of sharing obligation and performance. . . . He is eager and able to make things cooperatively, to combine with other children for the purpose of constructing and planning, and he is willing to profit from teachers and to emulate ideal prototypes. (p. 258)

If the child has had positive experiences and development has been relatively healthy, the child enters the fourth stage, the stage of industry, which is closely linked to the tasks of the school proper. The major developmental crisis at this period is *industry versus inferiority*, in which the child's task is to learn the skills society considers important: productivity and the development of pride in work accomplishments.

> To bring a productive situation to completion is an aim which gradually supersedes the whims and wishes of play. His ego boundaries include his tools and skills: the work principle . . . teaches him the pleasure of work completion by steady attention and persevering diligence. (p. 259)

Since in our literate society learning to read is the major educational task of the elementary years, improving reading performance becomes one of the major developmental tasks of this period. Learning to read, then, provides for increased environmental mastery and contributes to learner feelings about self. Problems in this area may lead to a sense of inadequacy and inferiority. "Many a child's development is disrupted when family life has failed to prepare him for school life, or when school life fails to sustain the promises of earlier stages" (p. 260).

Erikson's stages are a refinement and elaboration of the general socialization principles enunciated by Anna Freud, the noted child psychoanalyst, with whom he studied. Anna Freud delineates normal developmental sequences as reference points for the assessment of child and adolescent development. In tracing the specific developmental sequence, she also emphasizes that a prerequisite for successful entry into the elementary school grades involves movement from an "ability to play" to an "ability to work." According to Anna Freud (1965), this transition occurs when the child learns to control, inhibit, or modify the impulses to use materials aggressively and destructively and learns to use them positively and constructively. The child learns not to throw, to take apart, to mess, or to hoard and instead uses materials to build, to plan, to learn, and to share. Further, the child learns to carry out plans so that immediate rewards are not necessarily the goal. The child learns to tolerate intervening frustrations and can delay maximum pleasure until plans are complete.

Implications for Learning

Psychosocial development, especially as it involves learning, has direct implications for the classroom. Although an accepting environment and positive learning experiences are important for all children, they are particularly important for those children who come to school unprepared to meet the demands of the formal school setting. Learning, for these children, tends to be difficult and problems are likely to arise. Providing special opportunities that will increase these children's sense of self and enable these children to achieve feelings of mastery in school-related activities is necessary to build a foundation for successful learning. This gradual process, which emphasizes successful school-related experiences, must be an integral part of all aspects of the school environment. To this end, the teacher recognizes and accepts as a starting point what these children can do, aids them in expanding what can be done, and presents new demands that are consistent with the learners' stages of development.

Child development, then, is dependent on increasing degrees of physical, cognitive, and social-emotional growth. Shapiro and Perry (1976) emphasize this intertwining of physiological, cognitive, and social-emotional development when they describe the child entering the period of industry.

> The normal child of 7 ± 1 has reached a level of maturation and development that permits autonomy. He is emotionally less dependent on his family, has at his disposal a neuromuscular apparatus that is ready for the challenge of environmental mastery; and he has a new set of cognitive strategies to outwit and control his environment. (p. 97)

As this period coincides with the period of early reading experiences, the importance of physiological, cognitive, and social-emotional processes in reading development becomes apparent. The influence of these interrelated and continuous processes affects the child's ability to learn during the early school years. This ability has a lasting influence on the child's personality development. Being able to read, to manipulate numbers, to absorb and apply information, and to question and explore do more than provide tools for future learning or skills for earning a living. The experience of learning and the perception of themselves as learners allows children to think of themselves as competent. Each time children experience successful learning, the world becomes more intelligible and children become more comfortable and confident acting upon and within the environment. This is crucial for success in school, and, further, children who have learned to learn stand a better chance of surviving even serious problems and deprivation than do children who have never had a chance for mastery on an intellectual level (Escalona, 1967). Thus, there is a reciprocal relationship between learning and personality development; between reading, a major tool of learning, and social-emotional development. Cognition influences affect, and affect influences cognition.

Koppenhaver's Work

Koppenhaver's (1976) work describes the reading behavior of children as it should develop ideally during the elementary and later school years. We view his work as an integration of the cognitive and affective domains. Although his work uses the Krathwohl, Bloom, and Masia (1964) taxonomy in the affective domain as a framework for describing the growth of a child as a reader, a study of Koppenhaver's taxonomy and of the descriptive behaviors of the reader at each level makes clear the inseparability of the affective and cognitive domains. Although each of the levels requires a specific level of affective functioning, the behavior could not occur without the requisite cognitive abilities. Proficiency and motivation are integrally related, and necessary for the development of mature readers.

Koppenhaver presents the development of a mature reader by describing five levels of functioning. At the *receiving level*, the lowest level of the taxonomy, a child displays some observable measure of attentiveness toward reading-related activities. The child is alert to reading activities and listens carefully to oral stories or related discussions. The child listens and performs the requested tasks when the teacher gives assignments. Receiving involves willing performance of an assigned reading task.

At the next highest level, the *level of responding*, the developing reader voluntarily and actively participates. The child may read beyond the assignment, seek further information about an author or topic, and actively generate questions to gain deeper understandings. The movement from responding to valuing is a subtle one.

Although the learner actively accepts and positively reacts to reading at previous levels, at the *valuing level* this commitment is sustained in that the learner shows a consistent appreciation for the worth of reading. At this level the choice of reading matter improves, characters in stories become very real, and the reader may incorporate viewpoints expressed in books into his or her point of view.

At the *organization level* the reader has begun to analyze written material in light of personal values and to resolve conflicts that may exist between personal values and those in the text. Such a reader will organize reading to fit into the demands of the daily activities. For this reader, books have become a source of information and joy.

At the highest level, the *level of characterization*, the learner is a confirmed reader. Behavior, attitude, and feelings about reading are positive, consistent, and predictable. Books, for this reader, are an integral part of life. Figure 2.1 illustrates this taxonomy as it relates to reading.

EARLY EXPERIENCES AND READING

Of course, as this chapter emphasizes throughout, learning and feelings about learning do not begin at school entry. The positive reading behaviors Koppenhaver describes have their roots in children's early experiences with oral language and print well before school age.

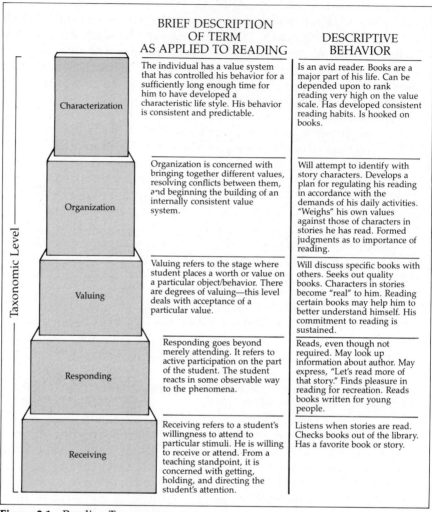

	BRIEF DESCRIPTION OF TERM AS APPLIED TO READING	DESCRIPTIVE BEHAVIOR
Characterization	The individual has a value system that has controlled his behavior for a sufficiently long enough time for him to have developed a characteristic life style. His behavior is consistent and predictable.	Is an avid reader. Books are a major part of his life. Can be depended upon to rank reading very high on the value scale. Has developed consistent reading habits. Is hooked on books.
Organization	Organization is concerned with bringing together different values, resolving conflicts between them, and beginning the building of an internally consistent value system.	Will attempt to identify with story characters. Develops a plan for regulating his reading in accordance with the demands of his daily activities. "Weighs" his own values against those of characters in stories he has read. Formed judgments as to importance of reading.
Valuing	Valuing refers to the stage where student places a worth or value on a particular object/behavior. There are degrees of valuing—this level deals with acceptance of a particular value.	Will discuss specific books with others. Seeks out quality books. Characters in stories become "real" to him. Reading certain books may help him to better understand himself. His commitment to reading is sustained.
Responding	Responding goes beyond merely attending. It refers to active participation on the part of the student. The student reacts in some observable way to the phenomena.	Reads, even though not required. May look up information about author. May express, "Let's read more of that story." Finds pleasure in reading for recreation. Reads books written for young people.
Receiving	Receiving refers to a student's willingness to attend to particular stimuli. He is willing to receive or attend. From a teaching standpoint, it is concerned with getting, holding, and directing the student's attention.	Listens when stories are read. Checks books out of the library. Has a favorite book or story.

Taxonomic Level

Figure 2.1 Reading Taxonomy

At home and in the community children engage in purposeful language communications to make their needs known, to direct and engage others, to question, to fantasize, and to share information (Halliday, 1975). Children establish these different uses of oral language through their daily interactions with adults and other children. As they see a need to communicate, they selectively use their language in different ways. By experiencing what language can do for them, children naturally expand their use of language and gain growing understanding of what language is all about.

These early uses of oral language are both social and cognitive experiences for the growing child. They help shape the child's understanding of people: how they can relate to other people, how others feel toward them, and in turn how they feel toward others. Early language experiences also enable children to seek information about the physical world around them and to use this information to further explore this world. Through these experiences children develop concepts of themselves and their environment that they bring to school.

When children function with oral language, they also experience print in their environment. They see print in the form of signs and print in the form of text. Signs they see include the print on television, the labels on food packages and other household products, the signs in the street and in stores, the print on toys and games, and print in such things as radio and television guides, telephone directories, and catalogs. These experiences with print add to their understanding of language as communication.

An important part of this experience with print is the special story time in the home. This shared situation—warm, relaxed, and absorbing—takes place between the child and another person. The child learns to attend for a long time, listening to language different from the usual conversational language. The physical closeness between the child and the reader allows the child to experience the flow of language without interference and to absorb meaning. This satisfying relationship and the visual stimulation the pictures provide soon become associated with books. This leads the child to strive to recreate this pleasurable experience by reconstructing the story independently.

A warm and accepting home language environment, as described, allows the child to use strategies of experimentation and approximation with no penalties for trial and error. The growth of language awareness and knowledge and the ability to take risks with print provide the base for increasing independence in reading (Doake, 1979).

Not all children have the same experiences at home. Although all children use language for communicative purposes, differences exist in the content and diversity of their communications and in their exposure to print in the environment, books, and the language of books. Therefore, schools must provide print-rich environments, encourage conversational language for varying purposes, and simulate the environment of the "at home" special reading time. Obviously, then, early shared experiences with language stimulate cognitive and affective growth and form the foundation for learning.

Reading Theory

In 1908, Edmund Huey stated that:

> . . . to completely analyze what we do when we read would almost be the acme of a psychologist's achievements, for it would be to describe very many of the most intricate workings of the human mind, as well as to unravel the tangled story of the most remarkable specific performance that civilization has learned in all its history. (p. 6)

Since the work of Huey, other experts have proposed many theories to explain the reading process. But even so, due to the many factors involved and the complexity of the task, reading theories and models are still in a developmental stage.

The following section will discuss those reading theorists whose views are prominent in reading instruction today. Historically, these theorists have been divided into two groups. Their views have come to be known as "top-down" models or "bottom-up" models of the reading process. Those theorists who expound a meaning-based or "top-down" model emphasize that readers begin with meaning and tend to use only minimal cues from the printed page. Readers rely predominantly on their prior knowledge of language and content in constructing meaning. This includes the child's knowledge of the order of words, phrases, and sentences of the language, and of the meaning of individual words, signs, symbols, phrases, sentences, and longer passages. The readers' knowledge of the world enables them to select only those parts of the text that they need to predict meaning. Phonological knowledge is not a crucial aspect. Only if the reading process breaks down does the reader resort to the sound-symbol correspondences of the language.

In contrast, some theorists hypothesize that to construct meaning the reader must progress through a step-by-step process. This "bottom-up" model of reading suggests that the reader must begin with the individual letters and the sounds of the language and move through progressively higher stages of processing in a set order. The emphasis here is on the printed page and what the reader extracts from the page rather than a focus on what the reader brings to the page.

Recently, an interactive theory of the reading process has surfaced. This model views reading as a process in which the reader simultaneously uses all levels of processing (visual, phonological, lexical, syntactic, and semantic) to construct meaning. Proponents of this interactive theory say that reading is neither "top-down" nor "bottom-up" but that the reader constructs meaning by the selective use of information from all the knowledge sources together.

Figure 2.2 illustrates those knowledge sources involved in the reading process. Meaning-based theorists view the reader as beginning at the semantic level and then sampling from the other knowledge sources as needed to construct meaning, whereas "bottom-up" theorists view the reader as gathering information from each knowledge source in a set hierarchical order beginning with graphic representations. Interactive theorists, on the other hand, view the reader as simultaneously using the relevant parts of each knowledge source without adherence to any set order. The following section elaborates on these three perspectives of the reading process.

MEANING-BASED THEORY

Two of the strongest proponents of the "top-down" approach are Kenneth Goodman and Frank Smith. According to Goodman (1973, 1976), reading is a psycholinguistic guessing game.

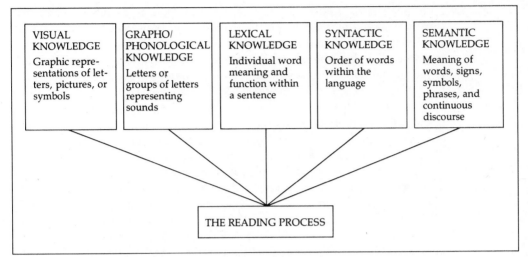

Figure 2.2 Knowledge Sources: Aspects of the Reading Process

> Reading is a psycholinguistic process by which the reader (a language user) reconstructs, as best he can, a message which has been encoded by a writer as a graphic display. . . . The receptive process does start with the phonological or graphic display as input, and it does end with meaning as output, but the efficient language user takes the most direct route and touches the fewest bases necessary to get to his goal. He accomplishes this by *sampling*, relying on the redundancy of language, and his knowledge of linguistic constraints. He *predicts* structures, *tests* them against the semantic context which he builds up from the situation and the on-going discourse, and then *confirms* or disconfirms as he processes further language. (Goodman, 1973, pp. 22–23)

Efficient reading results from skill in selecting the fewest, most productive cues necessary to produce guesses that approximate the author's meaning the first time. Readers, as users of language, interact with the graphic input as they seek to reconstruct a message encoded by the writer. They concentrate relevant prior experience and learning on the task, drawing on experiences and concepts previously attained as well as on language competence.

Frank Smith (1971, 1975), through his analysis of visual processing, also arrives at a "top-down" theory of reading. He states that:

> . . . overattention to the words, or the letters of the words, will simply clog the visual system with visual noise, information that cannot be used.
>
> To be able to read a child must be encouraged to predict, to use prior knowledge, or even have nonvisual information provided. . . . The child who predicts . . . by eliminating unlikely alternatives in advance, by making use of meaning and everything he already knows about language, is the only one likely even to recognize foolish mistakes if they are made. (1975, pp. 59–60)

Like Goodman, Smith describes comprehension as a sampling process during which the reader selects from the written message those cues needed to test predictions and resolve uncertainty about underlying meaning. Both Goodman and Smith propose that people comprehend written language similarly to the way they comprehend speech. In other words, they view reading and language as parallel processes.

SOUND-SYMBOL BASED THEORY

Gough (1972) exemplifies those theorists associated with linear or "bottom-up" models. For Gough, visual perception initiates the input of printed material, and processing proceeds step-by-step to higher stages moving from letter recognition to decoding (reader converts letters into systematic phonemes), to word recognition, and to syntactic and semantic rules. The reader must have the information gained at one level to move to the next higher level of processing. Thus, according to Gough, the reader "plods through the sentence, letter by letter, word by word" (p. 354), moving in a left to right linear progression. His emphasis is on decoding prior to obtaining meaning. Thus Gough sees skill in phonics as giving "the child a means of naming a word. . . . It provides him with a valuable means of data collection" (p. 350). As children learn to associate letters with sounds, they search their memory to name the word that has meaning for them. He, therefore, advocates an approach in which the emphasis is on decoding although he acknowledges that decoding alone does not "make the child a reader" (p. 353). As opposed to Goodman and Smith, Gough believes readers use guessing strategies only when they are unable to decode rather than as an approach to getting meaning from the printed page.

Similarly, LaBerge and Samuels (1974) view reading acquisition as a series of skills that for the fluent reader have become automatic. "When the decoding and comprehension processes are automatic, reading appears to be 'easy.' When they require attention to complete their operations, reading seems to be 'difficult'" (p. 314). In their "bottom-up" model of the reading process, readers move through visual, phonological, and episodic memory systems to reach the semantic memory system where they achieve meaning. LaBerge and Samuels theorize that learners use an episodic memory system in the earliest stages of learning, and this system is a store for related experiences and language meaning. For a child just learning word meanings, the linkage between a spoken word and its meaning must first be coded in episodic memory. However, the theory is that with increased exposure and proficiency in reading, direct links form between visual and phonological units and their meaning, to bypass episodic memory.

Although Gough and LaBerge and Samuels are considered "bottom-up" theorists, the LaBerge and Samuels' model is not as strict a "bottom-up" model as Gough's, in that bypassing a stage in processing is possible. For example, when a reader

. . . encounters a word he does not understand, his attention may be shifted to the phonological level to read out the sound for attempts at retrieval from episodic memory. At other times he may shift his attention to the visual level and attempt to associate spelling patterns with phonological units, which are then blended into a word which makes contact with meaning. (LaBerge & Samuels, 1974, pp. 313–14)

They believe that since children have extensive experience with spoken language "most of the connections between phonological word codes and semantic meaning codes have already been learned to automaticity" (p. 307). Therefore, as readers process information at the phonological level, they can focus attention on the decoding process. After readers decode the word, they associate it with meaning that is in their experiential repertoire. The fluent reader's attention can continuously focus on the meaning units of semantic memory, since decoding from visual to semantic systems proceeds automatically. In summary, this model assumes that written stimuli are transformed into meanings through a sequence of stages that are different at different levels of reading proficiency.

These differing theoretical positions become clearer if one looks at some of the implications for teaching reading. Those theorists classified as "top-down" would emphasize a naturalistic language approach to early reading instruction. Focus would be on comprehension without undue emphasis on the accuracy of oral reading. Children would be encouraged to attempt predictions on the basis of prior experience and language knowledge. Oral reading errors (or "miscues" as Goodman calls them, since they are not errors in terms of meaning) would be considered a natural part of the reading process. In fact, undue emphasis on word accuracy, according to these theorists, produces miscues that are phonemically similar but are contextually inappropriate. For these theorists the most important questions for the reader are:

Does it make sense?

Is it language?

On the other hand, theorists classified as "bottom-up" emphasize the teaching of sound-symbol correspondence prior to focusing on meaning and are most concerned with the accuracy of oral reading. In a classroom in which this view predominates, the teacher tends to correct all errors, even those that make sense within the context of the material being read.

INTERACTIVE THEORY
The issue is not which of the above theories is correct but rather is it possible for readers to use both approaches under different conditions? That is, to view reading as either a "top-down" or "bottom-up" process appears inconsistent with teachers' experiences with children and how they learn to read and function as fluent readers. In watching children

read, observers note that on some occasions a child will make errors consistent with the context and on other occasions the same child will hesitate and actually sound out an unfamiliar word to arrive at meaning. That is, a reader may substitute a synonym that retains the same meaning as the original word (uses syntactic and semantic knowledge) or may use grapho-phonological knowledge to process the word and to help obtain its meaning. In both cases, the reader reaches understanding of the text, although in the first instance the reader uses a "top-down" approach and in the second instance a "bottom-up" approach. Another example occurs when we observe a student read for different purposes. When the purpose in reading is general understanding of the material, the student uses the fewest cues to predict meaning, but when the purpose is studying technical material, the same reader will plod through the printed material step-by-step. This suggests that reading may be either a "top-down" or "bottom-up" process or perhaps a combination of the two.

Research literature, as interpreted by Rumelhart (1976), lends support to this position. He discusses research showing that the gathering of information at one level of analysis may be partially determined by higher levels of analysis, that is:

1. The perception of letters often depends on the surrounding letters.
2. Our perception of words depends on the syntactic environment in which we encounter the words.
3. Our perception of words depends on the semantic environment in which we encounter the words.
4. Our perception of syntax depends on the semantic context in which the string [of words] appears.
5. Our interpretation of the meaning of what we read depends on the general context in which we encounter the text. (pp. 7–17)

In examining the above five statements, one notes that a higher stage (as defined by "bottom-up" models) may influence processing at a lower stage. This suggests that readers in processing print may rely on any one or more of the following information sources as their primary clues to meaning: the general context, the semantic context, the syntactic environment, or the surrounding letters.

An example to illustrate how one's perception of syntax may depend on the semantic context in which the word string appears will help to clarify this interaction. This effect may be observed in syntactically ambiguous sentences. An example from Rumelhart's work follows:

They are eating apples.

The children are eating apples.

The juicy red ones are eating apples.

In the first sentence, the word *they* could refer to either children or apples, semantically as well as syntactically. In the second sentence, though syntactically *the children* could be apples, semantically we are led to another conclusion. Similarly, in sentence three, it is our good sense that stops us from believing that *the juicy red ones* have a good appetite. In this example it is essential to place the sentence within a broader semantic context to understand the syntax.

An additional example illustrates how our interpretation of the meaning of what we read depends on the general context in which we encounter the text.

The *run* through the park was exhilarating.

The *run* caused them to lose the game.

The *run* was closed for repairs.

The *run* of the play was extended.

The meaning of the word *run* is different in each of these sentences even though the syntax does not change. The remainder of the sentence gives us the meaning of the word *run* in each case. In fact, the meaning derived from whole sentences may depend on a broader definition of context; that is, what an individual brings to the text from his or her environment. Anderson and others (1976) give the following example to illustrate this concept:

> Imagine the statement *The bull is in the field* in each of the following circumstances. (1) You are driving past the field in your car. (2) You are sitting in the field having a picnic. (3) You have brought your pure-bred cow to be inseminated. (4) The sentence comes up on a screen in a memory experiment in which you are participating. (p. 369)

How a person interprets the meaning of the sentence clearly depends on the individual and the environment in which the sentence is read. Therefore, supporting a linear or "bottom-up" model in which the reader moves in a direct progression from graphic representation to the phonological level, to the lexical level, to the syntactic and semantic levels seems difficult to justify.

Since reading is probably neither a strictly "top-down" nor "bottom-up" process, referring to models such as Rumelhart's interactive model in looking at the reading process and the implications for teaching reading seems most logical. Rumelhart's work can encompass "top-down" as well as "bottom-up" models. His interactive model of reading indicates that all the different information sources interact simultaneously. That is, as a reader perceives the graphic information, he or she will make hypotheses about the message using one or more knowledge sources—feature, letter, letter cluster, lexical, syntactic, semantic—in any order.

Reading as Language Interaction

Rumelhart's concept that views the processing of text as a flexible interaction of the different information sources adds importantly to knowledge about the reading process. But although his work describes the components of the reading process that interact with one another, his model does not provide information about the type or extent of these interactions. The major benefits from such a model will occur only when experts can specify "just which components interact and when and why" (Anderson, 1976, p. 2). Thus, although Rumelhart's model emphasizes the interactions among the various knowledge sources used during the processing of print, other factors also interact during this process and influence reader comprehension. Specifically, we need more information about the influence of reader background and the requirements of the text. Researchers are now examining the influence of preexisting knowledge on reading performance. This prior knowledge involves the experiential base of the reader and includes what the reader knows and feels. The reader's knowledge includes general information and understanding of concepts related to the written message and familiarity with text structure. Feelings include the reader's motivations, attitudes, and interests as they relate to learning, to reading in general, and to the reading of specific texts.

Researchers are also examining the written message and its specific organizational structure and content. The written message reflects the writer's cognitive base and affective base. Although Rumelhart does not consider affective factors when examining what the reader brings to the text, some other theorists have acknowledged the influence of social-emotional factors in their models of the reading process. Experts recognize that understanding all the diverse factors involved in reading and integrating what is known into the development of comprehensive models of the reading process is difficult. Part of the problem is due to the great variability in individual reader functioning and the numerous combinations of factors that can influence reading performance. This implies that we may need multiple models to explain the interactions of the learner and text at different levels of learner development and that such models must acknowledge the possibility that alternate routes to reading acquisition may exist for different learners.

Thus, full understanding of the reading process requires that theorists incorporate the way in which the various knowledge sources of the reader interact with one another and with the text and the way personality factors influence this interaction. As Huey (1908) noted, full understanding of the reading process is an awesome task; consequently, it is no wonder that experts in the field are still far from accounting for an interaction of all of these factors.

In keeping with the current state of knowledge, Mackworth's (1971) statement is most appropriate; reading "can only be defined in terms of *who* is reading *what*, in *what* state, for *what* reason" (p. 67). Implicit in this statement is that reading is comprised of the reader, the text, the reader's feelings, and the reader's specific purposes. Because the text reflects the writer's knowledge, feelings, and ability to communicate through written language, we can understand reading best if we expand Mackworth's definition of reading to include writing. Writing can only be defined in terms of *who* is writing *what* in *what* state, for *what* reason. These definitions jointly account for the many interactions between reader and writer and highlight the complexity of reader-text interactions.

Although the focus of this book is on reader/writer interactions, we need to consider the full range of language communication areas. Listener/speaker interactions are the earliest forms of verbal communication and provide necessary experiences for understanding print. These interactions continue to influence learners as they interact with print throughout life. In the listener/speaker interaction, as in the reader/writer interaction, listeners bring their knowledge and feelings to communication as they interact with the message. Thus, listening can only be defined in terms of *who* is listening to *what*, in *what* state, for *what* reason; speaking can best be defined in terms of *who* is saying *what*, in *what* state, for *what* reason. The oral message reflects the speaker's background and use of language just as the written message reflects the author's background and use of language. As we have already said, all messages are most easily shared—and thus meaning constructed—when communicators and receivers have similar backgrounds (see Figure 2.3).

Although people think of listener/speaker interactions and reader/writer interactions as parallel processes, some important differences exist. In face-to-face listener/speaker interactions such nonverbal cues as facial expressions, gestures, and intonation aid communication. Also, listeners may communicate directly with speakers, commenting or questioning when meaning breaks down. Perceptive speakers may notice nonverbal clues from listeners when they are having some problems understanding and may choose to restate or elaborate the message. These direct communications between listeners and speakers have some advantage over the more isolated reader-text interactions. Readers do not have direct access to the writer when meaning breaks down. They are dependent on their own resources or searching for external sources of information. Some advantages for readers include the freedom to set their own pace, to read at whatever rate is comfortable, and to have the message always available to return to and to rethink as needed. Being aware of these similarities and differences between oral and written communications is essential for teachers.

To develop good communication skills, the child must interact with teachers and other learners. The role of the teacher in facilitating communication (oral and written) is to bridge any gaps that may exist between the communicator (speaker/writer) and receiver (listener/reader) so that messages are easily constructed. Teachers—guided by their knowledge of

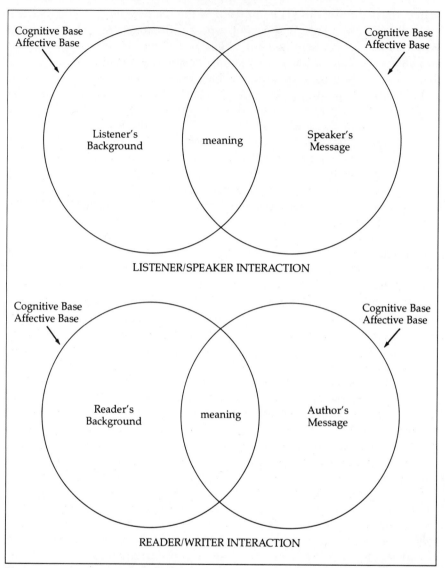

Figure 2.3   Constructing Meaning

learner development, language, and the reading process—interact with learners by assessing learner needs, structuring learning experiences, and evaluating learner performance. Learners, too, are active participants in this process. They interact with other learners and the teacher as they participate in listening, speaking, reading, and writing activities. Ongoing interactions between teachers and learners, using oral and written language, are what reading and reading instruction are all about.

Summary

This chapter presents background information about child development and the reading process. Teachers use knowledge from these areas as they make decisions about instruction within a language-thinking approach to reading. The chapter focuses on those aspects of cognitive and affective development that interact with reading, discusses different theories of reading, and suggests an interactive model. The reader uses information from a variety of sources more or less simultaneously—visual knowledge, grapho-phonological knowledge, lexical knowledge, syntactic knowledge, and semantic knowledge. The chapter places reading within an overall communication framework and describes both readers and listeners as active constructors of meaning as they interact with writers and speakers.

Concept and Language Development

Language and Thought

Language Development
HOW HUMANS USE LANGUAGE
HOW LANGUAGE IS STRUCTURED

Implications for the Classroom

Summary

C oncept development and language are integral parts of the child's overall cognitive development. Cognitive development is the way children organize their world: how they use experience, language, and thinking to make sense of their world. As children develop, they constantly face the task of perceiving information from the environment, organizing and storing this information, and applying this information to new situations. To make sense of the overwhelming amount of information available in the environment, the child must actively organize and store information by inferring relationships. The child uses categorization to organize these relationships or concepts; as a result, the child expands and refines concepts and forms new concepts.

> Once a concept develops, it serves as an experiential filter through which impinging events are screened, gauged, and evaluated, a process that determines in large part what responses can and will occur. (Harvey, Hunt, & Schroder, 1961, pp. 2–3)

Thus, concept development is the base for thinking, serving as a mediator between environmental input and performance. The use of language enhances and focuses this process. Language enables us to communicate and share ideas with others through listening, speaking, reading, and writing. Thus, cognitive development is a changing, expanding process beginning at birth and continuing throughout life.

Shortly after birth, the infant responds to objects and events in the environment. The infant hears, sees, and touches. These experiences and increasing maturation provide background for organizing sounds, sights, and feelings into predictable patterns. These, in turn, enable the child eventually to distinguish specific words, to associate them with experiences, and to speak them with meaning (Klausmeier & Ripple, 1971). This awareness of the objects and events in the environment, with their verbal labels, leads to expansion of the child's store of ideas through the preschool years. The results are a background of meaningful concepts and understandings and an ability to communicate with others that provide the foundation for learning to read. Not only does the reader bring this store of experiences and ideas to the printed page, but the reader also expands knowledge and ideas from information acquired through reading. This reciprocal process allows for the fullest development of language and ideas: Concepts continually grow and expand through experiences with the physical environment, through experiences with the medium of print, and through thinking about information from both these sources.

For the classroom teacher, concerned with the development of proficient readers, the important question is: What is known about language development that is relevant to reading instruction? This chapter will discuss the relationship of language and thought and language development, how language is used and how language is structured, and the impact of these on reading. The chapter will also suggest ways to create a language-thinking environment.

Language and Thought

The use of language to organize a person's own environment is an integral part of cognitive development and is most highly developed in the human species. Piaget and Lenneberg, although approaching the study of language development from different perspectives, both share the view that the human development of language is traceable to basic cognitive abilities: They agree that there is a biological predisposition to language development in people. According to Lenneberg, people develop language as they derive relations about things and other people in their physical environment and see the connections between these relations. Although he describes words as discrete entities, he emphasizes that words represent underlying continuous cognitive and physiological processes (1971). The important point made by Lenneberg is that learning the meaning of even a single word is not a passive process but requires intellectual activity on the part of the learner. The idea that words are simply labels is an oversimplification. For example, as children learn the word *book*, they are actively thinking by asking questions such as:

"What does the word *book* stand for?" and

"Is this physical object an example of a book?"

They know an object is a book because they have related the essential attributes of a book to the word *book*. Similarly, Piaget talks about young children's early experiences with the physical environment as the base for the development of cognitive structures. This early accumulation of information forms the indispensable base for the growth of additional cognitive structures, one of which is language. For Piaget, language is seen as a specifically human creation. Language is made possible by the more general cognitive capacity for organizing experience in a way that allows people to produce genuine language novelties which far surpass a copy-type knowledge of our environment (Sinclair-de Zwart, 1973). Piaget calls this biological capacity assimilation and accommodation. He views language as but one of the manifestations of the human capacity for representing things and events in their absence.

The work of Lenneberg and Piaget leads to the logical conclusion that biological as well as environmental components contribute to language development. The biological component provides the young child with the capacity to organize and to respond to experiences in the environment, to learn the language system, and to use it as a mode of communication. The environmental component gives the young child the necessary sensory and linguistic experiences for language growth. However, experts have not yet agreed on how to delineate the specific processes involved in this growth, particularly in regard to the development of language and thought.

The major issue is whether concept formation requires language. The fields of psychology and linguistics have an ongoing controversy regarding this relationship between language and thought: the role of language in concept formation. Theorists such as Kendler (1972), Sapir (1921), Vygotsky (1962), and Whorf (1956) believe that language is crucial to concept formation, whereas others such as Furth (1964) and Sinclair-de Zwart (1973) deny language this central role. Interestingly Bruner and Piaget, who agree that overall cognitive development is a sequential progression (see Chapter 2), disagree on this issue. Although both allow that language and thought are related processes, they view the role of language in concept formation differently. Bruner (1956, 1966) believes that language is a major tool in the advancement of cognitive development, whereas Piaget (1960) suggests that the development of language follows, rather than precedes—indeed *is grounded in*—the development of cognitive structures.

This controversy is theoretically important, but it does not affect the instructional procedures the classroom teacher follows. However, the very existence of such a long-standing and intensively studied issue emphasizes the close interrelationship of language and thought and suggests the need for teachers to consider both in planning for language-related activities.

Language Development

The relationship of language and thought becomes clearer when we trace the development of language. In the beginning, the baby uses language either as an emotional response or to proclaim the need for biological or psychological satisfaction. As children mature, the purposes for speaking that once served them well are no longer sufficient. Satisfying personal needs, exploring the environment, and proclaiming what one sees, hears, touches, and feels continue, but using language for these purposes becomes less dominant as the world becomes more complex (Berry, 1969). At this time, the child begins to share ideas and expand them through listening to the spoken language of others. The child uses language more intensively to explore relationships with people and things in the environment. The developing child asks questions, stores information about the ways language is used, increases vocabulary, and expands concepts. Language gradually becomes freed from the immediate environment, and the child begins to use language to think about and express ideas about people, objects, and events that the child no longer experiences directly through the senses. As a result, the child's memory store expands; the ability to rely on past experiences and language to identify and categorize new objects and events grows.

The language development of children is a continuous process with many aspects of language developing simultaneously. We shall consider how humans use language, and how language is structured.

HOW HUMANS USE LANGUAGE

Humans use language to communicate with others and to communicate with themselves. They also use nonverbal means to communicate with others.

Communicative Aspects of Language

Halliday (1973), Jakobson (1960), Trough (1977), Weeks (1978), and others have studied the communicative uses of language—language directed to others. Weeks has synthesized this work on language development. Table 3.1 adapted from her work represents this synthesis. The first seven functions noted in this table come from the work of Halliday. He hypothesizes that these functions appear approximately in the order listed and despite any possible variations in the first six the informative function appears last. Halliday further suggests that young children tend to use only one function at a time, but as their language develops and matures, they use several functions jointly. The other functions shown in Table 3.1 are from the work of Jakobson, Trough, and Weeks respectively. Brief descriptions of these functions of language follow.

1. Children use the *instrumental function* to satisfy their own material needs in terms of goods or services. These communications tend to be in the form of demands or protests.

2. Children use the *regulatory function* to exert control over the actions of other people in their environment. Although both instrumental and regulatory uses involve demands on other people, an important difference exists between them. In the regulatory function the demands are to direct another person to act in a particular way as opposed to satisfying a particular need by the giving or not giving of something in the instrumental function.

3. The *interactional function* refers to the child's attempts to establish and maintain contact with important people in the environment. This includes attempts to prolong a conversation even at the risk of losing meaning (Jakobson, 1960).

4. The *personal function* includes language used to express feelings and intensify awareness of one's individuality. It represents the child's attitude about self, and how the child feels others in the environment view him or her.

5. Children apply the *heuristic function* as they explore their environment and learn about things. Questioning, starting with "what" and "where" questions and progressing to "who," "how," and "why" questions, exemplify the use of language to acquire knowledge.

6. The *imaginative function* of language is the children's language of fantasy as they pretend and create, used most when children play or create stories or rhymes.

7. Communicating new information to a listener is the *informational function* of language. Children typically use declarative sentences to convey and discuss knowledge that the listener does not have.

8. The *poetic function* of language is the use of language in ways that allow enjoyment of the language itself. For example, when young children repeat utterances, they may be doing this for the purpose of enjoying the sounds and feel of the language.

9. When children use their language to tell about and interpret immedi-

Table 3.1 Communicative Functions of Language

Name of Function	How Child Uses It	Examples from Child Speech
1. Instrumental—I want	Makes requests to fulfill needs. Protests	I need a cookie! No!
2. Regulatory—Do as I tell you	To control activities of others.	Sit back and watch me
3. Interactional—Me and you	Greeting, issues summons to talk, keeps channels of communication open	Hewo, widdo Miss Pretty, Byebye, Know what?
4. Personal—Here I come	Expresses feelings and individuality	You're funny Yukky!
5. Heuristic—Tell me why	Explores reality, uses language for learning	Why are the doors locked?
6. Imaginative—Let's pretend	Plays games, makes up stories in interaction with others	Peekaboo! Let's play house
7. Informational—I've got something to tell you	Offers information that the listener does not have, and makes comments	I went to the store today
8. Poetic—(aesthetics)	Focuses on the message for its own sake	He put him in a little boat, little boaty boat
9. Interpretive	Recalls experiences, plans experiences, solves problems, interprets experiences	I took some trucks to the park last time. What can I take this time?
10. Performative—I promise I bet	Promises, bets	I'll be good!

Source: Adapted from T. E. Weeks. *Born to talk*, p. 3. Copyright © 1978. Used with permission of the author.

ate experiences and to recall past experiences, they use the *interpretive function* of language. This includes reasoning, recognition of causal relations, understanding sequence, and determining important ideas. These represent children's attempts to understand their experiences. Weeks includes reasoning about the future in the interpretive function. It involves thinking beyond the immediate or recalled experiences to anticipate consequences, predict solutions, and recognize problems.

10. The *performative function* of language is a small part of the language production of children. It includes promises, threats, bets, and curses, and the child may direct these toward inanimate objects such as dolls as well as toward people.

Noncommunicative Aspects of Language

As the communicative functions of language develop, language directed to oneself also develops. Some of these noncommunicative aspects of language appear in Table 3.2.

Table 3.2   Noncommunicative Functions of Language

Name of Function	How Child Uses It	Examples from Child Speech
1. Language play	Amuses self; creates interesting language patterns	bink ben bink, blue kink
2. Metalingual (language practice)	Repeats language segments as though "practicing" language, talks about language	bag^h bukth (Adult: box?) bak bak bak
3. Concept formation	Uses language as an aid to forming concepts	(trying to decide what color something is) Black. Kinda blueth (bluish). Blackshish
4. Self-directing (directive, private speech, egocentric speech)	Uses language to control and direct own behavior	This paper gonna be good all right, I think I gonna cut it
5. Self-image formation	Private speech that functions to define the child's roles and self-image	(decorating cookies) Arrow. I'm doing a good job.
6. Avoidance	Uses speech to avoid something worse, such as sleep	ba ba rattit ba ba rattit
7. Magical	Considers words to have qualities or powers in themselves	No, Greg. Cat. Our cat.

Source: T. E. Weeks. *Born to talk*. Copyright © 1978, p. 19. Used with permission of the author.

Children use language to stimulate and entertain themselves. This *language play function* includes sound play, nonsense words, rhyming, poetry, alliteration, similes, puns, and changing the names of objects. Language play is different from language practice. In the *metalingual* or *language practice function*, the purpose is to use language to improve use in some way, which may include monitoring language usage by talking about it. Although language play and language practice may sound the same to the listener, they have very different functions for the speaker.

The *concept formation function* of language is the use of language as children explore their environment and think about the attributes of objects and people. This allows children to classify and label things in their environment, forming concepts that guide further explorations in the environment. Children direct their own activities by using language to help focus their attention on a particular activity. This directive or *self-directing function* of language helps children monitor, direct, and plan their actions. As they direct comments about their actions to themselves (*self-image function*), they may influence their own self-image. These comments about themselves reflect how they hear others refer to them and can be powerful forces on the development of children's self-image.

Children may direct language to themselves in order to avoid an unpleasant experience. They often use this *avoidance function* of language to escape from such things as going to sleep, being punished, or cleaning up. The *magical function* of language grows out of children's need to control their environment. They often behave as if words are inseparable from the objects that they name. The name appears to the child to be an attribute of the object rather than a label, giving the word much more power than it really has. Experience with words forbidden by adults can also give children the sense that words somehow have magical powers.

Nonverbal Communication

At the same time that children are using language to communicate with others and to communicate with themselves, they are also using nonverbal behavior to communicate. This nonverbal behavior includes the use of vocal sounds, body movement, and personal space (Weeks, 1978). Some aspects of this nonverbal communication are listed in Table 3.3. The first aspect of nonverbal communication is the use of vocal sounds, or *paralinguistics*, to communicate meaning. Vocal sounds include pitch, volume, stress, lengthening, hesitation, tempo, and other factors that go into tone of voice. These paralinguistic features of language can be observed in infants as they cry, coo, and babble. Parents and caretakers quickly recognize meaningful messages in some of the sounds produced. Tone of voice continues to carry meaning as vocabulary develops and as the communicative functions of language expand.

Body movement, or *kinesics*, the second aspect of nonverbal communication, includes explicit gestures, body postures, and facial expressions. Gestures include such familiar movements as waving goodbye, putting one's finger to the lips to indicate quiet, and putting up one's hand as a signal to stop. Body postures are not as well defined by society as explicit gestures but do convey unconscious messages. How one stands, sits, or orients the body toward others communicates how one feels about others.

Table 3.3 Nonverbal Communication

Aspect	How Child Uses It	Examples
Nonlanguage vocal behavior (Paralinguistic)	Crying, cooing, babbling, whispering, baby talk	Mommy! gagaga gaga gagaga!
Body movement (Kinesics)	Explicit gestures, body postures, body rhythms	lifting up both arms—pick me up, waving goodbye
	Facial expressions, eye contact, gaze	frowning, smiling, glancing
Personal space (Proxemics)	Distance, facing	standing far apart, standing close together, facing a speaker

The rhythm of the body in relation to others, the total body or just the head, is another way of communicating to others through body movement.

Nonverbal communications are most readily transmitted through the face and the eyes. The basic emotions of happiness, anger, fear, sadness, surprise, and disgust have been identified in facial expressions. Eye contact and gaze direction are learned at a very early age. Connecting with another person through eye contact conveying affection is an important part of emotional growth in the infant. Eye contact continues to convey messages throughout life and informally to control conversation or more formally, at meetings or in a classroom, to recognize someone or to gain attention. Meaningful glances between people also convey different messages.

The third aspect, the way in which an individual stands or uses personal space, is called *proxemics*. The proximity of one individual to another communicates attitudes about interacting or conversing with others. Experts have found that culture influences how an individual places the body in reference to others and the distance maintained from others.

Implications for Reading

Although most children enter school at the point where they use language both for private purposes and to communicate with others verbally and nonverbally, their language development continues throughout the elementary school years. During these years teachers have opportunities to help children grow in all aspects of communication. This growth includes

> . . . expansion of communicative need, expansion of experience, expansion
> of confidence in the use of language, expansion of conceptual ability,
> expansion of control over the structure of language, expansion of
> vocabulary, expansion of the range of language that is understood,
> expansion of the range of language used in expression and the ability to
> communicate with many different people. (Smith and others, 1976, p. 66)

To foster the expansion of language and thinking, reading programs must integrate listening, speaking, reading, and writing activities to build on the natural overlap of these areas. Active participation by children in a variety of oral and written language experiences is necessary to expand their understanding and use of language to prepare them for the many demanding communicative situations in school and society.

Children need to experience familiar and useful activities and freely use their language to communicate their feelings, understandings, and questions to others. The language and the experiences that children bring to school provide the foundation of the reading program. Children's knowledge of how language functions and how print is used in their out-of-school environment must relate to their early school experiences for children to make sense of the school environment and perceive school and reading as an expansion of their familiar world. In their familiar world language is always part of a context. Children speak and listen for real purposes. Children see print in many situations at home and in their community. Many children "read" and "write" before school entry. This ranges from reading signs in the environment, to sharing stories with adults, to actually reading stories independently. Writing experiences range from early scribbles and pictures, to using invented spellings, to using closely approximated and accurately spelled words. These out-of-school reading and writing abilities, to whatever degree children develop them, grow out of real needs to explore the environment and communicate. This natural progression in communicative ability must continue in the classroom. Starting with the child's competence in oral and written language, the curriculum should set goals to increase this competence through experiences that foster the use of language to communicate and to understand the communications of others. These experiences should include many opportunities to use oral language in informal and formal speaking situations, to hear, create, and react to stories, to compose a variety of written communications, and to read continuous discourse of various types. As children read, they use private language to think about what they read, to organize reading behaviors, and to evaluate their own performances. All of these language-reading experiences increase children's understanding of the communication process and build on their natural inclinations to be language users.

Goodman and Goodman (1979) suggest using Halliday's functions of language as a framework for planning some learning experiences. Use of this framework can help the teacher to build upon children's familiarity with language and to serve as a link to reading. Table 3.4 on page 56 describes some experiences and activities that relate to the functions of language.

HOW LANGUAGE IS STRUCTURED
The continuous development of spoken language involves the close interaction of the communicative functions of language (how humans use language) with how language is structured. The structure of language includes three major components: the phonological system or the sounds of language, the syntactic system or the organization of words within sentences, and the semantic or meaning system.

Phonological Development
Phonological development "refers to the emergence of rules for combining sounds into pronounceable sequences in a language" (McNeill, 1970, p. 130). Although there is data available to describe the sequence and time at which particular sounds emerge in the child's development, experts know little about how rules develop for combining sounds into pronounceable units in a language.

The sequence of development in this area begins with the nonlinguistic vocalizations of early infancy and includes the early cries and cooing in response to physiological and psychological needs. During the babbling

Table 3.4 Language Functions and Learning Experiences

Function	Experiences and Activities
Instrumental (I want)	Sign-ups for activities or interest centers Picture collages with captions: *Things I Want* Play stores and gas stations Orders for supplies: *Things I Need*
Regulatory (Do as I tell you)	Signs Directions Rules for care of class pets, plants, materials Instructions to make things
Interactional (Me and you)	Message board for notes from teacher to children Class post office Games involving reading
Personal (Here I come)	Books about self and family with captioned pictures Individual language-experience stories
Heuristic (Tell me why)	Question box Single concept books Science experiments
Imaginative (Let's pretend)	Storytelling Picture-story sessions with class participation Creative dramatics activities Read-along books and records Comic strips
Informative (I've got something to tell you)	Message boards and bulletin boards Notes to pupils paralleling school messages to parents Class newspaper Community newspaper and *TV Guide* Content textbooks Resource books

Source: K. S. Goodman & Y. M. Goodman. Learning to read is natural. In L. B. Resnick & P. A. Weaver (Eds.), *Theory and practice in early reading* (Vol. 1), p. 152. Copyright © 1979 by Lawrence Erlbaum Associates. Reprinted by permission of publisher.

period, which begins at about 6 months, sounds become better defined and begin to take on some of the characteristics of the native language.

Jakobson and Halle (1956) propose that this development is invariant and universal and is organized so that any language can develop through a process of differentiation of sounds. Toward the end of the first year, the child begins to discriminate and produce the vowel and consonant phonemes of the native language in a systematic way. The first word usually follows at about age 1. From this time on, the use of the phonological system increases markedly. By age 4 most of the phonemes can be produced in at least some words. However, it may be several years before a child has complete mastery of the production aspect of language. According to Templin (1957), a child may be 7 or 8 years of age before this occurs.

In regard to rule development for using phonemes, it appears from informal observations that children continue working on phonological rules even longer than on the production of sounds, but there are few actual studies to support these observations (McNeill, 1970).

Syntactic Development

This is the acquisition of the grammar of one's language—that is, the rules that determine the structure of sentences. This rule knowledge is evident in children from the very first combination of words that they produce. Brown (1972) illustrates this point well in Table 3.5 in which he describes children's imitations of model sentences spoken by their mothers. In their imitations children preserve the word order of the model sentences and are highly systematic in their selection of words to be retained. Nouns and verbs are most frequently retained whereas adjectives are retained less often. The forms most frequently omitted are inflections, auxiliary verbs, articles, prepositions, and conjunctions. Thus, early combinations are governed by order and are systematically constructed/reconstructed.

In listening to early speech, experts recognize that some combinations cannot be based primarily on imitation from adult models since children produce novel sequences not heard in adult speech. For example, "allgone cookie," "more read," and "off hat." These early combinations change and expand until they take on the more familiar characteristics of adult syntax. The development of this rule-governed grammar by children is first evident with the production of two-word constructions at about 18 months to 2 years and continues with the production of three-word constructions in the second year. In these constructions, the main words of sentences are present but certain specific elements are systematically missing.

> By the time a child is 3½, a child has learned the essential creativity of language: he can produce sentences that are indefinitely long, for once he has learned that a sentence can be made bigger by adding a clause on with *and* . . . he comes to repeat the process often ad infinitum. (Crystal, 1976, p. 47)

Table 3.5 Some Imitations Produced by Adam and Eve

Model Utterance	Child's Imitation
Tank car.	Tank car.
Wait a minute.	Wait a minute.
Daddy's briefcase.	Daddy briefcase.
Fraser will be unhappy.	Fraser unhappy.
He's going out.	He go out.
That's an old time train.	Old time train.
It's not the same dog as Pepper.	Dog Pepper.
No, you can't write on Mr. Cromer's shoe.	Write Cromer shoe.

Source: Reprinted with permission of Macmillan Publishing Co., Inc. from *Psycholinguistics: Selected papers* by Roger Brown, p. 81. Copyright © 1970 by The Free Press, a Division of Macmillan Publishing Co., Inc.

For example, "Daddy gone shopping *and* he get cookies *and* he drive car," shows this pattern. The use of the conjunction *and*, which appears in children's language by age three or four follows a developmental trend which exemplifies the continuous development of children's syntax. The work of Athey (1977) illustrates the hierarchical development of children's use of the conjunction *and*. At the bottom of the hierarchy the presence of common elements would seem to be a minimum requirement. As we proceed up the hierarchy, the relationships become increasingly intricate and diversified. The following sentences illustrate this hierarchical development. They represent a few of the ways in which *and*, probably the easiest and most familiar conjunction, may imply a relationship that is not explicitly stated but must be inferred between two or more ideas.

1. *It was growing darker, and the rain was coming down heavily.* No intrinsic relationship exists between the two ideas. It may grow darker without rain, or rain without growing darker. The similarity of the elements is that they contribute to the description of a gloomy evening and do, in fact, often occur together.

2. *He dreamed about growing up and becoming a famous scientist.* Here the relationship is the "similar element" of dreaming common to the two ideas. There is no inherent, necessary relationship between the content of the two ideas (one can grow up without becoming a famous scientist), but there is a relation of temporal sequence combined with "appropriateness." A sentence such as, "He dreamed of growing up and eating a delicious supper that evening" would be inappropriate.

3. *Jim is tall, and John is short.* The relationship is one of opposition within a given context, e.g., comparing brothers or friends.

4. *He said he would come, and I believed him.* The relationship is not exactly causal, but reflects the social convention that we believe what someone says, unless and until we have sufficient grounds for not believing.

5. *The dog bared its teeth and Billy ran in terror.* Here the relationship is clearly causal. (pp. 73–74)

These examples are in keeping with developmental trends Hutson and Shub (1974) found, showing a random use of the conjunction *and* at grade one, an ordered use of the rule of similar elements at grade four, and the use of more complex rules at grade ten. Thus, the child's development of the grammatical system continues with a high degree of control achieved at about school age, with the process of completing this knowledge of the syntactic system continuing well into the school years (Chomsky, 1969; Crystal, 1976; Athey, 1977). Like most adults, children cannot state the rules of their grammar although they certainly use them in a consistent, systematic way.

Semantic Development

Semantic development involves the learning of the meaning system of the language. This system includes "the dimensions and categories of meaning, the definitions of words, the manner in which combinations of words gain meaning in sentences. . . ." (Slobin, 1971, p. 68). That is, semantic rules involve knowing the multiple meanings of words, recognizing subtle distinctions of words within a variety of contexts, and understanding phrases, whole sentences, and continuous discourse. "Meaning . . . arises from the way in which forms are used in relation to the extralinguistic world of objects, ideas and experiences" (Crystal, 1976, p. 51).

According to Halliday (1975), this means that humans use both ideational and interpersonal components in an integrated way to arrive at meaning.

> . . . (1) ideational, embodying the speaker's experience and interpretation
> of the world that is around him and inside him, and (2) interpersonal,
> embodying his own involvement in the speech situation—his roles,
> attitudes, wishes, judgments, and the like. (pp. 261–62)

The development of the semantic system is the aspect of language acquisition least understood, because it is so closely related to broader areas of cognition (McNeill, 1970) and involves a number of intangibles. Traditionally, experts have most frequently measured knowledge of the semantic system by the number of words in a child's vocabulary. However, this approach does not take into account the quality of the words, knowledge of multiple meanings of words, their subtler characteristics, or the fact that semantics involves considerably more than individual word meanings.

What experts know at this time is that initial meaning arises from the young child's base of experience and knowledge. These initial meanings of words are restricted by the young child's relatively limited experiential background and perspective. That is, a child first acquires only a partial awareness of the meaning of a word. Initially, the child experiences word categories as being global but as the child's semantic system expands, the categories increase in number and become more precisely refined. The semantic system continues to develop throughout the school years and into adulthood.

Meaning and Concept Development

The ongoing development of the semantic or meaning system is closely related to the development of concepts and reading growth. Concepts form the base from which the meanings extracted from the experience combine into an organized cognitive knowledge store. Therefore, concepts form the base from which the reader constructs meaning from text. As meaning is the goal of reading, understanding concept development provides the teacher with increased knowledge of the developing reader.

Klausmeier and Goodwin (1975) define a concept as:

> . . . ordered information about the properties of one or more things—
> objects, events, or processes—that enables any particular thing or class of
> things to be differentiated from and also related to other things or classes of
> things. (p. 44)

Carroll (1964) points out that because of the continuity of the physical,
biological, and social environment in which people live, they share words
and are able to understand concepts. When children learn that a word
stands for or names a concept, they are learning concepts shared among
the members of their language community. For the most part, it is these
societally shared meanings, referred to as denotative or dictionary meanings, that people generally use in spoken or written communication. Denotative meanings develop from a base of shared experiences and shared
language. Klausmeier and Goodwin (1975) state that an individual's concept becomes related to the concepts of other people at this denotative level
of word meaning.

A second type of word meaning, referred to as connotative meaning,
comes from the individual's personal store of unique experiences and
perceptions and may be based on feelings as well as cognitive information.
Communication at the connotative level is much more difficult than at the
denotative level because it involves idiosyncratic meanings of words rather
than commonly shared meanings. For example, the denotative meaning of
the word *read* is to construct meaning from print, whereas it may have
different connotative meanings for different readers. For some people the
word *read* connotes a pleasurable experience, whereas for others the word
may connote negative or unpleasant associations.

Klausmeier's work on concept development emphasizes the denotative
meanings of words. Like Carroll, he stresses that word meanings are based
on the societally accepted or public concepts people who speak the same
language share.

As individuals function in society, the meaning of words and concepts
continues to expand and new concepts develop. During the school years
this growth is rapid; therefore, knowledge of how concepts develop is
relevant for the teacher concerned with knowing individual child development as it relates to reading growth. As yet no definitive hierarchy of
concept development exists although a number of theorists (Bruner and
others, 1956; Vygotsky, 1962; Piaget, 1964; Taba, 1965) have hypothesized
stages of concept development. The work of Klausmeier, Ghatala, and
Frayer (1974), which is consistent in many respects with the work of these
theorists, offers a model of conceptual learning and development. Their
model clearly delineates levels of concept development and provides one
way of organizing observed behaviors, so that trends in the development
of meaning can be inferred. An adaptation of Klausmeier's model of concept development follows, accompanied by an example illustrating the
gradual development of a concept; in this case the concept of *book*.

Concrete Level

Description

The individual recognizes an object encountered on prior occasions by attending to perceptible features of the object, discriminating the object from other objects, and remembering the object. The individual may or may not acquire the name of the object at this level.

Example

The child recognizes a *book*, based upon a visual image stored in memory. To recognize it, the child must experience the book with the same essential features as initially experienced. That is, if the child first saw the book closed and facing the child, it must be in this same form for the child to recognize it and distinguish it from surrounding objects.

Identity Level

The individual recognizes an object as the same one previously encountered even though it is observed in a different physical perspective (spatial orientation) or in a sense modality other than the initial modality. At this level an individual both discriminates various forms of the same object from other objects and generalizes that different forms of the same object are equivalent. The name of the object may or may not be acquired at this level.

The young child recognizes a *book* as the same object previously seen and discriminates it from other objects even though the book may now be open or closed and combined with different objects than the child has seen it with before. It may also be in a different position spatially, that is, upside down or sideways.

Classificatory Level

The individual responds to two different examples of the same class of objects, events, or actions as being equivalent. Individuals correctly classify a large number of instances as examples and others as non-examples but can neither define the word that stands for the concept nor explain the basis of the specific classification. The individual may or may not have acquired the name of the object at this level.

The child recognizes that a paperback book and a hardcover book are both *books* and that a storybook and an alphabet book are two different examples of *books*. In addition, the child can correctly classify a large number of objects as being *books* or *non-books*. At this level the child cannot yet define the word that stands for the concept *book* and may not yet have acquired the concept name.

Formal Level

The individual can give the name of the concept and define the concept in terms of its attributes. The individual can differentiate between examples and non-examples of the concept in terms of similarities and differences by using hypothesis-testing strategies.

The child can now give the name *book* upon seeing a book, defines a book as something to read, something that has printed sheets of paper put together with a cover, and can differentiate between books and other objects.

These four levels describe the course of concept growth at all ages. According to Klausmeier and Goodwin (1975), the attainment of any new concept moves in an invariant sequence:

> A concept attained only to the concrete or identity level may be used in solving simple perceptually-based problems. Concepts learned at the classificatory and formal levels can be used in generalizing to new instances, cognizing supraordinate-subordinate relations, cognizing cause-and-effect and other relations among concepts, and in solving problems. (pp. 51–52)

That is, humans may use concepts developed at the higher levels in recognizing that two or more things belonging to the same class are similar, in noting relationships between concepts and distinguishing those that are more general and thus inclusive of the more specific concepts. Humans also may use higher level concepts in understanding if-then relationships, in using probability and correlational information to make predictions, and in problem solving through the use of previously obtained rules. The acquisition of labels or names which represent specific concepts facilitates the expansion of concept development. This expansion enables the individual to use symbolic thinking (language) rather than imagery and, therefore, to attain new concepts through spoken or written language as well as through the experiencing of actual objects and events.

> In sum, concepts perform a dual service: (1) they identify and classify input information; (2) they make it possible for the organism to "go beyond the information given" in all manner of adaptive ways. (Flavell, 1970, p. 986)

Implications for the Classroom

Although this book discusses the functions of language and the linguistic systems of language separately, remembering that children build up knowledge of all areas of language at the same time is very important. As children learn more about the linguistic system, they learn more ways to convey different functions, and as they learn more about functions, they expand the uses to which they can put the linguistic system (Clark & Clark, 1977). To encourage learning, the teacher arranges a classroom environment that fosters language-thinking growth. Teachers can create this environment in many ways, such as by:

1.   Accepting children's language to facilitate their participation in classroom activities. This involves recognition that the message or meaning the speaker intends is foremost—not the form of the presentation.
2.   Attending to children as they speak so that they become aware that they are important, that what they say (the message) has importance, and that a speaker needs a listener.
3.   Emphasizing natural language usage in conversation by accepting

single word or partial sentence constructions similar to those that children use at home and in the community.

4. Fostering talking as an important school activity so that children feel free to explain ideas, describe experiences, participate in discussions, and hold conversations with their peers and adults. This involves teacher recognition that classroom noise reflects communication and is a positive part of the environment.

5. Encouraging children to share out-of-school experiences with peers and adults so that they feel that they can verbalize all experiences—be they teacher-generated, home-generated, or child-generated.

6. Encourage children to share experiences and ideas in an audience situation, so that children become aware of the shared responsibilities in communication while they enrich their language base through both speaking to others and listening to others.

7. Planning experiences that will expand the children's base of ideas and thus expand their use of language as they describe, explain, and react to their experiences.

8. Exposing children to a wide variety of language through the use of story telling, television, radio, films, and other verbal media, in order to expand their concepts and language experience.

9. Providing centers of interest in the classroom that will encourage verbal interaction. These centers would include areas with a variety of reading materials; areas with a variety of listening-speaking materials (cassette tapes, records, filmstrips, etc.); and areas with drawing and writing materials.

10. Providing opportunities for experimentation with language through the use of rhymes, jingles, and the natural language games of childhood.

11. Planning opportunities for play that encourage verbal interaction among children and give children opportunities to use nonverbal aspects of communication.

A classroom in which teachers and children accept each other's language, freely communicate ideas and questions using their language, participate in diverse experiences and see print as useful provides the base for continued interest and growth in all aspects of language.

Summary

Chapter 3 describes the relationship of language and thought and the developmental nature of language. Also the chapter discusses the communicative functions of language, the noncommunicative functions of language, and nonverbal communication. The chapter relates these aspects of communication to reading. The structure of language is described including the phonological, syntactic, and semantic systems with an emphasis on concept development. Implications for the classroom teacher include a list of suggestions for creating a language-rich school environment.

The Teaching-Learning Environment

Teacher-Directed Experiences

Three Stages of Teaching
PREACTIVE TEACHING
INTERACTIVE TEACHING
EVALUATIVE TEACHING

Independent Learner Experiences

Integrating Teacher-Directed and Independent Learner Experiences

Overview of Assessment
INFORMAL OBSERVATION
STRUCTURED ASSESSMENT
FORMAL TESTING

Summary

T he teaching-learning environment is an active print-rich one. Teachers and learners are continually listening, speaking, observing, and doing. The door to a third-grade classroom opens, and an observer notices the following: The room abounds with print related to the day-to-day functioning of the children and teacher. The children and teacher are actively communicating in a variety of situations.

Six children are listening to a story from a tape recorder.

Ten children are reading silently.

Three children are in a writing center where they are drawing pictures, writing, and talking quietly with each other.

Nine children are engaged in a discussion with the teacher. The teacher writes down some notes as the discussion proceeds.

After approximately 10 minutes the situation has changed:

Of the six children who were listening to the tape recorder, three have moved to the writing center, and three have moved to the library corner.

Two of the ten children who were reading silently go to the library corner and begin to look at books and magazines.

The three children who were drawing, writing, and talking continue this activity.

The nine children who were engaged in discussion with the teacher begin to read silently.

The teacher moves to the writing center and interacts with each child with a brief comment or question and then calls one child to a quiet corner for an individual learner-teacher conference.

The questions uppermost in the observer's mind are:

How does this classroom environment facilitate learning?

How did the teacher plan for the observed activities?

How does the teacher implement the planned activities?

How will the teacher evaluate learners' progress?

This teacher has established an environment that encourages listening, speaking, observing, and doing. Children are motivated to participate in purposeful activities, have opportunities to engage in a variety of experiences both with the teacher and independently, and thus have a good chance to succeed in learning. They are learning to function as members of a group as they communicate their ideas to each other and understand that there are many ways to learn. As they share their learning, they experience that what they think, say, and do has value. They also learn that learning can be an independent activity; that they do not need the direction of others to experience, to question, and to solve problems.

Teachers as shapers of the environment model active learning, facilitate learning by participating with children in a variety of activities planned to meet their specific needs, and guide learners to become independent. Teacher behavior serves as a model for children and, therefore, teachers should demonstrate those behaviors they wish to stimulate in learners. If children perceive discrepancies between what teachers say and what teachers do, they will be less likely to follow teachers' words (Good & Brophy, 1978). Teachers need to listen attentively to students, to communicate their own ideas clearly to students through speaking and writing, and to exhibit their own personal reading habits. As modeling occurs at all times, not just when specifically planned for, teachers need to be aware of their own actions at all times. Along with modeling appropriate language and reading behaviors, the teacher creates an environment by actions and words that indicates acceptance of children's background, language, feelings, and opinions and relays the message that learners are important and that other adults and children take them seriously. The teacher transmits these messages to children by attending to their verbal and nonverbal communications, responding positively to their efforts and guiding or criticizing them in ways that encourage them to participate further. Within this accepting atmosphere children feel free to take part in new experiences and to express themselves even where the chance exists that their responses may not be the ones the teacher expects. Thus in this environment the teacher encourages risk-taking and views learning with enthusiasm.

In designing this learning environment, the teacher must simultaneously consider the learner, the curriculum content, and the goals of reading instruction—reading for enjoyment and reading for information. The teacher plans reading experiences, some of which are primarily teacher directed and some of which are primarily learner independent, with the active role of teachers and learners in mind. *Teacher-directed reading experiences* involve those language and reading activities in which learners specifically interact with text, teacher, and other children following a structured plan. Learners engage in those activities outlined in plans that the teacher has developed. This direct teaching is different from structuring the learner and the environment so that independent learning can take place. *Independent experiences* involve those activities in which children explore their environment through observing, listening, doing, and reading in a self-directed manner. Learners interact with specific materials provided in the classroom and with other learners to apply and expand reading/language abilities. In this case, instead of planning specific structured lessons, the teacher structures the environment to encourage independent explorations and experiencing on the part of learners.

This chapter will describe the three stages of teaching involved in teacher-directed experiences. It will discuss independent learner experiences and relate them to teacher-directed activities. An overview of assessment, as it relates to both teacher-directed and independent learner activities, also appears in this chapter.

Teacher-Directed Experiences

The teacher bases decisions about the content of teacher-directed experiences on informal observations and structured assessment of reading performance. Depending on reader and teacher purposes, these experiences or teaching plans will incorporate language experience materials and text materials, either narrative or expository. The goal of direct teaching is for children to learn to understand continuous discourse. Strategy teaching supports this goal. This approach to teaching reading develops readers who have both the ability and motivation to read because their concept of reading builds on their experiences with real materials that demonstrate that reading is enjoyable and purposeful. Teachers recognize that children need to learn some specific strategies to read effectively, but they do not confuse strategy teaching with purposeful reading. They view the teaching of any specific strategy as being important but subsidiary to reading for enjoyment and reading for information; strategies are only means, not ends.

In planning reading activities, the teacher begins with curriculum objectives and then analyzes the structure and content of the material. The teacher also determines the match between the concepts in the material and the curriculum goals. Once teachers have this knowledge, they can plan for reader-text interactions involving the design of activities to develop each of the aspects of effective reading delineated below (Brown, 1980, aspects 1, 3–8, p. 456).

Children who read effectively

1. understand why they are reading a particular text;
2. associate their background knowledge with the text content and structure;
3. identify the important ideas in a message;
4. allocate their attention so that they can focus their concentration on the major content area rather than trivia;
5. monitor their own reading to determine whether comprehension is occurring;
6. engage in review and self-questioning to see whether they are achieving goals;
7. take corrective action themselves when they find they are having failures in comprehension;
8. recover from disruptions that occur during reading;
9. organize the information gained from reading to fit their purpose(s); and
10. apply the information constructed from the text to fulfill their purpose(s).

As you can see, an effective reader uses reading for many different purposes. An effective reader is aware that reading is language, reading is communication with a writer, reading is information gathering, and reading is pleasurable. This reader recognizes that reading is integrally related to learning, that reading is a process to be used throughout life, and that reading is not a product or task done just to satisfy teachers or parents. In this context, children understand that the learning of specific strategies is not "reading" but a support they may need to increase their ability to construct meaning from real texts.

Three Stages of Teaching

To create and implement language/reading experiences, the teacher progresses through three related stages in a cyclical pattern. These stages are preactive teaching, interactive teaching, and evaluative teaching (Shavelson, 1976; Clark & Yinger, 1978; Yinger, 1978) and involve decisions made prior to teacher-learner(s) interaction, during teaching-learning activities, and following learning experiences.

PREACTIVE TEACHING

The first stage, preactive teaching, is the planning stage. During this time the teacher, taking into account variations in the way different learners function and the accompanying differences in their needs, creates two different types of teaching-learning plans. The teacher develops the first type, *general teaching-learning plans*, for all learners to structure their interactions with narrative and expository text. These plans provide opportunities to expand learners' understanding of the content and structure of stories and content area materials. The teacher develops the second type of plan, referred to as a *specific strategy plan*, when observations and assessments indicate that there are learners whose functioning with continuous text will benefit from focusing on a specific skill in isolation.

General Teaching-Learning Plan

In developing general teaching-learning plans, the teachers' focus is on learners' understanding of and reacting to an author's ideas and on how the author organized the ideas. Because authors use particular patterns of organization and forms of language to communicate their ideas, teachers may select particular elements of an author's writing for focus. Also, teachers may develop a general teaching-learning plan to reinforce previous learning. That is, some plans introduce concepts or ideas, and some plans review information that was previously introduced by applying the concepts in new reading situations.

For example, in using narrative materials, the teacher may choose to focus on the author's use of flashbacks in the development of plot, the author's use of figurative language to create vivid pictures, or the author's presentation of a character through the character's actions and behaviors. In using expository text, the teacher may have readers focus on the author's use of temporal relations in historical writing or on how the author distinguishes between major and minor ideas in the text. In all cases readers have clearly established purposes for reading and read real materials.

Specific Strategy Plan

The teacher develops specific strategy plans using ongoing diagnostic information about individual children. A child or a small group of children may need to learn a specific skill that will increase competency in reading continuous discourse. For example, readers who have difficulty understanding temporal relations in historical materials would form a small group and participate in a structured strategy lesson. This lesson would develop the concept of temporal relations using concrete experiences and examples. The teacher would select and develop reading materials so that readers would progress from sentences to paragraphs to longer discourse. In all strategy lessons learners would apply their knowledge in natural reading situations. In the above case the group would read and discuss an excerpt from a history text in which temporal relations were prominent.

The need for specific strategy teaching varies. For some children, learning to read is an easy process, and for the most part specific strategy teaching is not a necessary component of their reading program. These children tend to read early, get meaning from the written text, and achieve reading proficiency with minimal direct instruction. A second group also comprised of able readers exhibits some unevenness in reading performance. Children in this group require more direct strategy teaching to increase their reading efficiency further. A third group of children are those for whom learning to read is a difficult process. This group requires intensive instruction in specific strategies. And they require just as many opportunities for ongoing application of their learning in natural reading situations as all other readers. Strategy lessons can be thought of as a prereading activity because they prepare readers to interact with continuous discourse, the goal of all reading-related instruction.

During the preactive stage, when teachers are creating plans, they choose, analyze, and evaluate relevant commercially prepared materials and/or construct materials. Children's background knowledge of a text's content and structure as well as their interest and feelings are primary considerations in the selection and construction of these materials. Thus, during this planning stage teachers apply their knowledge of the readers in order to design reading experiences that will facilitate effective reader-text interactions and that will enable readers to extend and restructure their knowledge base to incorporate new information. According to Shavelson (1976), these

> . . . decisions made while planning instruction may be the most important ones teachers make. Unlike decisions during interactive teaching, decisions made in planning can be pondered—they have the advantage of time. (p. 392)

INTERACTIVE TEACHING

During the interactive stage of teaching the teacher makes decisions while working with and observing readers. This stage involves three related aspects of interactions: prereading experiences, reader-text interactions, and postreading experiences. See Figure 4.1 for an overview of this interactive stage of teaching.

Prereading Activities

Prereading experiences can be thought of as enabling activities because they provide a reader with the necessary background to organize activity and to comprehend the material. These experiences involve understanding the purpose(s) for reading and building a knowledge base necessary for dealing with the content and structure of the material. Readers need to know why they are reading and need to have a certain amount of familiarity with the topic and understanding of the author's language and organization. Some prereading activities can elicit students' knowledge of the content and structure of the material to be read. A major way to do this is to have learners share their personal experiences and knowledge related to the topic. In those cases where learners' backgrounds need expanding, teachers can plan activities such as participating in relevant experiences, viewing films/filmstrips or listening to stories, records, or tapes. To focus reader attention on important ideas in the material to be read, teacher-and/or student-generated questions or outlines can be helpful. Prereading activities may also include specific strategy lessons geared to student needs. The kind of prereading activities that the teacher selects depends on the purpose for reading, the reader, and the material. Readers, by participating in well-planned prereading activities, become aware that they need to assess their knowledge base before undertaking independent reading. This is an important component in developing students' ability to monitor their own readiness to interact with a particular piece of text.

Reader-Text Interaction

Reader-text interaction includes self-awareness on the part of learners of their comprehension and the ability of learners to regulate their reading by engaging in self-questioning and any needed compensatory strategies. Age, overall reading functioning, and experience relative to the task influence a reader's ability to self-monitor comprehension. Thus, being able to recognize if comprehension is occurring is a developmental process and young children apparently do not undertake it routinely (Brown, 1980; Baker & Brown, 1984). Research suggests that both young readers and poor readers focus on decoding when reading and tend not to be aware that the primary goal of reading is to construct meaning (Flavell & Wellman, 1977). Some other research suggests that this focus on decoding may also be a function of the instructional program and the theoretical orientation of the teacher (Harste & Burke, 1977; Meyers & Ringler, 1980). Although research in this area is in its infancy, it makes good sense to

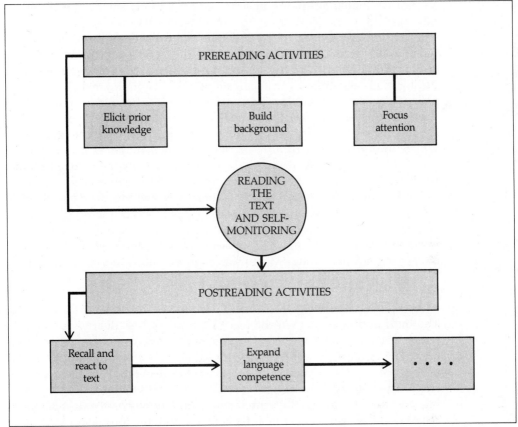

Figure 4.1 Overview of Interactive Teaching

consider that as with most things, more than one factor may influence developmental differences. Whatever the reasons that some readers focus on decoding rather than meaning, the teachers' responsibilities are to expand children's understanding so that they realize that reading must make sense and to help them expand the concept of self-monitoring.

Postreading Activities

Postreading activities like prereading activities are integrally related to specific learning purposes. The first activity following reading is either reacting to the text or recalling or reviewing information constructed from the text.

Although an important postreading activity involves a review of the text information, frequently an additional related purpose is to be able to retain and recall information for a specific objective. When this is the case, prereading activities focus the learner on important information that becomes the focus during postreading. For example, if student-generated or teacher-generated questions are a part of prereading activities, these questions should be the focus of any postreading discussion.

In addition, activities to expand oral and/or written language competence and reading competence involve the whole class, small groups and/or individuals. Teaching to expand oral language competence occurs during such activities as dramatization, role-playing, simulating experiences, reporting on and/or debating about ideas related to the reading material. The teacher facilitates written language competence by stimulating the writing of reports, essays, letters, notes, stories, and poems—all of which should use the content of the reading material as a jumping-off point. Finally, reading competence extends as learners read additional narratives, expository material, or poetry on the same or related topics.

Teacher decisions made during interactive teaching may be planned, spontaneous, or a combination of both. The success of these planned and spontaneous interactions depends on the teachers' training, prior experiences in teaching reading, and growing knowledge of readers' cognitive and affective functioning. Most interactive decisions are modifications of decisions made during preactive teaching (Shavelson, 1976).

EVALUATIVE TEACHING

The third and final stage in the teaching process is evaluative teaching in which teachers reflect on their planning and the success of the implementation. This process involves thinking about the teaching and learning experiences and evaluating any products that resulted from these experiences. The teacher assesses reader interactions with the text, how prereading activities facilitated this interaction, and how postreading activities clarified and/or extended this interaction. Children, too, take part in this process. The teacher encourages them to reflect on their own functioning and that of others through structured observations, discussions, and critical appraisals of their work. The evaluative stage provides teachers with an opportunity to expand their understanding of learners' strategies as these learners construct meaning from text and apply information during a variety of oral and written experiences. This knowledge is the basis for creating additional general teaching-learning plans and specific strategy lessons.

Independent Learner Experiences

As teachers create their general teaching-learning plans and specific strategy lessons, they need to consider the complementary role of independent learner experiences. These learner experiences involve independent or small group activities centered on curriculum areas or special interest areas designed to stimulate and expand learners' thinking and language functioning. The teacher is responsible for creating the environment that will stimulate this independent learning. Classrooms should be set up so that individuals or small groups can function on their own in areas often referred to as interest or activity centers. These centers are often thought of for use in the primary grades, but their value extends throughout all the grades. Students of any age can and should help the teacher plan the organization and materials for these centers. This shared planning will ensure that these areas reflect children's concerns and will foster the feeling that they are able to have an impact on their environment. As teachers and children develop activity centers, they think about activities that will stimulate language use—listening, speaking, reading, and writing—and they plan and design a print-rich environment that includes materials of varying levels of difficulty so that all children can share related experiences. As these centers are planned, teachers should keep in mind that some centers will be permanent whereas others will be temporary. Reading, writing, listening, and viewing centers should be a permanent part of the classroom, whereas topical centers would be temporary as curriculum and student interests change. The permanent centers provide opportunities to use language in both curriculum-related as well as interest-related areas.

The reading center should have a permanent collection of narrative books, non-narrative books, magazines, and newspapers. These can be related to general curriculum areas or particular areas of student interests. In addition, student-generated stories, poems, plays, and expository material have a temporary spot in the reading center.

The writing center has stimulating materials such as suggestions for writing and art work in curriculum-related and personally motivated areas. Student writings and drawings are on display in this area. The area also includes specific materials with which to write and draw.

The listening-viewing center has materials such as books or stories with accompanying tapes, filmstrips, slides, records, and so forth. Both teacher-prepared and student-prepared materials are stored there along with commercial materials.

The content of these permanent centers changes and expands as curriculum changes and topical interests evolve. Every subject area or student interest offers opportunities for creating activity centers and thereby extends learner knowledge and communication skills. The curriculum areas of science, social studies, mathematics, art, music, and health education provide topics for setting up temporary centers for language and reading expansion. Student interest can lead to additional temporary centers in any of the curriculum areas or provide supplementary areas of focus.

The teacher frequently introduces activities to the whole class in these centers; then individuals or groups of learners carry out such activities at different times: when they have completed structured reading activities, when they have extra time throughout the day, or when the teacher specifically sets aside time for independent work. In all activity centers, as in the rest of the classroom environment, print is available in many forms. There are lists, directions, schedules, labels, signs, books, and student writings. All materials are easily accessible and designed to stimulate active use.

Integrating Teacher-Directed and Independent Learner Activities

In keeping with a teaching-learning environment that encourages learners to construct meaning from experience, both teacher-directed experiences and student-directed experiences are planned and implemented to stimulate listening, speaking, observing, and doing. The following example illustrates the integration of these types of experiences during the three stages of teaching—preactive teaching, interactive teaching, and evaluative teaching.

A typical first-grade curriculum includes a unit on the neighborhood. During *preactive teaching* the teacher considers specific information about learners and knowledge of the neighborhood in which they live to plan experiences and activities in preparation for developing language experience charts. For example, the teacher plans a neighborhood walk as a starting point for this unit. The teacher plans diverse activities and selects various levels of material so that learners at different levels of functioning can learn about their neighborhood together. At the same time the teacher gathers materials such as books, pictures, filmstrips related to the neighborhood to be used in setting up a temporary interest center. The teacher thinks about possibilities for other materials and other temporary centers and plans ways to involve the children in establishing these centers. During the *interactive teaching* stage, the teacher and the learners develop a series of individual, group, and class language experience charts about different aspects of living, working, and playing in the neighborhood. These charts form the basis for teacher-directed language and reading experiences and may focus on different but specific purposes such as sequence of events, descriptive language, and/or classifying information. In conjunction with these activities, children will use materials in the activity center independently. The teacher guides children to add materials to the existing center and/or establish additional centers related to the neighborhood such as a neighborhood store.

During the final teaching stage, *evaluative teaching,* teachers and children assess what they have learned during teacher-directed and independent learner activities. The teacher assesses learners' functioning in the development, reading, and follow-up activities related to the language experience charts. The teacher also analyzes learner use of activity centers by noting those learners who participate in independent activities and the amount and quality of their interactions with other learners. In doing this, the teacher differentiates between those learners who use available materials and those learners who develop materials, noting the appropriateness and quality of these materials. Learners also participate in the evaluative process. They analyze their work, discuss what they have learned, and talk about what else they want to know.

Overview of Assessment

The teaching-learning environment provides many opportunities for getting to know the learner. These opportunities occur as learners interact with self-authored materials, texts, teachers, and other learners. Assessment will vary from daily informal observations as learners listen, speak, read, and write, to structured assessment procedures involving in-depth analyses of students' responses to print materials. Informal observation is the primary way of assessing learner functioning. The teacher observes all learners' behaviors as they function in reading-related activities. Diagnostic questions may guide the teacher's observations. Learners who appear to be having difficulty in comprehending written materials will require added evaluation using structured assessment procedures that provide in-depth analyses of their reading performances. Also, when learners with special needs are a part of the class—gifted learners, bilingual and bidialectal learners, and the learning disabled—using additional diagnostic questions to further understand the functioning of these learners may be appropriate. Chapters 14 and 15 discuss learners with special needs.

INFORMAL OBSERVATION

The teacher has the best opportunity to observe learner functioning informally during the interactive stage of teaching when general teaching–learning plans and specific strategy lessons are implemented. Also, during the evaluative stage of teaching, the teacher can reflect on observations and think about modifying instruction. Although most observations occur during interactive teaching, any situation in which a teacher interacts with a learner or learners interact with each other provides opportunities for observation of learner functioning.

Observation of learners who are just beginning to read focuses on interactions with print materials developed by using the readers' own experiences and language. This match between real life experiences and reading contributes to reader development by promoting verbalization of learners' understandings and insights (Athey, 1977). Thus, in early reading experiences the reader is the author, and assessment focuses on the reader's use of language and the quality of the interaction of the reader with reader-produced text. Educators generally refer to this approach to beginning reading as a Language Experience Approach (LEA). The teacher develops language experience charts on an individual and group basis as part of the regular classroom activities and analyzes these charts using a series of questions that focus on using oral language, relating language to print, and constructing meaning from print. The teacher uses data from these learner-developed materials to get to know these learners.

For learners already reading continuous discourse, the teacher uses published materials for the assessment. Although text may take the form of both narrative and non-narrative writing, we suggest that narratives form the basis for this assessment because most readers are familiar with story-type material. The teacher evaluates readers' performances through silent reading of text, using a retelling procedure. Structured questions are then used if they are needed to gain additional understanding of learners' functioning.

STRUCTURED ASSESSMENT

Those readers who in the teacher's opinion are having difficulty constructing meaning from print, require in-depth analysis of performance. The teacher sets up a reading situation specifically for assessment purposes. Although this type of assessment uses regular classroom materials (LE charts and/or narrative text), it differs from the previously described informal observation of reading functioning in that the specific purpose for reading is assessment, and the assessment occurs on an individual basis. The learner is aware of the purpose, and generally an individual teacher-learner conference follows the assessment. In these conferences the teacher and learner discuss the learner's self-perceptions of functioning, the teacher's analysis of the reader's performance, and some plans for instruction. This type of assessment will often take place close to the beginning of the school year, particularly for those learners who appear early on to be having difficulties comprehending written materials. In-depth analysis may also occur at selected times during the school year as part of teacher monitoring of reading progress.

In-depth analysis based on a LEA uses individually constructed experience charts as reading material. The teacher develops these charts from experiences specifically planned for assessment purposes. The teacher analyzes chart development and reading of the material to note the learners' conceptual understandings, language facility, overall understanding of the chart, and knowledge of word identification strategies. This type of analysis differs from informal observation using LEA in that it is always an individual experience and a series of charts allows for a broad-based and detailed picture of a learner's functioning.

For those learners reading textual materials, in-depth analysis consists of silent reading of text followed by a retelling procedure and structured questions as needed. Although similar to procedures described for informal observation, the major and important difference is that this assessment takes place with only one learner at a time. In this way the individual reader retells the story and responds to all of the questions. This allows the teacher to understand how the reader processes the text and where the construction of meaning breaks down for the particular reader. In addition, for some learners an oral reading analysis is necessary. This analysis focuses on miscues or oral reading errors at the sentence level and word level.

During both types of assessment (informal observation and structured assessment) the teacher must keep in mind that a reader understands written materials most successfully when the reader's purpose complements the writer's purpose. "A key assumption is that whatever the readers do is not random but is the result of the reading process, whether successfully used or not" (Goodman, 1975, p. 20). The assumption is that the reader has successfully processed material when the reader gains meaning from the text. Another assumption is that one or more aspects of processing may have been ineffective when performance indicates that the reader is constructing incomplete or inaccurate messages from the text. The role of the teacher, through informal observation and structured assessment procedures, is to find out in what ways this process has succeeded or failed. Chapters 5 and 6 will present examples of both types of assessment. Additional examples of informal assessment occur throughout the teaching chapters.

FORMAL TESTING
The misinterpretation of standardized tests has led to considerable controversy over the fairness and value of formal testing programs. Numerous political and social issues have been raised involving both community groups and educational institutions. Certainly, questioning the results of tests used inappropriately for making decisions about learners is necessary. For example, reading achievement tests primarily compare a group of students with the general population and in this way are useful to school administrators. Educators should not use such tests for instructional decision-making, yet sometimes they do use reading achievement tests for this purpose. This type of misuse of formal test measures has led to much of the controversy surrounding the use of standardized tests in schools.

Understanding that even with careful test selection and use test results are only a small sample of behavior at one point in time is essential. Teacher judgment of a learner's reading performance based on day-to-day classroom observations is the most important element in any assessment process and can yield the most relevant information for instructional planning. Therefore, teachers should only use the results of formal testing in conjunction with their observations of learners as they interact with text in a variety of reading situations.

Summary
This chapter discusses a teaching-learning environment in which both teachers and children interact in the classroom to facilitate active learning. Teaching within this environment focuses on purposeful reading in natural situations, provides opportunities for recreational reading, and includes specific strategy teaching only as needed. The emphasis in this approach is on reading narrative and non-narrative texts, and the application of strategies while reading continuous discourse. That is, children at all levels of functioning require extensive opportunities for reading meaningful material. Only in this way do readers come to understand the purpose and values of reading. Within this framework the chapter describes three stages of teaching—preactive teaching, interactive teaching, and evaluative teaching. Implementation of this teaching-learning environment depends on a combination of teacher-directed reading experiences and learner-directed experiences. Finally, the chapter discusses assessment as an integral component of all language/reading experiences.

PART
II

LANGUAGE AND READING

Language Experience as a Base for Reading

P revious chapters provide general guidelines for creating a classroom conducive to fostering language–thinking growth and appreciation of oral and written communication. This chapter will expand on these by discussing specific diagnostic and teaching activities to illustrate the application of a language-thinking curriculum. Teachers should take advantage of children's backgrounds and language as a bridge to reading; this chapter will focus on using student authorship as a base for reading experiences. This approach is generally referred to as a language experience approach (LEA). Although a language experience approach is most commonly thought of as a beginning reading approach, student authorship can be a valuable tool at all levels of reading function. The more proficient reader must also explore new experiences, and master new concepts and vocabulary; therefore, oral communication can also provide the necessary bridge to the written text for somewhat more advanced readers. As the LEA will expand to include readers of all ages, this chapter will apply the basic concepts of the LEA to both beginning reading experiences and subject area reading experiences to illustrate how learners can relate new experiences to print.

This chapter focuses on those aspects of student authorship in which children dictate their own ideas to others for reading. Remember that children's own writings are also an important part of the language/reading program. This aspect of student authorship is integrated throughout the teaching chapters and expanded upon in Chapter 16. Further, published materials such as basal readers, trade books, and content area texts and materials are also an integral part of the classroom reading program. Chapters 7–10 will describe reader interactions with narrative materials, and Chapters 11–13 will discuss reader interactions with expository materials.

Rationale for Language Experience Approach (LEA)

When children approach language/reading experiences, they bring a composite of knowlege, ways to apply this knowledge, and feelings acquired from past interactions with significant adults and children, objects and things, and print and other media. This cognitive and affective base varies for different children as early environmental interactions differ. Thus, children react to reading experiences differently because their language concept foundations have grown from their unique experiential backgrounds. Recognition of the uniqueness of children involves understanding that reading experiences need to vary according to reader backgrounds, requirements, and interests. Implicit is that reading should be personalized and begin with what the child already knows. This approach allows for retaining the language characteristics of individual children and incorporating their conceptual knowledge, while expanding their language awareness, knowledge, and usage. The teacher plans classroom interactions to build upon children's present language and concept functioning and creates a positive communication environment, both oral and written.

Through this oral and written language speakers and listeners, writers and readers, share experiences productively.

Within this framework readiness for reading is a building process with no clearly defined point at which time the learner is "ready to read." Rather, a gradual accumulation of experiences, knowledge, and abilities allows children to approach print with increasing understanding and facility.

> Children begin to learn to read from the time they begin to hear language and more particularly, from the time they hear their first nursery rhymes, jingles or stories. They begin to learn that books have pages and that the pages can be turned. They learn that books have a right and a wrong way up. They become fascinated with the pictures on the pages and will begin, at a very early stage, to use these pictures to help them "read" the story. They will soon learn that books mean "story time," a period of warm human sharing, enjoyed utterly by both the reader and the listener. Through this experience they will start to establish, and continue to extend, critically important positive attitudes towards books and reading that will influence their reading behavior for the rest of their lives.
>
> At some stage they will make an important discovery about the stories they are hearing and often repeating for themselves. They will become aware, although not necessarily with a conscious realization, that the source of the story they are hearing is not in the pictures or in the reader's head, but is actually on the pages in the black squiggles that the reader has been pointing to from time to time. They will begin to learn a whole lot of things about books, written language and reading which will set them on the road to literacy very early in their lives. (Doake, 1979, p. 2)

Since children have achieved a high degree of language competence in at least one language by the time they come to school and this language is their means of expression and communication, their medium of thought, and the central tool of their learning (Smith and others, 1976), classroom interactions must build upon the background experiences and language of the learner. This ensures learner familiarity with the specific content and vocabulary used in language and reading activities and facilitates the bridge between the learner and print. This approach to beginning reading recognizes the developmental aspect of reading growth and establishes a continuity between the mental operations that characterize children's responses to life events in the early years of development and the processes brought into play when the child first encounters reading.

Thus, beginning reading, far from being a formal process that is new and alien, should represent a continuity of the child's earlier cognitive and affective experience (Athey, 1980). Children listening to stories, children dictating stories, and children writing their own materials are all part of a LEA and enable children to approach print from a familiar base. As children share their ideas through drawing, talking, and writing and "read" their drawings, their talk written down, and their own writings, they expand their understanding of reading. These initial school experiences are a natural extension of their familiarity with language. Recognizing and incorporating what children know about language and print into the initial reading program provides the bridge between home and school.

Framework for Diagnosis and Teaching

As children see their spoken thoughts put into written form they can understand the nature of communication in reading in addition to recognizing words. Communication is stressed as children speak, see the speech represented by printed symbols, and then read the written representation of their speech. The association of meaning with the print is built into the reading of the personally created materials of the language experience approach. (Hall, 1976, p. 2).

The sequence of communication in the language experience approach is represented in Figure 5.1 adapted from the work of Hall (1976).

The use of this approach to reading not only provides a natural way for the learner to interact with print, but also provides an informal setting that facilitates teacher observation of the learner. As the learner expresses ideas through the use of language, as these ideas become written words by being visually recorded, and as the learner reads the print, the teacher is in a position to note the learner's understanding of the communication process. "The language experience approach to learning need not be confined to early reading, for children of all ages are faced with the problem of relating reading to their experience, albeit at different levels" (Athey, 1977, p. 91). Therefore, diagnostic procedures suggested in this section are appropriate for readers who are first approaching text and for readers who are using a combination of language experience activities and textual reading.

The three steps of the communication sequence involve a number of language/reading competencies. Table 5.1 shows the relationship of the language experience approach and language/reading competencies. This information provides a framework for diagnosis and teaching.

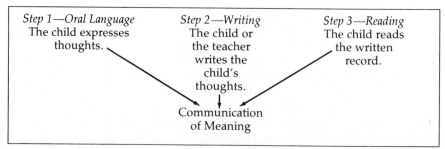

Step 1—Oral Language The child expresses thoughts.

Step 2—Writing The child or the teacher writes the child's thoughts.

Step 3—Reading The child reads the written record.

Communication of Meaning

Figure 5.1 The Communication Sequence in the Language Experience Approach

Table 5.1 Relationship of Language Experience Approach (LEA) and
Language-Reading Competencies

Language Experience Approach	Language-Reading Competencies

Step 1. Oral Language:
    Child expresses ideas
	Step 1. Expressing Ideas Orally:
	    a. indicates conceptual
	        understandings
	    b. shows language facility through
	        listening and speaking

Step 2. Writing:
    Teacher or child records ideas
	Step 2. Writing:
	    a. associates spoken language to
	        print
	    b. understands that written lan-
	        guage has permanency as
	        compared to oral language
	        which is temporal

Step 3. Reading:
    Child reads individual or
    group charts
	Step 3. Reading:
	    a. constructs meaning from
	        print
	    b. recognizes printed words
	    c. uses left-to-right direction
	    d. identifies letter-sound
	        correspondences

Using LEA for Diagnosis

For diagnostic purposes the steps can guide the teacher in observing all
learners in order to better understand their use of language. The teacher
records observations over an extended period of time and may maintain
them for each individual child in a format similar to the sample provided in
Figure 5.2 on page 86. The teacher periodically reviews the observational
data recorded for each child; and the teacher determines those children
who seem to be progressing in the LEA without any apparent problems
and those children whose performance indicates some difficulty in one or
more of the three broad areas under consideration. If the teacher notices
patterns of difficulty, those learners and their particular language/reading
problems will need special attention through the use of additional language experiences structured for the purpose of diagnosis. This involves
teacher awareness of what pupils require to function in each of these areas,
planning and developing specific language experiences for an individual
learner, and appropriate questioning to yield additional diagnostic
information.

DIAGNOSTIC QUESTIONS

In the area of oral language (Step 1 in Figure 5.1), the information in
Chapter 3 (Language and Concept Development) provides the basis for

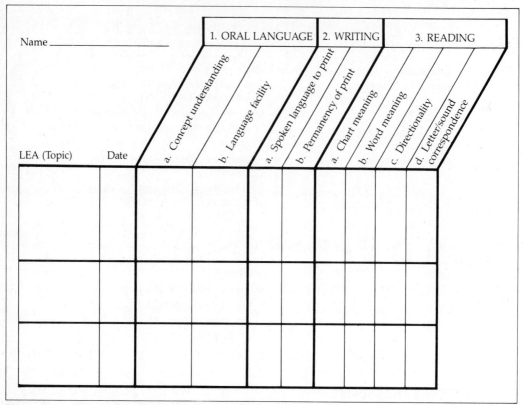

Figure 5.2   Observation Chart of Beginning Reading

formulating appropriate diagnostic questions. Examples of specific questions in this area are:

Application of Conceptual Understandings

What is the breadth of experience the child brings to the activity?

Are the presented concepts logically related?

Are the presented ideas/events organized in a sequential order?

Is a variety of words used to express ideas?

Do the words used show depth of conceptual understanding (denotative and connotative meanings)?

Is there difficulty either understanding or expressing particular groupings of concepts (time, space, quantity, etc.)?

What is the level of understanding for the major concept(s) discussed?

Language Facility

Is the level of sentence usage appropriate to the developmental level of the child (syntax and semantics)?

Is a variety of sentence patterns used?

Is there a disparity, greater than would be expected, between the child's reception of language and expression of language?

Is English a second language for the child?

Is the learner using a dialect of American English?

If the answer to either of the latter two questions is yes, refer to Chapter 15 (Bilingual and Bidialectal Learners) for further information.

In the area of writing (Step 2 in Figure 5.1), that is, relating language to print, the teacher asks questions such as:

Does the child understand that the written words represent the child's ideas, words—or the words of others?

Does the child understand that writing language gives it permanency?

In the third area (Step 3 in Figure 5.1), which involves the actual reading of learner-prepared materials, the teacher asks questions such as:

Chart Meaning

Is the child able to state (paraphrase) the overall meaning of the experience chart?

Does the child focus on details rather than the main point of the chart?

Is there differentiation between the main point and the details of the experience chart?

Are both explicit (stated) and implicit (inferred) meanings evident in discussion of experience charts?

Does the child understand the concept of *word, sentence, paragraph, story*?

Does the child express ideas that, while based on story content, show uniqueness and originality?

Does the child read material critically (personal evaluations and reactions)?

Word Meaning

Does the child use surrounding words as clues to determine word meanings?

Does the child understand words that have multiple meanings within the story context?

Does the child understand connotative as well as denotative meanings?

Are words that are used figuratively understood?

Directionality

Is there confusion between left-to-right in reading continuous discourse? If so, does the child confuse left-to-right in other activities?

Letter-Sound Correspondence

Does the child recognize:

rhyming words?

spelling patterns?

that letters represent sounds?

individual letter sound(s) as they occur in initial, medial, final positions in syllables or words? (consonants, short vowels, and long vowels)

words that begin with the same sound(s)?

that combinations of letters represent one or more sounds? (consonant blends, consonant digraphs, vowel digraphs, vowel diphthongs)

DIAGNOSTIC PROTOCOLS

To illustrate the interrelationship of teaching and informal diagnosis, two original children's stories presented in language chart form appear along with the teacher's diagnostic notes, in Figures 5.3 and 5.4. The purpose of these illustrations is to note the type of diagnostic information that teachers can obtain from analyzing language experience charts developed by individual learners. These charts are samples from second graders living in an urban area, based on the learners' own experiences following a snowstorm. The teacher recorded the stories verbatim during regular classroom activities. The teacher has written in manuscript rather than cursive writing to approximate the print that children read in books. Using manuscript writing facilitates children being able to read their own stories. In reading the analysis that follows each of the charts, understanding that the comments are based on only one sample of the children's work is important. The teacher would need to analyze additional samples of these children's dictated stories and writings on an ongoing basis before making any definitive diagnostic judgments.

Using the categories provided in Table 5.1 on page 85 as a framework, an analysis of George's performance is summarized in Figure 5.3.

The learner, George, shows excellent conceptual understanding in that

When the snow was starting my mother wanted to go to work. So she asked my father if he could take her. Then they came back in and said the car won't go. Then we put some snow salt on the snow so the snow could melt.

George, Age 7

he is able to present logically related concepts in a sequential order. He begins his story with an introductory sentence that helps the reader to understand what follows. George understands that snow can be changed to another form through melting and that melted snow would allow the car wheels to move, whereas other forms of snow could prevent movement. He also indicates awareness that there is a cause-effect relationship between snow salt and melting. He has learned the expressed concepts during experiences with the out-of-school environment, and they illustrate an ability to extract relevant information from the environment. Sentence usage is appropriate to the developmental level of the child, and he uses a variety of sentence patterns. When the teacher writes the story, George recognizes that his story is being transcribed into print from his oral language. He indicates this awareness when he voluntarily points to words as the teacher writes them. After the story is complete, George asks to be allowed to take it home to read, thus indicating an understanding that written words have permanency and communicative value beyond the immediate situation.

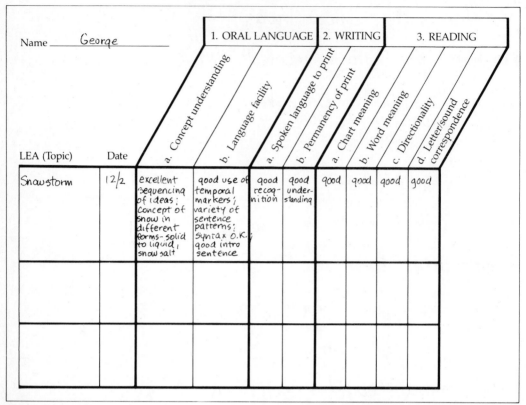

Figure 5.3   Individual Language Experience Chart with Teacher's Notes

In reading and discussing the chart, George reveals good understanding through his ability to tell another child what his story is about using some different words which express the same ideas. He reads the chart spontaneously from left to right and is able to locate several words upon request. The analysis using this chart indicates no particular difficulty in any of the areas evaluated. However, this conclusion is limited to this one experience and must be placed in the context of ongoing assessment.

On analyzing the second chart in Figure 5.4, the teacher notes that Edith is able to tell a story about her experiences in the snowstorm. However, her ideas are not adequately expressed. While she is able to remain focused on the topic snowstorm, she omits any reference to the snowstorm—information important for a reader. Further, the ideas in sentence one and the ideas in sentence two may be related, but Edith does not indicate any relation between these ideas as she presents them. There is a question whether Edith is monitoring her oral expression to take into account the communication needs of the reader. Edith evidences understanding of size in describing the boots that were too small. She also exhibits an under-

I fell down and
I fell on my head.
My family stay in
because they don't have
no boots because they
too small and they
can't come out.

Edith, Age 7

standing of causal relations when she refers to needing to wear boots and in her telling that the family had to stay in because their boots were too small. The reader can understand these relations even though Edith does not use the word *snow* if the reader is aware of the context.

Edith uses a dialect of American English with double negatives ("don't have no boots"), omission of the copula ("they too small"), and omission of the inflectional ending -*ed*. These dialect variations reflect the child's language community. However, the other syntactical deviations are not dialect related and are inappropriate. For example, in sentence one *I* is repeated unnecessarily, and in sentence two ideas that should be separated are combined in one structurally inadequate sentence. This sentence reflects immature use of conjunctions (*and, because*) to construct a run-on sentence. In addition, the pronoun (*they*) in sentence two does not have clear referents in two cases.

In discussing the chart and the related experience, Edith and her teacher recognize that Edith tends to focus on isolated details and has some difficulty organizing experiences and thoughts for oral expression. She

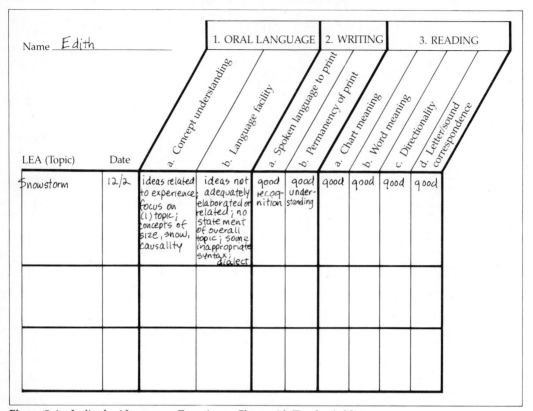

Figure 5.4   Individual Language Experience Chart with Teacher's Notes

does recognize that the teacher is writing down her oral language and by writing is making a permanent record of her story. Edith is able to read her story and tell other children about it.

Thus the analysis, using this chart, indicates that Edith can express her ideas orally, does understand some concepts related to snow and size, and is using causality in a meaningful way, although she elaborates on her ideas insufficiently for readers. Edith uses a dialect of American English. She often uses inappropriate syntactic structures, and tends to present details without a statement that ties them together. These findings would need confirmation through repeated observations and analyses of Edith's work.

A comparison of the two readers shows that their experiences related to the past snowstorm are quite different: Their descriptions of their snow-related experiences display different levels of conceptual functioning in regard to this experience, and their ability to organize their experiences and to use language to describe their experiences vary. Based on this preliminary assessment, the first learner, George, does not appear to need any structured assessment at this time. He would participate in the development of group language experience charts, read self-authored materials, materials authored by other learners and simple narratives. During these activities the teacher would continue to observe his performance and periodically record these observations to determine if he functions similarly in a variety of reading situations. The second learner, Edith, would require structured assessment in order to further understand her language and reading functioning. Since one of her major problems appears to be organizing ideas so they relate logically to each other, she would participate in a series of experiences with opportunities to describe these experiences as they occurred. Simple temporal sequence would be a starting point for the structured assessment, moving to other relations as diagnostic information warrants this. Edith would discuss the experiences with the teacher and through questioning, the teacher would elicit Edith's ideas and record them in an experience chart. The teacher would note if Edith can reconstruct information in an organized way when she experiences it in a sequential order and if sufficient detail is included. For example, Edith and her teacher would look out of the window and observe activities on the street. They would discuss the activities as they occur, and after a short time the teacher would ask Edith to relate all she has observed. Of course these experiences that the teacher has specifically structured for assessment purposes would also be learning experiences for Edith.

Language/Reading Experiences

As the previous section points out, a way in which children discover that print has meaning is through the use of a LEA. Allen and Allen (1969) have summarized the concepts children gain from a LEA.

> I can talk about what I think about. What I can talk about I can communicate in some other way. Anything I can dictate or write can be recalled through speaking or reading. I can learn to read some of what I dictate and some of what other people have written. Most of the words I speak and dictate other people use when they speak and write things for me to read. (pp. 7-8)

Learner understanding of these concepts leads to recognition of the interrelatedness of speaking, listening, writing, and reading and their inseparability from thinking. A LEA expands learners' understanding that print is a medium of communication and that text represents a message the writer wants to share with the reader. This concept is most easily understood when experiences with reading print begin with the reader's own writing and progress to reading books.

> Beginning reading should be *induction* rather than instruction, a gradual introduction of the children into the world of books. Beginning reading should be fun and exciting. Children should be encouraged to discover that print has meaning, that people write because they have something to say, something children may want to know about. (Hunter-Grundin, 1979, p. 22)

As helping children to "know" the world of books can best begin by using the learner's own language, the language experience program should incorporate not only dictated stories but also all aspects of student-authored materials. This expansion of LEA to include children's writing is part of the beginning reading program and continues throughout the grades. Through the experiences of being writers, reading their own writings and those of other children, children expand their understanding of why and how authors write. Such activities are necessary for learners to develop proficiency in constructing meaning from text. Using a LEA involves planning, implementing, and evaluating activities to stimulate oral language interaction and growth as learners share experiences and ideas; activities to foster the awareness that spoken language may be associated with print as ideas are written down; and activities to encourage reading for meaning as recorded experiences are read.

Activities associated with the three steps in the communication sequence (oral language, writing, and reading) can be thought of as, first, activities that occur prior to the recording of learner language; second, activities that occur while the ideas and experiences of the learner are being written; and, third, activities that follow writing. Although all of these activities will result in a language experience chart of some type, there are variations in both the process and the product depending on the purpose for which the chart is developed and whether the LEA involves a group or an individual learner. The general sequence of activities is the same for working with either a group or an individual learner. That is, the teacher stimulates oral language interactions, the teacher writes group/individual communications, the teacher and learner(s) read the communication, and the teacher plans for specific follow-up activities. Although many of the procedures are similar, interactions will of necessity differ as group and individual situations are different. However, in all situations in which a language experience chart is being developed, the teacher-learner(s) interactions are the crucial component of the process.

Using the LEA as the base for language/reading activities in the classroom requires a balance between flexibility and structure. This balance is necessary both in selecting those activities to be implemented and in grouping learners for participation in activities. That is, teachers plan activities but are sufficiently flexible to take advantage of spontaneous classroom interactions that may lead to other activities. Also, teachers are able to flexibly shift learners from whole-class situations to small-group situations, to individual situations, taking into consideration the type of grouping pattern conducive to carrying out specific activities and the specific needs of learners. Grouping patterns may be used singly or in combination, depending on the teacher's objectives.

The variety of learners found in a classroom and the diversity of ongoing classroom activities necessitate introducing learners to classroom routines in an organized way and guiding them so they can adjust to the many different activities available to them. This implies a structured approach to

Table 5.2   Teacher-Directed Whole-Class Activities

Reading stories, poems, and other oral communications
Guiding learners to compose class language experience charts or class books
Providing opportunities for children to write on topics of their own choice
Encouraging the reading of self-authored stories, poems, or other communications
Stimulating discussion on a topic, idea, event, or book (story)
Fostering the sharing of feelings and ideas
Showing films, filmstrips, slides, and other audiovisual presentations
Planning for classroom and out of classroom activities
Introducing activities such as games, new learning centers
Leading language word games, songs, etc.
Building class word banks
Observing language/reading functioning

learning as a means of achieving the desired flexibility in which learners can move purposefully around the room interacting with both other learners and materials. Classroom physical space should facilitate this mobility for both teacher-directed and independent learner experiences so that the variety of activities basic to a LEA can take place efficiently and happily.

As noted, some activities will occur with the whole class, some will occur within small groups and some will provide for individual learners. Examples of teacher-directed whole-class activities appear in Table 5.2.

Although the teacher may adapt all of the whole-class activities in Table 5.2 to work with small groups, significant differences exist in dynamics. First, small groups are not permanent groups as is a class. Groups may form to participate in specific reading strategy lessons based on diagnostic information; groups may form based on learner choice of an activity topic or other learners; groups may form to reinforce whole-class or group strategy lessons.

Additional teacher-directed activities are specific to small group work. Examples of these activities appear in Table 5.3.

In addition, the teacher serves as a resource for the individual learner working on an activity or project by guiding the learner as independent activities or materials are chosen; suggesting ideas for individual charts; discussing individual ideas prior to the writing of the charts; and writing

Table 5.3   Teacher-Directed Small Group Activities

Teaching specific reading/language lessons on reading for meaning, word
    identification, and sight word vocabulary
Developing language experience chart(s) based on specific diagnostic information
Using dramatization to expand concepts
Reinforcing language/reading concepts through games
Building group word banks for follow-up activities

word cards for individual word banks. The teacher also helps with spelling as learners compose their own charts; furnishes words, as needed, for independent reading and writing; and confers with learners about their progress. Of course, as needed, the teacher also teaches a reading/language strategy lesson to an individual learner.

TYPES OF LANGUAGE EXPERIENCE CHARTS

As noted, the development of an experience chart may be a whole-class activity, a group activity, or an individual activity. For each grouping pattern the teacher plans experiences to stimulate oral language interactions and encourage instances of spontaneous communications between teacher and learner(s) and between learner(s) and learner(s). This interactive environment can lead to the development of a variety of types of experience charts. The major types of language experience charts are narrative charts, work charts, and strategy charts.

Narrative Charts

The most frequently developed chart is the narrative chart. This type of chart is generally based on the description of a shared or individual experience, or the relating of an idea or event that an experience may stimulate. But the description expands the original experience in a unique or imaginative way. For example, an experience in which children have observed a hamster in class can form the basis for three different narrative experience charts. In one case, the learner might specifically describe the hamster's characteristics and actions as observed. In the second case, the experience of observing could lead to the creation of a chart in which the learner shares feelings about the hamster or goes beyond the observed experience to figuratively describe how the hamster looked or acted. In a third chart, a learner could create an imaginary story about a hamster.

Figure 5.5 illustrates the first variety of narrative chart.

Our Hamster

Our new hamster is called Hammy. He has two brown eyes. Hammy has four legs and a tail. His whiskers are funny. He runs around in his cage.

Figure 5.5 Example of an Individual Narrative Chart

Hammy looks like a little rat. (Larry)
Hammy runs fast like a mouse. (Judi)
Hammy feels soft like a ball of cotton. (Gilbert)
Hammy feels like my blanket. (Iris)
Hammy's whiskers look like wire. (Esther)

Figure 5.6 Example of a Group Narrative Chart

I wish that this whole board was real. Then I could go from gumdrops to lollypops to ice cream floats and to the gingerbread house. I would eat everything on the way. No, maybe I could freeze some and save it.

Figure 5.7 Individual Narrative Chart Based on "Candyland"

Figure 5.6 above describes the hamster imaginatively. Further, narrative charts may be developed from spontaneous discussion about a learner's feelings about people or objects, a learner's wishes or dreams, and other unique ideas or thoughts. For example, a chart may evolve from discussion of scary dreams, secret wishes, or fantasies. The following chart was developed by an individual 7-year-old playing the board game "Candyland" after she spontaneously described her wish to the teacher who recorded it (see Figure 5.7) above.

Work Charts
Work or planning charts are another type of experience chart. These are generally developed with the whole class or a group of learners. Their major function is to provide a written summary of directions to be followed, or plans for class or group activities, or of delegated classroom

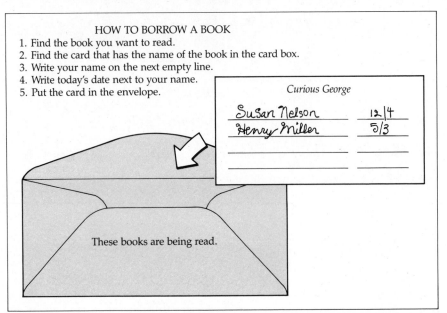

Figure 5.8   Example of a Work Chart

responsibilities. These work charts direct learner activity and may be of a temporary or permanent nature. Illustrative work charts may include a summary of directions for borrowing books from the library or directions on how to perform a science experiment (see Figures 5.8 and 5.9). Figure 5.10 work chart shows plans for a party and delineates the responsibilities of various students in the class.

Strategy Charts

The third category of experience charts is the reading strategy chart. This chart is an outgrowth of a teacher-directed activity in language/reading and has as its purpose reinforcement of a specific aspect of reading for meaning, word identification or basic sight word strategies. Reinforcement may occur through illustrating the concepts developed in a lesson, through a summary statement of the major concepts presented to guide future independent language/reading activities, or through stimulating independent teacher-planned activities directly related to the lesson. For example, a teacher-directed lesson developing the concept of multiple-meaning words could result in at least three different charts. One chart could simply reinforce the concept by containing a series of sentences or a paragraph that illustrates a multiple-meaning word used in a variety of contexts. To illustrate, the following chart (Figure 5.11) summarizes a class discussion of the many meanings of the word *run*.

Or upon completion of a strategy lesson on multiple-meaning words, the teacher may elicit from students a summary chart as in Figure 5.12.

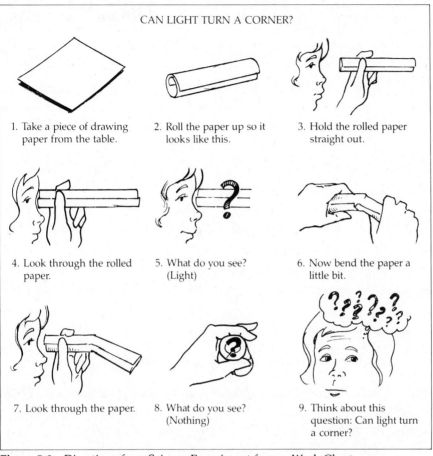

Figure 5.9 Directions for a Science Experiment from a Work Chart

THINGS TO BRING FOR THE PARTY	
Paper plates	Lee
Paper cups	Marcia, Bob
Napkins	Alyce, Allan
Cookies	Arnold, Gwen
Apple juice	Carol, Marilyn
Raisins	Adam
Carrots	Ruth, Bill
Records	Myrna, Lisa, Michael
Games	Eddy, Barbara, José, Gene

Figure 5.10 Work Chart of Party Plans

The word _run_ has many different meanings.

1. I like to _run_ in the park.
2. The baseball player scored a _run._
3. My dog uses a dog _run_ in the park.
4. We saw a woman with a big _run_ in her stocking.
5. The sun was hot and the ice cream began to _run_ down the baby's face.

Figure 5.11   Example of a Strategy Chart

Words Have Many Meanings

We learned that some words have more than one meaning. I can tell the meaning of a word by reading the whole sentence. Sometimes I need to read the other sentences in the story. Sometimes I need to use a dictionary to help me find the meaning of a word.

Figure 5.12   Example of a Summary Chart

Or a chart could stimulate an activity that reinforces the concept of multiple-meaning words and encourages further group interaction and/or independent activity (see Figure 5.13).

Table 5.4 summarizes the types of language experience charts which may be developed in whole-class, group, or individual settings.

The word <u>hand</u> has many different meanings just like the word run.

My <u>hand</u> is dirty.
<u>Hand</u> me the book.

Next to your name write a sentence using the word <u>hand</u>. Underline the word <u>hand</u> in your sentence.

Maria   1.

Betsy   2.

John   3.

Bruce   4.

Sally   5.

Figure 5.13   Example of a Strategy Chart to Stimulate Student Activity

Follow-Up Activities

The product or completed language experience chart leads to a number of follow-up activities that are either teacher-designed to meet specific learner needs or are learner-created as the learner spontaneously interacts with the written communication.

Word banks.   One major component of teacher-designed activities is the creation of word banks for individual learners, groups of learners, or the whole class. These word banks include familiar words or phrases written on word cards that can then be used in a variety of ways such as forming new phrases and sentences or as a reference when writing.

Ongoing assessment strategies.   Also important in follow-up is teacher planning of specific strategy lessons based on ongoing assessment of learner needs to develop reading for meaning, word identification strategies, and sight-word vocabulary.

As appropriate to the content of particular charts, the teacher may encourage such activities as art work and other written communication, dramatization, listening activities, and the reading of related picture books and easy-to-read books.

DEVELOPMENT OF GROUP AND PERSONAL CHARTS

Teachers and learners are active participants in all three steps of the communication sequence involved in the development of a specific LE chart and related activities. Teacher and learners interact during the oral

Table 5.4 Summary of Types of Charts

Narrative Charts	1.	Describing an observed experience.
	2.	Expanding upon an observed experience in an imaginative way.
	3.	Relating feelings, wishes, dreams, unique ideas, and thoughts.
Work Charts	1.	Summarizing directions to follow.
	2.	Listing plans for activities.
	3.	Delineating delegated responsibilities.
	4.	Establishing goals/problems and means/solutions.
Strategy Charts	1.	Illustrating the concept(s) developed.
	2.	Summarizing the concept(s) developed as a guide.
	3.	Stimulating independent activities directly related to the concept(s) developed.

language stage, which occurs prior to recording spoken language; during the writing stage, which occurs as ideas are recorded; and during the final stage, reading, which occurs after oral language has been recorded. A teacher uses the same steps to develop a language experience chart with a group of learners as when the teacher works with only one child. The major difference is that when a teacher works with only one learner, the learner may share a personal experience with the teacher, and the teacher may observe and assess functioning in greater depth than when working with a group. Table 5.5 details the steps and activities for creating a group experience chart.

For example, when the teacher works with only one child to develop a personal language experience chart, the teacher records all of the learner's responses rather than having to guide the group to select one response from the many responses the teacher has elicited. This provides the teacher with a much larger sample of the child's performance than when working with a group. Whether the teacher is working with a group of children or an individual child, both teacher and learner are actively involved.

The interaction between teacher and learner(s) fosters the learning process. Another way of describing these interactions is as the interactive teaching stage in the teaching/learning framework described in Chapter 4. Planning or preactive teaching has occurred prior to this step as the teacher used knowledge about learners to plan the specific content of the LE (a shared experience or recall of an experience) and follow-up activities. Evaluative teaching, the final stage in the teaching/learning framework, occurs as both teacher and learner(s) reflect on the quality of their interactions (the process) and evaluate the chart (the product).

ILLUSTRATION: PERSONAL EXPERIENCE CHART

The following illustration, using the personal experience of a child, demonstrates how the three steps of the teaching/learning process function in a language experience approach. During *preactive teaching* (Step 1) the

Table 5.5 Group Experience Chart

	Teacher	Learners
Prior to Recording	Provides an experience or stimulates recall of an experience.	Observe and/or participate in experience or recall and share ideas and events.
	Encourages thinking and elicits oral language through appropriate probe and structured questions.	Respond and listen to responses of others and interact with others.
	Observes and assesses language functioning.	
	Writes keywords and phrases on chalkboard.	
During Recording	Elicits the major idea/events to be recorded.	Respond by recalling and elaborating on major ideas/events discussed.
	Guides selection of statements to be recorded from the multiple responses.	Select the response(s) to be recorded.
	Writes learners' responses using *exact* language of learners.	Observe the left-to-right progression of written material.
	Says each word as it is written.	Listen to and associate oral language with writing.
	Uses appropriate punctuation, capitalization, and spelling.	Observe the conventions of written language.
After Recording	Reads chart orally indicating left-to-right progression of the written material.	Listen, associate oral language with written language, observe left-to-right progression.
	Leads group in oral reading.	Read with teacher.
	Asks learners to read their own sentences, providing help as needed.	Read and listen to others read.
	Encourages individual learners to read parts and/or entire chart.	Read chart including parts not self-authored.
	Reinforces major ideas and concepts through appropriate questioning.	Respond by reading appropriate parts and/or elaborate upon or paraphrase information in chart.
	Duplicates chart for class and individual learners and plans follow-up activities.	Participate in follow-up activities.

teacher uses knowledge about a student, a 7-year-old named Marjorie, to plan a language experience. The teacher knows that Marjorie plays chess with her older brother. Also, Marjorie has had many experiences in listening to and retelling stories and has demonstrated a good sense of concepts related to size and weight. The teacher, therefore, plans to expand Marjorie's understanding of the relations between size and weight of objects and to reinforce her knowledge of the sequential order of oral and written communication.

To attain these short-range goals, the teacher plans an experience for Marjorie in which she will play chess with oversized pieces. The teacher also constructs questions to guide the language experience. These questions might include:

1. How do these chess pieces compare with the ones you usually play with?

    Follow-up questions:

    1a. How do the pieces look to you?
    1b. How do they feel to you?

During this planning stage the teacher plans a follow-up activity to reinforce Marjorie's understanding of the relations between size and weight.

Interactive teaching (Step 2) begins as the teacher stimulates Marjorie's thinking by providing an oversized chess game and playing the game with her. As the game progresses the two discuss the physical atttributes (size and weight) of the chess pieces and the experience as it is occurring. As soon as the experience is concluded, Marjorie, with teacher guidance, recalls the experience and the teacher records it. After the chart is completed (see Figure 5.14), the teacher reads the chart as Marjorie observes and listens, and then Marjorie reads her story and tells what it is about. The teacher than asks Marjorie some questions, such as these, to reinforce her concepts of size, weight and sequence of events:

1. Are things that are as big as these chess pieces usually so light?
2. What do you think makes these pieces so light?
3. Can you think of anything else that is big and light?
4. What happened first in your story?
5. What happened next?
6. How did your story end?

As a follow-up activity to this language experience Marjorie would categorize and classify objects according to their size and weight. For example, she might bring in pictures of objects or write the names of objects that fit the following categories: Heavy and large; light and large; heavy and small; light and small.

The Chess Game
by Marjorie, Age 7

Once upon a time, there was a big boy and a little girl. After lunch they ran outside to play chess. Me and Tim played a big chess game. The pieces were big and light. We put the chessmen on a big board. We played chess with them. We moved them around in different places. Then I beat Tim. And then we went back inside.

Figure 5.14   Individual Language Experience Chart

Throughout the interactive teaching step the teacher has observed Marjorie's oral language functioning, her reading of the chart, and her responses during the discussion. This information is used during *evaluative teaching* (Step 3) in which the teacher assesses Marjorie's performance in the areas of oral language, writing, and reading based on this experience.

The teacher's analysis of Marjorie's work yields the following: In the area of oral language, Marjorie exhibits the ability to express ideas about the chess game fluently in a logical, sequential order. She indicates a concept for story beginnings—"Once upon a time . . ."—which seems to be based on her prior knowledge (schema of how fairy tales begin). However, while this is common for children of her age, in this instance it is inappropriate for relating a realistic experience. Her vocabulary usage and syntax are age-appropriate. She shows a good understanding of the spatial relations denoted by *outside, inside, on , around,* and understands the concept of light in relation to weight. Furthermore, it is clear that she understands that the word *light* is a multiple-meaning word by her description of the chess pieces in response to structured questions. That is, she describes the pieces as feeling *light* and some pieces looked *light* and other pieces were dark. As the teacher records her story, Marjorie follows the writing with her eyes and points to some of the words indicating that she associates her oral language with print. Also, her intonation during oral reading is good, with appropriate rhythmic patterns. After reading her chart, Marjorie indicates by her response to questions that she has a good sense of the main point of the story, can elaborate on the events, and understands the sequential nature of the events.

Many experiences lend themselves to the writing of language experience charts and related follow-up activities. The above illustration is only one of a number of personal charts Marjorie and her teacher developed. Furthermore, Marjorie, as any learner, is also involved in group experiences, the development of group charts, and the reading of simple narrative texts. Her teacher will analyze all of these reading experiences to put together a more complete picture of Marjorie's functioning.

Thematic Approach to Language Experience

Some language experience activities focus on relevant but isolated topics, and the teacher may also integrate others through the use of a thematic approach in the classroom. A thematic approach is one that builds classroom experiences around a particular topic or theme of interest to both teacher and learners. The teacher selects the theme with reference to grade level curriculum and integrates listening, speaking, reading, and writing activities. Although the theme may be common for all learners in the classroom, this type of program allows for variations in learner functioning and encourages learners to interact with each other, sharing experiences and ideas, even though there may be individual differences in communication abilities. Of course, although many classroom activities may revolve around one theme, many non-theme-related activities go on at the same time.

In selecting a particular theme, the teacher needs to consider the relation of the topic to the school curriculum and the appropriateness of the topic to the learners' ages, developmental levels, and experiential backgrounds. The curriculum areas frequently incorporated into school programs provide natural organizers for a thematic approach to language/reading experiences. The curriculum units from areas such as social studies, science, health or mathematics provide opportunities for a wealth of experiences for learners to explore, share, speak about, write about, and read about, providing a purposeful way to build language/reading experiences into the entire school day.

For example, elementary level curricula in the area of health education often focuses on maintaining good health, including concepts related to cleanliness, nutrition, medical care, exercise, safety, and first aid. Topics such as weather, animals, plants, and the environment are common units of study in the science areas. Social studies curricula frequently include units on how people live, work, and play in the family, the neighborhood, and larger community such as cities, different regions of the country, and world. Some areas of study in mathematics that lend themselves to use in a thematic approach to language/reading activities are geometry and measurement including concepts related to shape and form, money, time, weight, and temperature. These few samples show the wealth of topics the teacher may develop through curricula that coordinate specific language/ reading experiences with content area information.

Although experts recognize that textbook reading is an important component in developing concepts in the content areas, the importance of self-authored materials cannot be overemphasized. As noted, learners at all levels of development face new information and learning experiences and can benefit from using their own language and experience as a base for integrating new knowledge. Thus, language experience activities which introduce new concepts and expand existing knowledge may facilitate learning of curriculum content at any grade level.

ILLUSTRATION: ECOLOGY UNIT
Ecology is a common area of study in the middle grades. This sample topic illustrates the planning (preactive teaching), teaching (interactive teaching), and evaluating (evaluative teaching) stages in which teachers and learners participate when a thematic approach is used.

Preactive Teaching
As part of preactive teaching the teacher would plan language/reading experiences based on the range of learners' abilities and needs within the class. For the sample unit on ecology assume that the class is a heterogeneous middle grade class with reading levels ranging from approximately 2nd grade to 6th grade. The long-range objective of this unit, as any other, is to increase language effectiveness through activities that will expand listening skills, conversational and formal speaking, reading comprehension, and writing competency.

In conjunction with concentration on language/reading goals the teacher will develop a number of concepts from the class curriculum specific to the theme of ecology. These may include:

1. Pollutants are waste materials that harm the environment.
2. Pollutants may also be thought of as anything that makes the environment unpleasant to the senses.
3. Air pollutants are gases or particles not usually found in air.
4. Air pollutants affect the health of people and plants, damage property and influence environmental conditions and weather.
5. Water becomes polluted by the addition of chemicals, organic waste, and heat.
6. Noise pollution affects people as they live in their environment.
7. People help to create a clean or polluted environment.

To carry out the language/reading objectives and to develop the specific concepts about ecology, the teacher will develop some key questions to guide learners' thinking and plan a number of learning experiences. Some key questions for this unit include:

1. What makes up your environment?
2. What are the major differences between your environment and a natural environment?
3. What are some of the problems in a man-made environment?
4. How can people help to solve some of these problems?

Some examples of learning experiences for the ecology unit are:

1. Relate experiences by presenting factual information in oral or written form.
2. Describe experiences by using both literal and figurative language.
3. Read/listen to information to paraphrase in oral or written form.
4. Read/listen to information to take notes for a written outline.
5. Read stories and poems related to the environment and share the experiences through retelling and discussion.
6. Write a business letter to obtain information from environmental specialists or agencies.
7. Learn to write questions and conduct an interview.
8. Plan for and participate in a debate.

Students use the experiences in a variety of ways. That is, some learners will participate in only some of the experiences as appropriate to their functioning. Other experiences will help to expand all learners' knowledge but will use varying types and levels of materials in keeping with learner needs. Regardless of specific experiences, all learners will gain understanding of the major concepts of this unit on ecology and expand their language/reading competence.

As the final step in preactive teaching, the teacher becomes familiar with those resources needed during interactive teaching to build the learners' concepts about their environment. This unit would include such resources as the following:

Trips—Neighborhood walk
       Factory and/or utility company
       Environmental Protection Agency

Books—Black, H. *Dirt cheap: The evolution of renewable resource management.* New York: Morrow, 1979.

       McCoy, J. J. *A sea of troubles.* New York: Seabury, 1975.

       George, G. *All upon a stone.* New York: Thomas Crowell, 1971.

       Pringle, L. *Energy: Power for people.* New York: Macmillan, 1975.

Pringle, L. *This is a river: Exploring an ecosystem.* New York: Macmillan, 1972.

Films/Filmstrips—*What on Earth?*
Meeting with the Sea
Let's Discover

Photographs—National Geographic Society
New York Zoological Society

Interactive Teaching

To stimulate learners' thinking about their environment, the teacher guides the class in planning a neighborhood walk. The neighborhood walk serves as a base for developing some of the concepts relevant to the theme of ecology as well as to developing and expanding specific language/reading abilities. Based on class discussion on the purpose and guidelines for a walk, the class develops a group experience chart.

As preparation for completing this chart, including directions for the walk, the class draws up a neighborhood map and pinpoints those areas that will be of direct concern in their study of the environment. The class might develop one similar to the one in Figure 5.15 on page 110.

Since the walk will be a class experience, the teacher and learners jointly use the information on the Figure 5.15 map in writing a group experience chart. Figure 5.16 on page 111 is a sample of a planning chart learners prepared by referring to the neighborhood map.

If a class trip is not feasible, an alternate plan would be for pairs or small groups of students to have a similar experience independently. In this case the class chart might look as in Figure 5.17 (pp. 112–13).

Upon return from either the class walk or the independent walks, members of the class discuss their observations using their notes and other materials. Learners engage in a variety of different activities. For example, following the class trip one group of learners works with the teacher to discuss observations and record them in a narrative-type language experience chart. A sample of this type of chart is shown in Figure 5.18 on page 114.

Another group, with teacher guidance, discusses the ways in which the pollutants it observed affect the senses. A strategy chart, using the skill of categorization, such as in Figure 5.19 on page 115, might evolve. Discussion of this chart would develop the concept that not everyone considers all of the things listed as pollutants. For example, for some people advertising signs are interesting to view, yet for others these signs clutter the environment. For everyone, uncollected and open garbage is seen as a pollutant that affects both the eyes and the nose. From this discussion the terms *universal* pollutants and *personal* pollutants would emerge.

Note that not all learners would be developing language experience charts following the neighborhood walk. Groups of learners or individuals

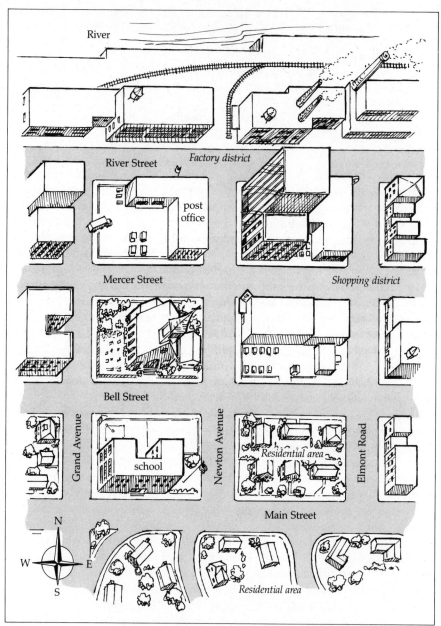

River

River Street   *Factory district*

post
office

Mercer Street   *Shopping district*

Bell Street

Grand Avenue

Newton Avenue

Elmont Road

school

Residential area

Main Street

N
W   E
S

Residential area

Figure 5.15   Illustrative Neighborhood Map for Ecology Unit

could be involved in a number of other activities. Dependent on learners' abilities and interests, some possible alternative activities are to

1.   draw pictures to illustrate pollutants in the environment.
(List of activities continues on page 113.)

Walking to Observe Pollutants

1. The walk will take place at 10 AM on Friday, March 5, 198 ___ .

2. We will begin at our school and walk north along Grand Avenue until we reach the end. Then we will turn east on River Street, walking past the factory district. When we reach Elmont Road, we will turn south past the shopping areas. We will return to the school by walking west once we reach Main Street, past the residential areas.

3. We will all carry our maps and paper and pencils to make notes about our observations.

4. The following students will bring special materials to help us remember what we see:

    Stanley   camera

    Jennifer   camera

    Marsha   tape recorder

    Robert   tape recorder

Figure 5.16 Sample of a Planning Chart

Walking to Observe Pollutants

1. Decide on a day and time for your walk.

2. Meet your partner or group in front of the main entrance.

3. Select a route for your walk from the following:

   a) Walk north along Grand Avenue until you reach the end. Go east on River Street to the factory district. Then return to the school building by walking west on River Street and south on Grand Avenue.

   b) Walk north along Grand Avenue until you reach Mercer Street. Walk east on Mercer Street to Elmont Road. Turn south on Elmont Road, walking past the shopping district, until you reach Main Street. Walk west on Main Street and return to the school building.

   c) Walk east on Main Street, past the residential areas to Elmont Road. Walk

north on Elmont Road to Bell Street.
Turn west on Bell Street to
Grand Avenue. Walk south on Grand
Avenue and return to the school
building.

4. Carry your map and paper and pencil
to make notes about your observations.

5. Those children who want may bring
cameras or tape recorders.

Figure 5.17   Sample of a Planning Chart

2. select pictures from magazines to illustrate different types of pollutants and categorize them.
3. write a description of one pollutant that affected the learner personally on the walk.
4. write a personal reaction to sights and smells in the environment using figurative language.

As the neighborhood walk is the motivating experience for study of the environment, the next step is for the class with teacher guidance to decide on what additional information it needs and what sources are available for obtaining this information. Discussions of this type might lead to a list of problems, appropriate activities, and materials to develop the concepts listed on page 107. The whole class, small groups, and individuals develop these concepts over time and would experience the type of learning experiences noted on page 108. For example, one resource a class might suggest is to interview different people concerned with the environment. Several students might choose to interview the manager of a chemical factory in the neighborhood and others might choose to interview the director of an environmental protection agency. These planned activities lead to a whole-class discussion of what information each individual can give the

What Pollutes Our Environment?

In the neighborhood we saw buses giving off black carbon monoxide fumes. The fumes made everything around look dirty and grimy. We also saw dogs and even a police horse making in the streets. Peter wasn't looking where he walked and he stepped in this dirt. His shoes smelled terrible and we laughed. Across the street from the post office we saw a factory. The smokestacks had black clouds of dirt pouring out of them. One factory smelled like bad eggs. Jim said it was probably the smell of sulfur. There was also a lot of uncollected garbage spilling into the street in front of one of the factories. We also saw people drop papers and garbage in the street as they walked by us. We really saw some of the ways that our neighborhood gets polluted.

Figure 5.18   Sample of a Narrative Chart

Pollutants That Affect My

Eyes	Ears	Nose
garbage	loud radios	garbage
graffiti	car horns	animal waste
street clutter	train wheels	chemical waste
advertising signs	truck engines	engine exhaust
smog	drilling / construction	smoke
smoke		
run-down houses		

Figure 5.19   Sample of a Strategy Chart

class and the questions necessary to obtain this information. Students prepare a list of questions (work charts) for each interview. In the process of writing the questions, students expand their knowledge about constructing questions. They learn such information as: Some questions lead to "yes" or "no" answers and provide little new information, whereas "why," "how," and "what" questions can produce more information (Haley-James & Hobson, 1980). The process of interviewing leads to increased skills in listening, speaking, writing, and reading competencies as students record and edit their interviews, interact with written materials, and share their information.

Figure 5.20 on page 116 gives questions for interviewing a factory manager. Responses to these "why," "how" and "what" questions can lead to considerable information gathering and thus increase students' knowledge bases. For example, when a group focuses on responses to question #3— "How do you dispose of these waste materials?"—the discussion could include the concepts of biodegradable materials, biodegradable agents, and biodegradable processes by focusing on those materials that do not pollute the environment (biodegradable materials) because people, animals, or plants (biodegradable agents) can separate these materials into simpler parts (biodegradable process) and put them to use. Students explore these

Interview Questions

1. What chemicals does your factory produce?

2. What waste products result from this production?

3. How do you dispose of these waste materials?

4. What effect does this disposal have on the environment?

5. What other ways could you dispose of your waste materials?

Figure 5.20   Sample of a Work Chart

concepts, important for any in-depth unit on ecology. As students share their information, they elaborate on the concepts and increase their understanding. As Klausmeier delineates (Chapter 3, p. 61), several levels of understanding are involved in concept attainment. Discussion and related reading help learners expand their understanding of critical attributes and recognition of irrelevant attributes as well as an understanding and recognition of examples and nonexamples of these concepts. Using the type of information provided in Table 5.6 as a guide for discussion, the teacher deliberately provokes exploration of the deeper and fuller meanings of the concepts (Athey, 1980). Of course, in any class, differences will exist among learners in levels of concept attainment and, therefore, in abilities to generalize and apply this information to new situations.

Evaluating Teaching
In using a thematic approach in the classroom, the evaluation of learners is an ongoing process in which the teacher notes learners' use of language in listening, speaking, reading, and writing activities. As data accumulate, a pattern of learning needs emerges, and the teacher plans specific reading and language experiences and reading strategy lessons. Examples of teaching plans may be found in Chapters 6 through 13.

Although this section has focused on how a teacher may use a language experience approach in the middle grades, note that using this approach to expand language/reading competence provides many opportunities for learners to read narrative text and non-narrative text related to the topic of the theme.

Table 5.6 *Analyses of the Concepts* Biodegradable Material, Biodegradable Agent, *and* Biodegradable Process

Concept Names: biodegradable material, biodegradable agent, biodegradable process

Relevant Attributes
  A. Biodegradable material
      Can be separated into simpler parts by living things
  B. Biodegradable agent
      A living thing
  C. Biodegradable process
      1. A living thing separates a material into simpler parts.
      2. The simpler parts are used by the living thing.

Irrelevant Attributes
  A. Biodegradable material
      1. Source of material—plant or animal
      2. Status of material—living or nonliving
  B. Biodegradable agent
      Type of living thing—human being, animal, or plant
  C. Biodegradable process
      1. Type of living thing—human being, animal, or plant
      2. Status of material
      3. Amount of time needed to separate the material

Examples and Nonexamples
  A. Biodegradable material

Examples	*Nonexamples*
1. Living things and products of living things	1. Rubber materials *a.* Car tire

2. Food
  a. Cream cheese
  b. Orange peel
  c. Hot dog
  d. Baked pork chop
	2. Plastic materials
	  a. Plastic spoon
	  b. Telephone

	3. Metal materials
	  a. Tin can
	  b. Razor blade

3. Plants and plant products
  a. Pine cone
  b. Leaf (e.g., maple leaf)
  c. Book
	4. Glass materials
	  a. Pop bottle
	  b. Window pane
	  c. Light bulb
	  d. Peanut butter jar

	5. Sand pile

  B. Biodegradable Agent

Examples	*Nonexamples*

1. Animal
  a. Insect
  b. Bird
  c. Bacteria
  d. Squirrel
  e. Caterpillar
  f. Moth
  g. Human being—boy
	1. Weather
	2. Breeze
	3. Scissors
	4. Warm water

2. Plant
  a. Mushroom
  b. Mold	

C. Biodegradable process

Examples

1. Human beings eating food
    a. Boy chewing a hamburger
    b. Girl eating lunch
2. Bacteria making garbage rot
3. Log rotting in the woods
4. Mold growing on a piece of bread
5. Moth eating a woolen coat

Nonexamples

1. Grandma cutting bread with a knife
2. Baking soda dissolving in hot water
3. Car running over an ice cream cone
4. Mother slicing a birthday cake
5. Ice cube melting in a glass
6. Sugar dissolving in warm water

Source: H. J. Klausmeier, E. S. Ghatala, & D. A. Frayer, *Conceptual learning and development: A cognitive view,* pp. 262–63. Copyright © 1974 by Academic Press. Reprinted by permission of publisher.

Summary

This chapter emphasizes the use of language as a base for teaching reading, describing the language experience approach and procedures to assess learners' needs and to expand their language/reading competencies. The chapter includes sample diagnostic protocols and warns that teacher judgments about reader functioning need to be based on many samples of reader performance. The development of a personal chart based on a child's individual experience and a thematic approach using content area subject matter in the middle grades serve as illustrations of the LEA.

Language as a Base for Word Identification

A language-based reading program incorporates a problem-solving approach to identifying unfamiliar words in text. As readers actively explore language in their environment, formulate and test hypotheses about language, expand their store of knowledge, and apply their knowledge to new reading situations, they expand their language facility and discover a variety of strategies to identify new words on their own. Readers discover these strategies as they encounter new words in their reading and either independently or with structured teacher guidance arrive at the appropriate meanings. The most common strategies learners use are focusing on the context, analyzing the meaning parts of words, and associating sound-symbol relationships. These strategies frequently occur in conjunction with each other, with context being the major consideration in the identification of a new word.

To facilitate learners' understanding that they can use specific strategies in approaching unfamiliar words, the teacher provides two types of reading experiences using student-authored materials, teacher-constructed materials, and commercially prepared materials.

The first type of experience occurs as learners read continuous discourse and indicate they have some difficulty in understanding the text because they are unable to identify one or more words. This problem gives the teacher an opportunity to initiate a discussion in which children are encouraged to question each other and share knowledge about particular word identification strategies that they have found to be effective. The teacher, as a member of the group, is ready to facilitate this interaction for discovery of strategies through appropriate questions and comments that guide learners' thinking. When meaning breaks down, the teacher can guide readers to discover those specific word identification strategies relevant to the reading material that can help them to identify the word and to construct meaning. Thus, reader miscues or oral reading errors direct the content of group discussions.

The second type of reading experience involves direct instruction in specific word identification strategies. In contrast to teacher-guided spontaneous discussions, the teacher plans this activity specifically for one or more learners who have exhibited a pattern of miscues and who could benefit from a structured reading experience focused on one specific word identification technique.

This chapter will provide background information on the components involved in each of the word identification strategies as a prerequisite for guiding interactive discussions and for planning specific word identification strategy lessons. Examples of teaching word identification strategies both in discussion situations and through the use of a structured teaching plan appear. The specific strategy plans use the three stages of teaching— preactive teaching, interactive teaching, and evaluative teaching, which we have described in greater detail in Chapter 4. The first plan which we will describe illustrates the teaching of phonic analysis; the second plan illustrates the teaching of morphemic analysis.

Components of Word Identification

The following section summarizes some of the basic background knowledge in the area of word identification that teachers may use as they function in their interactions with learners.

CONTEXTUAL ANALYSIS

Contextual analysis refers to a reader's use of clues provided by the surrounding words or graphics in text to understand individual words or groups of words. Contextual clues are primarily of four types: typographical, pictorial and graphic, syntactic, and semantic (Johnson & Pearson, 1978). These four types of clues are generally used in combination with each other and frequently in conjunction with morphemic analysis and phonic analysis to ensure accurate meaning and appropriate pronunciation.

Typographical clues such as parentheses, dashes, and commas are often signals to indicate that the author has provided a synonym, description, definition, or explanation of a preceding word. Authors also occasionally use quotation marks to highlight a special or unusual use of a particular word.

In addition to typographical clues, authors may provide *pictorial* and *graphic* aids in forms such as pictures, maps, charts, tables, graphs, and diagrams that may clarify or supplement the written text. Although typographical and graphic clues provide some help to the reader, in general, syntactic and semantic clues provide the most aid in identifying unfamiliar words.

Syntactic clues used in conjunction with semantic clues limit the possible alternatives in identifying an unfamiliar word by restricting the reader to a word that "fits" the structure of the sentence. Speaking and listening experiences provide the knowledge base that enables the reader to use syntax as a clue to word identification: Knowledge of the grammar or rules that determine the form of sentences or longer discourse assists the reader in predicting unknown words.

Separating syntactic clues from semantic clues is not possible because they operate together within written text. *Semantic elements* are the most helpful of all types of contextual clues in identifying unknown words since they are the meaning-breaking components of text. Summaries of the major kinds of semantic clues used by authors follow.

Synonyms

Writers use signal words such as "or," "that is," or "called" to indicate synonyms, or synonyms may be set off by typographical aids such as commas, dashes, colons, or parentheses. Further, the richness of our language frequently provides synonyms within the text.

For example, in the sentence—"The force, or pressure, of an electric current can be measured."—the words *or pressure* provide a synonym clue to the meaning of *force*.

The sentence—"The hatch was torn away during a storm at sea so another cover was used."—is an example of how rich our language is. *Cover* in this sentence is a synonym for *hatch*.

Definitions or Examples

When the meaning of an unfamiliar word is found in the same sentence or paragraph, writers may indicate such definitions by signal words such as "is called," "that is," or "means" or the definition may be set off by commas, dashes, or parentheses. At other times, the writer provides a definition without any specific signal words or typographical cues. For example, in the sentence—"The marsh was a swamp where the land was low and wet."—the writer has provided a definition of the word *marsh* without any specific cues. In the sentence "A voltmeter—an instrument used to measure electrical pressure—is used in a number of science experiments," the writer has provided a typographical cue and a definition within the text.

Antonyms

The meaning of particular words and phrases may be indicated by words such as "instead," "although," "but," "yet," "not only," "however," "neither-nor" that clue the reader to expect the opposite meaning of an unfamiliar word.

In the sentence "Although Mary was very thin, her sister was obese," the writer has provided a signal word, *although*, to cue the reader to the antonym for *obese*. Knowing that thin is the opposite of fat serves as a clue to the meaning of obese.

Summary Clues

The reader can often determine the meaning of an unfamiliar word or phrase from the context that precedes or follows it by using a number of clues in combination. For example, in the following passage the reader obtains the meaning of *disheveled* from a number of clues:

> The room was completely disheveled. Books were torn and thrown on the floor. Chairs were overturned and lamps were broken.

Inferences

The reader can obtain the meaning of an unfamiliar word by inferring the meaning based on information in the text and the readers' experiential background. For example:

> The wind was blowing furiously, and the rain was pouring down. It must have been a hurricane.

The readers' familiarity with different types of weather and the first sentence provide clues to what a hurricane is. Although writers provide other semantic context clues such as comparisons, figures of speech, idioms, cause and effect, the reader's knowledge as it interacts with the text allows the reader to infer the meaning of unfamiliar words. Readers' constant monitoring of their reading comprehension, so that using context to identify unfamiliar words becomes a natural strategy, is more important than their knowing the specific types of context clues writers use.

MORPHEMIC ANALYSIS

Morphemic analysis refers to a reader's use of the meaning units of words. These morphemic units include roots, inflectional variants, and affixes. *Roots* or bases that carry the major part of word meaning are of two types. There are *free bases* (root words) such as *walk* and *play* that can stand alone and enter into combinations with inflectional variants and affixes, and there are *bound bases* (word roots) such as *tele* and *dico* that cannot stand alone. *Bound morphemes* or bases must always join with other morphemic units to form a word such as *telegraph*.

A *compound word* generally is an example of two free bases joined together, as in *firehouse*. However, many compound words appear as separate words but operate as compound words such as in *living room* as contrasted with *bedroom*.

Also, in analyzing the meanings of compound words, the two free bases (root words) will not always relate to each other in the same way. Relations between root words will take forms such as one is *of* another, one is *from* another, one is *for* another, one is *like* another, one *is* another, one *does* another (Johnson & Pearson, 1978). For example, the compound word *fireplace* means a place *for* a fire, whereas the compound word *catbird* means a bird that sounds *like* a cat, and the compound word *policewoman* means a woman who *does* police work.

A *contracted word* has as its origin two free bases. This combination of two words is one in which an apostrophe indicates that one or more letters have been omitted. One type of contraction combines a personal pronoun and an auxiliary such as *I have* expressed as *I've* and *we will* expressed as *we'll*. A second type of contraction combines an auxiliary and a negative particle, such as *should not* expressed as *shouldn't* and *cannot* expressed as *can't*.

Inflectional variants are new forms of a root word that indicate a grammatical or syntactic change but not a change in the meaning of the word. Inflectional endings are added to roots and suffixes and are the final morphemic element in a word. Inflectional variants include noun inflections indicating plurality such as the *s* in *toys* and the *es* in *boxes*; noun inflections indicating possession such as the *'s* in boy's (singular) and *s'* as in girls' (plural); verb inflections such as the *ing* in play*ing*, the *s* in plays, and the *ed* in play*ed* to indicate person and tense; and adjective and adverb inflections to indicate comparative and superlative as the *er* in tall*er* and *est* in tall*est*.

Affixes are always attached to a root or a combination containing a root and an affix. In contrast to inflectional variants, affixes can affect the grammatical category of a word and often change a word's meaning. Affixes include *prefixes* that occur at the beginning of a word such as the *pre* in *pre*test, the *un* in *un*able and the *re* in *re*play; *suffixes* such as the *ful* in care*ful*, the *ly* in playful*ly*, and the *able* in comfort*able* that occur at the end of words. Both prefixes and suffixes are bound morphemes since they cannot occur independently of a root. Teacher knowledge of common prefixes, common suffixes, and Greek and Latin roots may be of some use during group discussions involving strategies for identifying unknown words. But the use of these morphemic units is most valuable in expanding and developing vocabulary when learners focus on using the meaning units of words to increase their vocabulary for both writing and reading.

The following example using the root word *print* illustrates some of the morphemic units.

The *print* was too small to read. (root word/free morpheme)

The *printmaker* was very busy. (compound word)

The *reprint* was widely distributed. (prefix + free morpheme)

The *printer* worked long hours. (free morpheme + suffix indicating agent)

The newspaper *printed* a special edition. (free morpheme + verb inflection)

The *printer's* tools were on the table. (free morpheme + suffix + noun inflection indicating possessive)

References such as Ives, Bursuk, and Ives (1979) and Johnson and Pearson (1978) are good sources for information in this area.

PHONIC ANALYSIS

Phonic analysis, like morphemic analysis, is used in conjunction with context clues to identify unfamiliar words. As reading materials are based on familiar language, phonic analysis should allow readers to understand the words once they "hear" them: Knowledge of letter-sound correspondences can enable readers to pronounce visually unfamiliar words. Phonic analysis refers to the identification of sounds and pronunciation units within written words. Such units include phoneme-grapheme correspondences, syllabication and accenting principles. In written English, 26 letters (symbols) represent the approximately 46 distinct sounds of the English language. Thus, the conditions under which a particular letter represents a particular sound must be specified.

Consonants represent those basic speech sounds in which the breath-stream passes through the speech organs with audible friction. These phonemes are differentiated by the place of articulation, the manner of articulation, and the presence or absence of voicing. Consonants always appear at the beginning and/or at the end of a syllable and appear in the middle of a syllable only when they are part of a consonant blend. There are more phonemes represented by consonants than there are consonant letters. Examples of phonemes represented by a single consonant are /d/, as in *door*; /t/, as in *table*; and /v/, as in *vote*.

Consonant variants include those single consonants that represent more than one sound, such as /s/ and /k/ both represented by *c*, as in *cent* and *car*; /j/ and /g/ both represented by *g*, as in *gem* and *gate*; and /s/ and /z/ both represented by *s*, as in *seen* and *busy*.

Consonant blends are combinations of two or more adjacent consonants without an intervening vowel. Each letter retains its own phonemic identity. Examples of blends are /br/, as in *brown*; /sl/, as in *slip*; /str/, as in *string*; and /nd/, as in *land*, and always occur in the initial and/or final position of syllables or words.

A *consonant digraph*, represented by two adjacent consonant letters, is a sound that is different from the sound usually associated with either of its consonant letters. For example, /sh/, as in *ship*; /ch/, as in *chop*; and /f/ represented by *ph*, as in *photograph*, are consonant digraphs.

Certain consonant letters may be silent in some words, such as the *k* in *know* and the *w* in *write*. When this occurs, the consonant is termed a *silent consonant* since it represents no sound in the word.

Vowels represent those basic speech sounds in which the breath-stream passes through the speech organs without audible friction. The different phonemes represented by vowels are produced by changing the position of the top of the tongue in the oral cavity and by changing the position of the lips. There are also more phonemes represented by vowels than there are vowel letters.

Short vowel sounds involve little or no shift in the tongue and include /a/, as in *cap*; /e/, as in *pet*; /i/, as in *bit*; /o/, as in *lot*; and /u/, as in *must*. *Long vowel sounds*, in contrast to short vowel sounds, require some amount of glide, or shift, in order to produce the sound. These vowel sounds include /ā/, as in *ape*; /ē/, as in *even*; /ī/, as in *line*; /ō/, as in *hope*; and /yōō/, as in *use*. A *vowel digraph*, represented by two adjacent vowel letters, is the vowel sound of one of them, such as /ā/ represented by the *ai* in *rain* and /ē/ represented by the *ea* in *meat*. A *vowel diphthong*, also represented by two adjacent vowel letters, is a vowel phoneme that is different from either of the vowel letters forming it. Vowel diphthongs include /ow/ represented by the *ou* in *house* and /oy/ represented by the *oi* in *boil*. *Vowel controllers* are consonants that control the sound of the preceding vowel. For example, *r* is a vowel controller in *bird*, *l* is a vowel controller in *bald*, and *w* is a vowel controller in *saw*.

Finally, the *schwa* represents a vowel sound in an unaccented syllable, such as /ə/ represented by the *a* in *about*; the *e* in *enough*; the *i* in *editor*; the *o* in *occur*; and the *u* in *upon*.

Syllabication refers to the visual identification of a letter or a combination of letters that form a syllable and, as such, can serve as an aid to pronunciation. Generally, linguists classify syllables as *open-syllables* ending in a sound represented by a vowel, such as the first syllable in *ti'* ger, or *closed-syllables* ending in a sound represented by a consonant, such as the first syllable in *cap'* tain. Syllables can also be described as accented or unaccented. A number of generalizations can aid the reader in visually syllabicating unfamiliar words (Ives, Bursuk, & Ives, 1979). *Accent* has to do with the intensity, or degree of force, with which the speaker utters a syllable. In words of more than one syllable, *stress*, or emphasis, is given to one syllable more clearly than the others. Words consisting of two or three syllables usually have only one that is accented. Words of more than three syllables have both *primary* and *secondary accents*. Table 6.1 summarizes the components in word identification.

A number of approaches to teaching phonics exist; however, the approach most consistent with a language-based program is the use of spelling patterns or phonograms within words. A *spelling pattern* is any "letter group which has an invariant relationship with a phonemic pattern" (Gibson, Pick, Osser, & Hammond, 1962, p. 30). This letter-group approach is a natural part of rhyming words, poetry, general language usage, and language play. Research (Glass, 1965; Glass & Burton, 1973; Gleitman & Rosen, 1973) supports the view that spelling units or syllables are more readily learnable than individual phonemes and that readers seem to group sounds by using various letter clusters. These *letter clusters* which begin with a vowel and end with either a consonant, a semivowel, or silent *e* are closed syllables and frequently are referred to as *graphonomes* (Jones, 1970). These spelling-sound units provide readers with letter sequences they can easily identify visually, avoid the sound distortions that result from pronunciation of individual phonemes in isolation, and allow readers to apply knowledge of letter-sound correspondences through blending (Ruddell, 1974).

The *phonograms* listed in Table 6.2 (pp. 128–30) are categorized by frequency of usage in the speaking vocabularies of primary grade children (Durrell, 1972) and by relative level of difficulty as Glass (1973) has determined. Level 1 presents the easiest phonograms, whereas level 5 presents the most difficult. The final list consists of high frequency phonograms not included in the Glass analysis of difficulty. Reference to these lists serves as a guide when the teacher previews commercial reading materials, analyzes student-authored material, and selects phonograms for specific instruction.

Teaching Word Identification Strategies

INTERACTIVE DISCUSSIONS

Teachers and students spend the greatest amount of reading time in reading continuous text and discussing it. These discussions focus on understanding the text and on developing problem-solving strategies when meaning breaks down. The teacher focuses on miscues that cause this

Table 6.1 Summary of Components in Word Identification

Component	Example
Contextual Analysis	
Typographical	parentheses, dash, comma, quotation mark
Pictorial/Graphic	picture, map, chart, table, graph, diagram
Syntactic	structure of the sentence
Semantic	synonym, definition, example, antonym, summary, inference
Morphemic Analysis	
Roots	
Free bases (root words)	walk, play
Bound bases (word roots)	tele, disco
Compound words	firehouse, living room
Contracted words	shouldn't
Inflectional Variants	
Plurality	to<u>ys</u>, box<u>es</u>
Possession	boy'<u>s</u>, girls'
Person and tense	play<u>ing</u>, p<u>lays</u>, play<u>ed</u>
Comparative and superlative	tall<u>er</u>, tall<u>est</u>
Affixes	
Prefixes	<u>pre</u>test, <u>un</u>able
Suffixes	care<u>ful</u>, <u>sh</u>ortly
Phonic Analysis	
Consonants	
Single consonant	/d/ in <u>d</u>oor
Consonant variant	<u>c</u> in <u>c</u>ent and <u>c</u>ar
Consonant blend	/br/ in <u>br</u>own
Consonant digraph	/sh/ in <u>sh</u>ip
Silent consonant	<u>k</u> in know
Vowels	
Short vowel	/a/ in c<u>a</u>p
Long vowel	/ā/ in <u>a</u>pe
Vowel digraph	/ā/ in r<u>ai</u>n
Vowel diphthong	/ow/ in h<u>ou</u>se
Vowel controller	<u>r</u> in bi<u>r</u>d
Schwa	/ə/ in <u>a</u>bout
Syllabication and Accent	
Open-syllables	<u>ti</u>' ger
Closed-syllables	<u>cap</u>' tain

breakdown and that form the content for teacher-guided group discussion in a problem-solving and supportive setting. The reader benefits from guidance in discovering techniques for identifying unfamiliar words in the form of teacher-guided questions and comments in conjunction with reading the text. Both the reader and other learners provide input in discovering appropriate strategies and constructing meaning. Prior to the reading

Table 6.2 Levels of Phonograms

Level (1)

Phonogram	Frequency	Example
ack	15	back, black, crack, jack, lack, pack, quack, rack, sack, shack, smack, snack, stack, tack, track
ad	9	bad, dad, fad, glad, had, lad, mad, pad, sad
ag	9	bag, drag, flag, sag, gag, rag, snag, tag, wag
an	12	an, bran, can, fan, man, pan, plan, ran, span, tan, than, van
ap	12	cap, chap, clap, gap, lap, map, nap, sap, scrap, tap, trap, wrap
ash	15	ash, cash, clash, crash, dash, flash, gash, gnash, hash, mash, rash, sash, smash, splash, trash
at	13	at, bat, cat, chat, fat, flat, hat, mat, pat, rat, sat, that, vat
ay	19	bay, bray, clay, day, dray, gay, gray, hay, jay, lay, may, pay, play, ray, say, spray, stay, tray, away
et	9	bet, get, jet, met, net, pet, set, wet, yet
in	15	bin, chin, din, fin, gin, grin, in, pin, sin, skin, spin, thin, tin, twin, win
ing	15	bring, cling, ding, king, ping, ring, sing, sling, spring, sting, string, swing, thing, wing, wring
it	12	bit, fit, grit, hit, kit, lit, mit, pit, quit, sit, slit, spit
op	14	chop, crop, drop, flop, hop, lop, mop, pop, prop, shop, slop, sop, stop, top
ot	14	blot, cot, dot, got, hot, jot, knot, lot, not, plot, rot, shot, trot, tot
um	9	drum, gum, hum, plum, rum, scum, slum, strum, sum
un	9	bun, fun, dun, nun, pun, run, spun, stun, sun

Level (2)

Phonogram	Frequency	Example
ake	13	bake, brake, cake, flake, lake, make, rake, shake, snake, stake, take, wake, mistake
ame	10	blame, came, dame, flame, game, lame, name, same, shame, tame
ank	11	bank, blank, crank, drank, frank, plank, rank, sank, spank, tank, thank
ate	10	ate, date, gate, hate, late, mate, plate, rate, skate, state
ent	9	bent, cent, dent, lent, vent, sent, spent, tent, went
est	10	best, blest, chest, guest, nest, pest, rest, test, vest, west
ip	19	chip, clip, dip, drip, flip, grip, hip, lip, nip, rip, ship, sip, skip, slip, snip, strip, tip, trip, whip
ock	14	block, clock, cock, crock, dock, flock, frock, knock, lock, rock, shock, smock, sock, stock
ug	11	bug, drug, dug, hug, jug, mug, plug, rug, smug, snug, tug

Level (3)

Phonogram	Frequency	Example
aw	14	caw, claw, draw, flaw, gnaw, jaw, law, paw, raw, slaw, squaw, straw, taw, thaw
ell	12	bell, cell, fell, hell, sell, shell, smell, spell, tell, well, yell, swell
ice	9	dice, ice, lice, nice, price, rice, slice, spice, twice
ick	13	brick, chick, click, kick, lick, nick, pick, quick, sick, stick, thick, trick, wick
ight	9	bright, fight, flight, fright, height, knight, light, might, night
ink	12	blink, brink, drink, ink, kink, link, pink, shrink, sink, stink, think, wink
ush	11	blush, brush, crush, flush, gush, hush, mush, plush, rush, slush, thrush

Level (4)

Phonogram	Frequency	Example
ale	10	ale, bale, gale, male, pale, sale, scale, stale, tale, whale
ave	10	behave, brave, cave, gave, grave, pave, rave, save, shave, wave
eat	10	beat, cheat, eat, heat, meat, neat, peat, seat, treat, wheat
ill	15	bill, chill, dill, drill, fill, grill, hill, ill, kill, mill, skill, spill, still, thrill, will
oke	9	broke, choke, coke, joke, poke, smoke, spoke, stroke, awoke
ore	11	bore, core, fore, score, shore, snore, sore, store, swore, tore, wore
ow	15	blow, bow, crow, flow, glow, grow, know, low, mow, row, show, slow, snow, stow, throw
ow	12	bow, brow, cow, how, now, plow, prow, row, scow, sow, vow, allow

Level (5)

Phonogram	Frequency	Example
are	11	bare, care, dare, fare, glare, pare, scare, share, snare, square, stare
ear	9	clear, dear, ear, fear, hear, near, rear, smear, spear
ound	9	bound, found, ground, hound, mound, pound, round, sound, wound

Noncategorized (Continued on page 130)

Phonogram	Frequency	Example
ail	15	ail, fail, frail, hail, jail, mail, nail, pail, quail, rail, sail, snail, tail, trail, wail

Noncategorized

Phonogram	Frequency	Example
ain	12	brain, chain, drain, gain, lain, main, pain, plain, rain, sprain, stain, train
amp	9	camp, clamp, cramp, damp, lamp, ramp, stamp, tamp, tramp
ide	10	bride, glide, hide, pride, ride, slide, side, tide, wide
ine	14	dine, fine, line, mine, nine, pine, shine, spine, swine, tine, twine, vine, whine, wine
int	9	flint, glint, hint, lint, mint, print, splint, squint, tint
uck	10	chuck, cluck, duck, luck, puck, shuck, stuck, suck, truck, tuck
ump	12	bump, dump, hump, jump, lump, plump, pump, rump, slump, stump, thump, trump
ung	10	clung, flung, hung, lung, rung, slung, sprung, stung, sung, swung
unk	10	bunk, chunk, drunk, hunk, junk, punk, shrunk, spunk, sunk, trunk

of a selection, the teacher previews the materials, becomes aware of those words and phrases with high potential for reader miscuing, and is prepared to ask appropriate guiding questions as part of the discussion. Some general questions and comments that guide group discussions are:

Using Context
What words help you to figure out the meaning of _____?

Look at the words in the parentheses (between the dashes). How do these words help you?

Read the next sentence. See if it helps you to figure out the word _____.

Read the sentence before it and see if it helps you figure out the word _____.

Read the rest of the paragraph. Look for another word that means the same as _____.

Read the words that follow the word(s) or *(that is, which is, means).*[1] Then reread the sentence and try to figure out the meaning of _____.

---

[1]Words in parentheses here are substitute words for the italicized word. Depending on context, the teacher uses the appropriate word.

Read the words that follow the word(s) *but (yet, however, not only, neither-nor)*[1]. Then reread the sentence and see if there is a word that is the opposite of _____ .

Think of an experience similar to the one in this story. It may help you to figure out the unfamiliar word.

Is there a word in the story to describe _____?

Using Morphemic Elements
A part of this word is the same as *(telephone)*. Think of what *(telephone)* means and see if it helps you figure out this word *(telegraph)*.

This word is made up of two words *(school)* and *(house)*. Think of the meaning of each word and see if it helps you figure out this word *(schoolhouse)*.

The apostrophe in this word tells you that a letter or letters are missing. What is the word including the missing letter(s)?

This word has the same beginning as *(reread)*. Think about the meaning of *(reread)* to figure out the meaning of *(rewrite)*.

This word has the same ending as *(careful)*. Think about the meaning of *(careful)* to figure out the meaning of *(hateful)*.

Using Phonograms
This word sounds like *(back)*, but begins differently. Say the word to yourself and then try to pronounce the new word *(hack)*. (Begins like *hat* may be used as additional clue if needed.)

Here the guided questions are separated by category, but remember that in actual practice the teacher uses them in an integrated way because using morphemic elements and phonograms to identify unfamiliar words is limited without reference to context. The following sample of a reader's miscues while reading text illustrates learner(s)/teacher interactions which focus on expanding word identification strategies. Note that the general guiding questions indicated above are much more specific in the context of an actual selection. Figure 6.1 is a sample of a reader's miscues and is followed by a spontaneous discussion between teacher and learners.

Reader Miscues
  Omission of "heaved"

  Mispronunciation of "strained"—(strĭned)

  Note: Repetition of word "and" (|and) coded but not considered a miscue

The wheels churned. . . .

The car sank deeper into the mud.

They all got out and pushed. They pushed and

strĭned

shoved |and (heaved) and strained and gasped and slipped.

Slowly the car began to move.

"Don't stop!" cried Mr. Grumpy. "Keep it up!

We're nearly there."

Everyone gave a mighty heave—the tires gripped. . . .

The car edged it's way up to the top of the hill.

Figure 6.1   Sample of a Reader's Miscues

Teacher-Learner(s) Discussion
T: What did you do when you saw the first word that you didn't know?
R₁ *(John)*:   I looked at it. I couldn't say it so I skipped it.
T: Is there anything else John could have done?
R₂: He could have tried to say it.
R₃: He could have thought of a hard word he knew that is like pushed.
T: Why pushed?
R₃: Because in the story it sounds like they're pushing and shoving and doing lots of things like that to get the car out.
T: That's a good idea. Often words with similar meanings are in the same sentence, and these words can help us to understand a word we don't know.
R₄: Heavy. He could have thought of heavy. It looks like heavy.
T: Let's try it.
R₄: They pushed and shoved and heavy and strained. . . .
T: Does that make sense?
R₄: No.
R₂: I know, the word is heaved.
R₄: I never heard of that word.
T: You're on the right track but it sounds like a word that I'm sure you know (teacher writes the word "leave" on the chalkboard).
R₄: Heave. I know, it's heave.
T: Now go back and reread the sentence.

John correctly rereads the sentence to the group including the correct pronunciation for strained.

T: What do heaved and strained mean?

R₁: It means pushing hard to get the car going.

T: How do you know they were working hard?

R₂: They were out of breath. I get out of breath when I work hard like riding my bike up the hill by my house.

This group interaction based on John's inability to identify the word *heaved* led to the discussion of a number of strategies that John could have used. In this example *heaved* is closely related to the meaning of *pushed*. In addition, knowledge of word families (leave/heave) was a helpful strategy.

This example shows that teacher questioning and comments as well as learner questioning and comments facilitate learner discovery of some techniques for identifying unfamiliar words.

STRUCTURED TEACHING

At this early stage of reading teachers can expect that some learners will require more direct instruction in developing word identification strategies. For those learners who require specific teaching, the teacher builds a base of diagnostic information so that teaching relates directly to learners' specific needs. Diagnostic data accumulate over a period of time through teacher analysis of learner miscues in oral reading of language experience charts and other reading materials (see Chapter 7 for miscue analysis). The teacher also collects data by observing how students use words generated during language experience activities in other language and reading situations. For example, a learner may recognize a word only within the context of a specific experience and be unable to read the same word in another context or use this word to develop new phrases or sentences. The teacher uses such data to establish learner patterns of reading performance for planning specific instruction in word identification strategies.

In the early grades instruction tends to focus on phonic analysis to a greater degree than on morphemic analysis. Knowledge of phonic elements allows the reader to pronounce or decode a visually unknown word. However, for the word to be meaningful it has to be part of the reader's listening/speaking vocabulary. In contrast, the use of morphemic elements allows the reader to expand vocabulary knowledge since the reader may combine morphemic elements to construct and understand new words. The reader will be able to understand these new words, that may not be a part of the listening/speaking vocabulary, if the reader has a concept of the meaning of the morphemic elements that make up a specific word. For example, a reader who has never used the word *thermograph* may understand it if the reader associates the root *thermo* with the word *thermometer* and the root *graph* with the word *telegraph*; or the reader may simply know that *thermo* refers to heat and *graph* refers to an apparatus that writes or records.

Instruction in phonic analysis and morphemic analysis appears to be isolated from context for purpose of emphasis, yet this instruction always includes application in context. Context clues, however, never leave the context. Learners understand them most effectively within the context of a story or expository material found in the natural reading environment and they should not be isolated for teaching purposes.

Specific Strategy Plans

The teaching/learning framework in Chapter 4 adapts well for teaching word identification strategies. The following section presents general teaching plans and specific illustrations for the structured teaching of phonic analysis and morphemic analysis.

PHONIC ANALYSIS: GENERAL TEACHING PLAN

As we have previously noted, the teaching of phonic analysis should begin with the learner's knowledge of rhyming words. Rhyming words are ideal for teaching phonic analysis because they incorporate letter clusters or phonograms familiar to the learner. A goal of this instruction is to focus learners' attention on the written features of words they already know auditorily. Teachers may use the following general outline with any phonogram selected for specific instruction. An illustration of teaching one specific phonogram follows this general outline.

Preactive Teaching

Teacher knowledge.   Background knowledge includes awareness of all aspects of phonic analysis: knowledge of the frequency and level of difficulty of letter clusters selected for instruction and knowledge of the learners' use of the selected phonogram during listening and speaking activities.

Teacher decisions.   Basing the choice on diagnostic information, the teacher selects the specific phonogram for instruction as well as the words to be included, and prepares materials (words, sentences, paragraphs) to use in interactive teaching.

Interactive Teaching

Focus attention.   Introductory materials such as word games, rhyming words, and/or poetry highlight the particular phonogram and focus learner attention on the instructional materials.

Learning activity/auditory-visual association.   The teacher pronounces a series of words. Learners respond when they hear a word with the selected letter-cluster. The teacher writes these words on the chalkboard and learners read them orally. The teacher emphasizes the letter-cluster by having learners box, underline, or circle the appropriate letters. The teacher encourages learners to notice that all the words have a common phonogram and different initial letter(s)/sound(s).

Learning activity/substitution or blending.   Learners substitute initial letter(s)/sound(s) for a given letter(s). They start with familiar words and proceed to the independent identification of new words. The phonogram remains constant as the learners form new words and read them orally.

Learning/activity application.   Application material includes texts of various lengths. The words using the particular phoneme appear in short sentences, paragraphs, short poems and stories. Learners read these materials orally so the teacher can note learner application of word identification strategies in context. Follow-up activity includes silent reading in natural reading situations.

Evaluative Teaching

The teacher reflects upon the lesson by thinking about such things as the appropriateness of the phonogram selected for teaching and of the words, sentences, and other materials used during instruction. The teacher determines if learners were able to move smoothly from one activity to another without problems and evaluates the oral reading of the application materials to note if learners can now independently read words with the phonogram that was the focus of the lesson.

ILLUSTRATION: PHONIC ANALYSIS

Preactive Teaching

Teacher knowledge.   Refer to the section on phonic analysis earlier in this chapter for information on all aspects of phonic analysis. Since this strategy plan focuses on the letter cluster *ight*, note that the phonogram *ight* is middle level of difficulty (level 3) for primary grade children. (See Table 6.2.) It occurs in nine different words typically found in the speaking vocabularies of these children. Therefore, this letter-cluster is fairly common in usage and is moderately difficult in relation to other common phonograms.

Teacher decisions.   This strategy serves those learners who would benefit from reading experiences that highlight words with the phonogram *ight*. Teacher observation indicates that this phonogram is in the listening/speaking vocabulary of the learners who participate in this experience. For example, one of the group, Marjorie, has used the word *light* in an experience chart (see p. 105). The teacher included her in this group because she can benefit from a structured experience to expand her knowledge of words with this phonogram. Other learners are in the group because they have shown a pattern of miscues of words with this phonogram. Material will include use of the nine words of the word family *ight* listed in Table 6.2 and additional words with the same letter-cluster.

Interactive Teaching

Focus attention. Teacher reads the following poem:

Star light, star bright
First star I see tonight
I wish I may, I wish I might
Have this wish I wish tonight.

Teacher encourages pupils to repeat the poem with the teacher.

Teacher-Guided Questions:
What words in this poem rhyme? (Sound the same at the end)
Elicit the following words: light, bright, might, tonight.
What part of the word sounds different?

Learning activity/auditory-visual association. Teacher reads the following list of words and learners respond by indicating those words that rhyme with (sound like) light:

*fight	swing
*slight	*fright
halt	*light
*might	goal
mild	*bright
road	*right
*knight	
*height	

The teacher writes the words with asterisks on the chalkboard as the learners respond and then the learners read these words orally. The teacher highlights the letter-cluster by having learners go to the chalkboard and circle the phonogram *ight*. The group discusses incorrect responses: If a learner responds that *swing* sounds like *light* the teacher may ask learners to listen to word pairs such as *swing* and *ring*; *swing* and *sing*; and then: *swing* and *light*.

Learning activity/substitution or blending. Present the following word on the chalkboard:

light

Have pupils substitute different initial consonants and/or consonant blends for the consonant *l* to form the following words:

night	fright
might	slight
fight	bright
right	tight
sight	flight
	knight

Learning activity/application. Present the following sentences for oral reading:

1. The stars were bright in the sky at night.
2. The bird in flight fell and had a fright.
3. My brother held onto the stick real tight with all his might.
4. Her right hand had a slight bump on it.
5. Marie wore glasses because of her poor sight.

Present the following paragraph for oral reading:

It was a bright and sunny morning. What a great day for a flight across the country. We would be able to see one sight after another. One passenger had a slight fright before taking off. She thought she had lost her luggage. But the luggage was right where she put it by the rack. Everyone calmed down and the flight took off.

Select a short poem that includes a sample of words with the phonogram *ight* for oral reading; follow this with silent reading in a natural reading situation.

Evaluative Teaching
The teacher thinks about whether the selection of the phonogram *ight* was appropriate for the group and if the words, sentences, and paragraph used in interactive teaching facilitated learners' understanding. The teacher evaluates the learners' oral reading during the application stage.

MORPHEMIC ANALYSIS: GENERAL TEACHING PLAN
As previously noted, an understanding of morphemic elements can help the learner to identify unfamiliar words and understand their meaning. A goal of this instruction is to expand vocabulary knowledge by building on the learners' conceptual understanding of the meaning units of words. Teachers may use the following general outline with any morphemic element selected for specific instruction. Accompanying the outline is an illustration for teaching one specific morphemic element.

Preactive Teaching

Teacher knowledge.   Background knowledge encompasses awareness of all aspects of morphemic analysis, including the meaning and use of the specific morphemic elements selected for instruction.

Teacher decisions.   The teacher selects the specific morphemic element for instruction based upon diagnostic information, chooses the words to be used, and prepares materials to use in direct instruction (words, sentences, paragraphs).

Interactive Teaching

Focus attention.   The teacher presents introductory material in the form of short sentences or a brief paragraph using familiar words containing the selected morphemic elements.

Learning activity/analysis.   The teacher writes a series of words containing the morphemic element on the chalkboard. Learners analyze the morphemic elements in each word and highlight the selected morphemic element through such devices as boxing, underlining, circling. The teacher and learners discuss the meaning of each word.

Learning activity/synthesis.   The teacher lists a series of words, this time without the selected morphemic element, on the chalkboard. Learners add the morphemic element under study, explain the meaning of the new word, and use it in a sentence. Learners may also fill in incomplete sentences using the specific morphemic element(s) in combination with a root word.

Learning activity/application.   Learners orally read sentences, paragraphs, and short selections containing the specific morpheme so the teacher can note learner application of word identification strategies in context. Follow-up activity includes silent reading in natural reading situations.

Evaluative Teaching

The teacher evaluates the lesson by considering the appropriateness of the chosen morphemic element and of the materials used during interactive teaching. The teacher considers if the transitions from one activity to another occurred easily. The teacher also evaluates the oral reading of the application materials to determine if learners can now independently read and understand words with the chosen morphemic element.

ILLUSTRATION: MORPHEMIC ANALYSIS

Preactive Teaching

Teacher knowledge.   The teacher refers to the section earlier in this chapter on morphemic analysis. As this strategy will focus on the morphemic element *er*, the teacher notes that *er*, a bound morpheme, is a suffix that means *a person who* or *one who*. Suffixes determine the part of speech of a word and in this case *er* denotes a noun suffix.

Teacher decisions.   This strategy is for those learners who would benefit from reading experiences designed to expand their knowledge of words with the suffix *er*. The teacher has observed that learners in the group have limited understanding of the meaning of the suffix *er* and how it modifies the meaning of the root word.

Material includes words in which the addition of the suffix *er* requires

1. no change in root word;

2. dropping of the final *e* of the root word;

3. doubling of the final consonant of the root word.

Interactive Teaching

Focus Attention. The teacher writes the following sentences on the chalkboard:

The ball <u>player</u> likes to <u>play</u> ball on Saturday.

The <u>teacher</u> planned to <u>teach</u> reading in the morning.

The <u>worker</u> was asked to <u>work</u> every Saturday.

The <u>singer</u> can <u>sing</u> many different songs.

Learners read the sentences to themselves, and then respond to the following questions:

In what way do the two underlined words in the first sentence look alike?

What does "play" mean?

What was done to the word "play" to form the other underlined word?

What does a "player" do?

Have learners analyze each sentence in the same way. Then write the list of the underlined words on the chalkboard:

player	worker
teacher	singer

Help pupils make the generalization that the suffix *er* in each word means *one who*.

Learning activity/analysis. The teacher writes a series of words on the chalkboard for analysis:

writer	thinker
dancer	speaker
doer	reader
killer	robber
	banker

Learners analyze each word by underlining or circling the suffix. The teacher points out that in some words the final *e* is dropped before the addition of *er*, whereas in others the final consonant is doubled before the addition of *er*. Learners then discuss the meaning of each word.

Learning activity/synthesis.   The teacher writes the following list of words on the chalkboard for synthesis:

help	ride
save	run
use	drive

Learners add *er* at the end of each word, explain the meaning of the word, and use it in a sentence. The teacher then writes the following incomplete sentences on the chalkboard, and learners respond by adding the suffix to root words and reading the sentences orally:

A person who writes is a _____.

Someone who dances is a _____ .

A person who reads a lot is a _____ .

Someone who speaks is a _____ .

Learning activity/application.   Present the following sentences for oral reading:

1. The mover lifted the heavy furniture onto his truck.
2. On a nice day he becomes a jogger.
3. When we moved to a new house we had to find a painter.
4. She was a good saver and put her money in the bank.
5. The farmer brought fresh fruits and vegetables to the store.

Present the following paragraph for oral reading:

The ball player was a great hitter. She was a fast learner. Her friend who was also a good batter and fielder practiced with her. They were both fast runners and good catchers. They enjoyed playing baseball together.

Select a short story which includes some words with the morphemic element *er*.

EVALUATIVE TEACHING
The teacher determines whether the suffix *er* was appropriate for the group and whether the materials used in interactive teaching facilitated understanding of words that contain the suffix *er*. The teacher evaluates learners' oral reading during the application step.

Summary

This chapter provides background information on the components of word identification and presents two approaches to helping learners discover strategies for identifying unfamiliar words. One approach involves group discussion of oral reading errors that affect meaning and group problem solving to discover appropriate strategies. The second approach uses a structured teaching plan for direct instruction in two specific aspects of word identification—phonic analysis and morphemic analysis.

PART
III

USING STORIES
FOR ASSESSMENT
AND TEACHING

Informal Assessment Using Stories

Overview of Assessment

Preparing for Assessment
PREVIEWING STORIES

Informal Observation
PROCEDURES: FREE RECALL, PROBE, STRUCTURED QUESTIONS
ANALYSIS OF CHILDREN'S RESPONSES
RECORDING OBSERVATIONS

Structured Assessment
ANALYSIS OF CHILDREN'S SILENT READING
ADDITIONAL DIAGNOSTIC STEPS
ANALYSIS OF CHILDREN'S ORAL READING
GUIDING TEACHER ANALYSIS OF DATA

Summary

T he teacher's informal assessment of learners takes place as learners interact with text. Reader interaction with text involves arriving at meaning through an integrated use of the reader's knowledge of the world and knowledge of oral and written language. As teachers observe a learner's interactions with text, they remember that the child's ability to use these sources of knowledge is influenced by the reader's experience or what the reader brings to the material, the reader's purpose, and the material being read. Thus, "the meaning of a communication depends in a fundamental way on a person's knowledge of the world and his/her analysis of the context as well as the characteristics of the message" (Anderson and others, 1977, p. 368).

This interaction between the reader and the author directs the reading process. Frederiksen (1975a) describes this process in five stages.

> First, a speaker or writer selects from his store of conceptual knowledge (or semantic memory) some organized set of information for transmission. Second, the speaker or writer encodes the conceptual message into a string of well-formed natural language productions. The third stage involves the physical transmission and reception of these natural language productions, either through speech or written text. The fourth stage occurs when a listener or reader transforms the natural language productions actually received into some semantic form or conceptual message. Finally, the listener or reader incorporates the interpreted semantic information into his semantic memory or general store of knowledge. Understanding, then, may be regarded as a process whereby a listener or reader attempts to infer the knowledge structure of a speaker or writer by using the available linguistic message, contextual information, and his own knowledge store as "data structures" from which the inference is to be made. (p. 371)

Textual reading is the interaction between the reader and an author's written discourse, and *discourse* refers to a text of any length that constitutes a coherent message. Discourse may take the form of both narrative or non-narrative writing and includes, for example, stories, drama, poetry, autobiographies, biographies, essays, and textbooks. In reading such materials, the reader derives meaning by interpreting the writing of others. *Assessment*, then, involves teacher monitoring of these reader-text interactions to determine those strengths readers bring to processing text and to note those factors (reader-based or text-based) that interfere with the construction of meaning. This chapter will describe two types of classroom assessment, informal observation and structured assessment, and the characteristics of narrative texts used to illustrate the assessments.

Overview of Assessment

When a classroom teacher begins to work with a new group of students, informal assessment must take place. This assessment involves initial informal observations of all learners and then structured assessment of learners who, in the teacher's opinion, require a closer look. The initial informal observations in which the teacher surveys the entire class provide the teacher with first impressions of learners and is the starting point for the year's program. The teacher limits structured assessment procedures to those learners whose reading performances are not yet characterized— readers whose strengths and needs are not evident to the teacher based on the initial informal assessment.

The teacher begins informal observation by examining standardized reading text data, when available, to determine the appropriate level of materials and selects reading materials approximately one year below the most recent standardized test scores to avoid unnecessary learner frustration. In selecting these materials, the teacher also gives consideration to pupil interests and level of maturity to facilitate the match between reader and author.

The teacher next analyzes the material to gain an understanding of text organization and requirements and observes reader-text interaction during silent reading. Depending on learner performance with these materials, the teacher then judges whether materials at other levels, either higher or lower, and of different content, may be more appropriate for particular learners. Using a hypothesis testing framework, the teacher may elect to change the level or content of materials for continuing these initial observations of children as they read stories and other materials during regular classroom activities.

As a result of these observations, the teacher differentiates between those learners who can begin to function immediately within a regular classroom reading program and those who need structured assessment before participating fully in the class reading program. The teacher proceeds to locate, in greater depth, the strengths and needs of learners selected for this structured assessment. In preparing for the use of structured assessment, the teacher selects and then analyzes appropriate materials in a process similar to the preparation for observing readers informally. In-depth observation of readers on an individual basis as they read text silently follows, and in some cases oral reading and the recording and analysis of oral reading errors (miscues) are also necessary. Based on this information, the teacher begins to plan for reading instruction. In special cases the teacher may judge that additional evaluation by a specialist will help in planning for a learner and will set up a referral for specialist services.

Following the teacher's informal observations and, if necessary, structured assessment, all learners receive observation on a continuing basis as they interact with their regular classroom reading materials. In contrast to structured assessment conducted individually, ongoing informal observation occurs during all reading activities: full class reading activities, group reading activities, and individual reading activities. That is, all reading experiences using the variety of materials encompassed in classroom work have diagnostic value. In keeping with this approach, at times during the school year some students may need additional structured assessment based upon ongoing observations.

As Figure 7.1 shows in the steps involved in teacher assessment of learners, the teacher observes all learners in initial informal observations, the classroom reading program, and ongoing observations. Only some learners require structured assessment, and a few learners may need evaluation by an outside specialist.

Preparing for Assessment

The first step in assessing learners' interactions with text, whether using informal observations or structured assessment procedures, is the selection and analysis of the material to use in monitoring reader-text interaction. Story-type text (realistic, mystery, imaginary, modern, science-fiction) makes suitable material for assessment purposes because it is most familiar to the majority of readers.

PREVIEWING STORIES

Analysis of text involves an examination of the discourse and an analysis of text-based questions, followed by the formulation of teacher-constructed questions. In surveying the material, the teacher notes:

1. the author and the author's relevant background;
2. the author's purpose;
3. the author's language;
4. the author's organization of the text;
5. the explicit information directly stated in the text; and
6. the implicit information based on what is presented in the text.

The teacher must be aware of the organization of the material and the possible information, both explicit and implicit, readers may construct from the text.

In addition to analyzing the material, the teacher analyzes text-based questions to determine the responses they may evoke, to determine if readers' responses can be explicit or implicit, and to determine the basis upon which the readers may formulate responses.

Teacher-constructed comprehension questions should follow the characteristics authors use to organize and transmit messages in story-type materials. The teacher should formulate each question with consideration of the message(s) the author intends and the type of reader interaction the teacher wishes to stimulate. These questions further elicit from the learner those characteristics of the story not revealed through spontaneous recall or teacher-aided recall. These structured questions need not cover all characteristics found in narrative text; the teacher selects those characteristics most appropriate to a given story and constructs questions based on these characteristics.

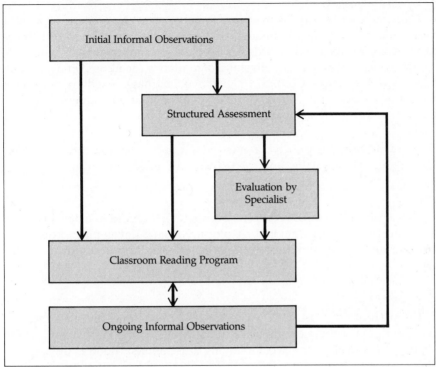

Figure 7.1   Teacher Assessment of Learners

The inclusion of question analysis and construction does not imply that teachers must always ask such questions. Frequently readers demonstrate sufficient understanding of both explicit and implicit meaning by freely recalling story information and responding to nondirective or very general probe-type questions so that the teacher does not have to impose additional structure with detailed questioning.

Story Characteristics
The following are the major techniques writers use in developing stories.

Genre
The type of story. The different categories of narratives appear in Chapter 8, pp. 186–88.

Point of View
The perspective from which the narrator observes or describes the action. Authors who use the first person identify with one of the characters or create a person involved in the action. Authors using the third person "stand outside" looking at the characters and situation. Some authors shift point of view from the first person to third person as different parts of the story occur.

Style and Language
The way a writer says something as opposed to the content of what is said (Lukens, 1982). Style includes the tone, sound, rhythm, word choice and usage, the order of words, and other specific devices of language. These devices include denotative and connotative meanings, imagery, and figurative language. Common figurative language used in children's stories includes similes, metaphors, exaggeration, and personification.

Characterization
The ways authors present characters through behavior, attitudes, feelings, thoughts, language, and the reactions of others toward them.

Plot
The significant actions or related events which unfold in a specific order and lead to the story outcome. A plot involves a developing problem or conflict, the climax, and the conflict solution or indication of future resolution.

Setting and Mood
The place, time, customs, and practices of people as revealed through the descriptions, the monologues and dialogues, of the narrator(s) and the characters, as well as the accompanying illustrations. Mood is the impression created by the setting, atmosphere, situation, and language.

Theme
The meaning of the story. Usually a theme includes a statement or a generalization about people and/or the world that emerges from the plot. Not all stories have such clearly defined themes but may be about an unusual person or unique situation from which the reader may perceive some general implications.

Developing Comprehension Questions
The following questions are representative of questions that can help to make clear each of the characteristics in any story material. These questions can serve as a guide to the teacher in developing specific structured questions.

1. *Genre and Narrator:*

    What type of story is this?

    Who is telling the story? How do you know?

2. *Style and Language:*

    What does the author mean by (word, phrase, or sentence)?

    What does the word _____ make you think of?

How does this (word, phrase, sentence) make you feel?

Explain the meaning of (simile, metaphor).

Why does the author compare _____ to _____?

Could (description of figure of speech) really occur? Why does the author use this description?

3. *Characterization:*

What do you learn about the most important character in the story?

What do you learn about other characters in the story?

What does (character name) do in the story?

What words does the author use to describe the character?

Why do you think the author uses these words to describe the character?

How do you know that this is a real (imaginary) character?

If you were this character, what would you do differently?

Which character do you like best? Why?

4. *Plot/Major Events:*

What is the main problem the characters face?

When does the problem begin?

What do the characters do to try to solve this problem?

How is the problem solved?

What happens after the problem is solved?

Was there another way that you might have solved the problem?

Does the end of the story fit with the rest of it?

5. *Setting and Mood:*

How does the author describe *when* the story takes place?

How does the author describe *where* the story takes place?

Does the description of the characters fit the place where the story is said to have occurred?

Does the language of the characters fit the time and place?

How does the story make you feel? What does the author do to make you feel this way?

6. *Theme:*

What is the main point of the story?

What does the story tell you about people?

What does the story tell you about the world?

As this chapter will show, the teacher modifies these questions in preparing specific questions for a particular narrative text.

Informal Observation

Informal observations of all learners involve the silent reading of text and an analysis of children's responses to the material. The information gathered during informal observation is the basis for teacher planning. This section will discuss classroom procedures to elicit students' responses to the material they have just read, a framework for analyzing their responses, and suggestions for recording the information.

PROCEDURES: FREE RECALL, PROBE, STRUCTURED QUESTIONS

Students' responses based on their interaction with text should occur initially without interference from the teacher. Therefore, readers' initial responses to the material should involve free recall of the text that they have read silently. Discourse recall is natural for children and does not necessarily bias learners to process text in a particular way. It provides the teacher with some diagnostic information about how learners are constructing meaning from text without external influence. The teacher can initiate this free recall of text with questions like:

Tell me what you have read using your own words.

What is this story all about?

Tell me as much information as you can about what you have just read.

Note that the teacher does not interrupt reader responses until readers have completed responding. In this way readers express what they have reconstructed during silent reading without any external cuing. This gives the teacher insight into how readers process the text.

Following free recall, probe questions elicit further recall. These questions minimally cue readers to recall additional information, thus adding to the teacher's understanding of reader-text interactions. This technique elicits additional explicit and implicit meaning from both good and poor readers (Tierney and others, 1979). The teacher constructs probe questions, based directly on the recall, and presents them immediately following recall. Examples of probes are:

Tell me more about what you have read.

Tell me more about what happened.

Tell me more about the people whom you just read about.

Tell me more about where this happened.

Teachers may include more specific reference to the text in probes to extend the information readers include in free recall.

In addition to free recall and probe questions, the teacher may also use author-constructed questions if available, teacher-constructed questions, or a combination of the two. Since structured questions impose the author's or teacher's view of what is important in the text, the teacher should avoid use of structured questions until students have provided all possible information during free recall and probe. In this way the teacher is able to distinguish between that information generated freely, information elicited with minimal cuing, and information generated through direct cuing.

ANALYSIS OF CHILDREN'S RESPONSES

The teacher analyzes readers' responses during free recall, probe recall, and structured questioning with reference both to the passage and to the readers in order to understand how readers reconstructed the author's message(s). Analysis of observed readers' responses during this assessment includes the important consideration of the type of thinking involved in reconstructing information. Pupil responses may be based on information directly stated in the text, or readers may infer relationships based on textually given information.

In addition, the teacher may observe other responses that are unique but appropriate, based on previous experiences and knowledge of readers as they relate to the information in the text. This type of inference in which the reader integrates prior knowledge (not stated in the text) with text information, has been referred to as scriptally[1] implicit (Pearson, 1976) because it brings the reader's own "scripts" or knowledge of the world to bear on reading between the lines. Thus, for example, two readers may respond to the same material or the same specific question in such a way that one response may be labeled as textually implicit, that is, involving inferences drawn totally from information provided in the text, whereas another response may be labeled scriptally implicit, that is, involving inferences which integrate the reader's prior knowledge and text information.

Additional responses to text may involve judgments in regard to "the goodness, suitability or workability" (Guilford, 1959, p. 476) of materials read. Experts often refer to this form of higher-level thinking, in which readers either spontaneously or through specific questioning evaluate text, as critical thinking. It involves readers' reactions to what they read.

In summary, readers' responses may be categorized as follows:

1. *explicit responses* based on information directly stated in the text;
2. *textually implicit responses* based on relating the explicit information stated in the text;

---

[1]*Scriptally* is a word that Pearson created to describe implicit inference in which readers integrate text information and their own scripts.

3. *scriptally implicit responses* based on integrating reader knowledge of the world and textual information (Pearson, 1976; Pearson & Johnson, 1978);
4. *evaluative responses* based on reader reaction to explicit and implicit information in the text (Guilford, 1959).

Thus, in their analyses of readers' responses during regular classroom activities, teachers must consider jointly the level of response (explicit, implicit, or evaluative) and how these responses came about. This involves determining how the child generated the information—free recall, probed recall, or responses to structured questions.

As a result of this analysis, the teacher distinguishes between readers who comprehend discourse without any apparent problems and readers who require structured assessment. For those readers who comprehend the text, the teacher begins to differentiate levels of reader response as a basis for planning general teaching/learning plans for this group. Readers who are having difficulty comprehending the text require additional diagnosis. In this case, the teacher selects additional narrative material, unfamiliar to the reader, for an in-depth analysis of the reader's silent reading comprehension and the reader's specific miscues or errors in oral reading as they affect comprehension.

RECORDING OBSERVATIONS

In order to be able to make these decisions, the teacher needs to keep careful records of observations. The following charts are some ways to organize information within the presented framework.

Figure 7.2 (Chart A) emphasizes the level of learner responses and enables the teacher to record how information is generated. For example, if a learner freely recalls some information directly stated in the text, the teacher indicates that information under the column Explicit Response and next to the line F (Free Recall). If, however, the teacher needs to ask a structured question to generate the information, a check mark indicates this next to the line S (Structured Question).

Figure 7.3 (Chart B) on page 156 focuses on the characteristics of stories and also enables the teacher to record how the information was generated. Chart B is most useful when the teacher has planned to emphasize only one or two story characteristics during a reading experience.

Teachers should record both initial observations and ongoing observations of readers as they process text to monitor pupil progress and to discern patterns of reader behavior. Remember that in observing a whole class or group of learners as they respond to text, a teacher cannot record *all* responses. Therefore, during any reading experience the teacher should select two or three learners for observation and focus attention only on these learners' responses.

Another way for teachers to focus attention during observations is to record learner responses to only one story characteristic. In this case the teacher records responses of all learners during a reading experience but

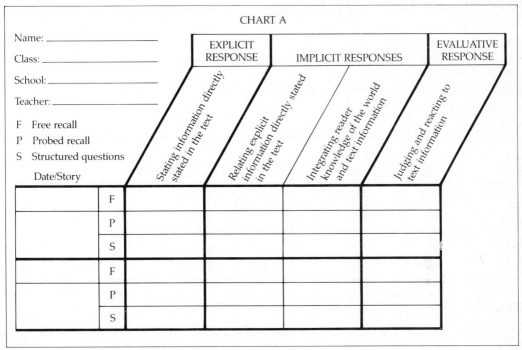

Figure 7.2 Observational Record: Levels of Learner Responses

only when they generate information about the one story characteristic the teacher selects for informal observation.

Informal teacher observation, then, should focus on either "who" (two or three learners and all their responses) or "what" (all learners and only selected responses). Using either of these approaches to observe learners as they process text or both of them at different times, will result in a pattern of reading performance that provides a basis for planning.

Structured Assessment
The teacher selects for structured assessment only those readers who need in-depth analysis of their reading performance. This assessment starts with silent reading and may be followed by oral reading. A teacher's analysis of silent reading performance indicates whether or not oral reading is necessary to further understand learner performance.

ANALYSIS OF CHILDREN'S SILENT READING
The teacher analyzes silent reading with the following steps. The teacher

1. selects the appropriate text;
2. analyzes the text using story characteristics;
3. has the learner read the material silently without any teacher interference; and

CHART B

| F Free recall | Name: _____ | | School: _____ | | | | | | | | | | | | |

F Free recall
P Probed recall
S Structured questions

Name: _____ School: _____

Class: _____ Teacher: _____

Date/Story	Style and Genre			Characterization			Plot			Setting/Mood			Theme		
	F	P	S	F	P	S	F	P	S	F	P	S	F	P	S

Figure 7.3   Observational Record: Learner Responses to Characteristics of Stories

4. conducts a teacher-learner conference during which the learner:
    a. recalls the content (meaning) of the discourse without cuing from the teacher (free recall);
    b. answers probe questions constructed by the teacher to elicit further information (probed recall);
    c. answers structured, teacher-made or textbook questions, if recall and probe did not yield sufficient meaning (structured questions).
5. records information obtained during free recall, probed recall, and structured questioning; and
6. analyzes readers recall according to level of responses, story characteristics, and amount of teacher cuing needed to generate responses.

Analysis of a Story
The following story, "Wait till Martin Comes," served as the material for analysis of the silent reading of two fourth-grade children. Because readers of this age typically enjoy adventure and suspense, a mystery provided suitable material.

Wait till Martin Comes
MARIA LEACH

That big house down the road was haunted. Nobody could live in it. The door was never locked. But nobody ever went in. Nobody would even spend a night in it. Several people had tried but came running out pretty fast.

One night a man was going along that road on his way to the next village. He noticed that the sky was blackening. No moon. No stars. Big storm coming for sure.

He had a long way to go. He knew he couldn't get home before it poured.

So he decided to take shelter in that empty house by the road.

He had heard it was haunted. But shucks! Who believed in ghosts? No such thing.

So he went in. He built himself a nice fire on the big hearth, pulled up a chair, and sat down to read a book.

He could hear the rain beating on the windows. Lightning flashed. The thunder cracked around the old building.

But he sat there reading.

Next time he looked up there was a little gray cat sitting on the hearth.

That was all right, he thought. Cozy.

He went on reading. The rain went on raining.

Pretty soon he heard the door creak and a big black cat came sauntering in.

The first cat looked up.

"What we goin' to do with him?"

"Wait till Martin comes," said the other.

The man went right on reading.

Pretty soon he heard the door creak and another great big black cat, as big as a dog, came in.

"What we goin' to do with him?" said the first cat.

"Wait till Martin comes."

The man was awful scared by this time, but he keep looking in the book, pretending to be reading.

Pretty soon he heard the door creak and a great big black cat, as big as a calf, came in.

He stared at the man. "Shall we do it now?" he said.

"Wait till Martin comes," said the others.

The man just leaped out of that chair, and out the window, and down the road.

"Tell Martin I couldn't wait!" he said.

Story Characteristics

As we have said, the teacher analyzes the text to note characteristics that learners may recall. For this story the following are characteristics to note:

Genre and Narrator

Mystery story told by the author using the third person point of view.

Style and Language

The author uses repetition of words (such as, "nobody") for emphasis; descriptive words for sensory impression (such as, "rain beating," "lightning flashed," "door creaked"); similes to emphasize size of cats (such as, "as big as a dog," "as big as a calf"); connotations of words (such as, "sauntering" to evoke in the reader more than a sense of *leisurely walking* [denotative] but a sense of superiority or confidence of the cat as he confronts the man); and personification—cats have the human attribute of speech.

Characterization

Man: does not believe in haunted houses or ghosts but gives in to fear of the unknown "Martin."

Cats: talk to each other; become increasingly larger and more frightening to the man.

Plot/Major Events

Man takes shelter from oncoming storm in haunted house. Four cats arrive, one at a time, in order of increasing size. With each arrival the cats question each other as to what to do with the man. Each time the response is "Wait till Martin Comes." With the arrival of each new cat, the man becomes increasingly afraid and conflict arises as to whether to stay or leave. The conflict is resolved when the man, giving in to his fear of the unknown, runs out of the house.

Setting and Mood

A haunted house during a storm at night creates a frightening, potentially threatening atmosphere.

Theme

People tend to be afraid of the unknown.

Structured Questions

The teacher then constructs structured questions to use depending on learner responses during free recall and probed recall and on the diagnostic information the teacher wishes to gain about a particular learner. The following questions illustrate structured questions based on the story characteristics in "Wait till Martin Comes."

1. What kind of story is this?
2. Who is telling the story? How do you know?
3. Where does this story take place?
4. What words helped you to gain a picture or feeling of where this story takes place?
5. What is the first problem the man faces?

6. What does he do to try to solve this problem?
7. Once the man is inside the house, what new problem does he have?
8. How does he solve this problem?
9. Does his solution of the problem fit with the rest of the story?
10. What does the story tell you about people?
11. How did you feel when you pictured a big black cat *sauntering* into the room?
12. Why did the author compare the cat to a dog?
13. Why did the author compare the next cat to a calf?
14. How does each new cat compare to the cats that were already in the house?
15. Why does the author do this?
16. Is this a true story? How do you know?

Diagnostic Protocols

A teacher used the story "Wait till Martin Comes" with two learners for assessment purposes. Both learners are children who in the teacher's opinion need individual assessment based on observations of their reading performances as they function with classroom reading materials.

Diagnostic protocol—Learner A. Learner A is a fourth-grade girl whose classroom reading performance indicates that she may have a problem functioning in the regular classroom reading program. The following describes Learner A's recall, responses to probe questions, and responses to structured questions.

Learner A

Free Recall:
T: Tell me everything you can remember about this story.
L: There was a big house, every time someone passed they would go past as fast as they can. Then when this man saw this house, he saw it was going to rain and he went into the house. So he went inside and he read a book. So he sat in a chair and read a book and then the cat came in. Then the door opened and a couple of cats came in. He got scared and ran out.

Responses to Probe Questions:
T: Tell me more about the man.
L: He was scared and he never would go back to the house.
T: Why was he scared?
L: Cause the cats kept coming and getting big . . . one was big as a dog and then the other, one of them, was as big as a cow.
T: Did anything else about the cats make the man scared?
L: They stared at him and they said to him, "Wait until Martin comes." This other cat, he talked . . . maybe Martin would kill him.

Responses to Structured Questions:
T: Who is telling the story?
L: The author.
T: How do you know it's the author?
L: Because he wasn't talking or anything . . . just telling.
T: What kind of story is this?
L: Scary.
T: Do you know the special name for scary stories?
L: Mystery stories—I like to read them.
T: Is this a true story?
L: No.
T: How can you tell?
L: Cause the cats talked and cats can't talk.
T: Does the end of the story fit with the rest of the story?
L: Yeah—he ran out of the haunted house cause Martin was coming.
T: Why was he scared of Martin?
L: Martin would be very big and could kill him.
T: Who do you think Martin was?
L: A great big cat or maybe a ghost who lives with the cats.

Learner A's free recall indicates a good understanding of the story development (plot and events). This includes recognition of the problems faced by the main character (man) and his resolution of these problems. Probe reveals further understanding of the story characters that include recognition that each cat is larger than the preceding one. In addition, she is aware that something else was yet to happen that could be harmful to the man. Structured questions reinforce the understanding she reveals during recall and probe as she indicates that if Martin were a cat, he would be very large. Further, her other prediction that Martin might be a ghost is in keeping with the story. She clearly recognizes this type of story and the role of the author in story telling. In summary, she displays clear understanding of this story and in conversation says she frequently reads mystery stories. It looks as though this learner has had prior knowledge of the structure of mystery stories that gives her a framework for relating to the material.

Further analysis of this protocol, in regard to levels of learner response, reveals that Learner A responds to the materials at all levels. That is, she gives responses that could be classified as (1) explicit responses as she relates the specific facts and details of the story as given, for example, "so he went inside and read a book;" (2) textually implicit responses as she sees relationships not directly stated between the explicit information given in the story, when asked why the man was scared she sees the relationship between the increasing size of the cats and the sequence of their appearance, "'Cause the cats kept coming and kept getting big . . . one was big as a dog and then the other, one of them, was as big as a cow;" (3) scriptally implicit responses as she integrates her knowledge of the world in which people in mystery stories frequently get hurt or killed and the text information about the haunted house, the talking cats, their size, and their reference to waiting for Martin before taking any action, "They stared at him and they said to him, 'Wait until Martin comes' . . . maybe Martin would kill him;" (4) evaluative responses in which she is able to judge that this is not a true story "Cause the cats talked and cats can't talk."

In summary, it appears, based on this structured assessment, that Learner A might function with materials of approximately fourth-grade level when they are story-type narrative materials based on familiar concepts. Depending on the learner's related background knowledge and her purposes for reading and the requirements of the text, the teacher needs to judge the suitability of other materials, which may lead to the selection of higher and/or lower levels of materials. The teacher will base judgments in regard to material selection on information gained from ongoing diagnosis during regular classroom activities.

Diagnostic protocol—Learner B. Learner B, a fourth-grade boy, is an example of another learner requiring structured assessment as a result of the teacher's observations of his reading. The following is a description of Learner B's recall, responses to probe questions, and responses to structured questions.

Learner B

Free Recall:
T: Tell me everything that you can remember about this story.
L: Story's about a haunted house . . . there was this man and there was this people that walking past it but nobody went in the house, there was this man and he said, "Who believed in ghosts?" So he went in . . . then, then the dark cat he, he kept on reading he didn't believe there was ghosts then, there was a dark cat came in, and the cat and . . . then the cat, then the . . . black cat and the cat came in and he got scared and went out.

Responses to Probe Questions:
T: Tell me more about the man.
L: He didn't believe in ghosts.
T: Tell me anything more you remember about the man.
L: He was reading.
T: Tell me more about the cat.
L: The cat sit on a window.
T: Tell me anything else you remember about the cat.
L: He was just big.
T: Tell me how big you think the cat was.
L: I don't know—big.
T: Tell me more about where this happened.
L: In a haunted house.
T: Tell me more about the story.
L: I can't remember.

Responses to Structured Questions:

T: Maybe these questions will help you remember. Who is telling the story?

L: Martin.

T: Why do you think Martin was telling the story?

L: Cause . . . a . . . the title was Martin and he comes in.

T: Who was Martin?

L: Just a man who wrote the story.

T: What is the first difficulty faced by the man in the story?

L: Everybody used to walk past the house and they got scared—and he says there's no such things as ghosts so he was going inside not like the other people.

T: Was there any special reason why he wanted to go into the house?

L: He was not scared of ghosts.

T: Once the man went inside the house, what new problem did he have?

L: See when the cats, when the big black cat came in he got scared and the doors went open all by itself and he went out.

T: Could this story have really happened?

L: No.

T: Why not?

L: Cause nobody believes in ghosts.

T: What kind of story is this!

L: Folktale.

T: Why do you think it's a folktale?

L: Cause folktales don't happen and who believes in ghosts?

Learner B's responses indicate that he is aware of the characters, although they are not clearly defined. He is able to give a general overview of some aspects of the plot and events in the correct sequence. However, his responses are at a very superficial level as are any attempts to relate ideas within the text. Based on his responses it appears that he totally misses the main point of the story and the specifics of plot development that could aid him in inferring the story theme. Although he is aware that this is not a true story, as shown by his calling it a folktale, he does not seem to have a clear sense of genre and narrator as this confusion and his confusion between Martin and the author indicate. The learner is unable to add much new information about the characters, the plot, and theme when the teacher guides his thinking through the use of probe and structured questions.

Further analysis of this protocol, in regard to levels of learner response, reveals that this learner predominantly gives information that can be categorized as explicit responses. His only response that indicates evidence of clear higher-level thinking (evaluative) is when he indicates that this is not a true story. However, this response is only partially correct because as previously noted, he classifies this story as a folktale. There is also some doubt whether he knows what a folktale is. It is important to remember that this analysis of Learner B's comprehension is based on a limited amount of data. Additional stories would be used with Learner B to see if a pattern of comprehension problems emerge.

ADDITIONAL DIAGNOSTIC STEPS

As a result of the assessment of comprehension during silent reading, the teacher may find that some learners (for example, Learner B in the preceding illustration) exhibit inadequate comprehension of the written material and require additional diagnosis. To help determine the next steps in diagnosis, the teacher attempts to answer the following questions with reference to the selection read by the learner during silent reading.

1. Does the learner have familiarity with the basic concepts and topic of the selection?

The answer to this question includes consideration of the general concepts upon which the story is based, the specific concepts and related vocabulary, and the relative importance to the story of the concepts which are or are not familiar to the learner.

2. Does the learner have familiarity with the format and organization of the selection?

The teacher needs to consider the author's writing style, use of language, and organization of ideas and events to answer this question.

3. Does the learner display or express interest in the selection or topic during the teacher-learner conference which follows the silent reading?

To examine how the learner reacts to the selection, the teacher notes if the learner has a positive attitude toward reading and has a positive feeling about reading this particular selection. Teacher observation during silent reading, during the teacher-learner conference, and during teacher questioning can give some insights into reader interest.

The teacher may elicit answers to the preceding three questions during the teacher-learner conference, and students probably will answer these questions only partially. Nevertheless, the teacher needs to consider these questions in choosing another selection for additional diagnosis. The teacher must also consider that different selections meet different purposes for reading. For reading a particular selection, learners should establish their own purposes. However, this is less likely to occur in a diagnostic situation. The very nature of the situation and presence of the teacher frequently lead to a reader purpose not directly related to the material but to the situation: The reader's purpose may include such goals as "to please the teacher," "to remember the story," or "to answer questions."

ANALYSIS OF CHILDREN'S ORAL READING

The purpose of the additional diagnosis is to note the specific strategies the learner uses in processing orally read text. This enables the teacher to infer aspects of the learner's processing of the written text. As Goodman (1976) has noted, "We can't see the reading process happening; we can not tune in on it directly; we must infer it from some kind of external behavior" (p. 65). Oral reading provides us with the external behavior needed for this analysis. However, it may provide us only with an approximation, since silent and oral reading are different.

The following steps implement diagnosis of oral reading. The teacher should

1. select the appropriate text;
2. analyze the text using story characteristics;
3. have the learner read the text orally without any previewing;
4. code reader miscues as the learner reads the material (the teacher may choose to tape-record oral reading to code the miscues at a future time or use the tape recording to verify coding done while reading is in progress);
5. have the learner freely recall the story; use probe questions or structured questions if needed; and
6. analyze reader recall and reader miscues.

The following example illustrates the steps outlined above as they apply to Learner B.

Step 1—Select a Story

Based on information gathered so far, the teacher decides to select fourth-grade material again since this level appears to challenge the learner, the learner is able to recall the overall plot and story characters, and although difficulty is evident, the learner does not appear to be frustrated. Based on a discussion with the learner in which he indicates that he does not particularly like mystery stories, the teacher chooses a realistic-type story using a school background—"A Common Bond."

A Common Bond
ALICE REEL

Mr. Perry was asking for volunteers to try out for the P.T.A. program to be given next week.

Miklos Nyari thought that Mr. Perry was looking at him, so Miklos looked the other way. Not for anything in the world would he let Mr. Perry know that he could play the violin.

Then his twin sister's hand went up, and Miklos' worst fears were realized.

"My brother and I sing Hungarian songs," said Juliska. "He plays the violin, and we both sing."

Mr. Perry seemed pleased. But Miklos wasn't!

"Fine!" said Mr. Perry to Juliska. "You and Miklos be in the auditorium tomorrow afternoon at three o'clock for the tryout."

Miklos frowned. Mr. Perry and Juliska will find out they can't count on me! thought Miklos. Boys just don't get up and perform with their sisters! None of my friends would.

It was one thing to play and sing with his family in his own home. Miklos liked the folk songs of Hungary, and he remembered them. His father had seen to that. Mr. Nyari and his family were American citizens now, but he wanted the twins to remember the nice things about their native land.

Delicious Hungarian pastries were one of the nicest things. Mrs. Nyari made them often.

Johnny Crane, Miklos' best friend, managed to be around whenever Mrs. Nyari made walnut and poppy-seed rolls or round cakes of many layers.

The Nyaris had been in the United States for several years. They had lived with their sponsor while Mr. Nyari had learned to be a tailor.

Then finally he and his family had moved to another part of the city, and Mr. Nyari had set up a little tailoring business of his own.

Miklos knew his parents were lonely. Miklos had made many friends at school. So had Juliska. But their parents knew very few people.

Miklos wished that Johnny's mother would go to see his mother. Mrs. Crane was so nice that a visit from her would make anyone feel at home in a new neighborhood.

At supper Miklos said to his sister, "You had no right to volunteer for me to be on the program!"

"But, Miklos," cried Juliska, "I thought that you liked to play and sing our folk songs!"

"I do!" said Miklos. "But not before a room full of people."

Mr. Nyari said, "You play the violin well, Son. It is time you played in public. Besides, it would make me very happy to have my boy and girl sing Hungarian songs before an American audience. Your mother and I and the little ones would be so proud of our Miklos and Juliska."

Miklos sighed. He'd have to try out, but maybe he and Juliska wouldn't be chosen for the program.

After the tryout Mr. Perry spoke to Miklos. "You and your sister are wonderful! I had been wondering what our room could do for the P.T.A. program, and I had two stars right under my nose. Plan to sing at least two numbers."

When Mr. Nyari heard the news, he insisted that the twins practice every night. The whole family helped decide what songs the twins would sing.

Miklos tried to be as happy about the program as the rest of his family, but he just wasn't.

On the night of the program, Mr. Nyari and his family were the first people to arrive at the auditorium. They were first because Mr. Nyari was afraid they might be late.

He and his wife and the younger children sat in the front row of seats. Juliska sat with them. But Miklos stayed at the door, waiting for Johnny.

At last the auditorium was filled, and the program began. Miklos found it hard to listen to the numbers that came before his and Juliska's.

About nine o'clock Mr. Perry stood and said, "The last number on the program will be given by two children who came from Hungary."

Miklos hated doing it, but he went with Juliska to the piano to tune his violin. Then they faced the audience and began their first song.

Juliska sang with such joy that Miklos began to feel better. He knew they were doing well.

As the twins started their second song, Miklos stiffened. A man was singing along with them. It could be no one but his father! Then his little sisters and brother joined in.

Miklos thought, What will Mr. Perry think? And my friends! What will they think!

When the song was finished, there was such loud clapping that Mr. Perry could hardly make himself heard.

"Won't the family of Miklos and Juliska come up and sing more songs with them?" he asked.

Mr. Nyari told the small children and his wife to stand with Miklos and Juliska. He stepped to the piano. "I would like to play for my family to sing," he said.

The whole family sang. Mr. Nyari's deep, rich voice filled the room.

Miklos looked at his father. To Miklos the voice sounded like that of a lonely man singing of happy times long ago in Hungary.

Suddenly Mr. Nyari stopped playing and got up.

"Enough of Hungary," he said to the audience. "Now my family will sing of our fine new country. We would like it if you would all join us."

The Nyaris played and sang American songs, and the audience sang with them.

Miklos really outdid himself playing and singing "Home on the Range."

When the Nyaris took their seats, Miklos felt a little dazed. Could all that clapping be for them?

Soon his parents were talking and laughing with other mothers and dads. Miklos heard Mrs. Crane say she would be over to call the next day.

Miklos and Johnny walked home together and talked about the evening. Johnny said that the singing had been the best part of the program.

"Say, Miklos, do you feel like an American or a Hungarian?" he asked.

"Why, both, I guess," said Miklos slowly. "I suppose part of me will always be Hungarian. But the biggest part is American."

Johnny laughed. "Well, right now part of me is Hungarian. Your mother said that if I stopped in, she would give me some walnut roll."

Step 2—Analyze the Story

For this story the following are characteristics to note:

Genre and Narrator

Realistic story told by the author using the third person.

Style and Language

Extensive use of names that would be foreign to American students. Connotative use of words (such as, Miklos *sighed* indicating reluctance and resignation to a situation rather than an overall reaction of sadness, weariness, or relief (denotative).

Characterization (main characters)

Miklos Nyari—plays the violin and Hungarian music but is not eager to perform. He is concerned with what people will think.

Juliska Nyari—twin sister of Miklos who is eager to perform.

Mr. Perry—teacher who encourages the Nyari children to perform.

Mr. & Mrs. Nyari—parents of the twins who are proud of their family and culture.

Johnny Crane—Miklos' best friend.

Mrs. Crane—Johnny's mother.

Plot/Major Events

Mr. Perry asks for volunteers for a PTA program. Miklos is angered by his sister's suggestion to take part by singing Hungarian folk songs. Miklos' conflicting feelings of family loyalty and a desire to merge into the American way of life surface. Miklos reluctantly agrees to audition and the twins are put on the program. Mr. Perry and the family are pleased and the twins practice for the performance. After the twins' first selection, the rest of the Nyari family spontaneously begins singing and are invited to come up to the stage. Miklos perceives loneliness in his father's singing of Hungarian songs. Abruptly Mr. Nyari stops playing the piano and singing and asks the audience to join with him in singing American songs. The singing together is followed by thunderous applause and then the Nyari parents begin socializing with the other parents. During the performance as Miklos watches the audience's reaction, he begins to realize that differences do not impose separation, and this leads to the emergence of a new-found pride in his family and background.

Setting and Mood

An American school and an immigrant family's home in America are the settings of a story that creates a warm, accepting atmosphere.

Theme

Music is one bond between people—and between nations. Both Hungarian songs and American songs help form a bond between Miklos' family and their new neighbors.

Step 3—Oral Reading

The teacher tells Learner B that the story is about a boy and his family and asks the learner to read the story aloud. The teacher tells Learner B he will not receive any help and should try his best. The teacher further tells him that if a word is difficult to read he is to try to read it, or guess the word and, if necessary, he may skip a word. He is also told that after he finishes reading the story he is to tell about it in his own words.

Learner B reads the story "A Common Bond" aloud.

Step 4—Recording the Miscues

The teacher may record the miscues as the learner reads the material or may choose to tape-record the oral reading for later listening. If the teacher codes reader miscues during oral reading without tape recording, the teacher must be adept at hearing and coding oral reading miscues to avoid information loss. When coding miscues, the teacher may use the markings in Figure 7.4 or any other system that will yield the same information.

To facilitate recording of the miscues, type the story triple-spaced and number each line as in the text. Figure 7.5 illustrates this typed form and the coding of Learner B's miscues on a sample taken from "A Common Bond."

Step 5—Diagnostic Protocol: Learner Responses

Free Recall:

L: Story's about a boy in school. The teacher wanted the boy and his sister to sing. . . . He, he didn't want to and so said none of his friends would. The boy's father made him practice. He practiced . . . he sang with his sister . . . and he had to sing in school. Everybody liked them and then . . . then, they clapped.

Responses to Probe Questions:

T: Tell me more about the boy.

L: The boy didn't want to sing.

T: Tell me more about his sister.

L: She wanted to sing.

T: Tell me more about the family.

L: They wanted them to sing, and they came to hear them sing.

T: Tell me more about the family when they came to hear the children sing.

L: They clapped.

Coding Symbols for Miscue Analysis

Type of Miscue	Code

1. Mispronunciation — Write the incorrect pronunciation directly above the word.

               twis
Example: twin

2. Substitution — Write the substituted word directly directly above the correct word.

               audience
Example: auditorium

*3. Omission — Circle the word or word part omitted.

Example: His father (had) seen to that.

*4. Insertion — Place a caret at the point of insertion insertion and write the word.

               living
Example: They had been in the
                  ^
United States for several
years.

*5. Repetition — Draw a line under the word or words that were repeated.

  a) Repetition to maintain continuity — Example: But their parents know very few people. ©

  b) Repetition to correct miscue — Example:
               know|
But their parents knew| very few people.

  c) Repetition that results in a miscue — Example:
               Ⓜ
               long|
A man was singing along| with them.

*6. Reversal — Indicate the change in word sequence as shown in the example.

Example: She wassonicethat . . .

---

*These deviations from the text are coded but are not considered miscues for purposes of analysis. Further, words repeatedly miscued are coded, although counted as only one miscue.

Figure 7.4 Coding Symbols for Miscue Analysis

band

A COMMON BOND
by Alice Reel

101   Mr. Perry was asking for volunteers to try out

Penny

2. volunterns
1. volems

102   for the P.T.A. program to be given next week.

pogrent

103   Miklos Nyari thought that Mr. Perry was look-

2. Marlinqus
1. Marlins Naqus
Penny

104   ing at him, so Miklos looked the other way. Not

Munqolos
Now

105   for anything in the world would he let Mr. Perry

Penny

106   know that he could play the violin.

2. vilint
1. villin

107   Then his twin sister(s) hand went up, and

twis

108   Miklos' worst fears were realized.

Marlins
tears ©
realed

109   "My brother and I sing Hungarian songs," said

2. Humagache
1. Humgan

110   Juliska. "He plays the violin, and we both sing."

2. Jurvilika
1. Jurv

111   Mr. Perry seemed pleased. But Miklos wasn't!

Penny
Milos

112   "Fine!" said Mr. Perry to Juliska. "You and

2. Jurkala
Penny
1. Jur

113   Miklos be in the auditorium tomorrow afternoon

Marklos
audience

114   at three o'clock for the tryout."

201   Miklos frowned. Mr. Perry and Juliska will

2. Markolt
1. Mar
fowned
Penny
Jukat

202   find out they can't count on me! thought Miklos.

2. Markolos
1. Mar

203   Boys just don't get up and perform with their

perom

204   sisters! None of my friends would.

205   It was one thing to play and sing with his family

        Markots

206   in his own home. Miklos liked the folk songs of

    Humaly

207   Hungary, and he remembered them. His father

                  2.Nakli

    has son   *1.Nak*   *whole*

208   had seen to that. Mr. Nyari and his family were

            citsen

209   American citizens now, but he wanted the twins to

                     natter

210   remember the nice things about their native land.

          2.Humagans 2.patries

    Deli   *1.Huma*   *1.part*

211   Delicious Hungarian pastries were one of the

         Namalaya

212   nicest things. Mrs. Nyari made them often.

        2.Markuleens

    Cane   *1.Marka*   *manged*

213   Johnny Crane, Miklos' best friend, managed to

        Naqalaya

214   be around whenever Mrs. Nyari made walnut and

     roll

215   poppy-seed rolls or round cakes of many layers.

    Mlayis   *living*

216   The Nyaris had been in the United States for

                       2.supum

    seven   *1.son*

217   several years. They had lived with their sponsor

    Conair

218   while Mr. Nyari had learned to be a tailor.

219   Then finally he and his family had moved to

              Nair

220   another part of the city, and Mr. Nyari had set

221   up a little tailoring business of his own.

                      2.Markos

    Markos   *family* *was*   *1.Mar*

222   Miklos knew his parents were lonely. Miklos

                      2.Juka

                      1.Juk

223   had made many friends at school. So had Juliska.

224   But their parents knew very few people.

225   *[Markos]* Miklos wished that Johnny's mother would go

226   to see *[him ©]* his mother. Mrs. *[Cane]* Crane was so nice that

227   a visit from her would make anyone feel at home

228   in a new neighborhood.

301   At *[As ©]* supper *[Markoos]* Miklos said to his sister, "You *[have]* had

302   no right to *[2.volate / 1.vol]* volunteer for me to be on the *[play]* program!"

303   "But, *[Marko]* Miklos," cried *[Jasnina]* Juliska, "I thought that you

304   liked to play and sing our folk songs!"

305   "I do!" said *[Marklos]* Miklos. "But not before a room

306   full of people."

307   Mr. *[Naklos]* Nyari said, "You play the violin well, Son.

308   It is time you played in *[school]* public. Besides, it would

309   make me very happy to have my boy and girl sing

310   *[2.Humin / 1.Huminia]* Hungarian songs before an American audience.

311   Your mother and I and the little ones would be so

312   *[happy with]* proud of our *[2.Marklits / 1.Markla]* Miklos and *[Jakisnia]* Juliska."

313   *[Markos signed]* Miklos sighed. He'd have to try out, but maybe

314   he and *[2.Jaklia / 1.Jak]* Juliska wouldn't be chosen for the *[play]* program.

Figure 7.5   Illustration of Miscue Coding

Responses to Structured Questions:
T: Who is writing this story?
L: Mr. Penny.
T: What problem did the boy Miklos have?

L: He didn't want to sing in school.
T: What did you learn about Miklos?
L: He was nice because he listened to his sister and his teacher.
T: How did Miklos feel when he sang?
L: He was happy 'cause everybody clapped.
T: What kind of song did he sing?
L: Humgin songs.
T: What are Humgin songs?
L: Happy songs.
T: How did his parents feel when the children sang?
L: They were happy. They clapped.
T: Why did the parents begin to sing?
L: Cause they liked the songs and practiced with him at home.
T: Why were they happy?
L: Cause the songs were good.
T: What does the story tell you about music?
L: Lots of people like music?
T: Could this story have really happened?
L: Yes.
T: How do you know?
L: Cause they're real people . . ., they play in school, and they have a family.

Step 6—Analyze Reader Recall and Miscues

A. *Analysis of responses.* Learner B indicates an overall understanding of the characters and plot of the story. However, this understanding is at a very global (nonspecific) and concrete level. His recall and responses to probe and structured questions indicate that predominantly he is sharing the author's message at an explicit level. Responses are typically based on textually explicit and low-level, textually implicit information. He did understand that the teacher in the story was planning a show and that he wanted the children to perform. Further, Learner B recognized that Miklos was not eager to perform but that his sister wanted to perform and involved Miklos in the program. Learner B also understood that the family was anxious for the children to sing and had them practice at home. Learner B knew that the children did perform and that they were very successful. At this one point he was able to relate *clapping* to his own knowledge that clapping is a positive response to a show. This protocol is consistent with Learner B's reading performance during structured assessment of silent reading. Thus, his understanding of narrative text would seem to be very similar during silent and oral reading. The addition of probe and structured questioning did not result in eliciting additional understanding in regard to story characters, plot, or theme.

Teacher discussion with Learner B revealed that because he was unfamiliar with some of the concepts upon which this story was based, his understanding of some points was limited. Although he knew that some people had moved to his neighborhood from other places, he was not familiar with the general concept of immigration and the more specific related concepts and vocabulary. For example, he did not know what is involved in becoming a citizen, learning a trade, the loneliness and the struggle inherent in adjusting to a new country, and the pride in one's culture coupled with a desire to belong in the new country. This lack of background knowledge appears to have limited the learner's depth of understanding of this selection. Learner B's limited background knowledge is further evident in the analysis of his oral reading miscues.

B. *Analysis of the miscues.*   The miscues are analyzed using a modified form of miscue analysis (Goodman, K., 1969; Goodman, Y., & Burke, 1972; Burke, 1973a, 1975; Hittleman, 1978). This analysis involves looking at reader miscues at two levels. The first level focuses on the whole sentence and how the specific miscues influence sentence and passage meaning. The second level focuses on the knowledge sources the reader brings to the identification of words not readily familiar. This procedure simplifies the analysis of oral reading miscues while retaining emphasis on reading for meaning. This simplified analysis provides the teacher with a way of obtaining some information about a reader's strategies in processing text and enables the teacher to plan reading instruction. This analysis is an important step in understanding a learner's specific needs, but ongoing diagnosis throughout the school year is still necessary to expand knowledge of learner needs and to recognize new needs as they arise.

For this analysis the teacher selects 20–25 sentences containing miscues from a logical portion of a story. The present illustration analyzes the first three pages of the text of "A Common Bond" (lines 101–314) (see Figure 7.6—Chart C).

First level.   The first level of analysis is at the sentence level. This involves viewing reader miscues in the context of the whole sentence and passage to answer two questions:

1. Does each sentence (as read) reflect accurate processing of the author's message? Is it semantically acceptable within the context of the passage?
2. Does each sentence (as read) reflect the reader's knowledge of the grammar of the language? Is it syntactically acceptable?

Figure 7.6 (Chart C) illustrates this first level of analysis based on the miscues made by Learner B. Note that in those cases where oral reading reflects the learner's use of a dialect of English the miscues are not considered reading errors (see Chapter 15).

For illustrative purposes, each sentence has been reproduced to facilitate teacher understanding of the recording and summary of miscue information at the sentence level. The teacher analyzes each sentence containing miscues using the two questions above. First, the teacher records semantic acceptability or unacceptability by placing a check in the appropriate column. If the teacher checks a sentence as semantically unacceptable (a √ in the "No" column), the teacher boxes the miscue(s) that change the message because this information will be the focus of analysis at the second level. Then the teacher records syntactic acceptability in a similar way. The data take on meaning as patterns emerge in the summary section of this chart. In this section the teacher summarizes the characteristics of the sentence just as the reader has read it. Each sentence may be characterized as:

A. *semantically and syntactically acceptable:* the sentence maintains the meaning of the message and is grammatically correct;
B. *semantically unacceptable but syntactically acceptable:* the meaning of the message has been significantly changed although the sentence retains correct grammatical form;
C. *semantically and syntactically unacceptable:* the meaning of the message is significantly changed and the grammatical form is incorrect.

The teacher summarizes these data by totaling the last three columns on the chart. From these totals the teacher can begin to see if the reader's miscues reflect accurate processing of the author's message or reflect loss of meaning. In the latter case the teacher can see if loss of meaning accompanies acceptable or unacceptable use of syntax in processing. When miscues reflect accurate processing of the message, they are not considered reading errors and, therefore, are not further analyzed. Those sentences that reflect loss of meaning are the focus of the second level of analysis. The specific miscues in these sentences (boxed words) are analyzed at the second level.

Second level.   The summary data in Figure 7.6 (Chart C) show that more than half of Learner B's sentences were not semantically acceptable. The miscues in these sentences are the focus of this second level of miscue analysis. Within each of the semantically unacceptable sentences, the teacher analyses only the miscues that change the intended message of the author. Therefore, a sentence that is not semantically acceptable may have several miscues but only one or two of them will need analysis (see boxed words in Figure 7.6 [Chart C]).

The knowledge sources or possible strategies a reader could use in identifying a word not readily familiar in print, form the basis for the analysis of the miscues. In keeping with an emphasis on meaning, the teacher begins this analysis by considering the reader's knowledge of the whole word and then considers reader knowledge of the linguistic units within the word. This involves looking at reader application of knowledge sources in the following order:

Chart C—Level 1 Analysis

Line #	Miscues	Number of Miscues	Semantic Acceptability Yes	Semantic Acceptability No	Syntactic Acceptability Yes	Syntactic Acceptability No	Summary of Data A	Summary of Data B	Summary of Data C
Title	band — A COMMON BOND (2. volunterns / 1. volems)	1*							✓
101	Penny — Mr. Perry was asking for [volunteers] to try out / pogrent	3		✓	✓			✓	
102	for the P.T.A. [program] to be given next week.	2	✓		✓		✓		
103	2. Marlinqus / 1. Marlins Nqqvs — Penny — Miklos Nyari thought that Mr. Perry was look-	2		✓	✓				
104	Monqolos / Now — ing at him, so Miklos looked the other way. [Not]	2				✓			
105	Penny — for anything in the world would he let Mr. Perry								
106	2. vilint / 1. villin — know that he could play the [violin].					✓			✓
107	twis — Then his [twin sister's] hand went up, and			✓	✓				
108	Marlins — realed — Miklos' worst [fears] [were] [realized]. / tears @	3		✓	✓			✓	
109	2. Humaqache / 1. Humqan — "[My] brother and I sing [Hungarian] [songs]," said	2		✓	✓			✓	
110	2. Juviiika / 1. Juvv — Juliska.								
112	"[You and]								
113	audience — Marklos — Miklos be in the [auditorium] tomorrow afternoon	1							
114	at three o'clock for the tryout."								
201	2. Markolt / 1. Mav — fowned — Miklos [frowned].	1		✓ ✓	✓ ✓			✓ ✓	
203	perom — Boys just don't get up and [perform] with their	1		✓ ✓	✓ ✓			✓ ✓	

Line #	Miscues	Number of Miscues	Semantic Acceptability Yes	Semantic Acceptability No	Syntactic Acceptability Yes	Syntactic Acceptability No	A	B	C
204	sisters!			✓		✓			✓
207	His father	2		✓	✓			✓	
208	had ⌐seen⌐ to that. Mr. Nyari and his family were *(2.Nakli 1.Nak) (has Son) (whole) (citsen)*	2			✓				
209	American ⌐citizens⌐ now, but he wanted the twins to *(natter)*								
210	remember the nice things about their ⌐native⌐ land.								
211	Delicious ⌐Hungarian⌐ ⌐pastries⌐ were one of the *(Deli) (2.Humagans 2.patries ①1.Humg 1.Part)*	1		✓	✓			✓	
212	nicest things.								
213	Johnny Crane, Miklos' best friend, ⌐managed⌐ to *(2.Markuleens 1.Marka) (Cane) (manged / managed)*	5		✓	✓			✓	
214	be around whenever Mrs. Nyari made ⌐walnut and *(Naqaleya)*								
215	poppy-seed rolls or round cake⌐s⌐ of many layers. *(roll)*								
216	The Nyaris had been in the United States for *(Mlayis living) (2.supurn 1.son)*	1		✓	✓			✓	
217	⌐several⌐ years. They had lived with their ⌐sponsor⌐ *(seven) (Conair)*	1		✓	✓			✓	
218	while Mr. Nyari had learned to be a tailor.								
219	Then finally he and his family had moved to *(Nair)*	1		✓	✓			✓	
220	another part of the city, and Mr. Nyari had set								
221	up a little ⌐tailoring⌐ business of his own.								

Continued on page 178

Line #	Miscues	Number of Miscues	Semantic Acceptability Yes	Semantic Acceptability No	Syntactic Acceptability Yes	Syntactic Acceptability No	Summary A	Summary B	Summary C
222	Markos · family · was — Miklos knew his parents were lonely.	2	✓		✓		✓		
226	Cane — Mrs. Crane was (so nice/that	1	✓		✓		✓		
227	a visit from her would make anyone feel at home								
228	in a new neighborhood.								
301	have — "You had"	2		✓	✓			✓	
302	2.volate 1.vol · play — no right to volunteer for me to be on the program!"								
308	school — It is time you played in public.	1			✓				
311	Your mother and I and the little ones would be so	2	✓		✓		✓		
312	happy with · 2.Marklits 1.Markla Jakisnia — proud of our Miklos and Juliska."		✓		✓		✓		
313	Markos signed — Miklos [sighed.] He'd have to try out, but maybe	1		✓	✓			✓	
314	play — he and Juliska wouldn't be chosen for the program.	1							
	Totals						5	13	3

A. Semantically and syntactically acceptable.
B. Semantically unacceptable but syntactically acceptable.
C. Semantically and syntactically unacceptable.

*A Common Band within the context of this story is not semantically acceptable. Since it is the title of the story and read, therefore, out of context, it is not recorded.

Figure 7.6   Level One Analysis of Reader's Miscues

1. Use of meaning or contextual clues.
   a. Is the word familiar to the reader based on experiential back-ground? That is, is the word part of the reader's listening/speaking vocabulary?
   b. Is the reader able to infer the unidentified word from context?

The teacher may gather some of this information as a part of learner responses during free recall, probe and structured questioning and during a follow-up discussion with the learner. Additional information may be-come apparent during a teacher-learner conference following the coding of the miscues and by observing the learner's language during regular class-room activities. This information is of extreme importance because even when the learner is able to apply knowledge of linguistic units within words to identify words, words take on meaning only if they are part of the listening/speaking vocabulary of the reader.

2. Use of morphological knowledge.
   Does the reader use the meaning parts of words (morphemes) to identify words? That is, does the reader apply knowledge of prefixes, roots, suffixes, and inflectional endings?
3. Use of phonological knowledge.
   a. Does the reader use knowledge of word parts (pronunciation units or syllables) to identify words?
   b. Does the reader use knowledge of phoneme/grapheme correspon-dence (sound/symbol) to identify words?

The teacher obtains information about the latter two areas by comparing the word given in the text to the miscue being analyzed. These compari-sons may readily reveal an area that is clearly a problem for the reader. In other cases the comparison may reveal more than one area of difficulty.

The miscues that affected the meaning of the passage (boxed—total #20) are listed in Figure 7.7 (Chart D). In listing these miscues only the first occurrence of a miscue appears for words that Learner B repeatedly missed in the story. The miscues are analyzed with reference to the three areas described above. Naturally, although lexical analysis is involved in the analysis of all miscues, analysis of morphemes and phonemes within words will vary from word to word.

The following examples illustrate how to analyze words using this chart. In the analysis of the first miscue *volunterns* for *volunteers*, the teacher determined during the teacher-learner conference that within the context of the sentence, Learner B did not know the meaning of the word *volunteers* since it was not a part of his listening/speaking vocabulary. In addition to not being able to use semantic knowledge as a cue, the learner also did not use knowledge available at the phonological level.

Another example to illustrate the analysis is the miscue *sister* for *sister's*. It was apparent during retelling that Learner B knows the meaning of

Chart D
Level 2 Analysis

Line #	Text	Reader	Lexical Knowledge Yes	No	Morphemic Knowledge	Phonological Knowledge Syllable	Phoneme V	C
101	volunteers	volunterns		✓			✓	
102	program	pogrent	✓					✓
104	not	now	✓					✓
106	violin	vilint	✓			✓	✓	
107	twin	twis	✓					✓
107	sister's	sister	✓		✓			
108	realized	realed		✓		✓		
109	Hungarian	Humagache		✓			✓	✓
113	auditorium	audience	✓			✓		
201	frowned	fowned		✓				✓
203	perform	perom		✓				✓
208	seen	son	✓				✓	
209	citizens	citsen		✓		✓		
210	native	natter		✓				
211	pastries	patries		✓				✓
213	managed	manged	✓			✓		
217	several	seven	✓			✓		
217	sponsor	supurn		✓			✓	✓
221	tailoring	tailing	✓			✓		
313	sighed	signed	✓					✓
		Totals	11	9	1	7	5	9

Figure 7.7 Level Two Analysis of Miscues That Affect Meaning

sister. However, the mispronunciation of *sister's* indicates a lack of application of knowledge of the morphemic element *'s*, indicating singular possessive. Although it is also possible that Learner B did not apply his phonological knowledge of the sound of /s/ in this case, since Learner B does exhibit knowledge of the sound of /s/ in other words it is hypothesized that the mispronunciation is due to lack of application of knowledge at the morphological level rather than the phonological level. These examples highlight the hypothesis-testing nature of diagnosis. Diagnostic information is confirmed only after repeated instances of similar problems occur, and patterns emerge. Therefore, the teacher need not be concerned when an individual word presents a problem in analysis. As we have noted, information that is important in planning for reader instruction will show up in repeated miscues involving application of a similar knowledge source.

To summarize Learner B's oral reading performance on "A Common Bond," the teacher considered the following:

1. the summary data based on analysis of whole sentences (Level 1 analysis);
2. the summary totals based on analysis of words (Level 2 analysis);
3. the specific miscues listed in Level 2, noting patterns within the three areas; and
4. the observations during oral reading.

Analysis of miscues at Level 1 indicates that Learner B has a good sense of language usage. For the most part his spontaneous insertions, mispronunciations, and substitutions retained the syntactic structure of the language of the author, giving evidence that he has an awareness of language structure.

Analysis at Level 2, in conjunction with teacher questioning, confirms that Learner B is not familiar with lexical items specifically related to the concept of immigration: native, citizen, sponsor. In addition, he is also unfamiliar with words (such as "bond," "volunteer," "realize," "pastries"). This lack of lexical knowledge affected the depth of his understanding of the selection. Although he did display some ability to apply his knowledge of the phonological system to words that were not readily identified, his ability tended to be limited to the initial syllable(s) in multisyllabic words or the initial phoneme(s) of single syllable words. Further, he displayed some evidence of difficulty in processing words in which there was an initial consonant blend. Also, when he made a concentrated effort to apply his phonological knowledge, he tended to ignore the context and made miscues that were illogical within the meaning of the selection (such as *signed* for *sighed, son* for *seen*). Viewing Learner B's performance on the total selection, the teacher realized that his use of context to gain meaning improved in the latter portions of the story. His miscues toward the end of the story tended to retain the author's meaning.

Based on this information, initial reading activities for Learner B in the future will focus on narrative text at approximately the same level or at a slightly lower level of difficulty provided that the content is within his experiential background or the teacher provides the background information to build the concepts and vocabulary he will need to understand a particular selection. The teacher will encourage him to interact with the text beyond the explicit level through guided reading and questioning. In addition, the teacher will provide strategies to help him use available phonological knowledge with reference to context as well as strategies to maintain his attention on an unfamiliar word in order to complete the phonological analysis of the word.

Ongoing diagnosis as Learner B reads a variety of materials in the classroom will further clarify the patterns noted during structured assessment, yield more detailed information about needed teaching strategies, and provide comparative information about his functioning with different types of reading materials. Only through ongoing diagnosis integrally related to the differing requirements of classroom reading, can the teacher fully understand Learner B's reading strengths and needs.

GUIDING TEACHER ANALYSIS OF DATA

After the teacher has completed assessment of comprehension through silent and oral reading of text for a given learner, a great deal of information becomes potentially available. After observing the reader, reviewing chart summaries of learner responses and miscues, and carefully examining the data, the teacher can gain a good sense of the learner's present reading performance. The following questions can guide the teacher in making use of this available information.

The teacher should keep the following questions in mind when

1. observing the reader during silent or oral reading;
2. evaluating reader responses;
3. analyzing data at the sentence level; and
4. analyzing data at the word level.

When observing: Does the reader

in silent reading indicate self-monitoring of comprehension by such devices as rereading, skipping a part of text and reading ahead, stopping to think?

in oral reading use a dialect of American English (bilingual/bidialectal variations?

recognize when a sentence or a word does not make sense? That is, does the reader verbalize this, show signs of increased anxiety, hesitate, display repetitions, or attempt to correct miscues?

display the sustained attention needed for comprehending the selection?

When evaluating reader responses: Does the reader

include most of the characteristics of the story?

give primarily explicit responses?

give textually implicit responses?

give scriptally implicit responses?

evaluate the selection?

show differences in the level of responses during free recall, probed recall, and structured questioning?

use concepts and vocabulary which reflect an understanding of the content of the selection?

exhibit differences in performance between silent reading and oral reading?

When analyzing data at the sentence level (Level 1 analysis): Do the miscues

reflect processing that is in keeping with the meaning of the sentence/ selection and maintain the structure of the language?

reflect processing that changes the meaning of the sentence/selection while maintaining the structure of the language?

reflect processing that changes the meaning of the sentence/selection and uses inaccurate sentence structure?

When analyzing data at the word level (Level 2 analysis): Does the reader

have the concepts and vocabulary necessary for understanding the selection?

have an adequate sight vocabulary?

have difficulty using morphological and phonological knowledge, relying mainly on sight vocabulary?

display a lack of knowledge of morphological elements; prefixes, roots, suffixes, inflectional endings, contractions?

display an overdependence on phonological knowledge as exhibited by:

a. using the tedious sounding out letter-by-letter approach?
b. repeatedly saying miscues of the same word without reference to context?

display a consistent pattern of miscues involving the phonological systems such as

a. miscues involving syllabication generalizations:
   insertion or omission of syllable(s) that reflect inappropriate use of one or more generalizations?

   miscues based on the position of syllables within words (initial, medial, final)?
b. miscues involving phoneme/grapheme correspondences (consonants, vowels, blends, digraphs, diphthongs):
   patterns of sound/symbol errors in a variety of words?
   inconsistent use of sound/symbol correspondences?
   position of phonemes within a syllable or within single syllable words (initial, medial, final)?

Following the structured assessment from which the teacher has gained a sense of the learner's overall functioning, learners read both narrative and non-narrative text. This provides opportunities for the teacher to observe learner functioning with a variety of materials in a variety of situations. This continuous ongoing diagnosis cannot be separated from teaching because different reading materials and reading situations have varying requirements. Demands on readers differ as they read narrative and non-narrative materials including all of the various types of text found within each of these two broad categories. In addition, the reader's purpose in reading a particular piece of text will alter reading requirements and the reader's performance. Therefore, ongoing assessment will take place within the context of (1) the purpose of the reader, (2) the knowledge sources that the reader brings to the specific reading task, and (3) the materials to be read. Chapters 9 through 13 on comprehending narrative and non-narrative text will discuss assessment and instruction as they both relate to the different purposes for reading, different readers, and different materials. Further, these chapters will highlight the requirements of different types of text.

Summary

This chapter presents informal observation and structured assessment procedures for use with readers in a classroom setting. The chapter introduces story analysis as a basis for both types of assessment. Informal observation involves silent reading and analysis of readers' responses during story retelling, probe, and structured questions. Structured assessment procedures include further analysis of silent reading and an analysis of oral reading. Diagnostic protocols demonstrate these analyses. The chapter emphasizes that the teacher can only establish the specific needs of readers by observing and analyzing their interactions with various types of text, in relation to readers' purposes, and during different classroom activities. The teacher needs to be cautious in overgeneralizing about learners' reading problems from limited data. Repeated instances of similar patterns are necessary to support the implementation of specific instructional plans.

8

Selecting and Analyzing Stories

Types of Narrative Text

Story Selection and Evaluation

Analysis of Stories
STORY CHARACTERISTICS AND INFERENCES

Applying Text Analysis: "Too Much Talk"
STORY CHARACTERISTICS
EXAMINING INFERENCES
USING STRUCTURED QUESTIONS

Summary

To facilitate students' comprehension of stories the teacher needs to be knowledgeable about types of narratives, criteria for selecting appropriate narratives for a given group, and ways of examining stories to determine their characteristics and possible interpretations by readers. The teacher with knowledge of narratives can plan instruction that will facilitate interactions between authors and readers and will be able to understand readers' responses to stories.

As noted, both author and reader are active participants in producing meaning. Authors select a message from their store of conceptual knowledge and choose the language structures they believe best suited to express the message. Authors rely on all of their resources in this process: conceptual knowledge and experiential background, language, and affective base. Similarly, readers have their own purposes for reading and their own resources that interact with those of the author. Thus the author and reader meet through the medium of print and share a message. The more compatible the backgrounds of the author and the reader, the more easily the reader can interpret the message.

This chapter briefly describes the different types of narratives, provides criteria for evaluating stories, discusses research on story analysis, and uses a simple story to illustrate some aspects of story analysis. Knowledge of this material helps the teacher to plan reading experiences that will bridge the gap between author and reader and facilitate comprehension.

Types of Narrative Text

Generally, stories from basal readers or trade books provide the major portion of the narrative text used in teaching comprehension because they form the core materials for most school reading programs and are readily available. The use of a variety of narratives in the teaching of reading comprehension expands learners' understanding of different genres. As learners become familiar with different genres, they have opportunities to internalize the characteristics of specific types of narratives and gain flexibility in constructing meaning from narratives of many different types.

The types of narratives from which teachers select materials include realistic stories, mystery stories, folklore, imaginary modern stories, science-fiction, poetry, and plays. These types are, briefly, as follows:

1. *Realistic fiction* includes stories that deal with the lives of people or animals. These stories may be set anywhere in the world and may be based upon modern or historical characters and settings. Events and situations are always possible; everything that happens could happen in real life. This category includes mystery and adventure stories.

2. *Modern fantasies* are contemporary stories in which the characters appear real but assume improbable characteristics. They frequently include tall tale exaggeration and incongruous situations, such as when talking animals and humans communicate or when humans exhibit superhuman powers or skills. Within the framework of a fantasy are logic and consistency that make the story an acceptable whole.

3. *Science fiction* combines scientific knowledge with fantasy to project the reader into a world that is not presently possible. Science fiction is closely related to modern fantasy. However, given future scientific advances, the events depicted in science fiction may become possible.

4. *Folklore* includes folktales, fairy tales, fables, myths, and epics. These stories have been transmitted from generation to generation by oral renditions and transcribed into written form. They are objective, understandable, and never abstract.

a. *Folktales* include stories about simple people, children, talking beasts; homely, imaginary beings; and animated forces of nature. These stories were communicated orally from one country to another and changed in the process.

b. *Fairy tales* were frequently created by special storytellers for entertainment in the royal courts and consequently focus on princes, princesses, palaces, giants, witches, and fairies.

c. *Fables* use talking animals, inanimate objects, and sometimes human objects to point out a moral which is often directly stated at the end. They evolved as people tried to socialize children into the culture's value system.

d. *Myths* represent early people's attempts to explain natural phenomena, such as the creation of the world and changes in weather and seasons, and as such belong to the world of the supernatural. They most often include stories of natural phenomena personified as gods: the sun, stars, fire and thunder, and the ways in which these personified phenomena were thought to influence people's destinies. Some myths are also described as being symbolic expressions of forces within individuals that are not understood. In such cases they explain human behavior in an unscientific way.

e. *Epic and hero tales* are tales of heroism, based on real or imaginary characters. The figures may be part of ancient history or mythology.

5. *Poetry* is the most compact form of narrative text. Most poetry uses words in a musical or rhythmic way and incorporates figurative language to communicate mood, emotion and experience. Poetry may be classified as:

a. *Formal verse* that is governed by rules of rhyme and rhythm. It includes narrative poetry that tells a story such as a ballad or epic and has a plot, and lyric poetry that expresses the writer's feelings and impressions and often is described as being similar to a song.

b. *Japanese haiku* that is a type of formal verse because it uses strict rules. However, these rules differ from traditional Western poetry and are not governed by rhyme and rhythm. The format of the haiku is usually 17 syllables divided into 3 lines of 5, 7, and 5 syllables, respectively.

    c. *Free verse* does not follow the rules of rhyme or rhythm and organization. Stanzas and lines vary.

    6. *Plays* are written to be seen but may be read. The reader must "perform" the roles of all the characters and must understand the conventions of playwriting including stage directions. Plays may be classified as tragedy, comedy (including musical comedy), and melodrama. (Cullinan, 1981; Sutherland, Monson, & Arbuthnot, 1981.)

Story Selection and Evaluation

Teachers select the majority of classroom stories from basal readers. But teachers should supplement these with other stories found in trade books and magazines. When using basal readers, teachers should feel free to select appropriate stories from different parts of the book even if they are out of sequence. Also teachers should not feel they have to use all the stories in a particular reader. Since many basal reader stories are adaptations, teachers should make sure the richness of the original story remains intact.

    Criteria for selecting stories from basal readers and from trade books are similar. Answering the following questions can help the teacher in evaluating stories for classroom teaching.

Characterization

1. Are the characters presented in depth so that their ideas and feelings are apparent?
2. Are the characters believable and consistent?
3. Are the characters' actions and traits consistent with the time and place of the story?
4. Are girls and boys and women and men presented as having similar human traits?
5. Are girls and boys and women and men presented as participating in similar activities and having nontraditional as well as traditional occupations?
6. Are minorities depicted in such a way as to indicate that society values their language, viewpoints, and culture?
7. Are disabled people portrayed as working at a variety of occupations and participating in a variety of activities?
8. Are older people characterized as having useful roles in life?
9. Are girls and women, minorities, disabled populations, and the aged sufficiently represented?
10. Do stories portray a range of family units including the nuclear family, single-parent households, and extended families?

Plot

1. Does the story have a beginning, middle, and end?
2. Does the plot have conflict, opposition, or a problem?

3. Is there a climax of action or a strong indication of future resolution?
4. Does the story have momentum?
5. Do the events move in a logical sequence?
6. Is the complexity of the plot appropriate to the developmental level of the reader?
7. If literary techniques such as flashback occur does the reader receive sufficient cuing?

Setting

1. Is the setting clear and believable?
2. Is the setting authentic if the story has a historical framework?

Theme

1. Does the theme reflect those developmental values that are inherent in the process of growing up?
2. Does the theme match the concerns of the specific readers given their developmental level?

Style and Language

1. Is the style (author's choice of words, sentence patterns, imagery used, and rhythm of the sentences) appropriate to the ideas the author wishes to communicate?
2. Is the language appropriate for the genre of the story?
3. Is the language appropriate for the characters of the story?
4. Does the dialogue sound like people talking?
5. Is the language appropriate for the developmental level of the reader?
6. Is the language appropriate for the experiential background and reading proficiency of the reader?
7. Are words or terms used that contribute to society's misconceptions about women, men, minorities, people with disabilities, and the aged?
8. Is the language nonsexist?

Illustrations

1. Do the pictures reflect the mood of the story, or do they conflict with it?
2. Do the pictures have any details that conflict with the text?
3. Do the illustrations extend the text without distracting from it?
4. Are girls and women, minorities, disabled populations, and the aged accurately and sufficiently represented in illustrations and pictures?

Technical Features

1. Is the size of the book appropriate to learners' physical development and reading proficiency?
2. Is the size of the type appropriate to the learners' physical development and reading proficiency?

3. Is the paper opaque, nonglare finish, and durable?
4. Are the color of paper and typography appealing for the reader?
5. Are the page layouts well-arranged and attractive?
6. Are the illustrations of artistic value and appealing to the developmental level of the reader?
7. Is the cover durable and well-designed?
8. Is the binding of good quality and strong enough for planned use?

The following sources have been referred to in the development of the preceding listing and give additional detail. They provide excellent resources for the teacher.

ERS Report. *Procedures for textbook and instructional materials selection.* Arlington, Va.: Educational Research Services, 1976.

Guidelines for selecting bias free textbooks and storybooks. New York: Council on Interracial Books for Children, 1980.

Sutherland, Z., Monson, D. L., & Arbuthnot, M. H. *Children and books.* Glenview, Ill.: Scott, Foresman, 1981.

Analysis of Stories

Analysis of text involves examination of the written discourse, careful study of text-based questions and preparation of structured questions for the teacher to use following reader-text interactions. In analyzing the written discourse, the teacher notes the type of narrative text, the author's view of audience, the author's background, and the author's purpose. Also, the teacher focuses on the organizational structure and language the author uses to express the message. Through this analysis the teacher becomes aware of some of the possible information that the reader might gain—information the author states explicitly and information the author implies.

Recent theoretical work on text analysis can help teachers as they attempt to gain insights into the interaction of reader and author. Researchers are studying the ways in which reader knowledge interacts with text characteristics, and this analysis is presently taking many forms. Text is being studied through the analysis of semantic structures and logical relations between ideas at the propositional and passage levels (Kintsch, 1974; Frederiksen, 1975a, 1975b, 1979; Meyer, 1975; Van Dijk, 1977; Kintsch & Van Dijk, 1978). Another approach involves the formulation of story grammars which are assumed to be representations of readers' schemata for story structures and organizations (Rumelhart, 1975; Mandler & Johnson, 1977; Thorndyke, 1977; Stein & Glenn, 1979). Other researchers have focused on the importance of drawing inferences in comprehending written discourse (Schank, 1975; Clark & Haviland, 1977). Recently Warren, Nickolas, and Trabasso (1979) have developed a way of examining stories in which they analyze the events that make up a story (event chains) and hypothesize types of inferences a reader might make to construct meaning.

Although all of this work is theoretically important, at this time direct application for instructional purposes is limited. No empirical evidence exists to support instructional programs or the construction of materials based upon the work of any one group of researchers. Rather, at this point in our knowledge, teachers can best use insights gained from the theoretical work in this area to expand their understanding of the demands of text on the reader and to serve as a basis for guiding their observations of learners as they read and discuss text. Thus, teachers should not limit analysis of stories from basal readers or trade books to the work of any one theorist. Rather, analysis should involve samples from the many different approaches to text analysis to develop sensitivity to the variations inherent in readers and in text. Implicit in this approach is teacher awareness of the variety of ways a reader may interact with text as readers vary in their functioning and text demands change.

STORY CHARACTERISTICS AND INFERENCES

We have used the work of Warren, Nickolas, and Trabasso (1979), Trabasso (1981), and Trabasso and Nickolas (1980) as a framework for examining stories. We have chosen their work because it focuses on inferences and because reader inferencing is an essential part of understanding a story. According to Trabasso (1981), inferences perform several functions. They allow the reader to resolve the meanings of those individual words that are ambiguous, to understand nominal and pronominal references, and to establish appropriate contexts in order to interpret text information.

The Warren, Nickolas, and Trabasso taxonomy distinguishes among three general categories of inferences: logical inferences, informational inferences, and value inferences. Since stories are organized around story characteristics, it is helpful to think about these inferences in relation to story characteristics. The story characteristics described in Chapter 7 (genre, point of view, style and language, characterization, plot, setting, mood, and theme) can be related to the specific inferences outlined in the taxonomy. Table 8.1 summarizes the major relationships between the categories of inferences and story characteristics. Viewing inferences within this framework provides a flexible guide from which teachers can analyze narrative text and study reader construction of meaning.

As children read stories, they make inferences about characters and plot events. All three categories of inferences (logical, informational, and value inferences) are used by children in their understanding of these two story characteristics. *Logical inferences*, the first information source in the Warren, Nickolas, and Trabasso taxonomy, refer to the logical relations between events specified in the text. These include the causes and conditions under which characters behave and events occur. In characterization, authors present characters through behavior, attitudes, feelings, thoughts, language, and the reaction of others toward them. Some techniques an author may use to describe a character include (1) telling about the character, (2) describing the character and surroundings, (3) showing the character in

Table 8.1 Summary of Illustrative Relations Between Categories of Inferences and Story Characteristics

Inference Taxonomy	Story Characteristics
Logical Inferences	Characterization
	Plot
Informational Inferences	Characterization
	Plot
	Setting and Mood
Value Inferences	Genre
	Point of View
	Style and Language
	Characterization
	Plot
	Setting and Mood
	Theme

action, (4) letting the character talk, (5) revealing the character's thoughts, (6) showing what others say to the character, (7) showing what others say about the character, (8) showing the reactions of others to the character, (9) showing the character's reactions to others (Hook, 1963).

Understanding characterization is dependent primarily on readers constructing two of the specific inferences within the general category of logical inferences—*motivational* and *psychological causation*. When readers make motivational inferences, they are inferring the reasons for a character's voluntary thoughts, actions, or goals; using these inferences they are predicting thoughts, actions, or goals based upon stated causes. On the other hand, when readers make inferences about psychological causation, they are inferring the reasons for the involuntary behavior, attitudes, feelings, or thoughts of a character.

Physical causation and *enabling inferences* are two other subcategories of logical inferences and are most closely related to plot development. In plot development, the significant actions or related events unfold in a specific order and lead to a story outcome. That is, plot involves a developing problem (conflict), climax, and the conflict solution in which efforts of the protagonist(s) lead to a resolution of the problem. When readers make inferences about physical causation they are thinking about the mechanical or nonhuman reasons for the unfolding of actions or events in a story. Sometimes readers make enabling inferences. In this type of inferencing they determine the physical or environmental conditions necessary but not sufficient for an event to occur. "How" and "why" questioning, which is either reader generated or, if necessary, teacher imposed, elicits those logical inferences required to understand the characters and plot events in a story.

Characterization and plot may also involve the second category of inferences, *informational inferences*. These inferences enable readers to determine who is doing what to whom, with what instruments, under what circumstances, and at what time and place. This involves readers in making inferences about specific people, things, objects, times, places, and contexts of events as they answer Who? What? When? and Where? Readers who make these informational inferences understand relations between an author's deliberate use of a word or phrase as a grammatical substitute for a preceding word, phrase, sentence, paragraph, or longer passage (anaphoric relations). A common anaphoric expression would involve *pronominal inferences*. These inferences involve relating pronouns to their antecedents, which occur earlier in the narrative. Common pronouns are *he, she, they, it,* and *them.*

A related type of informational inference is *referential inference*, in which the reader connects ideas by selecting the proper antecedent from those given in the text or by supplying an appropriate antecedent. These inferences differ from pronominal inferences in that pronouns are not given. The reader must infer the relationships between ideas without these stated cues.

As children make informational inferences they also make *elaborative inferences* about characters and situations. Although these inferences do not contribute to the logical unfolding of a story, they add details.

Understanding setting and mood also involves readers in constructing informational inferences. Setting includes the place, time, customs, and practices of people revealed through the language of the characters, character descriptions, and accompanying illustrations. Mood refers to the impression the author creates by the setting, atmosphere, situation, and language. Through the use of *spatial and temporal inferences,* which are additional subcategories of informational inferences, readers locate a specific event or series of events in place and time and determine their duration. Familiarity with events similar to those in the story provides readers with a context of place or general activity leading to further understanding of story events.

The last category of inferences, *value inferences*, requires the reader to infer the intentions of the author and make judgments about the thoughts and actions of the characters and the validity of events of the story. Thus, *evaluative inferences* are involved when readers react critically to all of the story characteristics inherent in narrative text. These inferences are based on a reader's value system and prior knowledge of situations related to story context. For example, construction of evaluative inferences is prerequisite to a reader's understanding of story theme, style, and genre. The theme of the story reflects the author's intentions, whereas the structure and organization reflect the author's style and use of genre. More specifically, theme may be described as a generalization about people and/or the world that emerges from the plot. Theme reveals the significance of the actions and is consistent with the plot and characters. The type of story and perspective from which the action is observed, are generally referred to as genre and point of view respectively. In developing a point of view, an author may serve as a narrator in two ways, as participant or as observer. Authors who use the third person "stand outside" of the narrative and look at the characters and situations. Some authors shift the point of view from the first person to third person as different events in the story occur. It is in this last category of inferences that readers make evaluative judgments to react to story content and structure.

The categories of inferences and related story characteristics we have just described are a suggested framework for examining narrative discourse and for analyzing readers' spontaneous responses to text and readers' responses to more structured questioning.

Applying Text Analysis: "Too Much Talk"

A first-grade story will illustrate some aspects of text analysis and reader-text interaction. The selected story, "Too Much Talk," is a fable that uses talking animals to point out the moral directly stated at the end.

Too Much Talk
A JATAKA TALE

Turtle lived in a small pond.
He liked to splash.
He liked to swim.

Best of all Turtle liked talking to his friends.
One friend was Duck.
The other friend was Goose.

One day Goose said, "There is a little pond over the mountain.
Duck and I want to live there."

"Please don't leave," said Turtle.

"Goose wishes you could go.
And I do too," said Duck.

"But I can't go," said Turtle.
"You will be flying.
I don't have wings."

"We will carry you," said Goose.
"Just hold onto this stick with your mouth."

"You must hold on tightly," said Duck.
"You can't talk when we fly."

Turtle wanted to go very much.
So he said, "I won't talk."

Goose took hold of one end of the stick.
Duck took hold of the other end.
Turtle took hold of the middle.
Then the three went up.

Soon Turtle looked down.
He saw a big lake.

"Let's stop here," said Turtle.

Down went Turtle.
He landed in the lake.
Duck and Goose just flew on.

Turtle had a new home.
But he had lost two friends.
Turtle had learned a lesson.

Sometimes even a little talk is too much.

The selection of this story assumes reader knowledge of some of the characteristics of turtles, ducks, and geese. Knowledge of the physical attributes and habits of each character and the relatedness of ducks and geese is crucial to understanding this story. If such knowledge is not part of the prior background and experience of the reader, the teacher would need to build the necessary concepts prior to reader-text interaction, making the reader more prepared to infer relevant information.

To illustrate fully the framework for text analysis, all types of story characteristics and related structured questions follow. Depending on teacher and reader purposes, readers may focus on only some aspects of story characteristics and the related inferences during any given reader-text interaction.

STORY CHARACTERISTICS

For this story, the following are characteristics that teachers would note and encourage learners to observe:

Genre and Narrator

Fable told by the author using the third person point of view. Animals take on human characteristics.

Style and Language

Dialogue is used in the unfolding of the story.

Characterization

Turtle—likes to splash and swim in pond; likes to talk to his friends; does not want to live alone; is unable to keep quiet when necessary.

Goose and Duck—are good friends and are friends of the turtle; want to move to a new pond; attempt to help turtle go with them; leave turtle to live alone in an unplanned new home.

Plot

Turtle, Duck, and Goose are friends. Turtle is happy in his home when Duck and Goose decide to move to a new home over the mountain. Turtle wants to go with them, but he cannot fly. Duck and Goose decide to carry Turtle on a stick so he can go with them. Turtle has to hold onto the stick with his mouth and, therefore, cannot talk. Turtle talks as they are flying over a lake, falls, and lands in the water. Turtle has a new home but loses his friends.

Setting and Mood

A country area with mountains, ponds, and lakes. The mood changes from happy to sad as the plot develops.

Theme

Sometimes even a little talk is too much.

EXAMINING INFERENCES

To illustrate some of the inferences required to construct meaning from this text, the first 14 propositional units (idea units) will be analyzed as suggested by the work on events chains (Warren and others, 1979). In this type of analysis each proposition is defined as an event that contains only one predicate relation.

1. Turtle lived in a small pond.
2. He liked to splash.
3. He liked to swim.
4. Best of all, Turtle liked talking to his friends.
5. One friend was Duck.
6. The other friend was Goose.
7. One day Goose said, "There is a little pond over the mountain.
8. Duck and I want to live there."
9. "Please don't leave," said Turtle.
10. "Goose wishes you could go.

11.   And I do too," said Duck.
12.   "But I can't go," said Turtle.
13.   "You will be flying.
14.   I don't have wings."

Since only part of the story is presented, it is important to recognize the focal event around which these propositions are organized. At this point in plot development, the focal event or moving point in the unfolding narrative is located in proposition 8 in which the main character is presented with a problem that needs to be resolved. If reader-text interaction was stopped at this point in the narrative, the reader could make inferences based on information already presented in the text or could predict events to come based on past story information and prior knowledge of similar situations. If, on the other hand, the entire story is read without interruption, the teacher may organize free recall around a number of focal events. Inferences in this case can be based on retrospective knowledge of the entire narrative. Dependent on the reader and the text, it may be facilitative to plan reading experiences around particular focal events rather than have readers process the entire story without reader-teacher interaction.

Based on the propositions listed above, some of the inferences that the reader can make appear in Table 8.2 according to inference categories. Table 8.2 gives a description of the specific type of inference, lists the proposition or propositions that it is dependent on, and indicates the related story characteristic(s).

USING STRUCTURED QUESTIONS

If the reader does not spontaneously infer important story information during free recall, the teacher may probe to elicit additional inferences or, if necessary, further cue the reader through the use of structured questions. Examples of structured questions to elicit logical inferences, informational inferences, and value inferences based on the total story follow. The questions are categorized by story characteristics, and the type of inferences expected in response to the question also appears.

Genre and Narrator

Who is telling the story? (Value inference: evaluative, understanding the narrator)

Could this story really have happened? Why? (Value inference: evaluative, validity of story events)

Characterization

What did Turtle like to do in the pond? (Informational inference: referential)

What friends did Turtle like to talk to? (Informational inference: referential)

Table 8.2 Sample Inferences based on "Too Much Talk"

Inference Categories	Descriptions	Sample Inferences	Propositions	Related Story Character- istics
Logical inferences				
a. Motivational	a. Inferring the reasons for a character's voluntary thoughts, actions, or goals (or vice versa)	a. Turtle didn't want to live alone	9	Plot Characterization
b. Psychological	b. Inferring the reasons for a character's involuntary thoughts, actions, or feelings	b. Turtle became sad	8, 9, 12	Characterization Mood
c. Physical	c. Inferring mechanical or nonhuman causes for given actions or events	c. Turtle couldn't go over the mountain with his friends	7, 13, 14	Plot
d. Enabling	d. Determining the physical conditions necessary but not sufficient for an event to occur	d. Duck and Goose had flown over the mountain before	7	Plot
Informational inferences				
a. Pronominal	a. Stating the antecedents or pronouns	a. Duck and Goose wished Turtle could go with them	9, 10, 11	Plot
b. Referential	b. Specifying the related antecedents of actions or events when the referents are not pronominally marked	b. Turtle liked to splash and swim in the pond	1, 2, 3	Characterization
c. Elaborative	c. Adding information which does not contribute to the story	c. Turtle wishes he had wings	14	Characterization
d. Spatial-temporal	d. Locating events or series of events in place or time	d. Turtle, Duck and Goose live in the country	1, 7	Setting
Value inferences				
Evaluative	Reacting critically to story characteristics inherent in narratives	Duck and Goose didn't like Turtle as much as he liked them	8, 9, 10, 11	Characterization

Why did Turtle want to go with his friends? (Logical inference: motivational)

How did Turtle feel when Goose and Duck said they wanted to live over the mountain? (Logical inference: psychological)

Why could Goose and Duck fly over the mountain, and why couldn't Turtle? (Logical inference: physical)

Why does Turtle use his mouth to hold onto the stick? (Logical inference: physical)

Why did Turtle fall into the lake? (Logical inference: physical or psychological)

Why do you think Duck and Goose flew on? (Value inference: evaluative, actions of characters)

How did Turtle feel in his new home? (Logical inference: psychological)

Plot

Why did Turtle have a problem? (Logical inference: physical)

How did Duck and Goose know that there was a little pond over the mountain? (Logical inference: enabling)

Why did Duck and Goose get a stick? (Logical inference: motivational or physical)

Why did they pick a long stick? (Logical inference: enabling)

Who wants to live over the mountain? (Informational inference: pronominal)

Where did Turtle want to stop? (Informational inference: referential)

What happened after Turtle said, "Let's stop here"? (Informational inference: referential)

When did Turtle get a new home? (Informational inference: temporal)

Setting and Mood

Where do Turtle, Duck and Goose live? (Informational inference: spatial)

Where was Turtle when he saw the lake? (Informational inference: spatial)

How did this story make you feel? (Value inference: evaluative story mood)

Theme

What did the author want us to learn from the story? (Value inference: evaluative, author's intention)

Sometimes questions yield more than one relevant response, depending on reader-text interaction. The type of inference that may be elicited by these questions may vary. To illustrate, a reader's response to the question, "Why did Duck and Goose get a stick?" may be "They wanted to help Turtle go with them" or "Turtle didn't have wings and couldn't fly with them." Both responses are appropriate; in the first case the reader has made a motivational inference whereas in the second case the reader has made a physical inference. Another example is two different readers' responses to the question, "Why did Turtle fall into the lake?" One reader responds by stating, "Turtle let go of the stick," whereas a second responds by stating that "Turtle couldn't keep quiet." The first response involves a physical inference while the second response involves a psychological inference.

Some questions may not readily yield any appropriate responses. In such cases the teacher may want to further structure the questioning situation. The teacher may break down the initial question into a series of questions to help the reader see the relationships necessary to respond to the original question. For example, the question "What happened after Turtle said, 'Let's stop here'?" may be structured further by the addition of questions such as:

Where was Turtle when he said, "Let's stop here?"

What was Turtle doing when he said, "Let's stop here"?

What did Turtle have to do before he could speak?

What happened when Turtle did this?

Note that although teachers may expect a certain response to a particular question, other responses may be just as relevant. The work of Pearson and Johnson (1978) addresses this issue when they discuss the relation between questions and reader responses. This relation between questions and responses depends on the interaction of the knowledge sources of readers with text. These researchers emphasize that when readers make inferences they either connect textually given information not directly related by the author or they create plausible responses based on the text but incorporate additional reader-based information. As the reader is an active participant when constructing meaning from print, reader responses will differ and readers can make different but relevant responses to the same story during free recall, probed recall, or structured questioning.

As Chapter 7 discusses, teachers should also examine reader responses to determine how readers arrived at meaning. That is, readers may base inferences on textually given information or such inferences may be idiosyncratic but relevant based on readers' previous experiences and knowledge related to information in the text. In addition, some responses may replicate directly the written material and not be considered inferences. Thus, to more fully understand reader responses, the teacher examines the textually given information and the related construction of meaning by the reader. Analyzing reader responses with reference to both the passage and the reader will illustrate this (Pearson and others, 1978).

For example, a teacher could classify the following reader responses either during free recall, probed recall, or structured questioning based on "Too Much Talk" as textually explicit, textually implicit, or scriptally implicit. Although we have listed structured questions in Table 8.3, learner responses may occur during free recall or probed recall.

Table 8.3   Sample Responses—"Too Much Talk"

Structured Questions	Learner Responses		
	Explicit	Textually Implicit	Scriptally Implicit
Where did Turtle live?	Turtle lived in a small pond.	Turtle lived where he could splash and swim.	Turtle lived in the country. Turtle lived in the water.
Who did Turtle like to talk to?	Turtle liked to talk to his friends.	Turtle liked to talk to Duck and Goose.	Turtle liked to talk to other animals.
What happened after Turtle said, "Let's stop here"?	Duck and Goose flew on. Turtle had a new home.	Turtle lost his friends. Turtle learned that even a little talk is too much.	Turtle was sad. Turtle was all alone to make a new home.
Why can't Turtle go over the mountain with Duck and Goose?		Turtle can't go because he doesn't have wings.	Turtle can't go because he can only crawl slowly.
Why did Turtle hold onto the stick with his mouth?		Because Goose told him to.	Because Turtle's mouth is the only part of him that could hold the stick.

Note in Table 8.3, those responses listed under the category explicit replicate information as stated in the text directly. These replicative responses are only a minor part of processing text; the major part of constructing meaning from text is inferring. Samples of inferential responses are categorized as textually implicit when the reader connects information or ideas presented in the text. That is, although all the information required to make an inference appears in the text, these responses require the reader to make a connection—infer a relation(s) between bits of information given in the text. In contrast, responses categorized as scriptally implicit require the reader to link prior knowledge with information presented in the text. That is, in order to categorize a response as scriptally implicit the reader has integrated relevant information not available in the text with information given in the text. To illustrate, the explicit response "Turtle liked to talk to his friends" directly replicates the information given in sentence 4 of the text. The response "Turtle liked to talk to Duck and Goose" is categorized as textually implicit because it connects information presented in sentences, 4, 5, 6 and requires the reader to understand anaphoric relations. The scriptally implicit response "Turtle liked to talk to other animals" requires the reader not only to connect the information in sentences 4, 5, and 6 but to integrate the prior knowledge that turtle, goose, and duck are classified as animals. Those responses categorized as textually implicit and scriptally implicit must be plausible in relation to the text in order to be considered appropriate.

In summary, the detailed analysis of "Too Much Talk" illustrates one framework that uses narrative discourse analysis as a base for instruction.

As readers' concepts, background knowledge, and interests expand, teacher selection of narrative discourse will expand to include different types of stories with different content and structure. The teacher may analyze these varied materials by applying the illustrated framework or by using different theoretical perspectives. Recognition that the relationships among readers, texts, and teachers are continually modified by experience is basic to meeting situational needs of readers and guiding reader development.

Summary

This chapter examines stories as a prerequisite to teaching reading comprehension. It describes types of narratives briefly and gives criteria for evaluating narratives. It presents a taxonomy for analyzing the possible inferences a reader can make, and a fable illustrates this taxonomy. This information is important background for teachers in planning for the use of narratives in teaching reading comprehension and in understanding readers' responses to narratives.

9

Teaching and Learning Using Stories

Teaching Stories
PREACTIVE TEACHING
INTERACTIVE TEACHING
EVALUATIVE TEACHING

Illustrative Teaching/Learning Plans
PLAN ONE: "TOO MUCH TALK"
PLAN TWO: "SU AN"
CHILDREN'S PROTOCOLS

Matching Assessment to Learning
DESCRIPTION OF ASSESSMENT ACTIVITIES AND SAMPLE RESPONSES
PREPARATION AND IMPLEMENTATION

Summary

W riters of narrative text may have many different purposes such as to inform, to entertain, to create a mood, to inspire, or to share an experience. For the reader, an important purpose of experiences with narrative material is enjoyment as the reader emotionally enters the writing and merges with the imaginative world of the author (Holland, 1973). Equally important, interaction with narrative materials extends learner capacity to relate to authors and expands learner understanding of human values, attitudes, and motivations. It also increases learner appreciation of language usage for the communication of ideas and feelings and increases learner knowledge through vicarious experiences.

Teaching Stories

The approach to teaching reading comprehension using stories is not very different from that described for assessing reading performance. Because assessment and teaching are integrally related, facilitating learners' comprehension of narrative text involves some of the same procedures used when working with learners to evaluate how they function in reading. However, there are also important differences. This chapter will expand upon the procedures outlined in Chapter 7 for assessing textual reading and present some specific suggestions for teaching reading comprehension. The focus will be on using short illustrated stories found in basal readers and in story books to help readers develop and apply efficient comprehension strategies.

This chapter will apply the framework described in Chapter 4 for teacher-directed experiences in using narrative text for teaching reading comprehension. The chapter will describe the three stages—preactive teaching, interactive teaching, and evaluative teaching—as they apply to the teaching of reading using stories.

PREACTIVE TEACHING

During the preactive or initial stage of teaching, the teacher selects and analyzes stories in preparation for reader-text interaction and plans specific purposes and related instructional activities to implement during interactive teaching. In selecting text, the teacher considers the general instructional purposes for which the text will be used. Also, the teacher considers the interests of the reader, prior knowledge and developmental level of the reader, and type and level of the material. The teacher should use the criteria for selection and evaluation of narrative text presented in the preceding chapter.

Recent research supports the commonsense notion that familiar and predictable stories are easier to comprehend then less predictable materials. Predictability involves factors like familiarity of story plot, characters, theme, language, and concepts. Furthermore, repetition of both events and language seems to aid predictability (Rhodes, 1979). Remember that the level of material cannot be determined solely by publisher designations that are based on traditional readability formulas. These formulas are limited because they do not make reference to semantic properties, to text characteristics, or to the background knowledge and experience of the reader. Rather, teachers need to be aware that they can select texts of varying levels of difficulty for the same reader because the quality of interaction will differ in different reading situations.

Once having selected the story, the teacher decides if the author's view of audience is consistent with the group who will read or hear the story: Is the story appropriate to the developmental level and interests of the group? Also, the teacher decides if the background of the writer and the language usage of the writer are familiar to the reader. If not, the teacher needs to bridge gaps between the reader and author by planning prereading activities.

During this planning stage, the teacher analyzes the written discourse with reference to story characteristics and types of possible inferences, evaluates any text-based questions, and prepares structured questions if necessary. Reader characteristics guide teachers in this analysis as they choose what to emphasize for a particular reader-text interaction. For example, depending on reader needs, the teacher may choose to emphasize only one or two of the characteristics of a story and the related inferences or only one focal event of a story with its related inferences. Similarly, teachers need to consider both the background of the reader and the reading material as they plan specific prereading activities to facilitate reader-text interaction and postreading activities to expand learners' language/reading comprehension.

INTERACTIVE TEACHING

This stage of teaching involves three sequences of learning experiences—prereading experiences, reader-text interactions and self-monitoring, and postreading experiences.

Prereading activities are considered to be at the "heart" of teaching comprehension. These activities assess readers' prior knowledge of story concepts, language and structure; build concepts and language background as needed; and focus learners' attention by having them reflect upon their knowledge and ideas in order to question and predict. The teacher structures these prereading experiences to stimulate group discussion. The discussion generally involves relating what learners already know about the structure and content of a selected story to any new information they need to construct meaning successfully from the print. In this process the teacher encourages learners to share their knowledge with others as they discuss and react to ideas relevant to the story they will read.

During reader-text interaction readers silently read the story to answer questions, to confirm hypotheses, to change hypotheses, and to make ongoing predictions and interpretations. As learners interact with the text, they use their knowledge of story structure to monitor their understanding of characters' feelings and actions, story events, and situations. They think about whether what they are reading makes sense in terms of their knowledge of what a story is and their knowledge of what the content of the story is.

This monitoring occurs simultaneously at the word level, sentence level, and passage level. By having questions in mind as they read a story, readers have a mental structure to guide comprehension monitoring. The teacher encourages readers to think about and ask themselves questions such as the following: Are there any new words in this sentence? Does the sentence make sense? What are the important events? Who are the important characters? Have I read something similar to this before? Given questions such as these, thoughts like the following might occur to readers:

Is this a new word? I know this word. Why doesn't it make sense?

This sentence (passage) makes no sense to me.

This sentence (passage) is not completely clear.

This sentence (passage) can mean several things, and I'm not sure which one the author intended.

This sentence (passage) doesn't make sense in view of what I already know about this story.

These sentences (passages) don't go together. They seem to mean different things.

This story doesn't seem to make sense, *or*

I don't understand the author's purpose in writing this story (Collins & Smith, 1980).

As the reader reflects on the specific comprehension problem, any one of the following decisions may be reached: The reader may decide to ignore the problem because it does not appear critical to understanding the story or to the reader's purpose. Another option is to wait by either suspending judgment in the expectation that the problem will be clarified further on in the story or to store the confusion in memory as a pending question with a tentative hypothesis that is tested as reading continues. A third option is to take some direct action by doing such things as:

1. rereading some part of the story to gather more information, to answer a pending question, or form a tentative hypothesis related to a pending question;
2. jumping ahead in the story to note if anything happens that refers to the pending question and might answer it;
3. thinking about the pending question and related information in the reader's repertoire of knowledge;

4. consulting an outside source such as reference materials or experts to increase the reader's store of knowledge.

At the extreme end of the continuum readers might decide to stop reading the selection (Anderson, 1980).

At those times when the reader chooses to take direct actions to solve a comprehension problem, these actions, beneficial as they may be, do break the flow of reader-text interaction. Therefore, the reader must be aware that a disruption has occurred and may need to stop and reflect in order to integrate the knowledge obtained in rereading, jumping ahead, or simply stopping to think. The reader should also be aware that to recover from a disruption, rereading a portion of the story is frequently necessary.

The first postreading activity involves responding to any questions or predictions generated during prereading activities. Following this, readers' responses to the story should take the form of free recall, probed recall, and answers to structured questions. These procedures and the rationale for their use are described in Chapter 7. Readers' spontaneous responses to the selected text and teacher's focus determine the amount of structured intervention required. This approach requires that teachers are able spontaneously to modify their planned actions to meet the immediate needs of readers. Thus, individual readers or groups of readers, specific story demands, and teacher focus all guide the teacher in selectively determining the type and amount of external structure to bring to reader-text interaction.

Although all readers are involved in the postreading activities just described, additional activities to expand language competence across the communication areas may occur with the whole class, groups, or individuals. These activities use the story content or structure as a basis for additional experiences in listening, speaking, writing, and reading.

EVALUATIVE TEACHING

The teacher examines reader reactions to the story and responses during free recall, probed recall, and structured questioning with reference both to the passage and to the reader in order to understand how the reader reconstructs the author's message(s). As Chapter 7 describes, reader responses may be based on information directly stated in the text, or the reader may infer relationships based on textually given information. In addition, the teacher may observe other responses that are idiosyncratic but relevant based upon the previous experiences and knowledge of the reader as this information relates to the information in the text. Teacher understanding of the depth and scope of reader processing of text depends on integrating the knowledge obtained from reader-text interaction within the framework of the demands of the text, purposes for reading, and the developmental level of the reader. Having a positive reading environment in which readers and teachers interact with each other and the text means that both readers and teachers will bring expanded and/or restructured knowledge to the next reading experience. Every reading experience leaves readers and teachers somewhat changed.

Illustrative Teaching/Learning Plans

The following plans use the framework just presented for teaching using narrative text. Plan One is based on the fable "Too Much Talk" analyzed in Chapter 8. Plan Two is based on a realistic story found in a fourth-grade basal reader.

PLAN ONE: "TOO MUCH TALK"

Introductory Comments

Teachers may use "Too Much Talk" in a variety of ways to meet the diverse needs of learners. It can provide the basis for a whole-class reading experience, a group reading experience or an individual reading experience. It can also serve different teacher and reader purposes. When teachers are developing their instructional plans for teaching a narrative, they consider the general purposes for reading a story as well as some specific purposes they feel are important for their children. To implement their specific purposes, teachers plan whole-class, group, and/or individual activities. To illustrate this planning, a first-grade class will be used. The reading performance in this class ranges from children who read language experience charts and picture books to children who independently read short stories usually found in primary level materials. Although the story provides the focus for whole-class interactions, some specific purposes and related activities meet group and individual needs of the learners.

The teacher's goals are

1.	to expand readers' understanding of the structure of a fable and
2.	to expand readers' understanding of characters' traits and behaviors.

Preactive Teaching

Teacher knowledge.	Chapter 8 has already provided an analysis of the content and structure of this story and offered structured questions.

Teacher decisions.	Diagnostic information indicates that "Too Much Talk" is appropriate to the developmental level of the range of learners in this class. Data also indicate that those children who read language experience charts and picture books can comprehend more difficult material through listening than through reading. Further, these readers are still developing a basic sight vocabulary and grapheme/phoneme correspondences. These children will form one of the groups; when planning for specific instructional activities for "Too Much Talk," the teacher places these children in Group C. A second group of children (Group B) who are now reading stories have some limitations in their ability to read independently for a sustained period of time. Some of these learners are just making the transition from language experience materials to story books; others need teacher guidance to predict/confirm as they interact with the text and others have limited attention spans. Readers in a third group (Group A) are reading story books and are able to do some monitoring of their own reading. These readers have developed specific strategies to use when the story does not make sense.

The teacher implements prereading activities with the whole class. Learners' interactions with the story are different for each of the three groups. Some postreading activities involve the entire class; others are planned for specific groups. The time needed to implement this plan varies based upon learners' performances.

Interactive Teaching

Prereading activities (whole class)

A.   The teacher assesses readers' prior knowledge of important story concepts by eliciting learner associations to the title of the story "Too Much Talk" and to the concepts *turtle, duck, goose, friends, lonely, country.* In the discussion the teacher uses learners' knowledge and personal experience and relates their responses to story concepts.

B.   The teacher builds story concepts as needed by the readers by having them

1.   observe and discuss related pictures (in this text and others);
2.   observe and discuss a filmstrip giving factual information about ducks, geese and other animals;
3.   observe and discuss the attributes of a turtle.

C.   The teacher encourages students to predict story characters' traits and behaviors by eliciting their hypotheses based on initial interactions with story material (such as title, pictures, and their knowledge of story concepts). The teacher may ask questions such as the following:

1.   How do turtles spend their time?
2.   How does a turtle move?
3.   How does a duck or goose move?
4.   What happens when there is too much talk?

Reader-text interactions (groups)
Learners are directed to interact with the text in the following groups:

Group A—reads "Too Much Talk" independently and thinks about the questions and predictions generated during the prereading activity.
Group B—reads "Too Much Talk" silently with teacher direction; reads only first 14 lines, stops, confirms hypotheses, makes further predictions.
Group C—listens to "Too Much Talk" either the tape or oral reading by

an adult or upper-grade student. Learners listen and think about the questions and predictions generated during the prereading activity.

Postreading activities (A-D: whole class; E: group)

A.   Learners respond and react to the questions and predictions generated during the prereading activities.

B.   Learners share information about characters' traits and behaviors by recalling the story and responding to probe questions.

C.   If needed, teacher asks structured questions specific to characterization (see pp. 197–99 for sample questions). Pupils respond to questions and may reread or refer to parts of the story to support answers. They discuss whether their answers are found completely in the story or if they used some other information (prior knowledge).

D.   Learners discuss the last sentence in the story, "Sometimes even a little talk is too much," and the fact that in this story the animals talk. (*Note:* The term fable would not necessarily be used at this level but this discussion can lead to an understanding of the characteristics of a fable.)

E.   The following group activities reinforce the concepts developed and expand reading/language competence:

Group A—reads another fable at approximately the same reading level or listens to a fable at a higher reading level, for example, "The Tortoise and the Hare." Pupils recall the story by either writing a brief description (traits, behavior) of the main characters or by answering teacher questions.

Group B—reads short descriptive paragraphs, each emphasizing a specific aspect of a character and answers multiple-choice or open-ended questions based on the paragraphs.

Group C—develops a group language experience chart based upon learners' retelling of the story "Too Much Talk." The teacher implements appropriate group and individual follow-up activities, such as word banks, sentence matching, story sequence, specific strategy lesson, art and craft activities.

Evaluative Teaching

During the interactive stage of teaching the teacher observes the process and product of the interactions and encourages ongoing evaluation by learners. This procedure leads naturally to evaluative teaching in which the teacher judges the quality of learners' responses following the listening or reading activity, learner-learner interactions and teacher-learner interactions. It is at this time that the teacher assesses learners' progress to aid in planning additional general teaching/learning plans and specific strategy lessons.

Summary Comments

As emphasized, the teacher determines the rationale for reading a story based upon diagnostic information gathered about learners and the particular text. In the teacher plan just outlined the focus was on expanding learners' understanding of characters' traits and behaviors. However, the teacher could have selected other story characteristics for emphasis using the same narrative text. As this story is a fable, learners are beginning to develop a concept of what a fable is. This concept will be expanded and reinforced as learners read and listen to other fables during their primary school years.

PLAN TWO: "SU AN"

Introductory Comments
At times the teacher will plan to introduce a story that requires understanding of very specific aspects of story characteristics. For example, for a group or class with limited work in the area of figurative language, the teacher may choose a story which is highly dependent on an understanding of figurative language. The teacher's rationale is both to expand the learners' knowledge of figurative language and to gain diagnostic information about those learners for whom this aspect of language may present difficulty. The story "Su An" readily lends itself to work with figurative language.

Su An
DORIS JOHNSON

Through the airplane door I step. I walk down the little stairs.

O! The wind is a tiger switching his tail and roaring in my ears. He tugs at my hair. It would please him also to have my sweater, but I pull it tight around me.

I put one foot on the ground of America. Then the other. A strangeness fills the inside of me. My heart wishes to be once more in Korea. My head says, "You are lucky to be a chosen child, Su An."

"Not so!" my heart answers. "Will you not look again upon your mother's face? Ah, Su An, I break in sadness."

My memory is like a picture that moves. My mothers' eyes are like two ponds at night in which the moon swims. But they do not spill their tears. Her voice is like the soft song of a bamboo flute and the steady presence of stones in a garden.

"Peace, little Su An," the picture speaks. "I must go away, so I leave you here with Madame Kim. She will take good care of you." My mother's lips are like blossoms trembling in a soft breeze. "My heart will always be with you," she whispers, "I promise."

Her kiss brushes my cheek lightly as a dragonfly's wing. And she is gone.

For many seasons I do not speak. I do not smile. I do not frown. I only wait.

Madame Kim is kind.

"Su An," she says, "your mother would have returned had she been able. But as the snow of winter melts in the summer sun, so does the past depart. Today is the day we must consider—and tomorrow. Think of the coming day of happiness when you will go to a new father and mother!"

I want no new mother. I want no mother but my own. A gray cloud descends upon my heart.

Now America burns beneath my feet. The tiger wind roars. Above the roar, Madame Kim calls, "Come, children. Your new parents wait!"

"No! No! No!" my heart cries. "No!" And while the others huddle, I turn to run away.

The crooked handle of Madame Kim's umbrella reaches out. It clutches my shoulder. My heart grows angry. "Honorable Lady of the orphanage, O daughter of a crow," it pounds. "You are as cold as snow and hard as ice. You have brought Su An across the sea and lost her to her mother forever!"

Madame Kim hands her name papers to Nurse Chi. She removes the crook and drops it over her arm. She takes my hand and says, "Enough of stubbornness!" She pushes holes in the crowd and pulls me through.

My heart weeps.

"Hush, Su An," commands my head. "The lady knows best. Trust her."

A door of glass opens and closes. The tiger wind is left behind. There are throngs of people. They are giants—pale, smiling giants with big noses and hissing speech.

"Mother!" calls my head. "Mother!" sobs my heart. "O little mother of the golden skin and moonlit eyes." On sticks of straw that once were legs, I run slip and slide.

Not once do Madame Kim's footsteps falter until now. They slow. They stop. She releases my hand.

"Greet your new parents, child," she says, and nudges me forward.

I must do what I must do! My head bows low, I stare at the feet of my parents. My father has the feet of a giant, my mother, the feet of a doll. I dare not raise my eyes.

"Su An." It is the song of a bamboo flute.

"Su An."

There is a rush of fragrance. My mother kneels. With her fingertips, she lifts my face. I see two ponds at night with the moon swimming in them. She smiles and places a little doll in my hand. It wears a happy face, and its hair is black like mine and shiny.

"Don't be afraid, Su An." My new mother speaks. Her voice is the steady presence of stones in a garden. "Your father and I love you and want to take care of you. We will have much happiness together. I promise."

I hear the sound of my own voice.

"O-mon-i," it cries. "O-mon-i!"

With a kiss light as a dragonfly's wing, my mother brushes away a tear that spills down my cheek.

I smile.

This story appears in both a fourth-grade basal reader (Fay & Anderson, 1978) and in a third-grade basal reader (Ruddell, Crews, & Livo, 1978). In the fourth-grade book it appears in narrative prose form whereas in the third-grade book it appears as a narrative poem. This difference in genre is not surprising because the predominance of figurative language makes this selection suitable for either genre. Further, both narrative prose and narrative poetry usually contain information about what happened, who or what was involved, and where it occurred, and sometimes includes why, how, and when an event took place.

It is also not surprising to find this selection in textbooks designated by the publishers for two different reading levels as different readability formulas have variations. Of much greater importance than these publisher-designated grade levels is the match between reader background and the text to be processed.

Preactive Teaching

Teacher knowledge.   Teacher analysis of "Su An" yields the following information:

Genre and Narrator: Realistic modern narrative. First person point of view as Su An, the main character, reveals her thoughts and feelings to the reader.

Style and Language: Extensive use of figurative language with emphasis on similes, metaphors, and personification; syntax may be unfamiliar to readers as it reflects Su An's Korean language patterns.

Characterization:
Su An—a young sad girl who was left in an orphanage in Korea by her mother and brought to America to meet her new parents.
Mother—a loving, caring and sensitive Korean woman who found it necessary to leave her young daughter at an orphanage.
Madame Kim—a kind woman who works in the orphanage and brings Su An along with other children to America.
American mother—a caring, affectionate and sensitive woman who, with her husband (Su An's new father), greets Su An at the airport.

Plot: Su An, along with other Korean orphans, arrives at the airport in America with Madame Kim and thinks about her mother whom she will never see again and her life in the orphanage. She feels that she does not want a new mother and tries to run away as Madame Kim calls the children to meet their new parents. Madame Kim stops her and takes her to meet her new parents. She is sad as she continues to think about her Korean mother but she moves forward to meet her new parents. Her new mother greets her with sensitivity and affection. Su An compares her to her natural mother, calls her "Mother," and smiles.

Setting and Mood: An airport in America that is cold and windy. The mood is initially unhappy, reflecting Su An's apprehension. The mood shifts to a happier one when she meets her new parents.

Theme: War creates hardship and changes the lives of innocent people. Terrible things may happen, but life goes on and sometimes things work out pretty well.

The teacher writes the following structured questions for use only if learners' free recall and probed recall do not indicate sufficient understanding of the figurative language used in this story. In some cases follow-up questions also may be necessary. Following each question we have included the specific figure of speech the reader needs to understand in order to respond appropriately.

1. How does Su An describe her Korean mother?
    Follow-up questions:
    a. What does she compare her mother's eyes to? (My mother's eyes are like two ponds at night in which the moon swims.)
    b. What does her mother's voice sound like? (Her mother's voice is like the soft song of a bamboo flute and the steady presence of stones in a garden.)
    c. What are her mother's lips like? (My mother's lips are like blossoms trembling in a soft tree.)
    d. What is her mother's kiss like? (Her kiss brushes my cheek lightly as a dragonfly's wing.)
2. How does Su An describe the wind as she arrives at the airport? (The wind is a tiger switching his tail and roaring in my ears.)
3. How does Su An describe her memory? (My memory is like a picture that moves.)
4. What words tell you Su An is sad when she is told she is going to meet her new parents? (A gray cloud descends upon my heart.)
5. How does she describe Madame Kim at the American airport? (Daughter of a crow, you are cold as snow and hard as ice.)
6. How do Su An's legs feel as Madame Kim pushes her to meet her new parents? (On sticks of straw that once were legs, I run, slip and slide.)
    Follow-up question:
    Why do her legs feel this way?
7. How does Su An describe the people she first sees at the airport? (They are giants, pale, smiling giants with big noses and hissing speech.)
    Follow-up question:
    Why do you think the people look and sound this way to her?
8. How does Su An's new mother appear to her?
    Follow-up questions:

a. How does she sound to Su An? (It is the sound of a bamboo flute. Her voice is the steady presence of stones in a garden.)
b. How does she look to Su An? (I see two ponds at night with the moon swimming in them.)
c. How does she feel to Su An? (With a kiss light as a dragonfly's wings.)

This last question, while not directly focused on figurative language, is important for understanding the story:

9. How would you compare Su An's feelings about her Korean mother with her new mother?

Teacher decisions. "Su An" is appropriate for this group of fourth grade children because they enjoy realistic fiction and are beginning to use figurative language in their writing. Reading a story that uses a great deal of figurative language should expand learners' understanding of figures of speech and increase their use of figurative language in their writing.

Prereading activities elicit and increase learners' understanding of the Korean War and its consequences because most learners have limited information about this topic.

Postreading activities focus on expanding learners' use of figurative language in writing.

Although understanding the flashback technique is not a specific objective for teaching this story, it is important in understanding the plot events and, therefore, the teacher will be aware of any problems in comprehension that may occur because of the flashback.

Interactive Teaching

Prereading activities
A. The teacher assesses readers' prior knowledge of important story concepts by eliciting associations to war, war orphans, Korea, adoption, new country. The teacher and class members discuss and relate associations to the content of the story.
B. The teacher builds story concepts as needed by

1. using film, filmstrips, or pictures to provide some factual information about the Korean War;
2. discussing factual information about war in general and the Korean War specifically;
3. having learners share personal experiences with adoption in general and the special circumstances of war orphans who were adopted;
4. having learners share personal experiences related to moving to a new neighborhood or new country;
5. having a Korean child visit the classroom.

C. The teacher encourages readers to predict how Su An feels about leaving Korea and coming to a new country. These hypotheses may be written on the chalkboard.

Reader-text interactions

Students interact with the story to confirm hypotheses, to change hypotheses and to make further predictions. They may refer to the chalkboard as they read and think about what is happening to Su An. Students reflect on the author's description of Su An's feelings and thoughts and consider how they would feel if they were war orphans.

If at any time during silent reading learners feel that the story does not make sense, they may use one or more self-monitoring strategies to aid comprehension. For example, they may stop and think about Su An, the events that have occurred thus far, and what is likely to happen to her. They then continue reading to see if the outcome confirms their prediction. Or a reader may choose to reread a section of the story, skip a section to see if continued reading clarifies the ideas, question a peer, or discuss the story with the teacher.

Postreading activities

A. Learners discuss the predictions made during prereading activities and share their ideas about why the story confirms some predictions and not others.

B. Learners recall the story, respond to probe questions, and to structured questions if necessary.

C. The teacher presents descriptions of people using figurative language, and learners illustrate the descriptions using various art mediums.

D. Learners collect pictures of people and select one or two to write brief descriptions of them using figurative language. Learners share these descriptions in groups and match the pictures with the written descriptions.

E. The teacher and/or learners give several figures of speech and write paragraphs about each. Learners share written materials for criticism, revisions, and editing.

Evaluative Teaching

The teacher reflects on the learners' reactions to the story and on their use of figurative language during free recall, probed recall, and responses to structured questions. The teacher keeps in mind learners' use of figures of speech while examining art work and writing and makes a comparison of the use of figurative language in these different types of communication. Further, the teacher compares the work following the story experience with previous work.

Summary Comments

An analysis of the major concepts in "Su An" makes it very clear that although 3rd and 4th grade children may use the selection, it is also appropriate to use this material with advanced readers and/or older children. Of course, understanding will be different based upon cognitive and affective developmental levels of the reader. For example, when dealing with story plot, there will be differences in children's abilities to understand flashbacks. This understanding increases as children's cognitive awareness of sequence and related abilities to hold more than one idea in mind grow. Also, an 8-year-old child's understanding of the concepts of war and the circumstances of war, and its impact on family life is considerably different from that of 11- or 12-year-old children. The increased experience and related understandings of older readers means that they can bring greater depth of understanding to processing the text. Based upon the different levels of understanding, educators can expect different degrees of abstraction as the reader interacts with the story, interprets the figurative language, and makes generalizations regarding the theme. For example, an 8-year-old child would appropriately conclude that the author's purpose is to share with the reader the idea that it is not easy to leave one's family and go to a new country. A more mature reader would generalize at a level of greater depth with responses such as, "Innocent people are often victims of the political actions of countries," or "War changes people's lives."

CHILDREN'S PROTOCOLS

The protocols illustrate how two readers at different levels of functioning responded to the story "Su An." The teachers, in both cases, implemented the teaching plan on a one-to-one basis. Student A is a third grade girl, age 8½, in a class for the gifted in a New York City inner city school. Student B is an 11-year-old boy in a regular sixth-grade class in the same school. During the prereading discussion with these readers, their teachers recognized that both of them were familiar with the major concepts related to the story except for the concept of "war orphans." Their teachers developed this concept by building upon the learner's prior knowledge of such concepts as "war," "orphan," and "adoption." The following transcripts present the free recall and probed recall of these readers.

Free Recall—Student A

A: I think the story is about a girl who was at home, right, and her mother had left her with a lady. The girl was talking about her mother, and she knew her mother wasn't coming back, and she knew she was going to an orphanage, but she really wanted her mother. She was more attached to her mother than other people, and she was afraid that she might never see her mother again, and she was very sad and lonely. She knew that her father wasn't her real father, and her mother wasn't her real mother, and she wanted to go back to her real ones.

Probed Recall—Student A

T: Can you tell me more about her mother?

A: Ah, her mother, she says her mother's eyes were like night ponds and she used to give her a kiss, her lips were like dragonfly wings and she misses her mother a lot. But later, when she was taking her, she stepped into America for the first time, but she missed Korea, that's where she used to live, and they had brung her to America where they had to take her to the orphanage. And the lady, she was Madame Kim, she was kind, and she grabbed her by the arm, and she took her to the orphanage where she saw her parents.

T: Anything more about her parents?

A: Her father's feet looked like a giant's feet and her mother's feet look like a doll's and her kiss was like a dragonfly's wings, like her mother's.

T: Anything else you remember?

A: The orphanage lady told her to go ahead, and she wanted to stay there, and she took her umbrella and took her over.

Free Recall—Student B

B: Well, the story is about this girl that, well she is a war orphan, and her mother had to go away for something, and she went to these people, and she really didn't want to go with them, but her mother made her go cause she had to go somewhere or something, and then at the end she was saying bye to her mother, and she had a new family, and she sort of acted like she was looking at their feet, and she wouldn't look up at them or anything, and I don't know really if she likes them because she didn't say in the story, but she was ashamed because she didn't want to look up at her new parents. That's really about it.

Probed Recall—Student B

T: Can you tell me anything about her real mother, her mother in Korea?

B: Just how her own real mother was nice.

T: Can you tell me anything more about her parents?

B: The father looked like a giant and the mother sort of like a doll.

T: Why do you think she said that?

B: Because, probably, like probably back in Korea life wasn't as fortunate and she was more prettier and he was more stronger and bigger.

T: Anything else about Su An?

B: I forgot.

The following are responses from Student A and Student B to selected structured questions that indicate reader understanding of the figurative language used in the story.

Text: "The wind is a tiger switching his tail and roaring in my ears. He tugs at my hair. It would please him also to have my sweater, but I pull it tight around me."
Question: How does Su An describe the wind at the airport?
Responses:
A. She means that the wind is very very hard, like it's very cold, and like when a tiger is mean and moving and is mean, he gets like the

wind. When the wind pulls, right, it's like taking off the clothes, it's like pulling things, and a tiger is like moving fast and hard and pulling things.

B. Because the wind was real mean and was like blowing wild and was just hard, and she wrapped her sweater around her cause it was cold.

Text: "Her kiss brushes my cheek lightly as a dragonfly's wing."

Question: How does Su An describe her mother's kiss?

Responses:

A. A dragonfly's wing is like a little touch so it would be like when she gives her a little kiss, it would be like a little touch.

B. Like a soft kind of kiss.

Text: "They are giants—pale, smiling giants with big noses and hissing speech."

Question: How does Su An describe the people she first sees at the airport?

Responses:

A. Because she's coming from another country and she comes from Korea.

   Follow-up question to Learner A:

   What did the people look like?

   A. They have different faces, they're a different color . . . white, and. . . . Yeah, they're white and the people in Korea look very different; they're not white.

   Follow-up question to Learner A:

   What did the people sound like?

   A. Because they're different, she don't know them very well.

B. Cause that's the first time she saw these people, because in Korea they don't have as much food as they have in America, and she wasn't as used to seeing as big people as those. Because I think in Korea they spoke with an accent, and here it sounds different.

Text: "On sticks of straw that once were legs, I run, slip, slide."

Question: How do Su An's legs feel as Madame Kim pushes her to meet her new parents?

Responses:

A. Her legs felt slippery, like trembling. They couldn't hold her good.

B. Like rubber and wiggly; they had a feeling in them that was sort of rubbery sticks of straw.

   Follow-up question to Learner B:

   What is a stick of straw like?

   B. Like a thin piece of straw, like straw is real thin and cracks easily; they'll crack down, and she'll fall down.

Question: How would you compare how Su An feels about her Korean mother with her feelings about her new mother?

Responses:

A. She's like her Korean mother, but not really.

   Follow-up question to Learner A:

How is she like her Korean mother?

A.   Because her lips are like dragonfly wings and her eyes are like night ponds and that's how her Korean mother looked, kind of, but they're not really alike. She just has to compare them a little more.

Follow-up question to Learner A:

What will she find out when she compares them a little more?

A.   Maybe people are different.

B.   Well, they're both kind of the same, cause the dragonfly kissing, like the other one had a dragonfly kiss, but her mother didn't have a rush of fragrance or anything like that. Well, the Korean mother was like sort of she was more kind of strict, and the new mother had just met her so she wouldn't like have been mean. She wasn't mean, the Korean mother wasn't mean; she was just a little more strict than the other was.

Follow-up question to Learner B:

In what ways was the Korean mother strict?

B.   She made her go to the new mother.

Analysis of Learner A's Responses

Learner A's background is in some ways similar to Su An's and influenced her focus when interpreting the story. Learner A has been separated from her natural mother for some time; she first lived with an aunt and uncle, and at present she lives with her grandmother. Her responses indicated that she identified strongly with Su An and focused on Su An's separation from her mother, her desire to return to her Korean mother, and the differences rather than the similarities of the two mothers. She downplayed Su An's acceptance of the new mother at the end of the story, and while noting physical similarities between the two women, she was unsure of the emotional similarities.

Learner A had good understanding of plot sequence. However, she confused time and place sequences in the plot (orphanage is in Korea not in America as recalled by reader) that may be related to the flashback technique.

Learner A indicated excellent understanding of the concepts of similes and metaphors by her spontaneous responses to these aspects of language usage that help describe characters and events in the story. Not only was she able to use figurative language in her free recall but was able to expand upon this knowledge in response to structured questions.

Analysis of Learner B's Responses

Learner B was able to integrate his knowledge of life in Korea to interpret figurative references to the descriptions of Korean and American people. However, he was somewhat culturally confused when he interpreted looking down as a sign of shame rather than respect. While he was not able to spontaneously incorporate figurative language during free recall and probed recall, when the teacher directed him to read and interpret similes and metaphors, he was able to do so with success.

Learner B missed the flashback sequence in which Su An's mother left her in an orphanage in Korea with Madame Kim. Relatedly, he confused the character of the Korean mother with that of Madame Kim, ascribing Madame Kim's traits to the mother.

Overall, Learner B's responses compared to Learner A's were more concrete and showed less elaborate use of language. Because Learner A is in a class for the gifted, we are not surprised that her performance is equal to or more advanced than Learner B's in some aspects of understanding this story.

As usual, educators should be very cautious about making judgments about these two readers because data is available for only one reading experience. Only through many observed experiences can teachers make generalizations about student reading with confidence. For example, teachers would have to explore both learners' understanding of flashbacks further before drawing conclusions about their knowledge of this technique. Teachers would monitor student responses to other stories using the flashback technique to determine if this writing technique really presents a problem for these students.

Matching Assessment to Learning

The preceding sections have focused on teaching reading comprehension using narrative text and informal observations of readers as they interact with this type of text. Informal observation of readers is the primary way for teachers to judge learners' growth in reading comprehension. As Chapter 7 describes, this method of evaluating readers' understanding of written materials occurs during regular classroom activities and whole-class or group reading experiences. Judging learners' performances in this way is a natural part of the reading program, and learners generally are unaware of when the teacher is monitoring their progress.

At certain times, however, teachers may find they want a relatively more structured approach to assessment than informal observation, yet they do not feel the need to use the in-depth structured assessment procedures from Chapter 7 that require a one-to-one situation. The procedure outlined below provides an alternative way of evaluating readers' understanding of narrative text. Using a group or whole-class setting, the teacher may assess readers' understanding of stories by having children recall and tell about the story events and respond to structured questions based on story characteristics. This procedure is similar to the type of questioning that we suggested teachers use during direct teaching except that children communicate in writing. Because this procedure incorporates similar student responses as in direct teaching (recall and structured questions), this assessment process avoids many of the problems inherent in testing. Unlike most tests, this approach to assessment provides a direct match between the requirements set up for learning activities and the requirements set up for assessment activities.

For this type of assessment, we suggest three levels of assignments because different learners will have different abilities in independent reading and recall of any selected story. The assignments advance in difficulty as learners move through the levels, requiring increased independence in responding, and increased writing. The teacher encourages readers who resist writing to demonstrate their understanding of the ideas by dictating responses to another child or adult, by tape-recording responses or by drawing. In this way even readers who are not yet able to express their ideas in written form can be assessed in a group setting. Also, an advantage in having three levels of assignments and flexibility in response modes enables the teacher to structure learning so that children can move from easier to more difficult tasks. For example, children who initially can only respond in writing to a level one assignment can practice responding to level two or three assignments orally or through drawing until they feel confident in responding in writing.

DESCRIPTION OF ASSESSMENT ACTIVITIES AND SAMPLE RESPONSES
The recall task in the three levels of assignment progresses from a simple recognition activity to an activity in which the reader writes freely about the story without any instructional cues from the teacher. In addition, at all three levels the reader is required to answer some open-ended questions which focus on characterization, story events, and personal reactions to the story. In their directions to learners, teachers emphasize that they are to write their ideas down and to write as much as possible and that spelling words correctly is not important. Also, teachers encourage learners to use as much time as they need since the assessment is not a timed task. The teacher uses the information from both the recall task and the readers' responses to structured questions to make judgments about children's understanding of stories. This type of assessment allows readers to tell their interpretations of a story without being unduly influenced by other children's responses or the teacher's thinking. As teachers read children's responses, they are able to gain valuable information about how their children think about a story, what they choose to focus on, and how they relate what they read to their world. Examples of the three levels follow.

"Su An"

Think about the story you have just read. Place a check next to each idea that you think was in the story.

✓ 1. Su An arrives at the airport in America.

___ 2. She thinks about her Korean mother.

✓ 3. Su An has come to this country with Madame Kim.

✓ 4. Su An feels that she does not want a new mother.

✓ 5. She tries to run away.

___ 6. Madame Kim stops her.

✓ 7. Su An meets her new parents.

___ 8. She keeps thinking about her Korean mother.

✓ 9. Her new mother kisses her.

___ 10. Then Su An smiles.

Choose __one__ of the ideas that you checked and write something more about it. Write the number of the idea that you pick here __4__

She did not want a new mother
Because she was afraid of leaving
her mother because she loved her.

Figure 9.1 Sample Level One Response

"Su An"

Read the sentences below which tell you something about the story you have just read. Then write some more about the story.

This story is about a girl named Su An. She has been brought to America from Korea.

> Her parents had to send her to America so that she wouldn't get hurt in the war. Su An's step parents wanted to love her the way her real mother and father loved her. Su An didn't know if her parents were still alive or not.

Figure 9.2   Sample Level Two Response

At level one, the teacher lists the major story events and instructs readers to check those events that they recall from the story, to select one checked event for expansion, and to write one or more sentences about the selected event. Figure 9.1 gives a sample of a level one assignment based on the story "Su An" and one reader's responses. This sample and the others that follow are the work of third-grade students in an urban public school.

At level two (Figure 9.2) the teacher gives readers one or two sentences about the story that are introductory and directs them to write as much as they can recall. The following is a sample of a level two assignment based on the same story and one reader's responses.

Finally, at level three (Figure 9.3) readers write about the story with no cuing. This last sample is one reader's responses to a level-three assignment after reading "Su An."

Upon completing the assigned recall task, learners answer open-ended

"Su An"

Think about the story you have just read. Write about it in your own words.

In this story Su An does not want a new brother or Mother She just wants her own, When she left Korea her head said that she is lucky to be chosen and her heart says she is not lucky to be chosen to go to America. Soon she had to go to the orphange and her new mother she does not want to go to her new mother.

Figure 9.3 Sample Level Three Response

questions about the story. Questions such as the following relate to the characteristics of stories and elicit students' own knowledge and reactions about story content.

1. Tell something about the characters.
2. What problem did _____ have in the story?
3. How did _____ solve the problem?
4. Did you like the story? Why or why not?
5. What part of the story did you like the best?
6. Did you ever have an experience like the one you just read about? Tell about it.

Using "Su An" as an example, the following is one reader's responses to these types of questions. Of course different children will respond differ-

"Su An"

1. Write something about the characters in the story.

The characters in the Story are good. Because they use there feelings

2. What problem does Su An have?

She did not want to leave her mother because she loved her.

3. How does Su An solve her problem?

Her mother has a little talk with her.

4. Did you like the story? Why or why not?

I like the story because the people show there felings.

5. What part of the story did you like best?

When her mother talked to her.

6. Did you ever have an experience like Su An's

*or do you know someone who had a
similar experience? Write about it.*

*Carly Did in my class she had
new parents.*

Figure 9.4   Sample Responses to Questions

ently based on their experiences, understanding of the story, and ability to communicate in writing. The sample presented in Figure 9.4 is taken from the work of the same child who responded to the level one assignment shown in Figure 9.1.

Although we have illustrated the assessment procedure with the work of third graders, this procedure has been used with whole classes in different grades. Teachers note that they are able to get an overview of everybody's reading performance with a particular story and can quickly spot those children who appear to have difficulty in understanding the story. Also, teachers report that this type of assessment provides them with insights about their children's language and thinking, in some cases going beyond what they learn during other group reading and discussion activities. Giving everybody the opportunity to express his or her ideas individually without being influenced by other children enables the teacher to better understand how a specific child is functioning in reading. Finally, using a written assessment procedure like the one described gives children an opportunity to express ideas and feelings which they might not share in a group discussion.

PREPARATION AND IMPLEMENTATION
As you can see from the samples we have presented, when teachers decide to use this type of assessment, they need to prepare materials for their students and implement a number of procedures. The following steps describe teacher preparation for and implementation of the assessment process:

1.   The teacher selects a story at approximately the same level as learners are reading during classroom activities.
2.   The teacher analyzes the story, lists the major events in preparation for level one assessment, prepares a one- or two-sentence introduction to the story for level two assessment, and writes structured questions for inclusion with materials at all three levels of assignment.
3.   The teacher prepares written instructions for the children. These instructions are similar to those illustrated in Figures 9.1 through 9.4.

4. The teacher matches learners to one of the three levels of assignment based on judgment of their ability to independently read and express ideas about a selected story. Learners will not necessarily receive the same level assignment for all stories; they will move from level to level in both directions.

5. The learners read the story silently and complete one of the three assignments, and the structured questions. Students may refer to the story because the assessment is focusing on understanding and not memory.

6. The learners and teachers review the completed assignments in group or individual settings. At this time learners may refer to the story again to support ideas presented and clarify any confusions. Some learners may profit from rereading the story after participating in the discussion. The teacher should follow up on this rereading by briefly discussing the story with the learner(s) once again.

This procedure is close to a natural reading situation in which learners read a story independently without preparation and think about what they have read. It differs in that learners are aware that the teacher is evaluating their reading performance and that the assessment generally involves writing. The use of this procedure periodically throughout the school year enables teachers and learners to assess reading and writing growth. The level of assignment would increase as readers progress. Readers and teacher jointly examine student writing and compare quality and quantity over time. The type of assessment just described can vary to meet the needs of different students. Teachers should experiment by using a variety of approaches within this framework to understand learners' comprehension of stories.

Summary
This chapter emphasizes teaching reading comprehension through the use of stories; illustrates a framework for teaching based on the general teaching/learning framework presented in Chapter 4; and describes prereading activities, reader-text interactions and postreading activities for two stories. The chapter presents and analyzes readers' responses to one of the two stories. In addition it describes and illustrates a classroom procedure for monitoring student progress in reading comprehension.

10

Specific Strategy Teaching

B ecause the natural communication of an author is connected discourse organized around particular ideas or experiences to share with an audience, whole stories form the base for the classroom reading program. Previous chapters have illustrated how teachers may use these narratives for gathering diagnostic information and for teaching whole classes and groups. Although most reader-text interaction is based on a complete narrative, at times reader performance will indicate the need for breaking down the demands of the text into specific elements. Indications for the need to plan specific strategy lessons come when the teacher notices learner difficulties with certain aspects of story characteristics. This chapter, then, will relate story characteristics to specific teaching strategies, will describe a guide for planning these lessons, and will illustrate several specific strategies.

Story Characteristics and Related Strategies

Examining stories shows that each story characteristic may relate to specific teaching strategies. For example, if diagnostic data indicate that readers are having difficulty understanding aspects of plot development, they may benefit from strategy lessons such as: sequence of events, anaphoric relations, causality, and anticipating or predicting events.

In the area of characterization readers may benefit from specific strategy lessons in related areas such as anaphoric relations (pronoun referents), dialogue cues, comparison and contrast between traits or actions, drawing conclusions about a character's behavior, understanding/predicting behavior based on characters' traits, emotional reactions and motives, and descriptive language.

Understanding theme is closely related to understanding the author's purpose. Specific strategy lessons that focus on forming generalizations about narratives and in inferring the main idea or general concept of a narrative may expand this understanding.

Strategy lessons which emphasize descriptive language and time and place concepts can help readers understand setting and mood.

Style and language, dependent on the author's background and purpose, vary from narrative to narrative. Therefore, specific strategy lessons that focus on different aspects of style and language may be necessary at different times. For example, a reader may need help in understanding the differences between denotative and connotative language, the use of figurative language, the inferences derived from author's tone and use of dialect.

Point of view reflects the perspective from which the events of the story are observed and will vary. A strategy lesson may focus on making readers aware of who is telling the story; for example, readers may benefit from learning that when an author writes a story in the first person the author becomes a character in the story. Readers must understand that the writer's use of the word *I* takes the place of a character's name.

Within narratives learners develop familiarity with genre by interacting with many different types of stories over a long period of time. With this knowledge as a base, strategy lessons can highlight the characteristics of particular types of narratives and lead to children's increased ability to predict the structure and characteristics particular to a specific type of narrative. For example, repeated experiences with different fables leads to reader prediction that a statement of theme will probably come at the end, giving the moral the reader should learn. Further, the reader will expect that the actions of talking animals, inanimate objects and sometimes humans will convey the moral. In contrast, experiences with realistic stories will lead readers to predict that they must infer the theme or author's purpose from the motives and actions of realistic people or animals.

Table 10.1 summarizes some of the specific teaching strategies that may be necessary to expand a reader's understanding of stories.

Although the strategy areas do relate to particular story characteristics, remember that the teacher needs to use a hypothesis testing framework in analyzing student performance and planning for student needs. The areas described may influence reader performance, or other areas may interfere with reading comprehension.

Table 10.1   Story Characteristics and Teaching Strategies

Story Characteristics	Examples of Related Strategies
Plot	Sequence of events Anaphoric relations Causality Anticipating events
Characterization	Dialogue cues Anaphoric relations Comparison and contrast Drawing conclusions Predicting behavior Emotional reactions and motives Descriptive language
Theme	Author's purpose Generalizations Main idea or general concept
Setting and Mood	Descriptive language Time concepts Place concepts
Style and Language	Denotative and connotative language Figurative language Dialect
Point of view	Storyteller's perspective
Genre	Characteristics and structure of a specific genre

Guide for Planning

As a guide to planning specific strategy lessons we have modified the teaching/learning framework presented in Chapter 4.

PREACTIVE TEACHING

Teacher Knowledge

The teacher should have background knowledge of all related aspects of the strategy to develop, including information about the broad topic area that the strategy lesson encompasses. Knowledge of the entire area related to the strategy lesson provides the teacher with a framework for planning a series of related strategy lessons based on continuing learner performance.

Teacher Decisions

Based on diagnostic information, the teacher determines particular strategies for development within a selected area. The teacher makes decisions about the content of the lesson, the level and type of materials, and the order of presentation.

INTERACTIVE TEACHING

Focus Attention

The teacher presents sufficient introductory material to illustrate the specific concept being developed and to encourage learners to make generalizations about the specific topic.

Learning Activities

Structured reading activities expand learner knowledge of the specific strategy. The teacher presents these activities in a sequential order with increasing length of discourse and increasing difficulty of task demands.

The teacher may construct the materials for these activities or select from appropriate commercially prepared material. These reading experiences encourage teacher and learner(s) interaction through guided questioning.

Application

Application material includes text of varying lengths. The teacher orders this material for presentation to provide for reader interactions with increasingly complex and longer text as the reader progresses through the application activities. The teacher may construct some material or may select them from appropriate basal readers, trade books, or magazines. Strategy lessons are not complete until readers apply the strategy in natural reading situations using complete narratives. The teacher will find a large number of narratives to choose from when selecting application materials for any topic area. Chapter 8 details criteria for selection of materials.

The use of a complete narrative for application purposes assumes that the teacher will establish prior knowledge of the readers and build appropriate background prior to learners reading the story. Further, although every strategy plan includes reader-text interaction using a complete narrative, we assume students will not complete this portion of the strategy plan during the same time period as the other reading experiences. Generally, the reading and follow-up discussion of the narrative consume at least one additional full period.

EVALUATIVE TEACHING
As diagnosis and teaching are cyclical, reader interaction with application materials becomes the basis for obtaining additional diagnostic information through informal observation. The teacher then uses this information to plan further instruction.

Illustrative Strategy Plans
The steps in the strategy plan described above serve for planning a series of specific lessons. Each specific lesson emphasizes one aspect of a broad area and relates to a selected story characteristic. Table 10.2 summarizes the illustrative strategy lessons.

Story characteristics not only relate to specific strategies but also to categories of inferences (see Table 8.1). Therefore, as teachers work with children on specific strategies, they keep in mind the category of inferences that is primarily involved in constructing meaning. For example, the strategy lesson on anaphoric relations between pronouns and noun or noun phrase referents involves informational inferences. Similarly, the strategy lesson on causal relations using signal words involves logical inferences.

Note that the section entitled *Teacher knowledge* includes information about the broad area. This background provides the base from which the teacher makes decisions about which specific aspects to teach. Although the teacher makes these decisions based on learner needs, the teacher's understanding of the general area provides a framework for planning specific strategy lessons and relevant sequences of teaching activities for particular students within a given area. Therefore, in the illustrative strategy lessons that follow, the section *Teacher knowledge* presents broad coverage of the topic as background for the specific strategy lessons. Because the

Table 10.2   Illustrative Strategy Lessons

Area	Specific Strategy	Level	Story Characteristic
I Anaphoric Relations	A. Pronouns—referent noun or noun phrase	2	Characterization
	B. Deleted nouns	4–5	Plot
II Causal Relations	A. Signal words—because, then, so, therefore	3	Plot
	B. Nonsignaled	4–5	Plot
III Figurative Language	A. Metaphor—Explicit	6–7	Style and Language

information in each topic area can provide background for the development of a number of strategy lessons, more than one sample lesson appears in two of the topic areas. Specific comments for evaluative teaching are not included. As we have noted, the teacher always reflects on the learners' responses to the application materials and always evaluates the products. Of course, every strategy lesson concludes with evaluation.

PLAN ONE: ANAPHORIC RELATIONS—PRONOUNS

Preactive Teaching

Teacher knowledge.   Anaphora refers to the deliberate use of a word or phrase as a grammatical substitute for a preceding word, phrase, sentence, paragraph or longer passage. Accuracy in relating anaphoric expressions and their antecedents is an important aspect of comprehending written discourse. Understanding or resolving an anaphoric expression refers to the process of determining its intended referent or antecedent. The reader derives antecedents through the use of syntax and inferencing. The form of syntax of the discourse determines some inferences; others depend on content or prior knowledge. If a writer uses an anaphoric expression with an inferentially derived antecedent or referent, the writer assumes that the reader can and will make the same inference. In sum, then, anaphoric expressions may be partly syntactic and partly semantic. Further, the referent of an anaphoric expression may be in the same sentence (intrasentential) or may be in a separate sentence (intersentential).

The following illustrates an anaphoric expression that requires inferring or world knowledge to derive the antecedent. In this example intersentential structure is used.

> Mary saw a pair of twins in the park. One was playing and one was sleeping.

In order to understand the anaphoric relation between "a pair of twins" (antecedent) and "one," prior knowledge of twins is needed by the reader. In this example knowing that twins equals two or that a pair equals two would enable the reader to determine that "one" refers to one twin, one child, or half the pair of twins.

We can categorize the preceding illustration of an anaphoric relation as deleted nouns. Other anaphoric relations have been analyzed (Menzel, 1970; Halliday & Hasan 1976; Nash-Webber, 1977; Pearson & Johnson, 1978) and appear summarized in Table 10.3. For each relation, examples using intrasentential and intersentential structures appear.

When teachers have theoretical knowledge about anaphoric relations they can use this knowledge to plan one or more strategy lessons in this area. The decisions they make involve selecting a particular anaphoric relation for emphasis (see Table 10.3) and preparing materials that will implement the lesson.

Table 10.3 Common Anaphoric Relations

Relation		Example		
1.	Pronouns: I, me, she, her, he, him, it, you, we, us, they, them	1.	a.	Ruth and *her* friend went shopping.
			b.	The girls planned a shopping trip. *They* chose to go to a large department store.
2.	Demonstrative adverbs: here, there	2.	a.	If I go to the store today, you will see me *there*.
			b.	We landed in Chicago. We plan to meet our friends *here*.
3.	Deleted nouns: few, many, several, one, others, some	3.	a.	The wind blew the kites hard, and (*one* was) *several* were broken.
			b.	The bicycle race took place on Saturday, and many people came to the park. *Some* came to to help the racers along the path. A *few* gave them water and juice. *Several* helped fix juice. *Several* helped to fix the bicycles when they broke down. *Others* only came to see the winner.
4.	Deleted verbs or verb phrase: so does, do so, will also, will too, does not, will not, cannot, would not, as does, as did, as will	4.	a.	Jerry read the storybook. *So did* Paul. Neil refused to *do so*.
			b.	Most of the boys will race in the swimming meet. A few boys will not. Some girls *will, also*.
5.	Deleted adjectives: so is, is also, is too, as is, was too, are too	5.	a.	Stan is a smooth and fast runner. *So is* Carol.
			b.	The baby is a sloppy eater. Her sister was, *too*.
6.	Synonymous anaphoric:	6.	a.	The *shrub* was dying. The dying *bush* was removed from the garden.
			b.	The *game* was played by four people. At the end of the *contest* the winner was announced.
7.	Arithmetic anaphora: the former, the latter, the first, the second, etc., the two, the three, etc.	7.	a.	Tina and Anna were reading. The *former* was reading poetry and the *latter* was reading a play.
			b.	Mary, Joe, and Pete were fighting. *The three* of them got hurt.
8.	Class-inclusive anaphora: inclusion of a subject in a general category—may be specific or non-differentiated	8.	a.	The beans were very dry. The *vegetables* did not taste good.
			b.	The rose was bright red. The *flower* was just picked.
			c.	The boys stepped on the worm and killed the poor *thing*.

(Continued)

Table 10-3 continued

Relation	Example
9. Inclusive anaphora: this, that, these, those, problems, the idea, the issue, the concept which refers back to a whole phrase, clause or multiple clauses	9. a. The President discussed problems inherent in formulating a workable nuclear energy policy. The *issue* will be debated in Congress. b. Children show different development at different ages. *This* is important in understanding children's behavior.

Teacher decisions. This strategy on anaphoric relations is planned for second-grade readers who have exhibited some difficulty in responding to questions that require relating pronouns to their appropriate referents.

The lesson will involve anaphoric pronoun relations. Because a reader can comprehend anaphoric expressions more easily when the referent is a noun or noun phrase rather than a clause or sentence, and when the pronoun follows its referent (Barnitz, 1979), this lesson will concentrate on:

1. anaphoric expressions with a noun or noun phrase as referent;
2. anaphoric expressions which follow the referent.

Material will include anaphoric expressions where both the referent and the anaphoric term are in the same sentence and where separate sentences contain the referent and anaphoric term.

Interactive Teaching

Focus attention

Present the following (2) sentences:

1. a. Sally likes to draw.
   b. Sally's drawing is getting better.

Teacher-guided questions:

Who likes to draw?

Whose drawing is getting better?

Present the following (2) sentences:

2. a. Sally likes to draw.
   b. Her drawing is getting better.

Teacher-guided question:

How is the second set of sentences different from the first set of sentences?

Follow-up questions:

What word appears in sentence 2b that is different from sentence 2a?

What word does *her* take the place of?

Has the meaning of the sentence changed?

Present the following sentence:

3. Mary liked the dresses and bought them.

Teacher-guided questions:

What did Mary like?

What did Mary buy?

How do you know that?

Follow-up questions:

What word does *them* take the place of?

In what way is this sentence like example 2 above?

In what way is example 3 different from example 2?

To ensure learner awareness of pronoun referents, elicit the following:

1. Some words can take the place of the exact name of a person or thing.

2. Sometimes these related words can be in the same sentence or in different sentences.

Learning activities

A. The teacher presents the following sentences with guided questioning:

1. Tom went to the movies because he likes to go.
    Is there a word in the sentence that we can substitute for *he*? (Tom)
    Now repeat the sentence substituting the word *Tom* for *he*. Does the sentence keep the same meaning?
2. Jane took the baby and put him on the bed.
    Is there a word in the sentence that we can substitute for *him*? (baby)
    Does the sentence change in meaning when we make the substitution?

B.   The teacher presents the following sentences, continuing to elicit the fact that the exact name of somebody or something may be substituted, and the meaning of the sentence does not change.

3.   Tom and Jane walked fast; they couldn't wait to get to school.
     Is there a word or words that we can substitute for *they*?
4.   The mother baked a cake for Tim and David. Mother said, "You will like it."
     What word or words in the sentence can we substitute for *you*?
5.   Johnny and Jane went to the library because they liked it.
     What word or words can we substitute for *they*?
     What word or words can we substitute for *it*?

C.   The teacher presents the following sentences. Pupil substitutes the appropriate referent for the anaphoric expression.

1.   The boy asked the policeman if *he* could ride in the police car.
     he *(boy)*
2.   The teacher sent a letter home with the child.
     It asked if *she* could come to school on Saturday.
     It *(letter)*
     she *(child)*
3.   The movie starred Jane and Tom. *They* were very funny in *it*.
     They *(Jane & Tom)*
     it *(movie)*
4.   Jane and her friend went to the movies. *It* was *their* favorite pastime.
     It *(movies)*
     their *(Jane and her friend's)*
5.   Mr. Brown called to Sam and Joe. *He* shouted and shouted to *them*.
     He *(Mr. Brown)*
     them *(Sam and Joe)*

D.   Present the following paragraph and have pupils select the appropriate anaphoric expression from among: he, she, it, them, they, us, we.

   Steve bought a new pair of skates. *Steve* took *the skates* to the park. The *park* was crowded. Steve saw Lisa. Lisa was with Michael. *Lisa and Michael* had new skates too.

Depending upon learner responses to Activity D, the teacher may need to review the concepts of pronoun number and gender.

Application
   A.   Present the following three paragraphs for silent reading.

   Nobody in Suzie's family knew that she was learning to ride a bike. It was her secret. Her birthday would come soon. They would give her a new bike. She would walk up to it, get on, and ride off! Suzie smiled as she thought of Jeff and Clem just standing there, watching her. They never thought she could do anything.

Suzie hurt all over from falling off the bike so much. Now her knee hurt from the new scrape. She thought she had better cover it up. She did not want anyone to know. She was surprised nobody had seen the scrapes.

Everybody was pretty busy, though. There was a lot of work to do on the farm this late in summer. Grandmother was canning tomatoes and other things from the garden. Clem and Jeff were helping her. Their father was busy all day outdoors. At night, he was in the kitchen, cooking dinner.

Source: D. Hasinbiller, 1978.

The teacher asks the following questions to determine readers' understanding of anaphoric expressions. Readers must respond with the name of a person or thing.

1. Who is learning to ride a bike?
2. Whose secret is it?
3. Who is going to give Suzie a new bike?
4. What will Suzie do when her family gives her a new bike?
5. Who never thinks Suzie can do anything?
6. What does Suzie want to cover up?
7. Has Suzie's family seen her scrapes?
8. Why hasn't the family seen her scrapes?
9. Who do Clem and Jeff help?
10. Who cooks dinner?

B.   Learners read "The Big Enormous Carrot" (Gordon, 1974) silently. Teacher checks understanding of story and specifically monitors understanding of anaphoric expressions—pronoun relation—through learner recall, probed recall and responses to structured questions.

The Big Enormous Carrot
DOROTHY GORDON

Vicki had a garden. She worked hard in her garden. She had lettuce and radishes. She had other things too. But the best things in her garden were her carrots. Her carrots were big and fat and orange.

One carrot was enormous. "It is the biggest carrot in the world," said Vicki. "I will take it to the fair. It will be the best carrot at the fair."

Vicki pulled her big enormous carrot. She washed it carefully. She laid it on the grass to dry. Then she went into the house to get a sack.

That day Wiggly, Mr. Jones's big rabbit, got out of his cage again. He hopped into Vicki's garden. He saw the big enormous carrot on the grass. He began to eat it. It was good.

Vicki came out of the house with her sack. She saw Wiggly eating her carrot. "Go away, you awful rabbit," she yelled. "Get out of my garden!"

Wiggly kept right on eating the big enormous carrot.

"Get out of here!" Vicki shouted again.

Mr. Jones came running. "Wiggly got out of his cage again," he said. "What has he done?"

"He has eaten my big enormous carrot. Now I can't take it to the fair," Vicki said.

"That's pretty bad," said Mr. Jones. "What can we do about it?"

"We can't do anything about it," answered Vicki.

Wiggly had just finished off the carrot. He sat there wiggling his nose and looking very happy.

Mr. Jones thought for a while. Then he said, "Your carrot can go to the fair."

"How can my carrot go to the fair?" Vicki asked. "It is inside of Wiggly."

"I will give Wiggly to you," Mr. Jones answered. "He is your rabbit now. You can take Wiggly to the fair. He is a good rabbit. He will win a prize for you."

So Vicki took Wiggly to the fair. He was the best rabbit there. Vicki got a blue ribbon and a trophy. On the top of the trophy was a little bronze rabbit. The rabbit was eating a carrot.

So Vicki's big enormous carrot went to the fair after all.

Sample structured questions and responses:

1. Who worked hard in the garden? (she/Vicki)
2. What will Vicki take to the fair? (it/carrot)
3. Who ate Vicki's carrot? (he/Wiggly)
4. To whom did Mr. Jones give Wiggly? (you/Vicki)
5. Who was the best rabbit at the fair? (he/Wiggly)

PLAN TWO: ANAPHORIC RELATIONS—DELETED NOUNS

Preactive Teaching

Teacher knowledge.   See section on p. 233 for teacher knowledge of anaphora.

Teacher decisions.   This strategy is for fourth- and fifth-grader readers who appear to have comprehension difficulties when reading anaphoric expressions other than pronoun referents. Previous strategy lessons for this group have emphasized anaphoric expressions of the class-inclusive and inclusive type. This lesson, therefore, is limited to anaphoric expressions involving deleted nouns. Materials include anaphoric expressions in which both the referent and the anaphoric term are in the same sentence and in which separate sentences contain the referent and anaphoric term. Application of the strategy in a natural reading situation includes anaphoric relations that are class-inclusive and inclusive as well as deleted nouns for purposes of review and reinforcement. Monitoring the readers' understanding of all anaphoric relations provides diagnostic data for future lesson planning.

Interactive Teaching

Focus attention
    Pupils read each of the following examples silently. Teacher guides discussion through questioning.

1. The food was left out in the sun, and some was spoiled.
    What was spoiled?
    What word was omitted in this sentence?
2. Although the children walked carefully on the ice, several fell down.
    Who fell down?
    What word was omitted in this sentence?
3. Two of the boys had gone home. The oldest one stayed in the park.
    How many boys were in the park?
    In the second sentence, what words were used in place of "boy"?

Guiding questions to elicit learner awareness of deleted nouns:

1. What clues did you use to answer the question?
2. Why did you have to use clues to answer the questions?
3. Does the meaning of the sentence change?

Elicit the following:

1. Writers use some words to take the place of other words. Some of these words are *several, one, some*.
2. Sometimes writers omit words but the sentence still means the same thing.
3. Sometimes the related words are in the same sentence, and sometimes they are in different sentences.
4. Readers often need to think about the connections between ideas to understand the author's message.

Learning activities
    A.   The teacher presents the following sentences with guided questioning. Pupils insert the appropriate referent that specifically takes the place of the deleted noun (italicized). Discuss each response.

1. The *women* went to work every day, and *several* traveled a long distance.

Who traveled a long distance?

What word has been omitted?

2. The *boys and girls* enjoy going to the movies, but a *few* prefer to go skating.

Who prefers to go skating?

What words have been omitted?

Why do writers omit words?

3. The children could not decide which friend to visit because *one* wanted to visit Bob, and *one* wanted to visit Paul.

Who wanted to visit Bob?

Who wanted to visit Paul?

What words could we add to this sentence? Do these words make the sentence clear?

B.   The teacher presents the following paragraphs. Pupils read each silently and discuss the writers' use of the following terms: *some, several, others, few, many, all, one*.

1. The men saw someone trying to break into a car. One said, "Let's call the police."

Sample questions:

Who said, "Let's call the police"?

How would you rewrite the second sentence?

2. Jane walked through the field filled with dandelions. Some tickled her legs. Some made her sneeze.

Sample question:

What tickled Jane's legs and made her sneeze?

3. All the children heard a loud noise. Several said it was a falling rock. Others thought it was a roaring river. A few started to run away.

Sample question:

In this paragraph the writer decided not to use the word *children* more than once. Reread the paragraph, and put in the word children where you think it belongs.

4. The airport was very crowded. Planes were lined up on the runways waiting to take off. All were headed for destinations in the United States. Many were carrying passengers. A few carried mail and freight.

Several kept their motors running as they waited for clearance from the control tower.

Sample question:

Discuss the writer's use of the words *all, many, few,* and *several*.

C. Have pupils cross out one or more words without changing the meaning of the sentence.

1. The people were shouting and laughing, and people were clapping.
2. All the cats were very hungry except for one cat who was sick.
3. The birds are kept in cages even though many of the birds could be flying about.
4. Children enjoy running and playing, but few children like to fall down.
5. Most automobiles use a great deal of gasoline, but several automobiles can use less gasoline.

D. Pupils are to rewrite the following sentences and paragraphs using one of the following terms for the italicized words:[1]

several	others	all
one	few	other
some	many	

1. The books were piled high on the shelf, and *the books* fell to the floor.
2. Two trains collided, and *ten trains* were late that morning.
3. The twins cried all night. The *boy twin* was sick. The *girl twin* was not sleepy.
4. The girls went on a camping trip. *Four of the girls* carried the food. The *rest of the girls* carried the tents.

Application
Learners read "The Cowardly Lion" (in W. Sutherland (Ed.), 1979) silently.

The Cowardly Lion
L. FRANK BAUM

A whirlwind has carried Dorothy and her dog Toto far away from Kansas to the Land of Oz. Dorothy wants to find her way home. A good witch has told her to follow the yellow brick road to Emerald City, where the Great Wizard of Oz will help her. On her way to the Emerald City Dorothy has met a Scarecrow and a Tin Woodman. Both have decided to travel with her.

---

[1]Teacher would underline words that are italicized here.

All this time Dorothy and her companions had been walking through the thick woods. The road was still paved with yellow bricks, but these were much covered by dried branches and dead leaves from the trees, and the walking was not at all good.

There were few birds in this part of the forest, for birds love the open country where there is plenty of sunshine. But now and then there came a deep growl from some wild animal hidden among the trees. These sounds made the little girl's heart beat fast, for she did not know what made them. But Toto knew, and he walked close to Dorothy's side, and did not even bark in return.

"How long will it be," Dorothy asked the Tin Woodman, "before we are out of the forest?"

"I cannot tell," was the answer, "for I have never been to the Emerald City. But my father went there once, when I was a boy. He said it was a long journey through a dangerous country, although nearer to the city where Oz dwells the country is beautiful. But I am not afraid so long as I have my oilcan, and nothing can hurt the Scarecrow, while you bear upon your forehead the mark of the good Witch's kiss, and that will protect you from harm."

"But Toto!" said the girl anxiously, "what will protect him?"

"We must protect him ourselves, if he is in danger," replied the Tin Woodman.

Just as he spoke there came from the forest a terrible roar, and the next moment a great Lion bounded into the road. With one blow of his paw he sent the Scarecrow spinning over and over to the edge of the road, and then he struck at the Tin Woodman with his sharp claws. But, to the Lion's surprise, he could make no impression on the tin, although the Woodman fell over in the road and lay still.

Little Toto, now that he had an enemy to face, ran barking toward the Lion, and the great beast opened his mouth to bite the dog. Dorothy, fearing Toto would be killed, and heedless of danger, rushed forward and slapped the Lion upon his nose as hard as she could, while she cried out,

"Don't you dare bite Toto! You ought to be ashamed of yourself, a big beast like you, to bite a poor little dog!"

"I didn't bite him," said the Lion, as he rubbed his nose with his paw where Dorothy had hit it.

"No, but you tried to," she retorted. "You are nothing but a big coward."

"I know it," said the Lion, hanging his head in shame. "I've always known it. But how can I help it?"

"I don't know, I'm sure. To think of your striking a stuffed man like the poor Scarecrow!"

"Is he stuffed?" asked the Lion in surprise, as he watched her pick up the Scarecrow and set him upon his feet, while she patted him into shape again.

"Of course he's stuffed," replied Dorothy, who was still angry.

"That's why he went over so easily," remarked the Lion. "It astonished me to see him whirl around so. Is the other one stuffed also?"

"No," said Dorothy, "he's made of tin." And she helped the Woodman up again.

"That's why he nearly blunted my claws," said the Lion. "When they scratched against the tin, it made a cold shiver run down my back. What is that little animal you are so tender of?"

"He is my dog, Toto," answered Dorothy.

"Is he made of tin or stuffed?" asked the Lion.

"Neither. He's a—a—a meat dog," said the girl.

"Oh. He's a curious animal and seems remarkably small, now that I look at him. No one would think of biting such a little thing except a coward like me," continued the Lion sadly.

"What makes you a coward?" asked Dorothy, looking at the great beast in wonder, for he was as big as a small horse.

"It's a mystery," replied the Lion. "I suppose I was born that way. All the other animals in the forest naturally expect me to be brave, for the Lion is everywhere thought to be the King of Beasts. I learned that if I roared very loudly, every living thing was frightened and got out of my way. Whenever I've met a person I've been awfully scared, but I just roar, and they always run away as fast as they can go. If the elephants and the tigers and the bears had ever tried to fight me, I should have run myself—I'm such a coward. But just as soon as they hear me roar, they all try to get away from me, and of course I let them go."

"But that isn't right. The King of Beasts shouldn't be a coward," said the Scarecrow.

"I know it," returned the Lion, wiping a tear from his eye with the tip of his tail. "It is my great sorrow and makes my life very unhappy. But whenever there is danger, my heart begins to beat fast."

"Perhaps you have heart disease," said the Tin Woodman.

"It may be," said the Lion.

"If you have," continued the Tin Woodman, "you ought to be glad, for it proves you have a heart. For my part, I have no heart, so I cannot have heart disease."

"Perhaps," said the Lion thoughtfully, "if I had no heart I should not be a coward."

"Have you brains?" asked the Scarecrow.

"I suppose so. I've never looked to see," replied the Lion.

"I am going to the great Oz to ask him to give me some," remarked the Scarecrow, "for my head is stuffed with straw."

"And I am going to ask him to give me a heart," said the Woodman.

"And I am going to ask him to send Toto and me back to Kansas," added Dorothy.

"Do you think Oz could give me courage?" asked the Cowardly Lion.

"Just as easily as he could give me brains," said the Scarecrow.

"Or give me a heart," said the Tin Woodman.

"Or send me back to Kansas," said Dorothy.

"Then, if you don't mind, I'll go with you," said the Lion, "for my life is simply unbearable without a bit of courage."

"You will be very welcome," answered Dorothy, "for you will help to keep away the other wild beasts. It seems to me they must be more cowardly than you are if they allow you to scare them so easily."

"They really are," said the Lion. "But that doesn't make me any braver, and as long as I know myself to be a coward I shall be unhappy."

So once more the little company set off upon the journey, the Lion walking with stately strides at Dorothy's side. Toto did not approve this new comrade at first, for he could not forget how nearly he had been crushed between the Lion's great jaws. But after a time he became more at ease, and presently Toto and the Cowardly Lion had grown to be good friends.

During the rest of that day there was no other adventure to mar the peace of their journey. Once, indeed, the Tin Woodman stepped upon a beetle that was crawling along the road, and killed the poor little thing. This made the Tin Woodman very unhappy, for he was always careful not to hurt any living creature. As he walked along, he wept several tears of sorrow and regret. These tears ran slowly down his face and over the hinges of his jaw, and there they rusted. When Dorothy presently asked him a question, the Tin Woodman could not open his mouth, for his jaws were tightly rusted together. He became greatly frightened at this and made many motions to Dorothy to help him, but she could not understand. The Lion was also puzzled to know what was wrong. But the Scarecrow seized the oilcan from Dorothy's basket and oiled the Woodman's jaws, so that after a few moments he could talk as well as before.

"This will serve me a lesson," said he, "to look where I step. For if I should kill another bug or beetle, it would make me feel so bad that I should surely cry again, and crying rusts my jaws so that I cannot speak."

Thereafter he walked very carefully, with his eyes on the road, and when he saw a tiny ant toiling by, he would step over it, so as not to harm it. The Tin Woodman knew very well he had no heart, and therefore he took great care never to be cruel or unkind to anything.

"You people with hearts," he said, "have something to guide you, and need never do wrong. But I have no heart, and so I must be very careful. When Oz gives me a heart, of course, I needn't mind so much."

They were obliged to camp out that night under a large tree in the forest, for there were no houses near. The tree made a good, thick covering to protect them from the dew, and the Tin Woodman chopped a great pile of wood with his axe, and Dorothy built a splendid fire that warmed her and made her feel less lonely. She and Toto ate the last of their bread, and now she did not know what they would do for breakfast.

"If you wish," said the Lion, "I will go into the forest and kill a deer for you. You can roast it by the fire, since your tastes are so peculiar that you prefer cooked food, and then you will have a very good breakfast."

"Don't! Please don't," begged the Tin Woodman. "I should certainly weep if you killed a poor deer, and then my jaws would rust again."

But the Lion went away into the forest and found his own supper, and no one ever knew what it was, for he didn't mention it. And the Scarecrow found a tree full of nuts and filled Dorothy's basket with them, so that she would not be hungry for a long time. She thought this was very kind and thoughtful of the Scarecrow, but she laughed heartily at the awkward way in which the poor creature picked up the nuts. His padded hands were so clumsy and the nuts were so small that he dropped almost as many as he put in the basket. But the Scarecrow did not mind how long it took him to fill the basket, for it enabled him to keep away from the fire, as he feared a spark might get into his straw and burn him up. So he kept a good distance away from the flames, and only came near to cover Dorothy with dry leaves when she lay down to sleep. These kept her very snug and warm, and she slept soundly until morning.

The teacher checks understanding of story plot and specifically monitors learners' comprehension of anaphoric relations—deleted pronouns—by noting responses during recall, probed recall, and structured questioning.

Responses to structured questions should include knowledge of anaphoric relations involving class-inclusive and inclusive expressions. Teacher observes learner responses as a part of ongoing diagnosis.

Sample structured questions and responses:

1. What was covered with dried branches and dead leaves? (the road; inclusive anaphora)
2. What will protect Dorothy from harm? (the mark of the good witch's kiss; inclusive anaphora)
3. Who is the great beast? (the lion; class-inclusive)
4. Whom does the Lion think is also stuffed? (Tin Woodman; deleted noun)
5. Who is a curious animal? (Toto; class-inclusive)
6. Whom does the lion think of biting? (Toto; class-inclusive)
7. What does the Scarecrow want the great Oz to give him? (a brain; deleted noun)
8. Whom did the Tin Woodman kill? (a beetle; class-inclusive)
9. Why was Tin Woodman unhappy? (Because he killed the beetle; inclusive anaphora)
10. What food will Dorothy probably eat for breakfast? (nuts; class-inclusive)
11. What did Scarecrow keep dropping? (the nuts; deleted noun)
12. What kept Dorothy snug and warm? (the dry leaves; inclusive anaphora)

PLAN THREE: CAUSAL RELATIONS—SIGNAL WORDS

Preactive Teaching

Teacher knowledge.   Causal relations refer to those inferences made by a reader as to the reason(s) or cause(s) for the occurrences of situations or events. The cause–effect relationship is built on the premise that "what happens" (effect) is the result of "what has come before" (cause). Understanding causal relations requires the reader to perceive one situation, event, phenomenon, or agent (person/animal) as causative of another situation, event, phenomenon, or agent. Logical reasoning and background experience are essential factors in understanding causal relations.

Causal relations may be found within one sentence (intrasentential) or within two or more sentences (intersentential). Within the sentence the structural expression of cause can go in either direction. That is, the structure functions as a whole, and in text the sequence *b* because *a* (*effect* then *cause*) is no less acceptable—in fact considerably more frequent—than because *a*, then *b* (cause, then effect) (Halliday & Hasan, 1976).

The following illustrate the two possible directions of a causal relation found within one sentence:

(*b*, because *a*)	1.	Mary's big toe really hurt because she dropped a book on her foot.
(because *a*, then *b*)	2.	Mary dropped a book on her foot, and her big toe really hurt.

Generally, in causal relations involving two or more sentences, the logical order of cause followed by effect is found. The reversed form of the causal relation in which the first sentence expresses the effect is less usual (Halliday & Hasan, 1976).

Causal relations may be either signaled explicitly by the use of special word(s) or may not be signaled at all. Both signaled and nonsignaled causal relations require the reader to infer the relations the writer implies. Nonsignaled causal relations require more prior knowledge and inferencing on the part of the reader than signaled causal relations.

Signaled causal relations are of two types, direct relations and conditional relations. Direct relations occur more commonly in text: "*a*, therefore *b*." The conditional type, although closely related, carries with it a probabilistic interpretation: "possibly *a*; if so, then *b*." The simplest form of conditional relations uses the word *then*.

Table 10.4, adapted from Halliday and Hasan (1976), lists some of the words and phrases explicitly used to signal a causal relation, both direct and conditional.

In addition to those causal relations noted in Table 10.4, some causal relations appear as time relations (Pearson & Johnson, 1978). The temporal relation is expressed in its simplest form by *then*, but other terms such as *next*, *afterwards*, *after that*, and *subsequently* may signal causal relations.

Table 10.4 Causal Relations

Relation	Examples

Direct Relations

General

1. Simple: so, thus, hence, therefore	1. (C/E)* It was cold so we put on our jackets.
	(C/E) It was a good harvest, and thus the settlers would be well-fed for another year.
2. Emphatic: consequently, accordingly, because of this (that)	2. (C/E) The country experienced a budget crisis and consequently raised property taxes.
	(E/C) Property taxes were high because of the budget crisis.

Specific

3. Reason: for this reason, on account of this, it follows (from this), on this basis	3. (C/E) On account of her shrewd investment, she became very wealthy.
	(C/E) She was a diligent worker. On this basis she was promoted to a new job.
4. Result: as a result (of this), in consequence (of this), arising out of this	4. (E/C) He became frightened as a result of the thunder and lightning.
	(C/E) Arising out of his strong motivation to succeed, he was over-conscientious in school.
5. Purpose: for this purpose, with this in mind/view, with this intention, to this end	5. (C/E) She planned to initiate a gubernatorial campaign. With this in mind, she hired a prominent advertising consultant.
	(C/E) The teacher planned to build a class library. To this end she canvassed the local bookstores.

Conditional Relations

6. Simple: then	6. (C/E) If there is a war, then many people will die.

*C/E—Cause/Effect
E/C—Effect/Cause

(continued)

Table 10.4 continued

Relation		Examples	
7.	Emphatic: in that case, that being the case, in such an event	7. (C/E)	A war is possible. In such an event many people would die.
8.	Generalized: under the circumstances	8. (C/E)	If inflation continues, people under these circumstances would have difficulty paying their bills.

Source: Adapted from M. A. K. Halliday & R. Hasan. *Cohesion in English,* p. 243. Copyright © 1976 by Longman Group Limited. Used with permission.

For example, look at this sentence:

Ellen earned some money selling magazines, and then she bought a new pair of boots.

Here is a clear temporal sequence of the two events. First she earned money; then she bought new boots. These two events have a causal relation.

Finally, written discourse often presents multiple causes for a single phenomenon. Sometimes the writer orders these causes sequentially, with each cause a partial explanation of the event or each cause related to the event but not dependent upon previously stated causes.

As noted, in many instances signal words do not cue causal relations. In these cases, the reader must infer that the text indeed indicates a causal relation and must then construct the relation without the aid of signal words.

Understanding how writers use language to express causal relations is important background knowledge for the teacher. Teachers use this knowledge to make decisions about what they will teach, what materials they will need, and how they will structure their lessons.

Teacher decisions.   The teacher plans this strategy for third-grade readers who have exhibited some difficulties in recalling story plot or in responding to questions related to story plot involving causal relations. In particular, students having difficulty in understanding causal relations in which terms such as *so, then, therefore* and *because* signal the cause–effect relation will benefit from this strategy lesson. Recent research suggests that the use of connectives (i.e., because, so) seems to facilitate comprehension and retention in memory of causal relations presented in written text (Marshall, 1977; Pearson, 1974–1975). This research reinforces the decision to teach this strategy.

The teacher limits the lesson to causal relations signaled by "so" and "because." Material includes causal relations which occur within one sentence and causal relations that occur in two sentences as well as causal relations using both directions. Further, application material specifically focuses on reader understanding of causal relations involved in plot development.

Interactive Teaching

Focus attention
Present the following picture:[2]

Children running with a dog chasing them.

Teacher-guided questions:

What are the children doing? (effect)

Why do you think they are running? (cause)

Have pupils complete the following sentences:

1. The children are running because *(the dog is chasing them).*
2. The dog is chasing the children, and, therefore, *(they are running).*

Present a second picture:

Children waiting to cross a street where the traffic light is red.

Teacher-guided questions:

What are the children doing? (effect)

Why are the children waiting? (cause)

Have pupils complete the following sentences:

1. The traffic light is red so *(the children are waiting to cross the street).*
2. The children are waiting to cross the street because *(the traffic light is red).*

Present the following material:

1. The dog is chasing the children. And so the children are running.
2. The traffic light is red. Therefore, the children are waiting to cross the street.

---

[2]The teacher may use any two pictures that depict a causal relation and are within the experience of the learners to focus their attention.

Teacher-guided question:

How are these last two sentences different from the sentences you completed after you looked at the pictures?

To ensure learner awareness of cause-effect relations, elicit the following generalizations:

1. An event or situation may cause another event or situation;
2. Some words help us to see the connection between a cause and its effect. Some of these words are *because, therefore, so;*
3. An event or situation and its cause may occur in one sentence, or it can be two sentences that show the connection.

Learning activities
   A.   The teacher presents the following sentences with guided questioning.

1. Bob missed his bus, and so he was late for school.
    Why was Bob late for school?
2. The snowplow was clearing the street because there was a big snow storm.
    Why was the snowplow clearing the street?
3. Joe went home from school sick and then went to the doctor.
    Why did Joe go to the doctor?

What signal words were used in these sentences? (*so, because, then*)
   Elicit through questioning that in sentences (1) and (3) the cause precedes the event, whereas in sentence (2) the effect precedes the cause, but all three sentences include a cause-effect relation. The teacher should point out that in real life (as opposed to language) cause always precedes effect.
   B.   Present the following clauses and have pupils match each event with a related cause.

Event (effect)	*Cause* (reason)
We stopped to play	It was dark out
The man fell down	It was snowing hard
The car lights were put on	We did not want to study
The train was late	He was dizzy

After each event is matched with a related cause, have learners compose sentences using different signal words—*because, so, then, therefore.* Learners may choose to relate the ideas using either direction (cause-effect; effect-cause) or may use two related sentences to express the causal relation.

Sample responses:

The car lights were put on because it was dark out.

It was dark out, and so the car lights were put on.

It was dark out. Therefore, the car lights were put on.

It was dark out. Then the car lights were put on.

C.   Present the following events/situations. Have learners select a signal word from the list below and complete each sentence. Learners are to ask themselves "What happened?" or "Why did the event/situation occur?" as an aid to completing the sentences.

1.   The men wanted to move some furniture _____

_____

_____.

2.   We planted some vegetable seeds in the spring _____

_____

_____.

3.   It was a very hot summer day _____

_____

_____.

4.   I caught a bad cold _____

_____

_____.

Signal words:

because	so
then	therefore

Learner responses will vary, as they may complete any sentences by adding a result of the event/situation or by adding the cause of the event/situation. Teachers can encourage learners to write more than one response to each statement. After responses are complete, have learners discuss the reasons for their completed sentences. This is a very good group activity since children learn to evaluate the appropriateness of others' responses, thereby learning about cause-effect relationships in the real world and about the language patterns used to describe these relationships.

Application

A.   Teacher tells the beginning of "Snow White and the Seven Dwarfs" and then presents the following paragraphs for silent reading.

> Snow White was hungry and thirsty, so she ate a little of the vegetables and bread on each plate and drank a little from every cup, because she did not want to eat all of anyone's meal.
>
> Then she grew sleepy, so she lay down in one of the beds, but she could not make herself comfortable, . . . [because] each bed was either too long or too short. Luckily the seventh bed was just right—so she stayed there, . . . and fell asleep.
>
> When it had grown quite dark, the masters of the house, seven dwarfs who mined for iron among the mountains, came home. They lighted their seven candles, and . . . [then] they saw that someone had been there.

Source: M. Carus, T. G. Anderson, & H. R. Webber (Eds.), 1976, pp. 49–50.

The teacher asks the following questions to determine readers' understanding of causal relations.

1.   Why did Snow White eat the vegetables and bread? (cause)
2.   Why did she only eat a little from each plate? (cause)
3.   What did she do when she grew sleepy? (effect)
4.   Why did she have trouble finding a comfortable bed? (cause)
5.   Why did she stay in the seventh bed? (cause)
6.   What happened when the Seven Dwarfs lighted their candles? (effect)

Note: Understanding the above events is important to the development of the plot. Encourage pupils to finish reading "Snow White and the Seven Dwarfs" on their own.

B.   Learners read "Robinson Crusoe" (M. Canis, T. G. Anderson, & H. R. Webber (Eds.), 1976) silently. Teacher checks understanding of story plot and specifically monitors understanding of causal relations through learner retelling, probed recall, and responses to structured questions. In the text some causal relations are signaled and others are not. Teacher notes learners' performance, particularly for nonsignaled causal relations, for use in planning future lessons.

Robinson Crusoe
DANIEL DEFOE

Robinson Crusoe was an English sailor who loved the sea. One time as he was sailing near South America, his ship struck a reef during a storm and was shipwrecked. The sailors climbed into a lifeboat, but that was soon dashed to pieces on the rocks. Everyone was drowned except Robinson Crusoe, who was luckily washed to the shore of a deserted island. There was no one to help him find food or shelter, and there was no way to leave the island.

But Robinson Crusoe knew how to do things for himself. He swam out to the broken ship, which was stuck in shallow water. From the ship he took food, guns, ammunition, water, clothes, tools, sailcloth, and lumber. Then he built a crude raft and returned to the island. He was able to make twelve trips to the ship before another storm destroyed it.

With the sailcloth he made a tent on the side of a small hill. Then he built a fence with sharp-pointed stakes to protect himself against enemies that might come to the island. He did not have much food, but with his guns he killed birds and small animals which he could cook and eat. He also found several springs on the island which gave him all the water he needed.

After a while, he made a bigger and stronger shelter in a cave that he found near the tent. The cave protected him from bad weather. He built shelves and racks for his guns, and he built a table and a chair.

He was able to grow corn and rice and barley so that he could make bread. He carefully saved the new kernels so that he could plant more grain the next year. He also found some wild goats on the island. He tamed the goats, and they gave him all the milk and meat he could eat.

On the ship he had found a pen and some ink, and he kept a diary of what he did every day. The diary also helped him keep track of the days and months and years. He also had found three Bibles on the ship, and he read them carefully. Every day he thanked God for all that he had.

One day he took a walk along the shore of the island. Suddenly he saw some strange footprints in the sand, and he became frightened. Someone else must be on the island! He went back to his shelter and prepared for an attack, but no one came. He searched the island, and he could find no one.

Some time later as he was looking around the island, he found many bones lying on the sand. They were human bones! Robinson saw where a fire had been made, but the men who had made it had left.

Robinson Crusoe lived alone on this island for twenty-four years. Many times he felt lonely, and he wanted someone to talk to, but no one came to visit him.

Then one time Robinson saw on the beach a group of savages from another island. They were cannibals who were preparing to eat their prisoners.

When Robinson Crusoe saw what was happening, he shot some of the cannibals, and the rest ran away. He was able to rescue one of the prisoners, and they became friends. Now Robinson Crusoe had someone to talk to. He called his new friend Friday because Friday was the day on which he had found him. He taught Friday to speak English, and Friday became his faithful companion.

Four years later, a ship passed near the island, and Robinson Crusoe and Friday were rescued. Together they sailed back to Robinson Crusoe's home in England.

The following structured questions concentrate specifically on causal relations signaled by the words *then, so,* and *because.*

1. Why was Robinson Crusoe able to return to the island from the ship? (cause)
2. What did Robinson Crusoe do to protect himself against enemies? (effect)
3. Why was he able to make bread? (cause)
4. Why did he call his new friend Friday? (cause)

PLAN FOUR: CAUSAL RELATIONS—NONSIGNALED

Preactive Teaching

Teacher knowledge.   See section on p. 248 for teacher knowledge of causal relations.

Teacher decisions.   The teacher plans this strategy for fourth- or fifth-grade readers who have exhibited some difficulty in understanding causal relations in narrative text when the relation is nonsignaled. This group of learners is able to recall story plot and respond to questions involving causal relations when the author uses signal words such as *so, then, therefore, because, thus,* and *accordingly.*

The lesson, therefore, uses the readers' knowledge of signaled causal relations to expand understanding of nonsignaled causal relations. Material includes causal relations which occur in two sentences, short paragraphs, and longer discourse. Application material focuses on reader understanding of causal relations involved in plot development.

Interactive Teaching

Focus attention
Present the following sentence:

Joan has a stain on her dungarees because she spilled some paint.

Teacher-guided questions:

What did Joan do? (cause)

What happened when Joan spilled the paint (effect)

Discuss causal relation and have reader note signal word "because."

Present the following sentences:

Joan spilled some paint. She had a stain on her dungarees.

Teacher-guided questions:

How are these sentences different from the sentence above?

Has the meaning the author intended changed?

Present the following sentences:

The school bus had an accident. All the children were late for school.

Teacher-guided questions:

What happened to the school bus? (cause)

What happened to the children? (effect)

To ensure learner awareness of nonsignaled causal relations elicit the following generalizations:

1. An author may indicate a cause-effect relation without the use of signal words;
2. The reader needs to link ideas together to understand the causal relation;
3. Logical reasoning and prior knowledge are important in linking cause and effect.

Learning activities
    A. The teacher presents the following short paragraphs with guided questioning:

1. Robert caught his leg on a wire fence. He tried to climb down. His leg began to bleed.
    Why was Robert's leg bleeding? (cause)
2. Marie and John spent all evening watching ice hockey on television. Ice hockey is their favorite sport. The home team won 7–5.
    Why did Maria and John watch the ice hockey game? (cause)
3. The traffic on the highway was bumper-to-bumper. Mr. Reid wanted to get home in time for dinner with his family. He arrived home so late that everyone had finished eating.
    Why was Mr. Reid late? (cause)

Elicit through questioning that the cause and effect in each paragraph is a logical relation between two things. Have learners note that in paragraphs (1) and (3) the reason (cause) for the event precedes the action (effect), whereas in paragraph (2) the *effect* precedes the *cause*.
    B. Present several paragraphs for silent reading. Have learners underline the *cause* and label it with a *C* and underline the *effect* and label it with an *E*. Discuss responses after completion of each paragraph.

. . . I was awakened by the violent tossing of a kite. I at once realized from the black and threatening clouds that a sudden thunderstorm was rapidly approaching, its preliminary gusts were already tossing the kite wildly about.

Source: R. Lawson, 1939.

I was the only one who could feed the fox. . . . I knew how to slip the food in the pen without being bitten. But one weekend I went camping with the scouts, so my brother had to feed him. When I got back my brother had thirteen stitches from gashes the fox made. Mother said I had to get rid of the fox.

Source: B. Williams, 1972.

When it was time to take the test, Pete felt his heart begin to beat faster. It seemed to thump loudly, echoing its beat in his throat. It set up a distant ringing in his ears. Pete closed his eyes and tried quickly to remember what he had learned so far. Nothing came to his mind—nothing at all. Suddenly he felt a little sick.

Source: M. Cone, 1965.

C. Present the following events. Have pupils construct brief paragraphs using the event in a causal relation. The event may be either the *cause* of an action or the *effect* of an action.

1. All the electric power lines were out.
2. The subway tunnel was filled with people.
3. Arnold was an hour late for the movie.
4. The runners practiced every day for two months.

The teacher may duplicate learner-constructed paragraphs for group reading and discussion. Have learners note particularly how different students use the same event as *cause* or *effect*.

Application
    A.   Learners read silently the first two pages of Part I of "The Seven Special Cats" by R. Koenig (1961).

The Seven Special Cats
RICHARD KOENIG

Part I

Late one night, not long ago, the door of a New York skyscraper opened, and a cleaning woman by the name of Mrs. Thwickle came out and closed the door behind her. And at the same moment a whisker came out of a hole in the wooden steps leading up to the bolted door of an old abandoned house across the street. Behind the whisker was a cat, black and white, with four black paws and a white tail and a black round spot on its white back. The cat sniffed to make sure all was safe, and then it came all the way out of the hole.

The cat saw Mrs. Thwickle across the street, and Mrs. Thwickle saw the cat. Mrs. Thwickle liked cats very much. She always carried some chopped meat and liver in her bag. On her way home from work as she walked through the silent streets, she would stop here and there to feed the stray cats.

"You are new here, aren't you?" said Mrs. Thwickle.

The cat didn't say anything.

You will frequently find that cats do not answer you when you ask them a question. Mrs. Thwickle knew this, and she was not angry when the cat did not answer.

"I am Mrs. Thwickle," said Mrs. Thwickle, "and you are Leonore." (She liked to give names to all the cats she made friends with.)

"You poor thing," said Mrs. Thwickle. "You're hungry and frightened."

Leonore said, "Eyowr." (Not "Meow.")

"You've had a bad time," said Mrs. Thwickle, who knew cats very well. "I can tell from your fur that you were well taken care of and haven't been stray long. That's the worst," said Mrs. Thwickle. "To be in a nice home and then suddenly become stray."

The teacher asks the following questions to determine readers' understanding of causal relations.

1. Why did the cat sniff?
   (To see if it was safe and she could come out of the hole.)
2. Why did Mrs. Thwickle carry chopped meat and liver in her bag?
   (She liked cats.)
3. Why wasn't Mrs. Thwickle angry when the cat didn't answer her?
   (She knew that cats frequently do not answer when you ask them a question.)
4. Why did Mrs. Thwickle call the cat Leonore?
   (She liked to give names to the cats she made friends with; the cat made a noise that sounded like Leonore—"Eyowr.")
5. How did Mrs. Thwickle know that the cat hadn't been a stray for long?
   (From the cat's fur.)

B. Learners read the rest of Part I and Part II of "The Seven Special Cats" silently. Table 10.5 is a summary of the plot for the remainder of the story.

Table 10.5   "Seven Special Cats"—Summary of Plot

Mrs. Thwickle feeds and protects Leonore. One day Leonore has six kittens. All the cats live in an old house and Mrs. Thwickle takes care of them. One day the old house is torn down to make way for a skyscraper. Leonore and the kittens are missing. Suddenly life in New York City is disrupted. The cats are tying up traffic in the streets and tunnels and creating chaos in the subway system, the Stock Exchange, and the United Nations. The people of the city are afraid and are not sure of how many cats are causing the problems. The mayor is forced to negotiate with Mrs. Thwickle in order to bring the city back to normal. Today, you will find Mrs. Thwickle and the seven cats living in the basement of the new skyscraper. Sometimes the mayor visits them because he really likes cats.

The teacher checks understanding of story plot and specifically monitors causal relations by noting learners' retelling, probed recall, and responses to structured questions which require comprehension of nonsignaled causal relations. The following are sample structured questions and responses which involve understanding of causal relations as they relate to plot development.

1. Why was the old house going to be torn down?
    (A new skyscraper was going to be built.)
2. What happened to traffic on Fifth Avenue?
    (Traffic stopped.)
3. Why were the subway trains backed up?
    (Matilda was walking along the train tracks, and Mr. Noonan stopped the train.)
4. What happened in the Lincoln Tunnel?
    (All the cars bumped into each other.)
5. Why do you think the cats were tying up the city?
    (They were angry that their old house was being torn down.)

Encourage pupils to read Part III to find out what happened to the cats and Mrs. Thwickle.

PLAN FIVE: FIGURATIVE LANGUAGE

Preactive Teaching

Teacher knowledge.   Figurative language refers to language usage that goes beyond the denotative meaning of words to intensify meaning; if interpreted literally, figurative language would not fit the context. Through the use of figures of speech—the basic tools of figurative language—authors create mental images, sensory impressions, and connotations which heighten the interaction between reader and text. This interaction is vivified as figures of speech aid in transferring impressions of ideas, objects, or emotions through comparison, association, and emphasis by providing for creative language usage. This opportunity to describe ideas and objects

Table 10.6   Figurative Language

Type	Example
1. *Simile*—involves a comparison of objects or ideas bridged by words such as *like, as, than*.	1. The wind was like a tiger, pulling at my sweater. The wind was as cold as ice, nipping at my nose.
2. *Metaphor*—involves either a directly stated or implied comparison.	
a. Topic and descriptive words are directly stated and connected by a form of the verb *to be*.	2a. The wind was a tiger pulling at my sweater.
b. The comparison is implied, and the reader must construct associations between a topic and its descriptors.	2b. The wind roared as it pulled at my sweater.
3. *Allusion*—reference to a famous person, object or idea—Biblical, literary, historical or current—that is real or imaginary.	3. She was Joan of Arc in all her glory as she stood up for her ideals.
4. *Personification*—involves giving life or human qualities to that that does not have life.	4. The Sun smiled as it rose in the sky.
5. *Symbolism*—concrete objects or events that represent something else, usually an abstract idea; it can be a universal symbol or author-created symbol.	5. Roast turkey—Thanksgiving "V" sign—peace or victory

in new and imaginative ways is essential for communicators to achieve the fullest sharing of their ideas. For readers to construct full meaning from figures of speech they must be able to understand stated comparisons and infer relations.

Figurative language takes many forms. Table 10.6 indicates some common figures of speech with examples of each.

Metaphors are among the most frequently used figures of speech. They often serve as vehicles to relate new knowledge to old knowledge and provide opportunities for creating more holistic and vivid impressions of phenomena. While metaphors focus mainly on comparative aspects of language, they may also serve as vehicles for understanding things in new ways and for expressing what is literally inexpressible (Ortony, Reynolds, & Arter, 1977).

Teacher decisions.   The teacher plans this strategy for sixth- or seventh-grade readers who show some understanding of figurative language during reader-text interactions but who rarely use figures of speech in their writing. The lesson builds on the readers' prior knowledge of similes. The lesson focuses on comprehending metaphors directly stated and connected by a form of the verb *to be*. As research indicates that recall of metaphors appears to be good when the descriptors are within the readers' store of world knowledge, this strategy limits material to metaphors using vehicles known to readers. Further, since research seems to support the view that metaphors can serve the function of bridging new and old information when the passage material is less familiar, the lesson that follows includes unfamiliar passages (Pearson and others, 1979). Other research indicates that the comprehension of metaphors is related to the degree of contextual support. That is, when there is sufficient context, the reader invokes several schemata in order to comprehend the metaphor (Ortony and others, 1978; Ortony, 1979). Therefore, materials selected for this strategy lesson are of sufficient length to ease understanding of the metaphors.

Interactive Teaching

Focus attention
Present the following paragraph to pupils for silent reading.[3]

> Hurt and unable to move, Fred might not survive the cold. Jimmy knew he must get moving fast. It was three miles back to camp, and *the path was a snake that slithered through the underbrush.* He would have to *stick to it like glue.* If only he could see the path, . . . [Suddenly he thought of the river.] The river ran right through the middle of the campground. He could not see the river, but he could hear it. He would follow it back to camp.
>
>   Jimmy began to move down the path. It was easy to hear the river now, but in places the water moved slowly. There, *trying to hear the trickle of the river would be like listening for the sound of a pin dropping.* [Suddenly he stopped in his path. A bear was in the brush. Jimmy's *feet were weights of lead.*]
>
> _____
>
> **Source:** B. J. Hanson, 1980.

Teacher-guided questions:

Why does the author compare the path to a snake?

What kind of picture does the author create?

How can the author describe the path in a literal way?

Would the picture be as vivid if the author used literal language instead of figurative language?

The teacher elicits the information that authors often represent one idea in terms of another to enhance communication. The teacher uses similar questions to guide reader understanding of the other underlined similes and metaphors.

Learning activities
   A. The teacher presents the following paragraph to pupils and directs them to read it silently.

_____

[3]Teachers would underline words that are italicized here.

And in a few minutes I was on the ladder, lowering myself into the cold water. . . . When I reached the bottom rung of the ladder I could see under the ship's hull, and I glanced around. [The scene was an abstract painting of vivid colors merging. It was a kaleidoscope of changing colors and forms. Slowly, my goggles cleared and I looked around.] I was over a thick bed of kelp. The ends of the long strands of orange-brown seaweed reached up through the murky green water just to my feet, as if I were standing on the tops of trees in this strange underwater forest. Every now and then, the kelp tops bent in unison like long grass in an open field when a breeze passes. I could feel the shift in the water current, too. It was like a cold draft. [The wind was a sharp cold knife piercing at my body.]

Source: E. Clark, 1951.

Teacher-guided questions:

Why did the author describe the kelp tops "like long grass in an open field when a breeze passes?"

What kind of a picture did this create for you?

How might the author have described kelp tops without using figurative language?

Would this description have created as vivid a picture for you?

What type of figure of speech did the author use? Teacher elicits that the use of figurative language helped to create a more vivid picture using fewer words than a literal description.

Teacher repeats the above type of questioning for each of the following similes and metaphors.

Similes
As if I were standing on the tops of trees in a strange underwater forest.

It was like a cold draft.

Metaphors
The scene was an abstract painting of vivid colors merging.

It was a kaleidoscope of changing colors and forms.

The wind was a sharp cold knife piercing at my body.

Teacher elicits the differences between similes and metaphors.
B.   Learners read the following paragraphs silently noting the italicized metaphors. For each metaphor they are to substitute a literal description. Learners write responses and share them with the group.

1. Tom was enraged at his friends. They had breached his confidence. *His face was a storm cloud* as he approached their room.
2. John planned his business ventures carefully. Before he made a decision he investigated both corporate matters and the people. *He was a fox.*
3. *Her life was a fishbowl.* Jane could not remain at home any longer. She wanted her own place. Seven brothers and sisters were just too much for her to handle.

C. Have pupils choose three metaphors from the following list and write a paragraph incorporating each metaphor. Remind pupils that words or expressions can have different functions depending upon context. Emphasize that to maintain the status of metaphor each expression must be used figuratively.

1. Her cheeks were red beets.
2. He was a breath of fresh air.
3. It was a three-ring circus.
4. It was a big parking lot.
5. She is a diamond in the rough.

Learners share completed paragraphs with each other in small groups.

Application
Select a narrative similar to "Su An" (see p. 211) or a poem such as "The Even Sea" for independent reading.

The Even Sea

Meekly the sea
now plods to shore;
white-faced cattle used to their yard,
the waves, with weary knees,
come back from the bouldered hills
of high water,

where all the gray, rough day they seethed like bulls,
till the wind laid down its goads
at shift of tide, and sundown
gentled them; with lowered necks
they ambled up the beach
as to their stalls.

Source: May Swenson, 1958.

The discussion following reader-text interaction focuses on the author's use of figurative language. The teacher begins by encouraging learners to react to the poem. Depending on student responses, the teacher may ask questions such as the following to stimulate thinking and discussion:

1. What is the poem all about?
2. How does the author describe the waves at sundown?
3. How does the author describe the waves during the daytime?
4. To what does the author compare the waves?
5. What different images do these comparisons create for you?
6. Why is the poem called "The Even Sea?"

The teacher uses these questions only when learners need direction in order to focus on the meaning of the figurative language.

Summary

This chapter presents specific strategy plans in the areas of anaphoric relations, causal relations, and figurative language. For each area, extensive teacher background information provides illustrations of the depth of knowledge required to plan and implement strategy lessons. The chapter presents a lesson plan format with a variety of student learning activities. Each plan is designed so that students move from an introduction to the strategy, through a series of activities planned to increase their independent application of the strategy, to applying the strategy in a natural reading situation.

IV

USING CONTENT AREA MATERIALS FOR TEACHING READING

Examining Expository Text

In many ways authors and readers approach writing and reading of non-narrative text differently than they approach narrative text. In non-narrative text authors usually provide information using exposition that has a heavier informational load than narrative material. Authors write exposition more succinctly, with less informational redundancy and may use technical vocabulary. These differences involve variations in both structure (how the author presents the material) and content (what information the author presents). Also, readers of non-narrative text approach such materials with very specific purposes in mind.

Within the general purpose of reading for information, readers read for different purposes at different times. These purposes include: (1) to develop new background knowledge or to increase familiarity in a specific area; (2) to recall and retain specific information in order to perform successfully on some future task such as participating in classroom discussion, giving an oral report, taking a test, or writing a paper; (3) to locate and select information relevant to a particular problem or topic; and (4) to follow directions in order to carry out a specific task. Although the demands of schooling lead to an emphasis on reading to recall and retain information, the four purposes noted above relate integrally and are supportive of each other. To become proficient at gaining information from non-narrative text, readers must be aware of how these purposes relate and how to use them in a coordinated way in real-life situations. Teachers should think of the purposes for reading expository text and their related processes as constant and applicable to different reading levels and types of materials. Of course, content varies across grades and subjects.

This chapter covers the different types of expository texts, criteria for textbook selection, and ways of analyzing content area texts. Chapters 12 and 13 focus on the teaching of subject matter using textbooks.

Types of Expository Text

The major portion of non-narrative text school-age learners read is *textbook material*. Textbook reading involves an objective presentation of informational material related to specific subject areas, such as science, social studies, or mathematics. Subject area texts generally include graphic representations (graphs, charts, tables, diagrams, illustrations, and figures), typographical cues (chapter titles, headings, subheadings, bold-faced type, and italics), questions that may be found either at the beginning or end and/or are interspersed throughout the text, terminal aids (index, glossary, and tables), and introductory and summary paragraphs or sections.

Texts vary in the amount of specific information the author provides. Some texts introduce major concepts and lead readers to expand on them through such techniques as questioning or suggested activities. These texts encourage active involvement of readers as they move away from the text, act on their own environment through the use of additional resources, integrate ideas gained through a variety of experiences, and then return to the text with an enriched base of knowledge. In these texts the reader is a "doer." Not only does the reader reconstruct the author's message actively, but also the reader expands the author's message by responding to questions, researching posed problems, following directions for specific activities, and thus participating in text-related experiences.

In contrast, other texts, although also relying on the readers' background knowledge as an aid to comprehension, provide the reader with most of the information the author wishes to convey. In these texts the author does not encourage the reader, although actively involved, to go beyond the text to other sources of information. That is, the author gives the major ideas and specifics related to these ideas in the text.

Although textbook materials consume a large part of school-based content area reading, teachers should be familiar with and incorporate all types of non-narrative materials. Material such as autobiographies and biographies, essays, manuals, and reference materials should be used as an important part of the school curriculum to supplement content-area texts. Brief descriptions of each of these types of non-narrative reading materials follow.

Autobiographies and *biographies* provide the reader with a comprehensive picture of an individual and emphasize human values, motives, and emotions. An autobiography is an account of a person's life written by that individual, whereas biographies describe the life of an individual written by someone else. Although autobiographies and biographies are generally written in a narrative style, the reader brings a different framework to the reading of these materials because they have no "true plot" but present a study of human nature based on the elements of a person's life. The reader follows the unfolding of the life story to gain an understanding of the person. The picture of the person comes from the writer's perspective: The writer's perceptions and attitudes influence both the material selection and the presentation of the person.

Essays generally focus on a single idea, experience, or person and express the opinion of the writer. That is, they deal with a limited or personal perspective and reflect the author's biases. Essays are analytic or interpretive in nature and may use a narrative, autobiographical, or nonpersonal style. Essays are written on a limitless variety of subjects, are relatively brief, and express a wide range of writer tones.

Manuals or *step-order reading* involves the presentation of procedural guidelines for the reader to follow in a sequential order. This type of reading is "how to" reading or following directions. It presents a step-ordered process that leads to an end product and is frequently found in science in the form of directions for experiments; in arts and crafts requiring constructions; and in such diverse reading as recipes, directions for magic tricks, and game rules.

Functional reading, required for participating in day-to-day activities, includes street signs, applications, advertisements, catalogs, directories, schedules, and maps. Some of these materials are found in newspapers and magazines; other aspects of reading newspapers and magazines are also important in everyday functioning.

Reference or *locational reading* involves the reading of reference materials with a focus on material evaluation and selection. The goal is the gathering of specific information appropriate to a given purpose. In this type of reading the learner must be able to skim diverse sources of information to locate relevant content. Books, newspapers, periodicals, and original source documents are sources of information. Locational sources also include indices, encyclopedias, dictionaries, atlases, almanacs, and other specific books containing specialized information such as *The Readers' Guide to Periodical Literature*, *Bartlett's Familiar Quotations*, and *Roget's Thesaurus of English Words and Phrases*. Knowledge of the arrangement and services of a library, including use of card catalogs, is an essential component of locational reading.

Textbook Selection and Evaluation

Although most classroom teachers do not have direct input into the process of textbook selection, some teachers do serve on district or school-wide selection committees. And all teachers have the responsibility for evaluating the textbooks used in their classrooms. Although ideally the teacher should read each textbook carefully and in its entirety prior to its selection and distribution to a class, the teacher can evaluate a text by skimming purposefully and reading selected portions carefully. Purposeful skimming allows evaluation of the text structure and organization and the technical features of the book. The evaluation of the text content—which includes the authenticity and accuracy of the material, the way in which the concepts are developed, the specific language used by the writer, and the graphic aids—requires reading selected portions to obtain an adequate sample for decision-making. Decisions involve judgments as to the positive features of the text and awareness of any lack or negative features. Teachers' evaluations that indicate shortcomings generally lead to proposals or decisions such as the following:

1. Discard the text because the type and quantity of negatives make the book inappropriate for the group.
2. Use the text and supplement the content with other related materials, both published and teacher-constructed.
3. Use the text and clarify the author's organization.
4. Use the text, make learners aware of negative aspects, and discuss ways to improve the text.

Of course, even when teachers decide that the best solution is to discard a text, they may still be required by their administrators to use a poor text. In such cases they should use the materials with the adaptations noted in numbers 2, 3, and 4 above.

The following questions can guide the teacher in evaluating content area texts for classroom use.

TEXT STRUCTURE

1. Does the table of contents demonstrate a well-organized and detailed book?
2. Does the index cover important topics adequately?
3. Are glossary definitions precise and is a simple pronunciation key given?
4. Does the bibliography list additional related materials either at the end of each chapter or at the end of the book?
5. Do appendices supply pertinent supportive information?
6. Do chapter and marginal headings relate logically to each other?
7. Do clear introductory statements begin chapters and sections?
8. Do clear statements summarize each chapter and section?
9. Does the author organize the information within each topic with clearly presented relations between ideas?
10. Does the placement of visual aids (pictures, maps, graphs, charts, diagrams, etc.) make referencing easy?

TEXT CONTENT

A. **Authenticity and Accuracy**
   1. Is the author a qualified expert in the field?
   2. Is the copyright date recent enough so that the content information is current and not superseded?
   3. Are graphs, charts, maps, and illustrations sufficiently current?
   4. Do educators recognize the publishing house as one that produces high-quality texts?
   5. Does the author take an unbiased approach in discussing controversial issues?
   6. Does the author present women and men with similar human traits?
   7. Do women and men in the text participate in similar activities and have nontraditional as well as traditional occupations?
   8. Does the author indicate respect for minorities' languages, viewpoints, and culture?
   9. Do disabled people in the text work at a variety of occupations and participate in a variety of activities?
   10. Does the author characterize older people as having useful roles in life?
   11. Do women, minorities, disabled populations, and the aged have sufficient representation in the text?
   12. Does the author fully include the contributions of women and minority groups to the life and culture of the U.S.?

B. Concept Development

1. Are the main concepts in accordance with the school curriculum?
2. Are the concepts appropriate to the developmental level of the reader?
3. Does the author develop the concepts in terms that learners will understand given appropriate prereading activities?
4. Does the author elaborate sufficiently on the concepts so that teachers and learners can use supporting material?

C. Language

1. Is the language appropriate for the developmental level of the learner?
2. Is the language appropriate for the experiential background and reading proficiency of the learner?
3. Does the author use appropriate technical vocabulary for the content area?
4. Does the author use words or terms that alleviate society's misconceptions about women, minorities, people with disabilities and the aged?
5. Is the language nonsexist?

D. Graphic Aids

1. Do the illustrations, pictures, and other graphic aids support the content consistently and accurately?
2. Are the illustrations and pictures accurate representations of events, objects, or ideas depicted?
3. Do accurate representations of women, minorities, disabled populations, and the aged appear sufficiently often in illustrations and pictures?
4. Do the illustrations or pictures expand and/or clarify the text content without distracting from it?
5. Do the titles and labels convey clearly the meaning of the graphic aids?
6. Does the author clearly define the symbols used in maps, graphs, and tables?

TECHNICAL FEATURES

Criteria for evaluating technical features of a textbook are the same as for stories listed in Chapter 8.

We have referred to the following sources in developing the above listing. They give additional detail and provide excellent resources for the teacher:

ERS Report. *Procedures for textbook and instructional materials selection.* Arlington, Va.: Educational Research Services, 1976.

Guidelines for selecting bias free textbooks and storybooks. New York: Council on Interracial Books for Children, 1980.

Sutherland, Z., Monson, D. L., & Arbuthnot, M. H. *Children and books.* Glenview, Ill.: Scott, Foresman, 1981.

Need for Teacher Analysis of Text

Following the selection of text, the teacher needs to analyze the text to become familiar with its organization and content. Text analysis also makes teachers aware of their own construction of meaning and how it may differ from that of students. This is an important distinction. Because of their sophistication and familiarity with content area subject matter and materials, teachers are often able to function so efficiently that they can draw high-level inferences without conscious awareness. Based on prior experiences and knowledge, teachers may unconsciously attribute ideas to text not really there. Teachers may not sense gaps in the text and may expect that students will construct understandings similar to their own (Herber, 1978). Therefore, teachers should examine texts carefully with a predetermined formal and/or informal analytic framework in mind because reference to this framework can provide an objective base for study of the interaction between student and text.

Viewing reading as information gathering enables teachers and learners to put textbooks in their proper perspective: Students gain information from many sources, as texts do not necessarily provide all of the concepts the teacher deems important. Thus, teachers need to integrate information gained from textbook reading with broad curriculum objectives, and they cannot view textbook reading as an end in itself.

As teachers examine content area texts, they need to be cognizant of the subject area and the specific concepts to develop within a selected topic. Of course, they must be sure that the textbook presents sufficient information so that the reader can understand the concepts. The next step is to determine how the author has organized and presented the information. This involves analysis of the text to note the important ideas and relations between these ideas. The organization of the text is an important component in reading comprehension because the reader must be actively involved in processing the ideas as presented by the author. Therefore, to understand readers' responses based on text information, the teacher must be aware of concepts and form of presentation in the text. Knowledge of the structure and content of the text will enable the teacher to:

1. decide if the text is adequate in content coverage,
2. decide on materials to supplement the text if needed,
3. prepare experiences and/or materials to assess and expand prior knowledge of readers both in structure and content,

4. construct prereading activities and materials that serve to focus reader attention to guide comprehension,
5. understand the demands of the text on the reader and how these text demands relate to reader responses,
6. construct structured questions and related postreading activities.

   To prepare teachers for these activities, the following section focuses on text analysis that forms the base for teaching. The next chapter discusses planning for instruction and teaching activities.

Analysis of Text

Since textbook reading forms the major portion of non-narrative discourse read by learners in school, this type of exposition can illustrate text analysis. Previewing text often yields sufficient information for the teacher to guide and understand reader-text interactions. However, sometimes the teacher finds that a text may be particularly difficult for readers and, therefore, chooses to analyze the text in greater detail. One technique called mapping enables the teacher to examine closely the relations between the ideas in a text. We present the same text to illustrate previewing and to demonstrate how a text is mapped.

PREVIEWING TEXT

A textbook, a section of a textbook, a chapter within a section, and subsections within a chapter generally share a similar organization: The writer provides introductory material, explanatory or informational material, and summary material. This basic organization allows the writer to present information in a coherent fashion and to relate the ideas logically.

   In analyzing a selected piece of expository material the teacher gives consideration to the overall message of the author and to the way different parts of the selection contribute to the totality of the message. Toward this end, the teacher examines the selected material to note:

1. the general or specific topic,
2. the major concepts,
3. the topics and subtopics used to develop these concepts,
4. the logical presentation of the author's ideas,
5. the organization and function of each paragraph in its relation to others.

The subject of a selection and the major topics are generally outlined in the table of contents. In addition, different size bold-faced type designates topics and subtopics of a selection within the actual text. Using both the table of contents and the headings within a chapter enables the teacher to preview an author's major ideas easily.

   In the text, the author may logically present the main ideas in a series of paragraphs or even in one paragraph using either deductive or inductive reasoning. In using deductive reasoning, the write moves from the general to the specific, from a presentation of the main point to the supporting evidence or specific items of supportive evidence. In contrast, in using inductive reasoning, the writer moves from the specific to the general, presenting supporting evidence first before leading the reader to the generalization. The latter presentation encourages more active participation than the former because the reader works with the author to piece together the information to construct the generalization.

Most frequently paragraphs or groups of paragraphs develop around a generalization or statement of the author's major ideas accompanied by supporting information. This statement most often comes at the beginning or end of a paragraph. However, the author's main point may appear in any position in the paragraph, or the author may not directly state it and require the reader to infer or construct it.

We may, then, consider that a well-written paragraph contains a specific idea or a specific purpose. Furthermore, we may describe paragraphs as serving four general functions: to introduce, to give information, to provide transitions, and to summarize.

Introductory paragraphs come at the beginning of a chapter or topic and help the reader to focus attention on the information to follow. These paragraphs generally do not have as heavy an informational load as the paragraphs that follow. *Content-bearing paragraphs* are the most information-filled paragraphs because they describe, explain, inform, or tell about the topic. Writers develop these paragraphs using one or more method(s) of idea presentation. *Transitional paragraphs* maintain the flow of the material by briefly restating what the author has already said and by preparing the reader for new information to follow. *Summary or concluding paragraphs* review important ideas. Although they most frequently appear at the end of a selection, the author may place them throughout the selection to summarize important points.

The author often labels the content-bearing paragraphs according to the major form of idea presentation. Although paragraph labeling may be a useful way to describe paragraph patterns, note that more often than not paragraphs are not pure in form even though a particular type may predominate. The following are among the more common descriptors for paragraphs.

1. *Illustrations* and *examples*—general or specific—support a major idea, or concrete particulars clarify a generalization or concept.
2. *Definitions* clarify phrases. Generally, the words to be explained are technical and need relating to the context in which they appear. Frequently typographical aids such as italics or bold-faced type aid the reader in focusing on the technical vocabulary.
3. *Classifications* divide a topic into its parts or divide large groups into smaller categories according to their explained or described characteristics.

4. *Sequences* or *chronological presentations* temporally order information by tracing the development of an idea or event or a series of steps to follow.
5. *Cause-effect/effect-cause* shows a relationship between an event and its consequences.
6. *Comparison/contrast* show similarities and/or differences between two or more ideas, events, objects or people.
7. *Problem/solution* discuss and answer or solve a problem or question.

Two other types of paragraphs may appear in textbook material, although they more frequently occur in literary work.

1. *Narrative* paragraphs tell a story, anecdote, or incident. When used with expository materials, these paragraphs may generate interest, introduce important concepts or ideas, or connect explanatory paragraphs that have a heavy information load.
2. *Descriptive* paragraphs describe something by painting a verbal picture of the physical world through an appeal to the senses.

To review, teachers analyze non-narrative text to determine the structure and content of a selection and to note if the text adequately covers concepts emphasized in the curriculum.

Illustration

A section of the textbook, *The Social Sciences: Concepts and Values,* Grade 4 (Brandwein and others, 1970) illustrates text analysis based on the above framework.

Table 11.1 shows the overall organization of this textbook including the titles of six units and some additional detail on Unit Four from which we have taken the specific illustration.

To note the subject and overall presentation of content, the teacher has to recognize that this textbook emphasizes the relations and interdependence of people and nations. The author organizes the text into six broad units. We have selected one of these units, entitled "Acting to Share Resources," to illustrate how a teacher applies text-analysis procedures.

This unit begins with the following introduction, which uses a question and answer format.

Introduction

What would you do if you had earned some money? Would you spend it? Would you save it? Would you give it to a friend?

If you decided to spend the money, what would you buy? There are probably many things that you would like to have. Maybe you would not

Table 11.1 Overall Organization of Textbook

The Social Sciences: Concepts and Values

Unit One:	Acting in a Group
Unit Two:	Acting as a Person
Unit Three:	Acting to Use Resources
Unit Four:	Acting to Share Resources

*Introduction
1. Some Money of Your Own
2. Choosing and Planning
3. A Fair Exchange
*4. What's It Worth to You?
    The Story of Money
    Setting a Price
    The Law of Supply and Demand
5. Help Wanted
Summary

Unit Five:	Rules for Interaction
Unit Six:	Interacting as a Nation

*Sections presented in total in this chapter.
Source: From *The social sciences. Concepts and values*, Orange, Grade 4, by Paul F. Brandwein *et al*. Copyright © 1970 by Harcourt Brace Jovanovich, Inc. Reprinted and reproduced by permission of the publisher.

have quite enough money to buy something you wanted. Could you save your money until you had enough money to buy it?

Perhaps you would choose to buy a ball with your money. If you did, you would have to pay the price that the storekeeper set on it. How does the storekeeper decide how to set a fair price on his goods? How do goods get into the stores where you can buy them?

In this unit, you will learn how people share resources. You will learn how people depend on each other for their needs and wants. You will learn how people earned and spent money in the past. You will learn how they earn and spend money today.

Let's begin our study by asking what you would do if you had fifty cents.

The teacher notes that the information in the unit is divided into five sections, each focusing on different aspects of the exchange of goods and services. A brief description of the major concepts included in all five sections of this unit appears below.

Unit Four: Acting to Share Resources
Section 1: *Some Money of Your Own*

      People earn income by producing goods and producing services.

Both goods and services depend on the human resources of the country.

People make choices on the basis of availability and personal values.

Economists study the use of goods and services.

Section 2:   *Choosing and Planning*

People must choose how to spend money and how to use their resources.

Families, communities and the country make plans for the present and future based on choices.

Section 3:   *A Fair Exchange*

Trading is one way to get needed or wanted things.

Because resources are limited, people, communities, and regions of the world depend on each other for them.

Section 4:   *What's It Worth to You?*

People have not always used the kind of money we use today.

Mediums of exchange take many different forms.

A number of things influence the price of goods and services.

Section 5:   *Help Wanted*

People with special skills produce goods and services.

Efficient use of human resources requires a division of labor.

Each generation shares skills and knowledge.

The unit concludes with a summary of the major concepts presented and a transitional piece that highlights some problems in the regulation of goods and services that leads directly to the next unit on government entitled, "Rules for Interaction."

The focus of reader-text interaction will be in Section 4 of this unit, entitled "What's It Worth to You?"

---

4. What's It Worth to You?

Look at the pictures on this page. [The pictures in the original are of the items the text talks about.] If you had a choice, which would you take to the store to buy food? You would probably take the twenty-dollar bill.

Why would you choose the twenty-dollar bill? That's easy, you say. The twenty-dollar bill is money. Of course, you could sell the cow or the horse and use the money to shop. Or you could lead either the cow or the horse to the store and try to use it to pay for your food. Perhaps you wouldn't like to do this. But at some time and in some place, each of the things pictured was money. In Massachusetts, the colonists paid their taxes with cows!

The Story of Money

1. People have not always used the kind of money we use today. Sometimes they have not used money at all. They have depended on fair trades through barter. In barter, no money is needed. Recall the trading of baseball cards and the trading of animal furs for household goods.

2. At other times or in other places, some kinds of animals have been used as money. The prices of goods could be given in terms of the animals. That is, the price of a pair of sandals might be one pig. The price of a horse might be several pigs. The pigs were a medium of exchange, a tool for making trade easier. How much was a pig worth? It was worth whatever it could be traded for.

3. How much is a dollar worth today? It is worth as much as it will buy. A dollar is a symbol, isn't it? It is really only a piece of paper, but it means whatever it can buy.

4. In many places and at many times—even today—cattle have been used as a medium of exchange. So have horses, buffalo, reindeer, camels, sheep, goats, and pigs. But animals can get sick or be injured or just grow old and useless. A thin, sick pig is not worth as much as a fat, healthy one.

5. Some other things that have been used for money do not work well, either. Flour gets moldy, and salt isn't easy to use if it gets wet. In most places, people tried to find things which last a long time to use for money. For example, North American Indians who lived along the seashore used shells for money. They polished the shells and put them on a string. The strung shells were called wampum. Even the English and Dutch settlers used wampum as money.

6. Of course, many kinds of coins have been used for money. Iron, brass, gold, and silver coins have all been used because these metals have been thought valuable by many peoples.

7. The coins we use today are not pure gold or silver. But no matter what metals are used, each coin has the same value as another of the same kind. That is, a dime has the same value as any other dime. Of course, you know now that any kind of money is worth only what it can buy.

8. What kind of money is easy to carry and will last a long time? Coins are easier to use than animals and food. But all coins are heavy, especially when there are very many of them.

9. Paper is good to use for money. Can you see why? It is easy to carry and can be made so that it will last a long time. The paper used for money is much stronger than the paper you write on. It is stronger than the paper page of this book. You know that, when you decide to spend your dollar, you can buy something priced at a dollar with it. The face value of a

dollar is the value it has marked on it. The face value will not change, even if you keep it for months and months.

10.   Many people put their dollars in a checking account in a bank, where the money will be safe. Then, if they buy a television set, they can give the salesman a piece of paper called a check. The storekeeper takes the check as payment. Then he takes or sends the check to the bank. He knows that he can get the dollars that have been put in the bank by the buyer of the television set. The storekeeper can spend these dollars or can keep them in his own checking account.

11.   Today, much trading and exchanging is done with checks. Why is a check a good way to trade for goods? Name one way in which a check might be more useful than dollar bills.

Setting a Price

1.   How much is a cow or a horse or a box of salt worth? How do you know how much to pay for a pair of shoes or a new coat or a baseball glove? When you go to the store, the prices are already marked on what you want to buy. The price tells you very clearly what you will have to pay for it. But how does a storekeeper know what price to charge consumers for shoes or a coat or the glove?

2.   Remember that the storekeeper, too, buys the goods he sells. The owner of the factory where the goods are made must pay for the materials, labor, and other resources used to make them. The factory owner must sell his products at a price which will repay him for the cost of making the goods. But the factory owner wants to do more than this. He also wants to have some money left over for himself.

3.   The money that is left over is his profit. Why must the factory owner make a profit? He needs to buy food and clothing for himself and his family. He must pay rent. He has other expenses, too.

4.   A factory owner usually sells his products to a middleman. A middleman often buys goods in large amounts from factories that make different kinds of products. He then sells the goods to department stores and storekeepers. The services of a middleman cost money. He wants to make a profit, too.

5.   When the storekeeper buys the goods, he must pay a certain price for them. What other costs does the storekeeper have? Name some of them. How does the storekeeper decide the price that he will charge the consumer for goods?

6.   Suppose that one warm day in the summer, a girl about your age went with her mother to a store. They bought a pair of sandals for five dollars. The girl liked the sandals very much and showed them to all her friends. Some of them wanted sandals, too. Suppose that, within a few days, twenty more consumers went to the same store. Each of them wanted to buy a pair of sandals. But there were only five pairs of sandals left in the store.

7. An economist would say that there was a demand from twenty people for a supply of five pairs of sandals. Twenty girls wanted sandals. There were only five pairs. As you can see, the demand was greater than the supply.

8. Of course, the storekeeper was very happy. His sandals were priced at five dollars each. He could make a reasonable profit and sell all that he had.

9. The next day, the storekeeper ordered more sandals for his store. But by the time they arrived, the summer was almost over. The storekeeper had a large supply of sandals, but nobody came into the store to buy them. There was no demand. Then the storekeeper put a sign in his window. The sign said, "Sale! Sandals at Greatly Reduced Prices! "Only $4.00 a Pair!"

10. He had lowered the price on the sandals. The storekeeper had made his profit smaller on each pair of sandals. Do you think there might have been more demand for the sandals at the lower price?

11. To learn more about supply and demand, try the investigation on the next page.

The Law of Supply and Demand

1. Of course, the story you read about the storekeeper was just a story. It didn't happen exactly like that. But economists tell us that supply and demand do help to set the price on goods. The factory owner, the middleman, and the storekeeper must each be able to make a fair profit on their goods.

2. When there is enough of something for everyone who wants it, then the price is often low. When there is more than enough supply to meet the demand, the price tends to be low. When there is not enough of something for all who want it, then the price is often high. That is, when the supply is not large enough to meet the demand, the price tends to be high.

In planning for this interaction, the teacher notes that the general subject of this section is the value and use of different mediums of exchange. The teacher also notes that the author organizes information into three major topics in this section. The following are the major concepts on each topic:

Topic I: *The Story of Money*

    1. People have not always used the kind of money we use today.

    2. Whatever the medium of exchange is, it does not have a set value but is worth whatever it can trade for or can buy at a given time.

Topic II: *Setting a Price*

1. A combination of (a) the manufacturer's cost of materials plus a profit, (b) the middleman's cost of service plus a profit, and (c) the storekeeper's costs plus a profit determine the final price of goods.
2. Supply and demand may also influence the price of goods.

Topic III: *The Law of Supply and Demand*

1. When there is enough supply to meet demand, prices tend to be low.
2. When there is not enough supply to meet demand, prices tend to increase.

Note that by presenting questions not answered in the text, this author encourages the reader to expand knowledge by exploring resources outside the text. For example, the author does not answer the question "What other costs does the storekeeper have?" Also, both inductive and deductive reasoning patterns are used within parts of the text. For example, under *The Story of Money*, paragraph one is deductive, whereas paragraph two is inductive. Further, this section illustrates some of the ways authors organize ideas within and across content-bearing paragraphs. Paragraph one provides an overall framework that introduces the topic and a definition of the word *barter*, and paragraphs one and two provide examples of this concept jointly. The author uses effect-cause relationship in paragraph six that describes why people have used iron, brass, and silver for coins.

The presentation of a problem-solution occurs in paragraphs eight, nine, and ten. The problem is: What kind of money is easy to carry and lasts a long time? The author presents the solution, paper or checks, in paragraphs nine and ten. In moving toward this solution, the author presents low-level contrasts and comparisons by showing that coins are different from animals and food in that they are easier to use, and all coins are similar because they are heavy.

Under the topic *Setting a Price*, we find another example of problem-solution relations. The first paragraph presents the problem: How does the storekeeper know what price to charge customers for goods? The following four paragraphs partially answer this question by highlighting the costs involved in dealing with factory owners and middlemen. The reader can only piece together the full answer by going beyond the text to discover the additional costs the storekeeper incurs.

Paragraphs four and five under the topic *Story of Money* demonstrate the presentation of a problem not directly stated that the reader must infer from the many examples that illustrate the limitations of animals and food as mediums of exchange. The text presents the solution directly in paragraph five that discusses wampum and coins. Paragraph ten under the topic *Story of Money* describing the use of a check to purchase a television set illustrates sequence/chronological order.

Now that we have listed the major concepts for each of the three topics in the section "What's It Worth to You?" and pointed out some typical ways authors organize their ideas, we will show how the teacher can use the information under the heading *The Story of Money* to plan classroom activities.

The teacher previews this section to determine if the text includes the major concepts of the curriculum with supporting information. For example, the concepts noted in a teacher's curriculum guide on this topic could be as follows:

1. Throughout history people have used different mediums of exchange to acquire goods and services;
2. Society has developed methods to produce, allocate, and distribute goods and services for needs and wants;
3. Consumer awareness and action can influence the purchase price of goods and services;
4. Supply and demand affect prices of goods and services.

Teacher analysis of the text can lead to note-taking such as the following:

Story of Money

Concepts: 1. People have not always used the kind of money we use today.
        2. Mediums of exchange can take many different forms.
Major Idea: Barter or fair trade as a medium of exchange.
Subtopic: Animals or food used to barter.
Major Idea: Symbols for money and mediums of exchange.
Subtopic: Shells, coins, paper, and checks are symbols of money.

Further, the teacher, in previewing text, could classify the different mediums of exchange and their attributes. In Table 11.2 is one way to illustrate the groupings.

Such note-taking as described above enables the teacher to make sure the text adequately explains the concepts needed for the curriculum and to determine if expansion is necessary. Furthermore, analyzing text in this way sensitizes the teacher to the author's particular organization and presentation of ideas. And this knowledge also allows the teacher to understand the reader's construction of meaning. As readers freely recall text content and respond to probe questions, the teacher is able to assess whether reader responses reflect text organization and content.

If reader responses deviate from the text, the crucial questions are:

1. Are reader responses scriptally implicit ones that are appropriate?
2. Are reader responses inappropriate because text content and/or structure confused them?
3. Are reader responses scriptally implicit ones in which the reader brings inappropriate knowledge to the text?

Table 11.2 Classification of Mediums of Exchange

Medium of Exchange	Examples	Attributes or Properties
Goods Definition: Worth whatever they can buy	Animals cattle horses buffalo reindeer camels sheep goats pigs	sick, injured, old, useless
	Food flour salt	moldy, wet
Symbols for money Definition: Worth whatever they can buy	Shells wampum	last a long time
	Coins iron brass gold silver	valuable, heavy
	Paper bills checks	easy to carry, strong

For example, if during free recall of *The Story of Money*, a reader includes the use of charge cards along with checks as a way of buying goods, this would be considered a logical deviation from text based on the prior experience of the reader. However, if a reader focuses on animals as a medium of exchange and their attributes (sick, injured, old, and useless) without indicating that these characteristics led to the use of other mediums of exchange, this would be a clue to the teacher that the reader may have missed the causal relation inferred in paragraph five. This clue should lead the teacher to ask probe questions or structured questions to determine where meaning broke down.

On a simpler level a reader might recall only the names of the animals and their attributes without indicating that the animals were a medium of exchange. This would be a clue to the teacher that the reader may have missed the major points presented in paragraphs one and two. This clue should lead the teacher to determine where meaning broke down by asking a probe question such as "Tell me more about the animals," or structured questions to elicit if the reader understood the definition of barter given in paragraph one and the illustrations of animals being used as mediums of exchange in paragraph two. The teacher would ask questions such as the following: What is barter? What is used for barter? What is a medium of exchange? How much is a medium of exchange worth? What was the main problem in using animals as mediums of exchange?

MAPPING TEXT

Recently, several researchers have conceptualized a technique for text analysis known as mapping (Anderson, 1978; Armbruster & Anderson, 1980; Anderson & Armbruster, 1984). Mapping primarily involves analyzing the relationships between ideas within the content bearing passages of text. Thus, mapping is a diagrammatic way of viewing the author's organization and can provide structure for the teacher when guiding the reader to understand the important ideas in the text.

There are seven basic relations that teachers can isolate for the purpose of mapping most texts. These are (1) example, (2) property or characteristic, (3) comparisons and contrasts, (4) temporal, (5) causal, (6) enabling, and (7) conditional (Armbruster & Anderson, 1980). These relations represent typical patterns authors use to connect ideas in written discourse.

The symbols used in a map to designate relations appear in Figure 11.1 along with an example for each symbol. These symbols and their accompanying explanations (legend) are adapted from the work of Anderson and Armbruster (1984).

Illustration

In previewing the section "What's It Worth To You?" several teachers indicated that they found the writing in the first topic *The Story of Money* confusing. Teachers noted that the relations between the ideas were often not clear, and readers might become confused as a result of the author's structure. For example, the author used a flashback technique without explicit cuing (see *The Story of Money,* pp. 281–82.) Based on this teacher feedback, we have selected this section for mapping. This visual mapping of relations between ideas, as the author specifically presents, helps the teacher in noting these points in the text that may present readers with problems in constructing meaning.

Probably educators will develop a number of paradigms for mapping text. For the classroom teacher, the recognition of the relations between the ideas presented in the text is of importance, and any one of several visual displays can serve this function. The map of *The Story of Money* (Figures 11.2A, 11.2B, and 11.2C) uses the symbols presented in Figure 11.1. It indicates visually that this section of the text has a number of related ideas, each of which is expanded by descriptive and explanatory material. The map is one way of illustrating the many relations readers should infer.

We will now present the ideas from *The Story of Money* that have been mapped beginning with the first section shown in Figure 11.2A. The *idea* that people have not always used the kind of money we use today provides

SYMBOL[1]		LEGEND
A. *Concepts*		
	B / A	1. Examples: A is an instance of B.
	B / A	2. Properties or Attributes: A is a property of B.
	B / Define A	3. Definition: A defines, restates, clarifies B.
B. *Causality*		
	A ⟹ B	1. A causes B.
	A ⟹⟫ B	2. A does not cause B.
	A and B ⟶ C	3. A and B cause C.
	A ⟶ B or C	4. A causes B or C.
	A ⟹ B ⟹ C	5. A causes B causes C.
C. *Comparison*		
	A ≈ B	1. A is similar to B.
	A ≉ B	2. A is not similar to B.
	A > B	3. A is greater than B.
	A < B	4. A is less than B.
D. *Temporal*	A ⟶ B	1. A occurs before B.
E. *Enablement*	A ⟹ B	1. A enables B.
F. *Adversative*	A / but / B	1. A but B

[1]The size of the symbols in this figure are much smaller than they would need to be in an actual map. Symbols vary in size to accommodate the amount of text.

EXAMPLE	MAP OF EXAMPLE

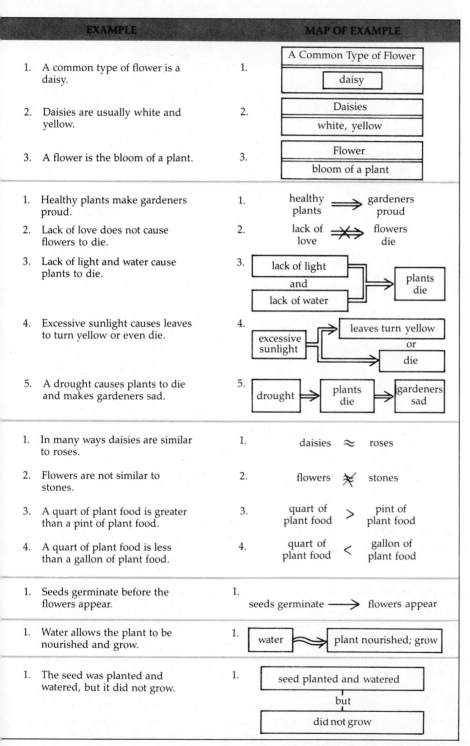

1. A common type of flower is a daisy.

2. Daisies are usually white and yellow.

3. A flower is the bloom of a plant.

---

1. Healthy plants make gardeners proud.

2. Lack of love does not cause flowers to die.

3. Lack of light and water cause plants to die.

4. Excessive sunlight causes leaves to turn yellow or even die.

5. A drought causes plants to die and makes gardeners sad.

---

1. In many ways daisies are similar to roses.

2. Flowers are not similar to stones.

3. A quart of plant food is greater than a pint of plant food.

4. A quart of plant food is less than a gallon of plant food.

---

1. Seeds germinate before the flowers appear.

---

1. Water allows the plant to be nourished and grow.

---

1. The seed was planted and watered, but it did not grow.

Figure 11.1   Symbols for Mapping

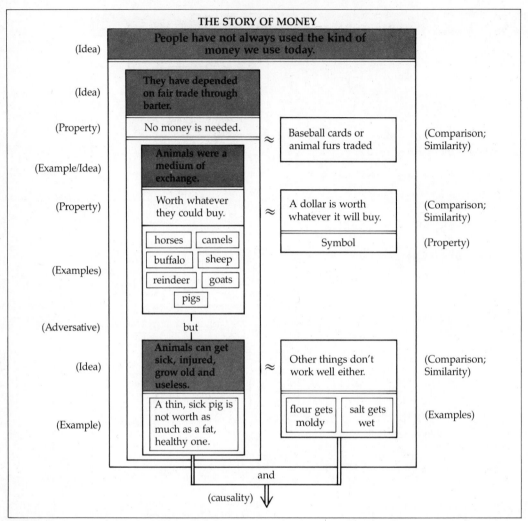

Figure 11.2A Beginning Section of Map

the historical framework for discussing mediums of exchange beginning with barter (Figure 11.2A) and concluding with checks (Figure 11.2C). The *idea* that people have depended on fair trade through barter is developed by providing a *property* of barter and *comparing* it to the trading of baseball cards and animal furs. This is followed by a concrete *example* of bartering (animals). This *example*, which also provides an additional *idea*, is then described by presentation of its major *property* and *examples* of specific animals. The text then *compares* the major *property* of animals used for bartering—worth whatever they can buy—to the present dollar that is also worth whatever it can buy and described, therefore, as having the *property*

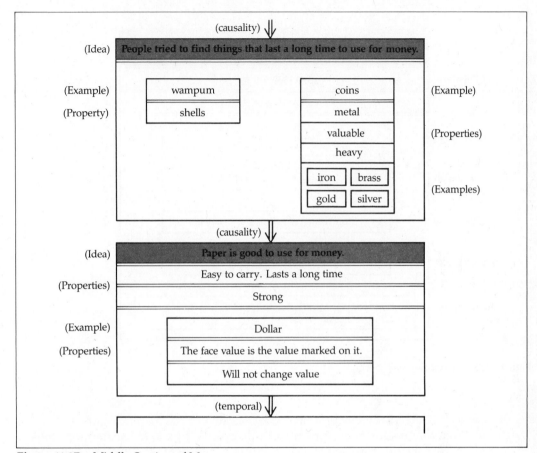

Figure 11.2B   Middle Section of Map

of being a symbol rather than having a set value. The author then returns to the specific *idea* of animals as a medium of exchange and gives us a new *idea* that points out a major limitation (*adversative*) and gives us an *example* to support this contrast. At the same time, the author notes that other items (flour, salt) used as mediums of exchange have also had problems similar to the use of animals (*comparison*).

We now continue with the next section of the map (see Figure 11.2B). All of the limitations of using animals and other items as mediums of exchange have led people to find other mediums of exchange that would last a long time (*idea*), and the author indicates these through a *causality* relation. The author also gives some *examples* and *properties* of these new mediums of exchange. The fact that coins were heavy (*property*) led to the *idea* of paper as a medium of exchange. *Properties* of paper money and an *example* with its *properties* are given.

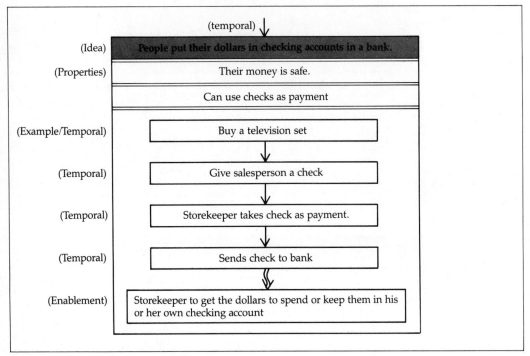

Figure 11.2C   Final Section of Map

And, finally, we present the last section of the map in Figure 11.2C. The author begins by relating the *idea* that paper is good to use for money to the *idea* of storing dollars in a checking account in a bank. This is a continuation of the sequence describing people's use of money (*temporal*). *Properties* of banks and checks are given with an *example* using a *temporal* sequence. This *example* is of the use of a check to purchase a television set. This temporal example concludes with a statement of *enablement* indicating how the sending of the check to the bank enables the storekeeper to make a choice about his money.

As you can see, mapping text gives the teacher a framework or schema for viewing the relations between ideas. It highlights the many different relations both presented and inferred in text and helps the teacher to become aware of how authors write content area texts. Once a teacher has internalized the basic patterns used in mapping a piece of text, this knowledge becomes useful in observing reader-text interactions even when the teacher has not formally mapped a particular piece of text. Knowing the categories involved in mapping enables the teacher to "map" (spontaneously break down) a piece of text mentally. This helps the teacher in interacting with readers to clarify the major ideas and their relations. This spontaneous "map" is not an array of the text but a mental guide to understanding reader responses and formulating questions. Thus, although visually mapping text as previously described may be a useful technique at certain times, teacher knowledge of how to map a text is most important because the teacher can apply this knowledge as required in many different reading situations.

Other Approaches to Text Analysis

Although a general approach to text analysis and mapping are the primary focus of this section, the work of other researchers is also relevant. Kintsch and van Dijk (1978) and Kintsch (1979) have formulated a method of text analysis based on propositions or idea units to describe those cognitive processes involved in text comprehension. Their analysis includes the phrase-by-phrase processing of text (microstructures) and the more global summary producing structures (macrostructures) that condense information into units that memory can store easily. Inferences based on world knowledge are an important aspect of this model. This model of text analysis is not limited to expository materials but may be used with any type of text.

Another researcher, Meyer, also focuses on propositions as idea units. She confines her structural analysis procedures to expository text and analyzes the text according to hierarchical content structures (Meyer, 1975; 1977). These content structures depict the major and minor relations the author uses to organize text. Her representation is similar to an outline of a passage but encompasses all of the ideas and their relationships. She classifies passages into different types of expository text on the basis of differences in top-level (overall) structures. A major difference between her text-analysis system and that of Kintsch is that Meyer's representations do not include any reader inferences since her purpose is to focus solely on the structure and content of the text. According to Meyer, the major relations in expository text are (a) response, which relates a problem or question to a solution; (b) adversative, which relates what did happen to what did not or one view to an opposing view; (c) covariance, which relates an antecedent condition to a consequence thus relating causal structure; and (d) attribution, which relates a collection of attributes or properties to an event or idea.

Some researchers have taken different routes. In contrast to propositional analysis, Halliday and Hasan (1976) base their work on cohesion in text on analysis of those relations of meaning that allow text to be a unified whole as opposed to an unrelated listing of ideas.

> Cohesion occurs where the INTERPRETATION of some element in the discourse is dependent on that of another. The one PRESUPPOSES the other, in the sense that it cannot be effectively decoded except by recourse to it. When this happens, a relation of cohesion is set up, and the two elements, the presupposing and the presupposed, are thereby at least potentially integrated into a text. (p. 4)

Thus, elements in text cannot be interpreted without reference to other text-based information; this relatedness of information allows for unity of a piece of writing or cohesion. The author expresses this cohesion through syntax and vocabulary. Halliday and Hasan's work provides a description of the cohesive elements or patterns in text—such as anaphoric reference or conjunctions. Their work adds a new and important dimension to the theoretical work on text analysis because previous work has not focused on cohesion.

Although we do not describe these other approaches to text analysis in detail, you can see that aspects of these paradigms are evident in the preceding illustrations. Although each researcher may focus on different aspects of expository text structure and function, they do overlap with the different paradigms often complementing each other. Whereas educators today view text analysis primarily as a research tool, such analysis does serve to increase understanding of the many relations inherent in text and provides a valuable basis for further inquiry.

Summary

This chapter focuses on examining expository text. Prior to describing ways of analyzing text, the chapter discusses the different types of expository texts and presents criteria for textbook selection and evaluation. The chapter describes two approaches to analyzing text, previewing text and mapping, in detail using social studies material to illustrate each analysis. In addition, the chapter presents a brief overview of other research on text analysis to stimulate further teacher inquiry.

Teaching Expository Text

The previous chapter discussed the selection of nonnarrative texts and some ways of analyzing informational material. This chapter builds on this knowledge and uses the teaching framework described in Chapter 4 to teach content area material. The chapter will describe and illustrate prereading activities, self-monitoring activities, and postreading activities using materials from social studies and science texts. Although some of these activities are similar to those used with story-type material, many are specifically for use with exposition.

Prereading Activities

These activities fall into three main categories: activities to elicit prior knowledge, to build background knowledge and establish purposes, and to focus learner attention (see Figure 12.1).

ELICITING PRIOR KNOWLEDGE

The major activity, eliciting learners' existing knowledge of a specific subject, is an open-ended discussion between students and teachers. This discussion uses teacher- and student-generated questions, pictures and/or other objects or materials to stimulate verbal interchanges. The questions encourage learners to associate their experiences and knowledge to the content of the prospective text. For example, prior to reading *The Story of Money* with the class, the teacher could bring in objects such as coins, checks, charge cards, or a picture of Indians trading with settlers. Questions such as "What have you purchased lately?" "How much did it cost?"

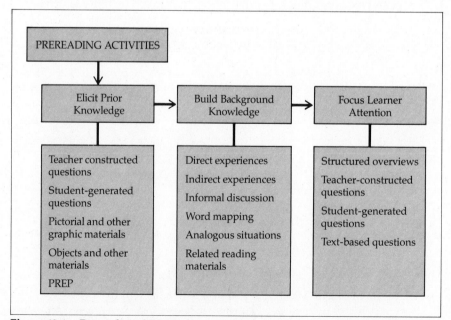

Figure 12.1   Prereading Activities

Figure 12.2   Material to Stimulate Discussion

"Did you ever get something without buying it?" would generate a discussion in which ideas relevant to the topic would come to the fore.

As part of this discussion, the teacher could use materials such as the advertisement in Figure 12.2 found in a local weekly newspaper.

A more structured group discussion to elicit prior knowledge involves a technique known as PREP (Langer, 1982). The first step is for the teacher to analyze the text and select a word, a phrase, or a picture that will stimulate discussion of an important concept in the text. For example, for *The Story of Money* the teacher would select the word *money* and would proceed as follows:

1. The teacher says: "Say anything that comes to mind when you hear the word *money.*" Then the teacher writes responses on the chalkboard.

This type of statement encourages students to probe as many links as possible about a given idea. Students may access ideas that may not be a part of the teacher's expectations. The teacher accepts these ideas non-judgmentally and may help students to refine or expand them during phases 2 and 3.

2. For each response given in phase 1, the teacher asks the respondent, "What made you think of _____?"

As students focus on why they thought of a particular response, they are becoming aware of their thinking strategies. Further, in this step they hear each other's ideas, interact, and evaluate their own and others' contributions as they relate to the concept under discussion.

3. The teacher says, "Based on our discussion, have you any new ideas about money?"

During this phase students expand their own ideas based on associations developed during group discussion and awareness of their own strategies.

Langer (1982) states that teachers may differentiate between the amount of prior knowledge a student has by noting kinds of associations a student makes. Responses that involve superordinate concepts, definitions, analogies, or a linking of two concepts usually indicate high knowledge. Responses that take the form of examples, attributes, or defining characteristics generally indicate a moderate knowledge, whereas low-level associations such as morphemes, words that sound like the target word, or first-hand experiences usually indicate limited prior knowledge of the concept being developed.

BUILDING PRIOR KNOWLEDGE

The teacher must help to build prior knowledge for those learners who indicate they possess insufficient background to understand a selection fully. The teacher can plan direct and indirect experiences to build needed concepts and vocabulary. Direct experiences include participating in related activities both in and out of the classroom. These direct experiences involve such activities as manipulating objects and things in the classroom, observing events and phenomena in the environment, participating in experiments, interviewing resource people, and taking trips within the school environment and the broader community. Indirect experiences include such things as listening to stories, guest speakers, recorded speeches, music, and plays, reading related narrative and non-narrative materials, and viewing films and film strips.

For example, direct experiences related to *The Story of Money* include visiting a store or a bank to observe the use of money or interviewing a storekeeper about how he sets prices for his merchandise. Indirect experiences include listening to *Jack and the Beanstalk* that introduces the concept of barter and fair exchange. Where appropriate, a guest speaker or film can add another dimension.

A second way to build background knowledge needed for reading is through vocabulary expansion. The teacher can accomplish this through informal discussions incorporating unfamiliar words within a familiar context and more formal structured presentations of new words in written context. For example, in giving background for *The Story of Money*, the teacher can relate her/his experience in going shopping, going to the bank, or having difficulties in cashing a check. In relating these episodes informally, the teacher incorporates those concepts and vocabulary that readers will encounter formally in the text.

Another way to build knowledge at the concept or word level is by building on Klausmeier's model of concept learning and development (see Chapter 3). As we have noted, experts have hypothesized that several stages of concept development exist. For example, objects or ideas may not be familiar, individuals may or may not discriminate various forms of the same object from each other or know examples and nonexamples or the attributes or name of an object. If learners have reached the classificatory or formal levels, they may be able to use their knowledge base to generalize to new instances, to categorize superordinate-subordinate relations, and to recognize cause and effect and other relations among concepts. Mapping learners' responses as they freely associate to a presented word can both indicate to the teacher the depth of prior knowledge related to the concept and provide the base from which to expand learner knowledge prior to text interaction. To do this, the teacher uses a simplified form of mapping technique discussed in Chapter 11 for text analysis. The teacher writes the word or concept on the board, elicits reader associations to the word(s), and visually lays out the learner-generated associations to clarify them for the group. This allows the teacher to guide readers in determining relations between different concepts, relations between classes of things, and relations between a particular concept and its examples and attributes (Pearson & Johnson, 1978). This simplified form of mapping is a particularly good tool for helping readers integrate prior knowledge with their expanded knowledge before reading.

Based on the associations elicited from learners, the teacher decides if expanding further learner knowledge prior to reading is necessary. The teacher can often determine this during mapping and class discussion. At other times the teacher will determine that the learners' knowledge base is too limited to benefit sufficiently from this type of interaction. The teacher then provides direct and indirect experiences as described above. Following these experiences the group then returns to the map to add newly learned associations. Adding to the map following reading provides an excellent additional technique that reinforces concepts gained from reading and assesses learners' knowledge gain.

A map for the word *money* that a teacher and a third-grade class developed prior to reading *The Story of Money* follows in Figure 12.3. Note the differences in the associations elicited from third-grade students as compared to the fifth graders as Figure 12.4 illustrates.

The teacher can help the class to expand these maps depending on reader-text interactions and follow-up discussions. The PREP technique described above and the word-mapping approach are similar: They both use word associations and share elements of elicitation and expansion of prior knowledge. The differences are that PREP primarily assesses prior knowledge, whereas word mapping expands prior knowledge. This latter technique permits the probing and expanding of relations within and between concepts in greater depth.

Further, background knowledge may increase through the use of analogous situations to relate existing knowledge to new knowledge. Since an analogy provides a comparison that can explain a difficult idea or concept by pointing out its similarities to something easier to understand, analogy

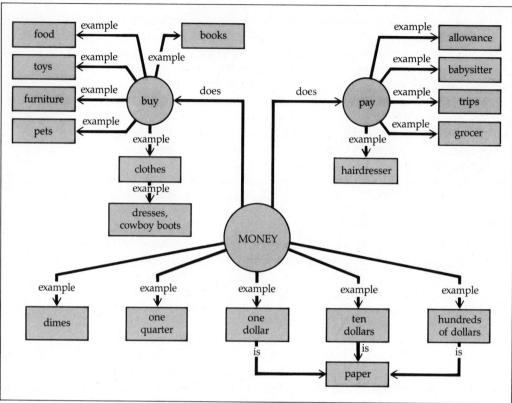

Figure 12.3   Semantic Map of Money (Grade 3 NYC public school)

can facilitate the expanding of learners' knowledge (Hayes & Tierney, 1980). For example, to help students understand the concept of bartering for goods during the early American period, the teacher initiates a discussion of situations in which children trade books, toys, games or other belongings. The discussion establishes the idea that both "traders" must be willing to exchange goods and that the goods must be of equal value to the traders. Ideally students set up their own bartering system in the classroom. This activity facilitates learners' ability to understand the trading of animals and food for other goods and services when they are reading about bartering in *The Story of Money*. And this concrete experience is analogous to an example given in the text.

At times, the teacher may find it helpful to provide related reading materials that incorporate new vocabulary. These reading materials are at a level of difficulty lower than the text to be read to enable the reader to focus easily on the concepts being developed prior to meeting these same concepts in the actual text. The teacher creates this context-rich material following group discussions with learners using a language-experience approach, or the teacher may prepare sentences, paragraphs, or short

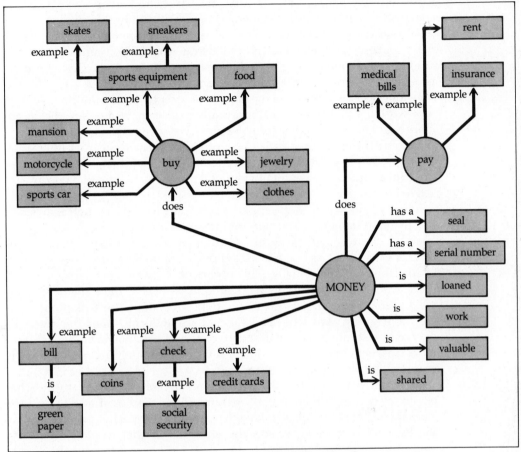

Figure 12.4 Semantic Map of Money (Grade 5 NYC public school)

passages in advance. Sometimes during prereading activities, encouraging learners to read expository material on the same topic but at a simpler level than they would ordinarily read is beneficial. This type of introductory exposure to the content provides an opportunity for learners to become familiar with the major concepts they will encounter in a form that is relatively easy for them to process.

FOCUSING READER ATTENTION

Another important component of prereading activities is establishing purpose(s) and focusing learner attention on those parts of the material that will facilitate achieving these purpose(s). Whereas students read material for many different purposes, the primary initial goal for reading expository text, as we have emphasized, is to learn to understand text information by reconstructing the major ideas. Some techniques for helping the reader to focus on the major ideas in text are structured overviews, teacher-constructed questions, and student-generated questions.

The structured overview technique uses key vocabulary to highlight the main concepts of a selection and to illustrate the relations among them. In addition to demonstrating the relationships among words, this technique provides a framework that helps learners focus on new ideas and information, develops a context using familiar words to clarify the meanings of new words, and provides an opportunity to learn or review specific vocabulary acquisition skills that some learners may need (Herber, 1978).

The structured overview may be a product of teacher-learner interaction (Herber, 1978) or a totally teacher-generated product (Earle, 1969). In keeping with an interactive point of view, the former technique that encourages active learner involvement is preferable.

Initial planning for a structured overview involves teacher analysis of text to determine major concepts and relations among ideas. Following this analysis, the teacher selects the words that represent key concepts. The teacher then arranges these words in one or more structured overviews to lay out the relations visually. This preliminary diagraming is primarily for the teacher to guide learners as they jointly develop the structured overview used during reader-text interaction. Of course, the structured overview the group develops may take different forms from the teacher's overview. Although some patterns of concept relations may follow the text more closely than others, any one of several is generally acceptable and the graphic display will vary in form.

To develop a structured overview for *The Story of Money*, the teacher begins by writing "mediums of exchange" on the board and asking the learners for words or ideas that come to mind. The teacher jots down all of the learners' responses, selects the word *money* that would be typically among the group of responses, and draws a line connecting the phrase "mediums of exchange" to the word *money*. In selecting the word *money* from among the learner responses, the teacher is careful to note that all the responses are good ones but that money was selected because the prospective text deals with money. The teacher then adds the word *barter* and tells students that barter is also an important concept because they will study about the history of money and how barter was a way to exchange goods before money was used.

At this point the structured overview looks as follows:

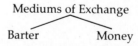

Mediums of Exchange

Barter   Money

The teacher elicits from the group their associations with the words *barter* and *money* based on prior knowledge and experience. From among the responses given, the teacher adds those words related to the major concepts in the text. For example, students might know that animals and food were used to barter and that coins, paper, and checks are forms of money used for purchasing goods. At this point the teacher makes a mental note that *barter* and *money*, although important concepts, are not equal level classifications. The teacher knows that money is used for purchasing in the same way that animals and food are used for bartering and, thus, that barter and purchase have equal weights, with money being on a similar level as animals or food. The teacher now makes one of two choices. If the words *purchase* or *buy* do not come up during further discussion, the teacher inserts one of these words at the same level as the word *barter* and discusses the relation between the two concepts and the idea that to barter goods and to purchase goods are both forms of trade. The word *trade* may also be added to the structured overview. Or the teacher knows that the text develops the concepts *barter* and *purchase* and may decide to wait until after the class reads the text to adjust the structured overview. This second choice is the one to make if the teacher judges the existing structured overview to be sufficiently detailed for the particular group of learners. Regardless of the options used, the teacher continues to construct an overview. The teacher may need to add the word *wampum* and indicate to the group that just as coins, paper, and checks are symbols for money, wampum—which the early settlers used to trade with the Indians—was also a symbol for money. At this point the teacher may add the word *symbol* to the diagram and discuss the concept. The teacher then introduces the idea that all mediums of exchange have value and discusses this idea using the learners' understanding of the term *value* from their past experiences. The teacher may tell them that as part of their reading they will learn about the value of money and other mediums of exchange. The final structured overview that the group will use may look as shown in Figure 12.5 if the teacher chooses to expand learners' concepts of barter and purchases prior to reading.

Teachers may also use questions to focus readers' attention prior to reader-text interaction. Forcing learners to attend to aspects of the text considered important leads to increased retention of the highlighted information (Reder, 1980). We emphasize that questions that highlight information should not just ask learners to duplicate information in the text but should require them to integrate important ideas in the text. This higher-level questioning encourages the learner to evaluate and integrate

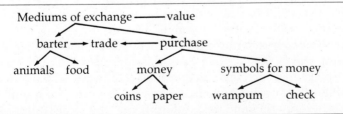

Figure 12.5   Structured Overview for *The Story of Money*

information rather than to process the material in a textually explicit or replicative way. Such questions may be teacher-constructed or learner-generated depending on the topic and learners' prior knowledge. Teacher-constructed questions develop during the planning stage and are specific and designed to focus reader attention on important concepts, to determine important relationships between ideas, and to integrate information during text processing. An example of a teacher-constructed question for *The Story of Money* is "How does the use of barter differ from the use of money?"

Student-generated questions generally follow activities designed to elicit prior knowledge and activities designed to build needed background. Sometimes to stimulate specific learner-generated questions, the teacher will pose general questions. In the case of *The Story of Money*, the teacher may ask, "What else do you want to know about the history of money?" or "Based on our discussion of bartering, what additional information do you expect to get from reading the text?"

The text may or may not answer the student-generated questions resulting from these teacher-posed questions. However, having learners ask questions encourages active processing and guides learners in assessing what information is and is not available in the text (Singer & Donlan, 1980).

If students have difficulty in stating questions, learning how to question becomes a part of the prereading activities. Teaching may consist of modeling of questioning techniques and discussing the "question words" such as *how, why, when, where, what,* or *who,* so that students learn to generate successful questions and to use question words. This activity also builds in teacher and student evaluation of questions. As the teacher writes questions on the board, students evaluate their relevance to the topic under discussion and predict what type of information they can expect in the answer, given the structure of the question.

Learning how to generate questions during group situations also has relevance for future independent reading situations. With practice in questioning and ongoing activities that encourage application of questioning techniques, learners can move from group generation of questions to independent production of their own questions. Independently formed questions are an integral part of most study formulas such as SQ3R (Survey, Question, Read, Recite, Review) designed for recall and retention during self-guided study of expository texts (Robinson, 1961). In learning how to apply SQ3R and other study techniques, students learn to generate questions based on introductory material, headings, and summary material. Experiences with creating questions in a group setting may enable students to develop better questions independently. Increased experiences in developing and evaluating questions should lead to lesser emphasis on textually explicit questions than on questions that require integrating ideas and applying prior knowledge to new knowledge.

Once learners understand text information, they can fulfill specific reader purpose(s). Thus, reading for specific purposes generally does not occur until a first reading has established familiarity with the content and structure of the text. Once the reader understands the major concepts and the author's organization is clear, the reader can narrow the focus and reread the material for specific purposes. These specific purposes fall into two broad categories: (1) to recall and retain text information and (2) to seek additional information in order to answer research questions or to solve problems stimulated by reader-text interaction.

Included in the category designated retention and recall of information are such specific learner objectives as following directions, conducting an experiment, taking a test, writing a report, engaging in discussion, or participating in a debate. Knowing why one needs to retain and recall information or knowing what one will do with information leads to variations in attention, effort, and focus.

Although the main goal of reading text is to construct meaning, knowing the specific purpose(s) for which the reader will use text information encourages the reader to simultaneously read for meaning, allocate special attention to certain parts of the text, and determine those parts of the text to reread. For example, if a reader knows that the specific purpose for reading *The Story of Money* is to participate in a debate on the relative merits of using checks as opposed to using money, the reader reads initially for the major concepts of the entire selection and notes where to find and reread specific information relative to the debate. In addition, the reader generates questions to guide information-seeking if information beyond that given in the text seems necessary to support the readers' point of view. If, on the other hand, the reader knows that a short-answer test on the entire selection is coming, the reader attends to the total text both in the initial and rereading stages and pays particular attention to how the details relate to the major concepts.

Monitoring Reader-Text Interaction

Once the teacher has elicited and developed background knowledge and focused reader attention on the purpose(s) for reading and the important concepts to be gained from the text, the reader is ready for direct interaction with the material. An integral part of this interaction is the self-monitoring of progress. This self-monitoring or metacognition consists of those strategies the reader uses to judge whether comprehension is occurring and those compensatory strategies that adjust the interaction between the reader and the text when the reader has problems constructing meaning (Brown, 1980, Baker & Brown, 1984).

These strategies are similar to those described for self-monitoring of reader interaction with narrative text (see Chapter 9, pp. 206–207). The major difference is that here teachers encourage learners to think about the specific word maps, structured overviews, teacher and/or student generated questions, and purposes generated during prereading activities. Further, readers think about whether the information that the author provides makes sense and is either consistent with or in conflict with their knowledge of the topic. As relations between ideas are of primary importance in comprehending expository text, readers reflect on the author's presentation of ideas and the relations between them. When the information in the text is not sufficiently clear to meet readers' purposes, readers can choose to consult an outside source such as a dictionary, glossary, encyclopedia, or resource person for an answer to a pending question.

Postreading Activities

If students are to become skillful in independently learning new information from text, they need exposure to both a variety of text structure and to a variety of postreading text-related activities. Those activities that follow reader-text interaction begin with a review of text information that takes different forms depending on the reader, the text and the purpose(s). This review includes reacting to and/or recalling major ideas as well as other activities. These other activities depend on reader responses to the text discussed and on those prereading activities that focus reader attention. Reader purpose dictates the specific type of activity. If the primary goal is recall and retention of information, the teacher will select one or more study-type activities. If reader-text interaction has stimulated the formation of research questions or problems relevant to learner purpose, the teacher selects activities that allow for the gathering of additional information to help answer the questions. Of course, this gathering of additional information can also follow study activities if study activities lead to the awareness that students have not answered all questions (see Figure 12.6).

Any of the postreading activities in Figure 12.6 can lead to related language-reading experiences that will increase oral and written language competence and/or reading competence. This expansion of language/reading competence extends the language-thinking approach discussed in Chapter 3 into the area of expository reading experiences.

REVIEWING TEXT INFORMATION

Generally the first activity designed to help both readers and teachers to assess information gained during silent reading is either an evaluative reaction to the author's ideas or a free recall of the major ideas. An evaluative reaction to an expository text has cognitive and affective components and involves a reader's reactions to both the content and structure of the text. When reacting to content, the reader responds to such things as the topic, elaboration of the topic, and the author's point of view on the subject. Reactions to structure involve such things as judgments about how the author organizes material, develops ideas, and uses language. The teacher can stimulate evaluative reactions through questions to judge both content and structure. Sample questions directed to *content* are:

1. Does the author present the topic in a fair manner? Why do you feel this way?
2. Does the author present information accurately? How do you know?

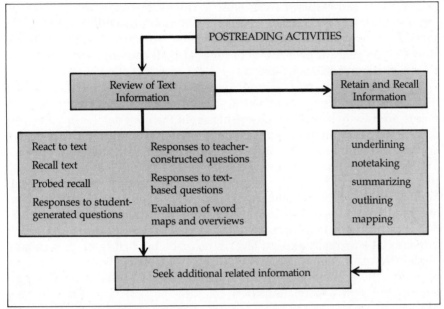

Figure 12.6 Postreading Activities

3. Does the supporting evidence prove the author's position? Why do you think so?
4. How does the information the author gives serve your purpose(s)?
5. How do you feel about the points the author chooses to emphasize in developing this topic?
6. Do you agree with the author's point of view? Why?

Sample questions directed to evaluate the *structure* are:

1. Do you find that the author organizes the material so that you can follow easily? Why do you think so?
2. Why does the author choose to use a _____ (temporal, cause-effect, comparison/contrast, and so on) pattern to organize this particular content?
3. Does the author develop the main concepts so that the ideas become clear to you? Explain.
4. Do you find that the author's use of _____ (illustrations, tables, graphics, figures, maps, diagrams) influences your understanding of the material? How? OR
   How does the author's use of _____ influence your understanding of the material?
5. What influence does the author's choice of language have on your understanding?

If students can respond completely to the evaluative type of questions suggested above, the teacher may not have to follow with free recall and probed recall of information. Generally, the teacher can assume that if students can react appropriately in judging both content and structure of text, they have processed the text.

Although reactions may sometimes follow directly after the reading of a text, many times the teacher chooses to have students recall freely the main points prior to their making judgments about the material. During this free recall the teacher monitors the specific content reconstructed by the learners and determines if the content as reconstructed includes the relevant and appropriate relations among the ideas. The teacher keeps in mind the relations used by the author—which can include such patterns as definition/example, problem/solution, cause/effect, comparison/contrast, and temporal arrangement—as learners are recalling the major ideas. In addition, the teacher also focuses on which parts of the text students interpret primarily at a textually explicit level, a textually implicit level, or scriptally implicit level. Depending on the learners' reconstructions, the teacher organizes the probe and structured questions so that the omitted or ambiguous concepts and relations between ideas become clear. These review procedures are similar to the procedures described in Chapter 7. The major difference is that instead of focusing on story line concepts such as plot, events, and characters, the free recall, probed recall, and structured questions used with expository text focus on the main content-related concepts and the relations between them.

To iterate, the teacher uses probed recall and structured questions only when reactions to the text and/or free recall do not produce sufficient information to judge learners' understanding of the text completely. In all review situations, the students answer the questions they generated during prereading activities to see if the text provided the information they hypothesized.

For diagnostic purposes the teacher analyzes all learner responses (reactions, recall, probed recall, responses to structured questions) to determine if students construct the relevant relations between ideas. Further, the teacher determines at what points students make textually explicit, textually implicit, and scriptally implicit responses and how relevant these responses are to the text information.

Some expository materials include questions for learner responses. The teacher may or may not include these questions in the review of text information. Their use depends on the teacher's judgment as to whether the text-based questions cover concepts deemed important in understanding the text and whether, based on the learner's previous responses to the text, the information highlighted in the questions warrants further emphasis.

If the class uses a word map to elicit prior knowledge or a structured overview to focus reader attention on the important concepts in the text, postreading review must definitely include a joint teacher-student(s) evaluation of these visual displays. This evaluation determines the relevance of the initial diagram to the overall text information and indicates whether deletions or additions are necessary or appropriate.

To illustrate this, the teacher would evaluate the structured overview in Figure 12.5 and would determine whether to make changes or additions. For example, if during prereading activities the teacher had not modified this structured overview to place the words *barter* and *purchase* on equal levels, the teacher would focus learner attention on this point and encourage learners to adapt the overview based on their reading of the text. Discussion could also lead to the addition of the word *trade*.

RETAINING AND RECALLING TEXT INFORMATION

Not only is learner monitoring of reading behavior an integral part of reader-text interaction, but it is also equally important in selecting and applying study techniques during postreading activities. Dependent on reader purpose, the learner will read the text in different ways, focusing on specific information located and selected to satisfy the criterion task. For example, during an initial reading the reader typically reads to determine overall topic information and to look for focal points in the text for retention. The reader returns to those parts of the text that are relevant and pulls out the information needed to select and organize for memory.

Learning to be an independent studier relates directly to the many aspects of thinking, language usage, reading narrative text, and reading expository text discussed throughout this book. Prior to school entry and during early school years, learners have many experiences that build knowledge needed to study effectively. The learner develops this knowledge base through many varied experiences in the environment. The expansion of knowledge is an ongoing process in which both the content of the experiences change and the level of learners' understanding of these experiences increases. As readers increase their knowledge of those functions needed to study effectively, they increase their abilities to organize and classify objects and events and to recognize such relations as super-subordinate, cause-effect, and temporal. Further, they will recognize that some ideas are more important than others and that some ideas are more relevant to the important issues than others. Learners will apply these abilities with increasingly difficult content, moving from concrete to abstract things and ideas, from simple to complex things and ideas. Also, they develop the ability to paraphrase through sharing and retelling experiences when dealing with informal language communications and interactions with narrative and expository text. Further, learners begin to understand that different types of text vary in their structure and organization and that understanding text organization helps in remembering important information. Thus, the integration of everything readers have learned about language and reading with knowledge of specific study purposes and activities enables them to move forward as they systematically attempt to organize and retain text information. The development of this integration allows readers to become independent studiers.

In summary, reaching the goal of effective studying involves a complex set of behaviors available through the flexible use and integration of a number of abilities: The young child needs guidance in piecing together the various components and in working toward this goal. Bearing in mind the complexity of studying, you can understand the reasons that experts have found efficient studying to be a late emerging ability (Baker & Brown, 1984).

Researchers have emphasized that for those students who are not developing these abilities spontaneously and are not able to apply study strategies effectively, specific instruction is relevant and necessary. Of course, as with all teaching, instruction should be in keeping with a learner's overall cognitive and reading functioning. When considering study techniques for instructional purposes, experts have found that almost any of them can be effective if the learner focuses attention and organizes and processes information in a form and manner appropriate to the criterion task (Anderson & Armbruster, 1984). A teacher's selection of one study technique over another depends as much on the text as on the learner. If an author has been "considerate" in writing the text and has made the relations between the major ideas clear, study techniques such as underlining, note-taking, and summarizing should be sufficient for retaining material. If, on the other hand, the author has been "inconsiderate" and the relations are not sufficiently explicit, techniques such as outlining and mapping, although time-consuming, may be more appropriate.

Therefore, to be effective studiers, students must know the demands of the text, the text organization, and a variety of study strategies. This knowledge combines metacognitive awareness of self as a studier with the ability to monitor the usefulness of the selected strategy.

We recognize that mature readers, having learned how to study text, are generally able to survey text and move directly to one of the study techniques that we are going to describe. However, we recommend that in teaching students to be independent studiers, teachers use a three-step process. First, students should learn to survey the text. This involves a teacher's guidance through appropriate questioning processes to familiarize learners with chapter titles, chapter subtitles, words, phrases, or sections the author deems important enough to highlight. Authors use typographical techniques, graphic aids, and introductory and concluding paragraphs to highlight and focus material. Students should be aware of an author's use of production techniques.

Following survey of a text, students read the text with full knowledge of the purpose(s) for which they will use the information. During this silent reading of the text, students are monitoring their understanding of the major concepts. Not until they have completed this step are learners ready to select and use a specific study technique.

Underlining

Underlining or highlighting is one of the more popular study techniques because it is relatively easy and quick. This technique permits the reader to delineate the important ideas in the text without the necessity of copying the information. The major facilitative effect of this technique occurs when students generate the underlining themselves as opposed to their receiving the text already underlined (Anderson & Armbruster, 1984). This process requires the student to focus on the content actively and make decisions about what is important and what is unimportant relative to the criterion task. Regardless of the task, students should underline the major concepts in the text. The amount of detailed information underlined depends on the specific purpose for which they will use text information. For example, if the criterion task following the reading of a selection is to take a multiple-choice test, the student will probably highlight main points and major and minor detail information. If the reader is preparing for a discussion or debate on selected aspects of the information, the focus will be on that information relevant to the pertinent issues. If a learner is reading to gain background knowledge prior to preparing an oral or written report, the reader underlines primarily the main points to note what information is available in the text and what information must come from other sources.

Although we realize that underlining in textbooks is prohibited in most schools, teachers can duplicate materials to use in teaching this study technique. Learners can then apply this technique to books that they own and to school materials that are consumable such as newspapers and magazines.

Note-taking

Note-taking, like underlining, is a popular study technique but more time-consuming. As a study technique note-taking condenses and organizes text information so that the student can use the information for the established purpose. In constructing notes, learners create a permanent record of information so that they can review important ideas at any time without direct reference to the text.

This permanent record or visual display of major concepts and related ideas depends on the purpose for note-taking and the individual study style of the learner. The purposes for note-taking are similar to those for underlining. The focus of the written notes as well as the quantity of notes varies depending on the learner's specific purpose (criterion task).

Also, the way the notes look varies from learner to learner. Learner's experience and personal study style influences the visual arrangement of the notes on a page. For example, some learners may choose to use a simple version of an outline format in which the main concepts appear as headings and the related ideas are indented under these headings. Other learners may prefer to use a column format in which column headings are the major concepts and related ideas are listed beneath. Frequently learners find that underlining specific information in their notes is helpful for highlighting ideas for future study. More important than the specific form in which students take notes is the knowledge that the relevant information needed for the criterion task is accurate and organized clearly.

In taking notes, students may either follow the author's structure and organization or, better, construct an alternate organization. Preliminary research in this area reports that students who reorganize text information recall significantly more material. The hypothesis is that in restructuring, learners are more involved because they must understand the author's organization and figure out new content organization in a way that facilitates the accomplishment of their own learning purpose (Anderson & Armbruster, 1984).

In teaching the specific study strategy of note-taking from written material, no matter what the purpose or form, emphasis is on the need for clarity, organization, and accuracy of content. Typically, teaching students to take notes begins within the organizational framework the author presents. Note-taking is a group or class activity until students recognize that this is a useful and productive use of study time: They will understand that taking notes helps them to recall text information when they successfully accomplish specific tasks based on experience with taking notes. In learning to take notes, students are taking a step toward becoming independent studiers. As a part of this development, they learn to select the major points covered in the text, to record these points in their own words, to add detail information relevant to their purpose, and to determine if they need additional information to clarify and/or expand text information. When students are comfortable with note-taking from an author's structure, they are ready to think about different ways to organize the same content. Their reorganization depends on their purpose and idiosyncratic styles of study.

Summarizing

Producing an adequate summary of text is a complex process. Research on text summarization describes five rules that, if applied appropriately, seem to lead to a precise and accurate gist of text information (Brown & Day, 1980; Brown, Campione, & Day, 1981; Baker & Brown, 1984). These rules involve deletion, superordination, and selection or invention of topic sentence(s). Deletion may occur in two ways. One involves omitting material considered unimportant or trivial. The second involves disregarding any redundant or repetitive material. The third rule in constructing a summary is to invent a superordinate category to encompass either a number of related items or a number of related actions or events. The last two rules for summarizing text deal with locating topic sentences and finally with constructing topic sentences when the author does not explicitly state them.

A series of developmental studies on the application of these rules found that students can be taught to summarize. In these studies the results of training related both to age and ability. Both younger children and college students with reading problems were able to apply the two deletion rules with considerable success. The studies showed considerably greater influence of both developmental level and reading functioning on the ability to apply the rules of superordination and selection and invention of topic sentence (Brown & Day, 1980; Brown, 1981). This developmental trend in the application of the rules of summarization is clear if we think in terms of the amount of cognitive intervention required to apply each rule. For example, the easier deletion rules require only that text information be omitted. In contrast, the most difficult rule, the invention rule, requires not just the deletion, selection, or manipulation of material already provided as in the other rules but necessitates the construction of a synopsis statement using the reader's own words. If we think about the differences in the demands required to apply each of the rules, we can understand that the ability to summarize text is related to cognitive level and reading performance.

When teaching learners to write summaries of material, keep in mind these developmental differences. Specific instruction should include direct teaching in the use of the rules of summarization, modeling the use of the rules in whole class or group situations and explicit instruction in checking to see if the rules were used appropriately. Initially teachers select and/or construct text material the author has organized around a clearly stated topic sentence that includes some detail information that is important but redundant. Learners would, with teacher modeling and guidance, select the main idea and delete those details and information judged trivial and repetitive.

This strategy serves as a clear way to begin to build the many concepts inherent in the rules of summarization. With increased skill in reading and a solid understanding of the specific content to summarize, learners should be able to deal with deletion of trivia, deletion of redundant information, and recognition of topic sentence. Learning the rule of summarization that involves substituting a superordinate term for a list of items or a superordinate event for a list of actions also is easier when a teacher selects materials heavily loaded with lists of related items or events. A teacher's modeling and guidance should lead learners to construct superordinate terms. At this point learners should be able to use the first four rules of summarization and should have many opportunities to apply the rules and to check, either with teacher direction or independently, if they have applied the rules correctly.

Questions such as the following guide learners in checking the accuracy and conciseness of their summaries.

1. Have I selected a topic sentence?
2. Have I omitted unimportant information?
3. Have I omitted repetitious information?
4. Have I replaced lists or related items with a general word or phrase?
5. Have I replaced a series of related events or actions with one sentence that incorporates all the ideas?

Students learn how to summarize material with no explicitly stated topic sentence when they have become adept at writing summaries using the first four rules of summarization.

Outlining

Outlining is generally more time-consuming than underlining, note-taking, or summarizing. It involves not only the location of the major ideas and related information but also the reorganization of the information in a visual representation so that the ideas and the logical relations between them are evident. This production of an alternate form of the text for study purposes is particularly effective when the author has not made the relations between the ideas sufficiently explicit. In creating an outline, the reader must specify both the explicit and implicit relations that serve to clarify and organize related information. Therefore, although outlining is a useful study technique for almost all types of text, it is particularly helpful when the relations in the text are not clear.

As in the case of notes and summaries, outlines become a permanent record of text information and vary in the amount of detail included depending on the specific study purpose. Of those study techniques we have discussed so far, outlining is most closely related to reorganizing the text as part of note-taking.

In teaching the specific strategy of outlining text material, the teacher begins by selecting text material that students have already read and reviewed for meaning. The first step in developing an outline involves skimming the material to locate main topics. The reader writes these topics down, leaving sufficient space to fill in the major concepts and related ideas. The next step involves a return to the text to examine each of the main topics and to read the information carefully to determine the relations between the explanatory and supportive ideas. The reader then fills in the related information for each topic and indicates the topic and the major and minor relations through indentation and the use of Roman numerals, capital letters, Arabic numbers, and small letters. The type of outline most commonly used for study purposes is illustrated in Table 12.3 on page 318.

In using an outline format, the amount of detail recorded by the learner is directly related to the purpose to which the outline will be put and the amount of detail the author gives. For example, a learner can construct an outline with several major topics and any number of related details or with only one or two major topics and a few related details or in some cases even no details.

Similar to other study techniques, at first outlining is a group or class activity with the teacher serving as recorder. Only after many shared experiences of this type can the learner begin to outline text independently. The foundation for understanding the concepts involved in outlining is built in the early school years through various experiences in organizing and classifying things and events with emphasis on relations. Although learning the conventions of outline format is necessary, early experiences with outlining should focus on content (ideas and their relations) rather than format.

Mapping

For the most part mapping should be limited to teacher analysis of text. However, sometimes a group of students—with teacher guidance—may want or need to diagram relations in text by using this mapping technique. This may involve small pieces of text in which the relations are implicit or particularly difficult for the students to construct, or larger pieces of text if the teacher feels that mapping is the most effective way to highlight the relations. Mapping uses the same symbols we described before. We emphasize again that the process for determining the relations between the ideas is of primary importance. The teacher can select any well-developed mapping paradigm for student use.

We will illustrate the study techniques described (excluding mapping) using the following text from *Elementary Science* (Abruscato and others, 1980).

People and Living Space

If all the people in the world were packed together, they could stand on the state of Delaware and still have a great deal of room left. But everyone does not live packed together in Delaware. *The population is spread unevenly over the earth.*[1]

In the deserts and the Arctic there are fewer than one person in 300 sq km (120 sq mi). In New York City, there are almost 70,000 people in 1 sq km (.4 sq mi). This does not mean that every person in the Arctic is hundreds of kilometers away from every other person. It doesn't mean that 70,000 persons live in each square kilometer in New York City. These numbers are averages. *Some people live closer together than the averages indicate. Other people live farther apart.*

Scientists have carried out experiments with small animals to see what crowding does to them. They found that *when animals are crowded together they become less healthy.* They *fight* more, they *don't eat as well,* and they *stop producing healthy young.* How does crowding make you feel? Do you behave any differently under very crowded conditions?

People need different amounts of space. The distance you keep from other people when you talk with them is sometimes called your personal space. Most people like to keep a *personal space* of about 60 cm (2 ft). They feel *uncomfortable if anyone moves inside that space.*

Other kinds of space are important too. For example, in a city, *parks*

---

[1]Students would underline material italicized here.

can be *peaceful quiet places* where a person can get away from others. It can be a place to *relax* or to *play*. What would happen if cities became so populated that no green spaces remained for parks? Would life in the cities be more or less pleasant?

The federal government has set aside large areas of land for citizens to enjoy. These areas are the *national parks.* They are *places of great beauty.* It is *against the law for people to change the land* in national parks. They cannot cut down trees, build on the land, or disturb the land in any way. Even though millions of people visit the parks each year, there are always *places to be alone* if you wish. Such places are the *wilderness areas.* Not many roads enter wilderness areas. If you wish to enter one, you may have to hike or ride a horse.

How would you feel if the human population increased so greatly that the national parklands would have to be used for natural resources and living space?

Wilderness areas in such places as natural parks, national forests, and wildlife refuges are important for another reason. They *provide secure, protected, natural environments* for *many organisms,* including *those in danger of dying and disappearing from the face of the earth.*

Plants and animals that are in danger of dying are called **endangered organisms** (en-**dane**-jerd). More than 170 kinds of animals and 1,700 kinds of plants in the world are endangered. The bald eagle is an *endangered organism* in the United States. So is the cougar.

Human beings have caused some plants and animals to become endangered. For example, many buffalo were killed so that their skins could be used for clothes.

Endangered organisms are now protected. It is a crime to hunt them. Once an endangered organism is gone, it can never be recovered.

Note that the learner influences the selection of a specific strategy in terms of preference and the text influences the chosen strategy in terms of author's organization and the criterion task. In the following illustrations, different purposes illustrate several ways to organize the same piece of text for study. To recall the text information for class or group discussion, one possible strategy is to underline the major ideas and important details. Note the italicized portions of the text above. A second illustration is of note-taking. Students have chosen note-taking since they will read and take notes to gain background information to help them decide on their position for a debate. The debate issue is: "Should national parks remain as recreational facilities and wilderness preserves, or should they be developed for their natural resources and as living space?" The students will read to determine what information the author presents to support each position and in which area they should consult further resources. Table 12.1 shows one student's notes. This student chose to take notes in a

Table 12.1 Student's Notes in Column Format

National Parks

Keep parks as recreational and wilderness preserves	*Develop parks for natural resources and living space*
people need space	(no information given)

national parks
  great beauty
  space to be alone
    (wilderness areas)
  recreation	

animals need to be protected	
plants need to be protected	
endangered organisms particularly need protection	

column format, using the debate issues as column headings. This was a personal preference of the student, and certainly the student could have organized the notes in one of several other formats.

If the purpose for reading and retaining text information is to share the major ideas with other students, summarizing is one way to organize information. Table 12.2 illustrates one student's written summary of the text information.

Although the illustrated strategies are useful given the presented purposes, they do not explicitly focus on the relations between the ideas. This latter type of approach is more complex and is used when students need recall of text information in greater detail. Outlining and mapping of the text are two strategies that delineate the relations among the ideas. Both include sufficient detail to be useful for students who are studying for a test. The following illustration (Table 12.3) is one student's outline of the text.

Table 12.2 Student's Written Summary

People and Living Space

The population of the earth is distributed unevenly. Some people live much closer to each other than others. Scientists have shown that when small animals live very close together, they fight, eat poorly, and stop producing healthy babies. Space is also important to people. They need a certain amount of personal space to be comfortable, and they need open space like city parks and national parks. Open space is important so that people can play, enjoy nature, or be alone. Wilderness areas in national parks provide both places for people to be alone and safe homes for endangered plants and animals. People have caused some organisms to become endangered, but now people are protecting these plants and animals.

Table 12.3   Student's Outline

People and Living Space

I.   Population spread unevenly
   A.   Arctic and deserts
      1.   less than one person in 300 sq. km.
   B.   New York City
      1.   700,000 people in 1 sq. km.

II.   Need for personal space
   A.   Animals
      1.   less healthy if crowded
         a.   fight
         b.   do not eat well
         c.   produce unhealthy young

   B.   People
      1.   uncomfortable if someone moves into personal space
         a.   about 2 ft. distance necessary

III.   Open space
   A.   City parks
      1.   peaceful and quiet
      2.   people can relax or play
   B.   National parks
      1.   set aside by federal government
      2.   places of great beauty
      3.   against the law to change the land
         a.   cannot cut down trees
         b.   cannot build on land
      4.   provide natural wilderness areas
         a.   for people to be alone
         b.   for plants and animals to be secure
         c.   for endangered organisms to be protected

SEEKING ADDITIONAL RELATED INFORMATION

An important potential result of postreading activity is a learner's developing awareness of the need for additional information related to text content to clarify or expand text information. This form of self-monitoring can lead to a reader's interaction with a variety of content-related materials, including other textbooks, biographies, encyclopedias, and other general reference books. Learners will find some of these materials at home, some in the classroom, some in the school library, and some in public libraries. Using a classroom library is the first step in learning how to use school and public libraries. All libraries are organized to facilitate locating information. Generally, classroom libraries require only a simple organization in which materials are either classified according to type or content or arranged alphabetically by author or title. This provides learners the chance to become familiar with library organization and forms a base for understanding the two library classification systems generally in use in this country—the Dewey System and the Library of Congress System.

Although understanding the overall organization is important, the ability to use the card catalog actually enables a learner to locate information efficiently within a given system. Card catalogs are organized by either the title, the author, or the subject area of the book. Sometimes separate catalogs are used for each type, or more frequently the three types of cards are integrated into one catalog.

Once the learner has located a particular book, the learner must become familiar with the book to determine if it is appropriate for his or her purpose. In this process the learner first checks for a book jacket to read the synopsis of a book's content on the front flap and something about the author on the back flap. In many cases the book jacket gives sufficient information to determine if a book is relevant to the needs of the reader. If a book jacket is not available or the information on the jacket is not sufficient, the learner skims the title page to find out about the author, the illustrator, and the publisher; the learner examines the copyright page to note the date of publication that tells recency of information in the book; the learner previews the preface, introduction and/or foreword, to learn the author's purpose for writing the book and become familiar with the organization of the book; and finally the learner reads the table of contents to note the topics included and gain an overview of the book. At this point the reader should make a decision as to the suitability of the book. If the book is appropriate, further skimming of the book includes noting if the author has included an index to help locate specific information, a glossary to help define words, an appendix for supplementary information, and a bibliography to locate further sources of related information.

Although learners most often use the library to locate content area texts and related trade books, many times they need to use the reference collection of the library. This includes use of encyclopedias, dictionaries, almanacs, atlases, the *Readers' Guide to Periodical Literature*, and other specialized reference books and materials. Libraries also house special collections including periodicals, pictures, newspapers, pamphlets, records, film strips, and tapes. In using any of these sources, you apply the same study strategies described for use in retaining and recalling text information. Although students will not be able to underline library materials, they may choose to take notes or summarize, and in some cases they may prefer to outline.

EXPANDING LEARNER COMPETENCE IN LANGUAGE/READING

Any one or more of the postreading activities discussed may lead to language/reading experiences planned to increase learner competencies in using oral language and/or reading. In this way learners enrich reading experiences with expository text, integrating all aspects of reading and the communication process discussed in previous chapters. The teaching/learning plans presented in the next chapter illustrate the integration of reading expository text with other language activities.

Summary

This chapter describes specific prereading activities, self-monitoring activities, and postreading activities to use in teaching content area materials. The chapter describes prereading activities to elicit prior knowledge, build background knowledge, and focus learner attention and illustrates them using social studies materials. The chapter also describes study techniques including underlining, note-taking, summarizing, and outlining to help students retain and recall text information and illustrates them using a section of a social science textbook. In addition, the chapter includes some discussion about obtaining additional information from other source materials.

13

Teaching/ Learning Plans

R eading expository text is only one part of teaching in the content areas. Content area teaching involves the use of many activities in addition to reading to gain information about a topic. Thus, while reading textbooks and other related materials is crucial in obtaining information about a subject, the teacher must integrate reading within the broad framework of learning.

We present three teaching plans using materials from social studies and science textbooks to illustrate the integration of reading and other activities. Each plan incorporates aspects of information gathering that go beyond the text. Remember while reading these plans that each one is part of an ongoing unit of study. For example, Plan Two that uses a biography of

Table 13.1 Overview of Teaching/Learning Plans

Teaching/Learning Plan	Type of Material	Purposes for Reading
"What's It Worth to You?" (Brandwein and others, (1970) 3rd-4th Grade Class	Social Studies Textbook	Expand knowledge to be able to write persuasive essays and participate in debates. Increase ability to use reference materials in the library.
Harriet Tubman, "Black Moses" (Risjord & Haywoods, 1978) 5th-6th Grade Class	History Textbook: Biographical Selection	Personalize study of American history in the 1800s. Expand understanding of the genre of biography.
"The Earth's Future" (Abruscato, 1980). 6th-7th Grade Class	Science Textbook	Expand knowledge about world population growth and its related problems. Increase ability to interpret bar graphs.

Major Prereading Activities	Major Postreading Activities
Respond to advertisement Interview people related to topic Listen and/or read story Discuss teacher related experience Develop word map and structured overview	Recall text information, probed recall and teacher constructed questions. Expand word map and structured overview Seek related information through library resources or personal interview and take notes Write a persuasive essay Plan/participate in debate
Listen to song Use of analogous situation Student generated questions	Recall text information, probed recall and student generated questions Listen and/or read narrative poem Write poetry, prose, personal journal Research on related topic
PREP PREP extended to word map Interpret graph	Recall text information, probed recall and text-based structured questions Write a business letter

Harriet Tubman as the reading material is part of a unit of study on the Civil War.

Table 13.1 outlines the material for each plan, the primary purposes for reading this material, and the major prereading and postreading activities.

In this chapter each plan includes relevant teacher background about the topic and the text, direct teaching activities, and comments on the evaluation of teaching. We use the framework for teaching introduced in Chapter 4 in each of these teaching/learning plans.

Teaching/Learning Plan One: "What's It Worth to You?"

PREACTIVE TEACHING

Teacher Knowledge
This article from *World Book* gives teachers some background information about money.

Related information. Money is anything that people agree to accept in exchange for the things they sell or the work they do. Gold and silver were once the most common forms of money. But today, money consists mainly of paper bills; coins made of copper, nickel, and other metals; and checking account deposits.

Each country has its own system of money. The bills and coins look different and have different names. In the United States, for example, the basic unit of money is the U.S. dollar. Canada uses the Canadian dollar, France the franc, Great Britain the pound, Japan the yen, Mexico the peso, and West Germany the mark. The money in use in a country is called its *currency.*

Money has three main uses. First, and most important, money serves as a *medium of exchange*—that is, it is something which people will accept for their goods or services. Without a medium of exchange, people would have to trade their goods or services directly for other goods or services. If you wanted a bicycle, for example, you would have to find a bicycle owner willing to trade. Suppose the bicycle owner wanted skis in exchange for the bike and you did not own skis. You would then have to find something a ski owner or ski maker wanted and trade it for skis to give the bicycle owner. Such trading is called *barter.* Barter can take much time and make it difficult for people to get the things they want. A modern, industrialized country could not function without a medium of exchange.

A second use of money is that it serves as a *unit of account*. People state the price of goods and services in terms of money. In the United States, people use dollars to specify price, just as they use hours to express time and miles or kilometers to measure distance.

A third use of money is as a *store of wealth*. People can save money and then use it to make purchases in the future. Other stores of wealth include gold, jewels, paintings, real estate, and stocks and bonds.

Any object or substance that serves as a medium of exchange, a unit of account, and a store of wealth is money. To be convenient, however, money should have several qualities. It should come in pieces of standard value so that it does not have to be weighed or measured every time it is used. It should be easy to carry so that people can carry enough money to buy what they need. Finally, it should divide into units so that people can make small purchases and receive change.

In the past, people used beads, cocoa beans, salt, shells, stones, tobacco, and many other things as money. But above all, they used such metals as copper, gold and silver. These metals made convenient, durable money.

Today most money consists of paper. The paper itself is of little value, but it is accepted in exchange. People accept pieces of metal or paper in exchange for work or goods for only one reason: They know that others will take the same metal or paper in exchange for the things they want. The value of money therefore results from the fact that everyone will accept it as payment.

Source: *The World Book Encyclopedia,* 1982, pp. 588–89.

To expand knowledge of a topic, teachers may use the entire article from which the above material was taken and other books and encyclopedias.

Concepts to develop. The four major concepts to develop in this lesson are that

1. throughout history people have used different mediums of exchange to acquire goods and services;
2. society has developed methods to produce, allocate, and distribute goods and services for needs and wants;
3. consumer awareness and action can influence the purchase price of goods and services; and
4. supply and demand affect prices of goods and services.

Summary of the text for students. A general summary of the major ideas in the three sections *The Story of Money, Setting a Price,* and *The Law of Supply and Demand* appears in Chapter 11.

Text structure. The author presents expository material with a relatively heavy information load and uses graphics and related questions as well as questions that encourage the reader to go beyond the text. For all three parts of this section, the overall organization is chronological. The relations in the piece *The Story of Money* that traces the history and use of money are not as clearly delineated as the relations in the other two sections and, therefore, we chose this section to map as a reference for understanding student responses.

The author adheres more clearly to a chronological sequence in *Setting a Price* tracing the events in determining price as goods move from factory to store. At the store level the author provides a concrete example of consumer influence on setting prices. The last section on *The Law of Supply and Demand* begins with a transition from the preceding section and then expands the concrete example to a generalized form.

Teacher Decisions

This lesson is for readers in a third or fourth grade class who are working on a social studies unit on sharing resources. They have read the three preceding sections in this unit and, therefore, have background knowledge about the general topic of money and its use. They have read about having money of their own, how money is earned, choosing and planning how to spend money, trading for goods that are not readily available, and the interdependence of people, communities, and regions.

The text to be read, Section 4, "What's It Worth to You?" encompasses some of the major concepts of the class curriculum and presents material in such a way that the students should be able to interact successfully by using their prior experience and the planned prereading activities. Through reading the previous sections, they have already become familiar with the author's presentation of ideas and language usage.

The general student purpose for reading this text is to expand knowledge of the topic and more specifically to gather information in order to write persuasive essays and participate in debates on the following issues:

1. the use of barter versus the use of money
2. the use of cash versus the use of checks, and
3. buying things as needed versus waiting for a sale.

An important part of reader-text interaction involves selection of appropriate information and determination of what additional information they may need to write a persuasive essay. A teacher's analysis of text content determines that the learners have to go to a school or public library to gain additional information to supplement the text. Teacher planning also involves the allocation of time so that these activities can occur with teacher supervision and, if necessary, direct instruction.

INTERACTIVE TEACHING

Prereading Activities

To elicit prior knowledge. Discussion based on advertisement and use of teacher questions (see pp. 296–97).

To build prior knowledge/direct experience. Interview local storekeepers and/or bank tellers;

To build prior knowledge/indirect experience.

1. Listen to or read *Jack and the Beanstalk* for concepts of barter and money;
2. Teacher relates an experience on using cash and a check to make purchases;
3. Develop a word map as described in Chapter 12 (see Figures 12.3 and 12.4).

To focus reader attention. Establish reader purpose related to the three issues learners will use in writing a persuasive essay. The teacher should point out the first two issues during the previously described experiences and arrange teacher/student and student/student interactions focused on barter, money, cash, and checks. Teacher-constructed questions related to children's experiences when purchasing items with family or friends stimulate the third issue. Teachers may use questions such as these:

1. How do you and your family decide when to buy something?
2. What things do you think about when you get ready to buy something?
3. Do you or your family look at advertisements before you go shopping? What can you learn from them?

As teacher and students develop the three issues, the teacher records them on the chalkboard, and some readers may choose to write them down in notebooks and keep the issues in view as a guide for silent reading. Students read the entire section for the main points and note where specific information relative to the three issues is located in the text.

Reader-Text Interaction

Students then silently read "What's It Worth to You?" Self-monitoring focuses on whether or not the author provides information related to the three issues recorded on the chalkboard. If so, the reader thinks, "Do I understand the information? Does it make sense? What other information do I need to know about this area?"

A further aspect of self-monitoring is a student's decision as to which of the three issues to pursue.

Postreading Activities

Review of text information. The teacher asks learners to retell in their own words what information the text gives on each of the three issues. The teacher probes learner recall to extend the retrieval of information and if necessary may ask structured questions such as the following:

1. What is barter?
2. What have people used for barter?
3. What is a medium of exchange?
4. What is the main problem in using animals as a medium of exchange?
5. What are some benefits in using money as a medium of exchange?
6. What are some problems in using cash as a medium of exchange?
7. Why may it be better to use checks instead of cash?
8. How can using checks be a problem?
9. How do storekeepers set their prices?

10. Why are prices different in different stores?

11. Why do prices change over time for the same goods or services?

Retain and recall information. Students select one of the three issues for their essay, return to the text, and underline or take notes on information relevant to their topic. At the same time, they generate questions they think are important and need answers in order for them to write good persuasive essays.

Seek additional related information. To answer the student-generated questions, learners will need to locate additional sources of information during structured library experiences. These experiences will include:

1. Use of the subject index in the library. Students generate key words such as *money, coins, barter, currency, checks, purchase, trade, supply and demand.* The teacher may add additional words such as *economics, treasury, finance, investment,* or *mint* depending on the level of the learners. Individual learners and/or groups use the key words noted above to locate books, related articles, film strips, records, pictures.

2. Use of the encyclopedia. Students use the key word *money* to begin their search for information. Using the Index and Research Guide of the *World Book Encyclopedia* (1982), students locate the following headings and subheadings listed by volume and page.

Money M:588 *with pictures*
  Coin Collecting **Ci:609** *with pictures*
  Convertibility **Ci:806**
  Counterfeiting **Ci:876**
  Devaluation **D:140**
  Exchange Rate **E:337**
  Free Silver **F:426**
  Gold (Money) **G:242**
  Gold Standard **G:244**
  Income **I:84**
  Indian, American (Money) **I:124** *with picture*
  Inflation (Severe Inflation) **I:204** *with picture*
  Investment **I:288**
  Legal Tender **L:160**
  Savings **S:138**
  Trade (The Use of Money) **T:284**
  See also the list of Related Articles in the
    Money *article*
Money [play by Bulwer-Lytton]
  Bulwer-Lytton, Edward George Earle Lytton
    B:586
Money income
  Income **I:84**
Money market fund
  Mutual Fund **M:810**
Money order M:599 *with pictures*
  Post Office (Money Order) **P:628**
  Telegraph (Special Services) **T:74**
Money-purchase plan
  Pension (Group Annuity Plans) **P:241**
Money supply
  Money (Money and the Economy) **M:598**
    with diagram
Money wages
  Wages and Hours (Wages) **W:2**

Source: *The World Book Encyclopedia.* © 1982 World Book-Childcraft International, Inc.

As students use this index, they recognize or become aware of the following:

1. There are eight major headings beginning with the word *Money.*
2. The first listing of *Money* indicates "M:588 with pictures." This means that the main article on the topic of money will be found in volume M beginning on page 588 and that pictures accompany the article.
3. The other subheadings under *Money* are references to more specific aspects of money, and students can find information in a number of different volumes.
4. Other related articles are available, and the list of these articles appears at the end of the main article on money.
5. The second listing of *Money* is a play by Bulwer-Lytton and is not relevant.
6. The remaining six headings indicate more specific areas related to money that students may or may not use.

After reading this index, a decision based on learner purpose would be to read the main article and then determine if further information is still necessary. Students would also skim information at the end of the article that lists related articles, an outline of the article just read and structured questions for review purposes (see Figure 13.1). They might decide to read additional material related to the topic of their essay.

Another way to generate related information, particularly for learners of this age, is through interviewing. Some learners may not be ready to function with library resources and will use interview techniques to obtain information to expand the material in the text.

In preparation for an interview learners

1. decide on the person or persons to interview;
2. list the information required in the form of questions. These questions are generally who, what, where, when, why, and how questions; and
3. choose a means of recording the information. Learners may decide to take notes as they receive answers to their questions or to tape the interview and then either play the tape for their group or take notes from the tape.

Expand language/reading competence. Learners read selected material or use interview material and take notes related to their debate issue, which should include information on both points of view. Learners write persuasive essays to convince other students of their points of view. Learners share their essays in groups formed around the three issues and their pro and con positions. Students share through oral reading to the group and through silent reading of other learners' writings. Each of the groups decides how to constitute the proposition to debate in the form of an affirmative statement that presents a clear-cut issue with pro and con

Related Articles. See BANK and ECONOMICS. See also the following articles:

MODERN CURRENCIES

Bolívar	Half Dollar	Pound
Cent	Kopeck	Quarter
Córdoba	Krona	Quetzal
Dime	Krone	Rial
Dinar	Lira	Ruble
Dollar	Mark	Rupee
Drachma	Nickel	Shekel
Escudo	Penny	Yen
Franc	Peseta	Yuan
Guilder	Peso	

HISTORICAL CURRENCIES

Denarius	Eagle	Greenback
Doubloon	Farthing	Guinea
Ducat	Florin	Piece of Eight
Pine-Tree Shilling	Shilling	Talent
Real	Sou	

NEGOTIABLE INSTRUMENTS

Bill of Exchange	Money Order
Bill of Lading	Negotiable Instrument
Bond	Note
Check	Savings Bond
Draft	Traveler's Check
Letter of Credit	

GOVERNMENT AGENCIES

Federal Deposit Insurance Corporation
Federal Reserve System
Treasury, Department of the

INTERNATIONAL FINANCE

Balance of Payments	European Monetary System
Bretton Woods	Exchange Rate
Convertibility	International Monetary Fund
Devaluation	
Eurodollar	Special Drawing Rights
European Monetary Agreement	

OTHER RELATED ARTICLES

Barter	Gresham's Law
Bullion	Indian, American (Money)
Coin Collecting	Inflation
Colonial Life in America (Money)	Investment
	Legal Tender

Counterfeiting	Mill
Depreciation	Mint
Depression	Silver (Uses of Silver)
Free Silver	Trade (The Use of Money)
Gold (Money)	Wampum
Gold Standard	

Outline

I. **How Money Developed**
   A. The First Coins
   B. The Development of Paper Money
II. **History of United States Currency**
   A. The First United States Currency
   B. The Rebirth of Paper Money
   C. United States Currency Today
III. **How Money Is Manufactured**
   A. Minting Coins
   B. Printing Paper Money
IV. **Money and the Economy**
   A. The Value of Money
   B. Definitions of the Money Supply
   C. How the Money Supply Is Determined
   D. The Role of the Federal Reserve System
V. **International Finance**
   A. The Balance of Payments
   B. International Reserves

Questions

How did people obtain the things they needed before they used money?
What organization controls the supply of money in the United States?
What motto appears on all U.S. coins and paper money?
Where was the first paper money used?
What were some things that people in the past used as money?
Why do certain coins have ridges called *reeding* on the edge?
How does inflation affect the value of money?
Where are U.S. coins manufactured?
How did the expression *two bits*, meaning 25 cents, originate?
When did the U.S. government begin to issue *greenbacks*?

Figure 13.1 Sample of Study Aids on Money in *The World Book Encyclopedia*

Source: *The World Book Encyclopedia.* © 1982 World Book-Childcraft International, Inc.

positions. For the three issues for this topic, the propositions may be as follows:

1. People should use money to purchase goods and services.
2. People should use cash to pay for goods and services.
3. People should wait for sales before they purchase goods.

Each of the above propositions is not necessarily true or false and, therefore, is debatable.

The learners then select two debating teams for each of the issues and pool the information in their essays to build arguments for both sides. They organize the information so that the debaters can use the notes efficiently while presenting their material. The debaters within each group practice presenting their ideas by having other members of the group take the opposing position.

During the three debates class members serve as the audience and participate in questioning the debaters and in evaluating the organization and presentation of the arguments.

For those learners who choose to do further reading in the area of economics, the following teacher reference is an excellent source of fiction and nonfiction material for children in grades K-6:

Nappi, A. T., Luksetich, W., & Dawson, G. G. *Learning economics through children's stories.* New York: Joint Council on Economic Education, 1978.

EVALUATIVE TEACHING

Since the purpose of this lesson is to read expository materials to gain and organize information for presentation in a debate, the job of the teacher is to reflect on classroom interactions and to evaluate the products. In reflecting on reader-text interactions, the teacher thinks about the reader's performance with the text, with related library materials, and with other information sources. The teacher records specific information relevant to students' abilities to underline important concepts, to locate information in the library efficiently, to take notes or to summarize from a variety of sources, and to apply this information in the writing of the essay and in preparing for the debate.

Also, the teacher reads selected essays, not for the purpose of correcting them, but to note whether readers are able to use the information to develop a persuasive argument. The final products to evaluate are the debates themselves. The teacher listens critically to the arguments each group presents and records any information helpful in planning further instruction: Content, organization of content, presentation, points made, credibility, and personal style may be important.

Further, the teacher analyzes the amount and quality of learner-learner interactions, particularly as learners work in groups, share their essays, and develop their debate positions. The teacher also considers self-evaluation; that is, the teacher's perception of success in teaching individual students or groups of students. This self-evaluation focuses on the process of questioning, elicitation from learners, type of feedback given to learners, number of learners the teacher interacts with, specific learners interacted with, and general learning climate in the room.

Teaching/Learning Plan Two:
Harriet Tubman—"Black Moses"[1]

A brief biography about Harriet Tubman from a history textbook is the basis for Plan Two. This text is appropriate for learners who are reading at approximately a fifth or sixth grade level. It may also serve as a listening activity for those learners reading at a lower level.

PREACTIVE TEACHING

Teacher Knowledge

The following article provides teachers with some background information on Tubman.

Related information.   Harriet Tubman was the most famous and successful conductor on the Underground Railroad. Her proud boast was "On my Underground Railroad I never ran my train off the track and I never lost a passenger." Born a slave on a Maryland plantation, Harriet Tubman knew at a very early age, that there was a way out of slavery. Determined to be free herself, she was not afraid to help others who dared to try to escape. When she was only thirteen, she interfered with efforts of an overseer who was trying to prevent a slave from escaping. She was struck on the head with a two-pound weight meant for the fleeing slave. As a result, she suffered violent headaches for the rest of her life. Quite often she would fall into a deep sleep that could last anywhere from a few minutes to several hours.

Harriet Tubman was a young woman in her twenties when she finally made her escape. Word had reached her that she and two of her brothers were going to be sold immediately. She left the plantation as soon as it was dark going straight to the farmhouse of a white woman who had promised to help her. The woman fed Harriet, gave her the names of two other people who would help her, and directed her to their houses. Thus Harriet began her first trip on the Underground Railroad. Both black and white people helped her on her way until she reached Philadelphia and freedom in 1849.

Twenty times in the next ten years Harriet Tubman made the dangerous trip back to the South to bring out 300 slaves. Whenever a slave became frightened and wanted to turn back, she would not hesitate to use the gun she always carried with her. Pointing her gun at the person, she would say, "You'll be free or you'll be dead."

The time came when it was too dangerous for Harriet Tubman to continue her trips South. The price on her head had reached forty thousand dollars. She worked on the Union side during the Civil War. She served as scout, nurse, and spy in the Carolinas.

After the Civil War, Harriet Tubman became active in the fight for women's suffrage. She also raised money to build schools for the newly

---

[1]Material for this plan was adapted from *EMBERS: Stories for a Changing World.* A supplementary reading comprehension program by R. S. Meyers, B. Banfield & J. Gastón-Colón. The Council on Interracial Books for Children and The Feminist Press. Copyright © the Council on Interracial Books for Children, 1983.

freed slaves. She died in Auburn, New York in 1913. A bronze plaque in front of the courthouse honors her memory.

Concepts to develop.   People working together create social change. Black and white people worked together to organize antislavery movements. Some individuals have leadership qualities that are a force in moving groups to action.

Summary of the text for students.   Harriet Ross Tubman was born into slavery in 1819 in Maryland. She had a hard life as a slave. In her twenties she married a free black named John Tubman.

She learned about the Underground Railroad and escaped from slavery in 1849. She took a job in Philadelphia to earn money to return to the South and bring her family North. Not all of her family wanted to come, but she did bring other slaves with her. This gave her the idea of extending the Underground Railroad to the South, and over the next 10 years she made 19 trips to Maryland. In the 1850s abolitionists learned of her work, and she began to speak publicly under the name *Moses*. She needed to use a false name because she was still a fugitive slave.

During the main part of the Civil War she was a guerilla leader; and toward the end of the war, she worked as a nurse on the battlefields. Following the war, she moved to Auburn, New York, and opened her house to southern blacks who were looking for work.

She became active in the Women's Suffrage Movement and worked actively in it until her death in 1913.

Text structure.   This selection is a biography written in narrative style. It gives a chronological account of the events in Harriet Tubman's life as the author perceives it. The selection is a study of her life within a historical context and highlights the interaction of personal characteristics and social conditions in the shaping of an individual's life.

The author uses exposition interspersed with descriptive and narrative paragraphs. Descriptive paragraphs create visual images of Harriet Tubman and her activities with the Underground Railroad, describing how she looked and acted as she worked. The author uses narrative paragraphs to relate anecdotes and incidents to help the reader understand Harriet Tubman's strength of character. For example, to illustrate her determination and bravery, the author presents an anecdote about a train ride in which Harriet Tubman refused to yield her seat. Elaboration, used throughout, clarifies information.

Teacher Decisions
This lesson is for readers at approximately a fifth or sixth grade level who are studying about slavery and the Civil War. They have read and discussed material that introduces the concept of slavery and life in the South during the early and middle 1800s. Some specific topics covered include life on a plantation, the hired slave in the city, how slaves managed to survive, attempts at escape or rebellion, the importance of family and religion in the slave community, and the Underground Railroad.

The teacher has selected the biography of Harriet Tubman included in the class textbook to personalize study of this period in history and to expand learners' understanding of the genre of biography. Depending on their knowledge of this time in history, the writing style of the biography, and their prereading activities, students will generate their own questions prior to reading the biography. They will also have an opportunity to compare information from different sources by participating in postreading activities centered on reading or listening to a narrative poem. Learners will understand that authors may select from a variety of writing forms and choose to emphasize different aspects of situations and relate different events and information about the same situation.

INTERACTIVE TEACHING

Prereading Activities

To elicit prior knowledge.   Have students listen to recordings of "Go Down, Moses." Discuss the lines: "Oppressed so hard they could not stand/Let my people go." Develop the idea of the overwhelming desire for freedom through questions such as the following:

What sentiments do these lines express?

What do you think these oppressed people wanted more than anything else?

Why do you think this song was created?

By whom?

Discuss with students the fact that Afro-Americans enslaved in this country many years ago composed this song. Develop the idea that freedom at any cost is important to any enslaved persons by asking questions such as the following:

How would you feel if you were enslaved?

What would be your greatest desire?

How would you try to achieve it?

If you planned an escape, what are some of the problems you might face?

How would you try to solve these problems?

What particular kinds of knowledge and skills would you have to have?

How would these help you?

What kind of assistance would you need? From whom might you get such assistance?

To build prior knowledge/indirect experience.   The teacher prepares students for understanding the difficulty of finding an escape route through discussion of an analogous situation cued by questions such as the following:

Have you ever taken an overnight hike or walked on nature trails?

What were some important safety rules you had to observe?

Why were these important?

In what ways was it necessary to have group cooperation?

How could one or two persons endanger the safety of a group?

How would escaping slaves face similar problems?

What would be the important difference between your situation and that of an escaped slave?

The teacher has students consider the following questions:

How would runaway slaves have to travel? Why?

What kind of qualities would runaway slaves have to have?

What kind of qualities would the people who helped them have to have?

What do you think would happen to runaway slaves who were caught? To the people who helped them?

Suppose slaves got frightened and wanted to turn back; should they be allowed to turn back? Why or why not?

Why was secrecy important?

Could slaves let people know their escape plans? Why or why not?

To focus reader attention.   Following this discussion of the difficulties in escaping from slavery, the teacher asks learners: What else would you want to know about Harriet Tubman's life? The teacher has students generate questions based on their knowledge of Harriet Tubman, the Civil War, and biography as a form of writing.

Learners may generate questions such as the following.

1. Where was Harriet Tubman born?
2. When was Harriet Tubman born?
3. Why is she an important person?
4. How does her life "fit" into the historical perspective?
5. How did Harriet Tubman help others?
6. How did she die?
7. When did she die?
8. What was her contribution to society?

Reader-Text Interaction
Students read the following biography of Harriet Tubman silently.

Brief Biography of Harriet Tubman

Harriet Ross was born a slave in 1819. At the age of six she was hired out to
a trapper, who made her wade into the swamps to recover his muskrats.
When she caught pneumonia, she was put to housework. She cleaned
house all day and took care of the children at night. She ran away so often
that she was sent into the forests to work with her father, a lumberjack who
worked for his master in the woods of Maryland's eastern shore. In her 20's
she married John Tubman, a free Black living in the neighborhood.

Then she learned of the Underground Railroad. Harriet Tubman
escaped by means of the Underground Railroad in 1849, when she was
about 30 years old. Instead of going on to Canada, she took a job in
Philadelphia, to earn enough money to return to Maryland for her family.

She went back in 1850, but found her aging parents unwilling to leave.
She took out her sister, though, and five other slaves who wanted to go.
That gave her the idea of repeated trips. Instead of waiting until slaves fled
to the North, why not extend the Underground Railroad into the South?
Over the next ten years, she made 19 trips back to Maryland. As her
tombstone says, "She never ran her train off the track and never lost a
passenger."

Her appearance helped. Short, heavyset and stooped, she would
waddle down a country road singing to herself. Slave patrols considered
her a half-wit who would eventually find her way home. But her songs
were messages to her "train" of refugees hiding in the woods. When the
patrol was gone, they would resume their journey.

In the late 1850's abolitionists learned of her adventures and made a
hero of her. She began giving talks to antislavery meetings, introduced
simply as Moses, after the Biblical hero who led his people to the Promised
Land. A false name was necessary because she was herself a fugitive slave,
and under the federal law of 1850 she could be taken back into slavery at
any time.

When the Civil War came, Harriet Tubman volunteered to work as a
spy, but the army refused her services. Her chance came when the navy
captured Port Royal, South Carolina, to use as a base for blockading the
South. The White planters fled the Union Army, but the Blacks remained
and eventually were allowed to form a regiment.

Harriet Tubman became a guerrilla leader, as the Port Royal Blacks
conducted raids into the heart of South Carolina, burning plantations and
freeing slaves. When northern troops under General Sherman arrived in
South Carolina, Harriet Tubman left. She spent the last months of the war
as a nurse on the Virginia battlefields.

When the fighting ended she was given a railroad pass home. But the conductor—this time a real one—refused to honor it because she was Black. Despite her advancing years it still took three men to wrench her out of her seat and throw her into the baggage car.

After the war she settled in Auburn, New York. She made her house into a haven for unemployed Blacks who had come north looking for work.

In her last years an Auburn neighbor, Susan B. Anthony, interested her in the women's suffrage movement. Though almost 90 years old, she brought to the movement all the strength and vigor of her years as Railroad conductor. She retained her strength to the very last. Having caught pneumonia, she summoned her circle of friends, conducted her own funeral service, led the group in singing "Swing Low, Sweet Chariot," and died. The year was 1913, seven years before women got the vote.

Student self-monitoring focuses on whether the text answers student-generated questions, and if not, what additional sources of information can learners use. Students also consider what additional information the text presents and how relevant it is to understanding Harriet Tubman as a person and evaluating her contribution to society.

Postreading Activities

Review of text information.   The teacher asks learners to recall the major events of Harriet Tubman's life. The teacher probes learner recall and asks learners to respond to higher-level student-generated questions. Students note any questions they are unable to answer due to lack of sufficient text information.

Seek additional related information.   If any student-generated questions remain unanswered, individual students or groups of students use reference materials and other biographies to find answers to their questions.

Expand language/reading competence.   The teacher has learners listen to or read the poem "Harriet Tubman" by Johanne Johnston. This material expands biographic information by focusing on the feelings of Harriet Tubman during a crucial experience in her life—her escape from Maryland to the North.

Harriet Tubman

The woods were dark all around her.
There was no road, no path,
no trail.
She could only tell what direction she was going
by looking up at the stars and following the
bright one that hung low
in the north.

When clouds covered the sky so that it was dark too,
she had to feel her way. She
put out her hands and felt the tree trunks.
Moss grew on the northern side of tree trunks.
She felt for the moss and where it grew it
showed her the way.

When day came, she had to hide
in bushes or behind rocks. When there were storms
she had nothing but bushes or trees
to cover her.
After a while, she had no more food.
Sometimes she found berries. And she drank
from brooks.
On and on she went, night after night,
covering mile after mile.
Sometimes, not often, she came near to a house
where she thought there were people who
would help her.
She would go to the house when it was day,
and the people would hide her for a day
while she ate something and rested.
Then when night came, she would
start on again.

At last, after many nights and days,
Harriet Tubman knew she was out of the South,
where she had been a slave.
She was in the North where Negroes could be free.
Soon she was in the city of Philadelphia
where there were white men and women who
would help her.
She made her way to those people and they
welcomed her with joy.
Harriet Tubman was safe and free.
"Now you must rest," they told her.
"After that, we will find you a place to live
and a job so that you can have a good life."

Harriet said, "Thank you. Yes I want a job
for a while. But as soon as I have earned
a little money, I must go back down South again."
"Go South again?" said her friends.
They were horrified.
"How can you think of making that terrible journey again?"
Harriet said, "I have brothers there, and
my mother and father. I have friends—all of them
still in slavery. Now that I know the way

I must go back and lead them to freedom also."
Her friends said, "You can't bring so many.
You will be caught."
Harriet said, "I will just have to make many trips."
Nobody could make her change her mind.
Before many weeks had passed, she was on her way.

The teacher focuses the discussion with questions such as:

1. How did you feel when you listened to or read the poem? How do you think Harriet Tubman felt on her first trip North?

The teacher encourages interaction and tries to elicit feelings of fear of the unknown, being alone, being hungry.

2. Compare your feelings when you read her biography and when you read the poem.
3. What did you learn about Harriet Tubman's character from the poem that added to what you already knew about her?
4. What differences are there between the information given in the biography and the poem? How can we verify the accuracy of the facts?

Reading about Harriet Tubman's life as a poet perceives it and comparing this form to past experiences with prose on the same topic become natural bridges to expanding writing competence through activities such as the writing of poetry or prose.

Teachers may suggest topics such as the following to learners:

I am someone who would help Harriet Tubman.

I am someone who would capture Harriet Tubman.

Or readers may want to keep a personal journal about events in their lives and about their feelings. This activity would increase learners' understanding of biographies and autobiographies.

Some students who are particularly interested in the life of Harriet Tubman and the historical times in which she lived may undertake a research project on topics such as: the Underground Railroad, the Abolition Movement, or Harriet Tubman's role in the Civil War.

Further, interested learners may choose to read additional materials about Harriet Tubman and her times. We suggest the following books.

Childress, A. When the rattlesnake sounds. New York: Coward, McCann & Geoghegan, 1975.

Epstein, S., & Epstein, B. Harriet Tubman: Guide to freedom. Champaign, Ill.: Garrard Publishing, 1968.

Freedman, F. Two tickets to freedom: The true story of Ellen and William Craft, fugitive slaves. New York: Simon & Schuster, 1971.

Lindstrom, A. J. *Sojourner Truth: Slave, abolitionist, fighter for women's rights*. New York: Julian Messner, 1980.

McGovern, A. *Runaway slave, the story of Harriet Tubman*. New York: Scholastic Magazines, 1965.

Petry, A. *Harriet Tubman, conductor on the underground railroad*. New York: Thomas Y. Crowell, 1955.

Sterling, D. *Freedom train, the story of Harriet Tubman*. New York: Doubleday, 1954.

Swift, H. S. *The railroad to freedom*. New York: Harcourt Brace Jovanovich, 1960.

EVALUATIVE TEACHING

The teacher reflects on the quality of class discussion following the reading of the biography and the poem. The teacher notes if learners were able to reconstruct the sequence of events in Harriet Tubman's life and relate these events to the times in which she lived. Further, the teacher analyzes the learners' ability to recognize Harriet Tubman's feelings and to relate her feelings during her life experiences to feelings learners have experienced in their lives. Also, the teacher thinks about the learners' performance with the two different types of biographical material and notes if the learners reacted differently to the materials and perceived differences and similarities between the materials. The teacher also examines the written products for both content and form as a first step in a student editing process.

Teaching/Learning Plan Three: "The Earth's Future"

The final lesson plan concentrates on a science unit which deals with the earth's future. It focuses on a particular aspect of the unit: the concept of population explosion. The background information for the teacher, the curriculum concepts, and the summary of text content cover the broad aspects of the earth's future to help the teacher place the lesson in proper perspective within the unit. Because the present lesson focuses on the section entitled "People and More People," we have analyzed only this part for text structure. This unit is for learners reading at approximately a fifth to seventh grade level, but teachers may use it with more capable readers and with other learners who may have some difficulty in reading the text but can benefit from the prereading activities, listening to the text or parts of the text, and using the graphic information.

PREACTIVE TEACHING

Teacher Knowledge

Related information. The following report, published by the New York Zoological Society, provides some relevant information about the earth's future. Teachers can obtain additional information about this and related topics by writing to the sources listed in the appendix under the ecology heading.

CONSERVATION IN THE 1980'S

The destruction of habitats and the depletion of species are proceeding so rapidly that in the decades ahead the nature of life on earth will be irrevocably changed.

At least 1,000 species of animals and 20,000 species of plants are currently threatened with extinction because of man. Not even this tally conveys the magnitude of the problem, however. Of the estimated three to ten million species, at most one million have been described scientifically. We mourn the loss of such species as the passenger pigeon and Steller's sea cow and decry the decline of the Siberian tiger and great whales, but we cannot mark the disappearance of those which remain unnamed and are so inconspicuous that their retreat is silent. With each loss an entire microcommunity of dependent organisms is altered and, ultimately, the natural balance of the ecosystem.

The most far-reaching cause for the loss of life is, perhaps, the least understood: the destruction of habitats. We understand the kind of damage wrought by indiscriminate hunting and environmental pollution. But as more people crowd the planet, wilderness itself is disappearing and is being replaced by habitations, crops, pastures, and forest plantations, leaving environments degraded of their former biological richness.

No habitat has been more severely affected than rainforests, fragile ecosystems supporting the greatest celebration of life on earth. At present rainforests are being felled at the rate of fifty acres a minute. Mountain habitats, too, are being destroyed at an alarming rate. As their forests are felled for timber and steep slopes are terraced into fields, wind and water soon erode the soils, leaving only bare rock.

As a rapidly expanding human population continues to exert pressure on remaining natural areas, the only hope of saving these pieces of nature lies with establishing a large network of reserves, a network providing a secure home for most of the world's plants and animals.

What reasons exist for preserving natural ecosystems, and how and where can the Animal Research and Conservation Center help?

Ecological problems are often described as scientific and technological, when in fact they are mainly social and cultural. The fight to preserve ecosystems cannot, of course, be separated from human poverty and the basic needs of an ever-increasing population. What arguments can conservationists pose, what information can they provide, to help convince government officials, especially in developing countries, to incorporate wildlife management at the highest levels of national planning?

We need to study ecological problems if we are to predict the consequences of our actions. As more and more wilderness disappears, nature preserves will provide planners with the only standards against which they can measure change over time. For example, studies have shown annual water runoff in a North American temperate forest region to be 40 percent greater in a felled area than in an unfelled area, and mineral losses, twenty times greater. Not only is this a compelling case against the practice of denuding hills, but also a graphic reminder of the fragile limits of our natural resources.

Burdened by ever-increasing populations, most governments are struggling to survive, and economic incentives for preserving wilderness and wildlife must be found. Reserves can, for example, sometimes provide a greater return per unit area from recreation than from any other form of land use. In addition, game ranching, whether antelope in Africa or capybara in South America, may in some areas provide greater profit than livestock alone. Native species may reproduce faster than cattle, thus provide more meat, or be more resistant to disease, need less management, and cause less damage to the environment.

Conservationists are understandably reluctant to assess the value of the black rhino or any other species solely in terms of its potential monetary value. Most wild species may never bring an economic return, although it is now estimated that an adult male lion is worth $515,000 in tourist revenues in Kenya. But what if its market worth changes? And, what of those species with no immediate useful purpose?

The world's conservation needs greatly exceed the combined resources of concerned individuals, scientists, and conservation organizations. Choices will have to be made. Some people pose the ethical argument that it is morally wrong to exterminate another species, perhaps any species, though more favorable arguments can be delivered on behalf of elephants than malarial parasites.

Some day we may want to rebuild what we have squandered, and from well-stocked reserves it would be possible to draw plants and animals. Thus, we need to build a genetic storehouse of species, and we need to do it soon. The continuing loss of species will affect our future seriously and directly. For example, nearly 50 percent of all prescription drugs are derived from plant and animal products. Recently, scientists isolated from pokeweed a chemical toxic to snails, a chemical which may help to battle schistosomiasis, the snail-transmitted disease which debilitates millions of people. Guinea pigs are now known to contain an anti-leukemic agent in their blood. What unknown agricultural crops and drugs await discovery among plants, and what wild animals could still provide us with food? Without the necessary genetic stock, we may never know.

In the final analysis, the wealth of a nation lies in its resources, including its land and the species it supports, and nations that abuse them will surely see their prosperity vanish. The task of preserving as much as possible of the earth's biological endowment must be assumed by this generation, and the next.

Concepts to develop

1. The interaction of people with the nonliving physical environment make up a complete ecosystem.
2. The population of the world is very large, is increasing, and is not evenly distributed over the land.
3. Many factors affect a population. They include food, water, sunlight, and space.
4. Increase in population affects the environment and increased competition for available resources (food, energy, and space).
5. Special farming techniques will result in increased food production.
6. Scientists in the future will use alternate forms of energy, including wind, moving water, tides, geothermal heat, and atomic fission and fusion.
7. Conservation will protect our natural resources and endangered species.

Concepts 1, 3, and 6 are adapted from Minimum Teaching Essentials, Grades K-9, Board of Education of the City of New York, 1979.

Summary of the text for students

The earth's human population is about 4.5 billion. It is growing so fast that some experts expect it to reach almost eight billion by the year 2000. The population began to rise rapidly in the late 1600's as industry grew and modern medicine developed. The earth can supply enough food for many more than its present population. But there may be problems in getting food from where it is grown to where people need it.

[Space is also a problem for the people and animals on earth][2] The human population is spread unevenly over the earth. Some people live much closer to each other than other people. Experiments have shown that when small animals are crowded together they fight more, do not eat as well, and stop producing healthy young. Open spaces are important because they are places where people can be alone, relax, and enjoy natural beauty. Wilderness areas are important because they provide homes for and protect plants and animals, especially those that are endangered.

The future of life on earth appears to be very encouraging. Population growth appears to be slowing. Fusion reactors and solar cells may supply much of our energy in the future. Materials needed to build new products will probably come mostly from recycled waste. Food may be produced in chemical solutions. [Most people think that having clean air and water, wholesome food, and open space for people are important.]

Source: J. Abruscato and others, 1980, pp. 261, 266, 271.

[2]Authors' insertions are in brackets.

Text structure. The author presents expository material that encourages learners to read independently for major concepts. The author begins with a series of questions to help learners relate prior knowledge to the topic and includes advance organizers to focus the reader's attention on the important concepts. Some interspersed questions encourage readers to integrate material with their previous knowledge; other questions focus learner attention on important concepts in the text. After presenting questions that focus attention, the author provides answers with concrete examples, an illustration using graphic material, and explanatory discourse.

A concrete example illustrates just how many people the world population of 4.5 billion really is. Graphic information illustrates the concept of population explosion, and an activity in the form of questions guides the reader in using the bar graph. The description of the graph that follows the activity is chronological, tracing population growth over time. Explanatory discourse then focuses on why the rapid increase in human population occurred and uses predominantly cause-effect relations with elaboration of details to aid in the explanation.

The final two paragraphs in this section present several problems in the form of questions to stimulate learners to think about solutions. The function of the last paragraph is to act as a transition to the next two sections of the chapter.

Teacher Decisions

This lesson is for members of a sixth grade class that has been studying the earth: Learners have studied content related to sources of energy and how energy is produced, the problems of pollution and the need for clean energy and new types of energy. They have also studied the importance of saving natural resources of the world including air, water, and sources of energy and food and are now ready to read about the earth's future. The teacher is aware that this text, as most content area texts, does not include all of the concepts that need developing for this curriculum unit. Therefore, the teacher supplements the material in the text with relevant materials from libraries and agencies and organizations active in this area of ecology such as films, film strips, newspapers, periodicals. The organizations and agencies listed in the appendix for the teacher are among those that students can also contact. The teacher encourages students to write business letters requesting information and to use reference materials in the library.

The first section of the chapter is entitled "People and More People." It introduces the concept of population explosion and serves as an introduction to the next two sections that discuss population changes and the interrelationship of population growth and our natural resources. The students' background knowledge of natural resources will help them to understand problems inherent when a population explosion occurs and limited natural resources are available. The author includes a bar graph to develop the concept of population explosion. However, the teacher may be unsure of the learners' ability to interpret bar graphs and plans a prereading activity about bar graphs for diagnosis and knowledge-building.

The students' purpose in reading this first section is to expand their knowledge base about world population growth and related problems. This should help them understand the next two sections of this chapter that focus on the interrelatedness of people, resources, space, and our future.

INTERACTIVE TEACHING

Prereading Activities

To elicit prior knowledge.   The teacher uses the PREP technique (Langer, 1982) and says:

1.   Tell me anything you think of when you hear the words "population explosion."

After each response is written on the chalkboard, the teacher asks:

2.   What made you think of _____ ?

After students have responded, the teacher closes with the question:

3.   Based on our discussion, have you any new ideas about the population explosion?

To build prior knowledge.   The amount and depth of knowledge elicited during the PREP determines if learners can process the text or if they need further background knowledge. In the latter case the teacher may choose to use the words elicited during PREP to build a word map.

Since understanding how to read a bar graph or histogram is crucial to processing this text, the teacher provides a graph (Figure 13.2) for analysis and discussion.

The teacher has selected this graph because it measures specific objects realistically represented for the reader. This concrete representation of the specific buildings, some of which are familiar to readers, provides an intermediate step toward reading bar graphs. The teacher uses the following questions to elicit specific information that then leads to generalizations about reading bar graphs.

1.   What is this graph all about?
2.   If the artist had placed labels along the bottom of this graph (horizontal axis), what do you think they would say?
3.   What do the numbers on the sides (vertical axis) of the graph stand for?

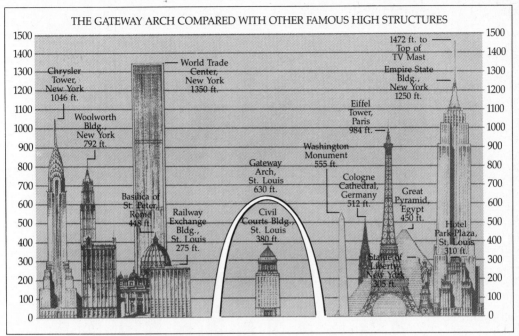

Figure 13.2 Graph Using Realistic Objects

4. What do you notice about the space between each of the intervals on the vertical axis?
5. Choose a structure and tell the group how high it is in feet.
6. Notice where the top of the structure you have chosen falls on the scale for feet. How does this relate to the number of feet listed under the name of the structure?
7. What is the tallest structure? Shortest structure?
8. Which is taller: the World Trade Center or the Statue of Liberty? The Cologne Cathedral in Germany or the Basilica of St. Peter in Rome? The World Trade Center or the Empire State Building?

To aid the readers in the transition from this graph to the standard form of a bar graph, the teacher presents a graph (Figure 13.3) that includes the same information without concrete illustrations.

Learners compare the two graphs, and then the teacher elicits the following generalizations about reading graphs:

1. Graphs usually have a caption or title that tells the reader the main point of the graph. If the writer has not captioned the graph, the reader must infer the topic from the data in the graph and the text.
2. Graphs have vertical and horizontal axes with specific functions.

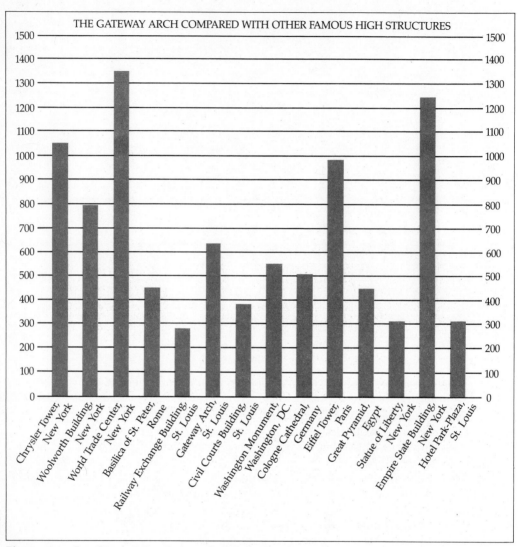

Figure 13.3 Bar Graph Representing the Information from Figure 13.2.

3. Frequencies are usually along the vertical axis and generally have equal intervals.
4. The horizontal axis lists or names the specific object, thing, situation, or time being described in frequency form.

To focus reader attention. For this section of the text, the author has provided some questions and advance organizers to focus attention on important points (see paragraphs one and two in "People . . . and More People" that follows). The teacher directs students to these textual aids and instructs them to read and think about the answers to these questions. In addition, the teacher directs them to attend to the interspersed questions to help them focus attention and integrate the knowledge.

Reader-Text Interaction
Reader-text interaction focuses on the following selection.

---

1 People . . . and More People

1. Have you ever been to an amusement park or street fair that was so crowded you could hardly get to where you were going? There are a great many people in this world, aren't there? Do you know how many? Do you know if the human population is increasing in size?
2. When you finish this lesson, you should be able to:

Tell the term used to describe the rapid growth of the human population.

Tell when and why the rapid increase in the human population began.

Identify two problems that the rapid growth of the human population may bring.

3. No one really knows exactly how many people there are in the world. Can you think of reasons why this is so? However, based on all the information obtained, the number is believed to be about 4.5 billion. Do you have any idea how many people that is? Perhaps this will help you. If you were to lay down 4.5 billion pennies as close together as possible, they would cover 226 football fields.
4. Not only is the human population of the earth very large, it is also increasing. The following activity will give you an idea of just how rapidly it is increasing.
    Study the graph [on page 348]. It shows how the human population of the earth has grown from A.D. 1 to the present.

1. How many people were living in the year 1?
2. How many years did it take the human population to double from the year 1?
3. When did the population reach one billion?
4. How long did it take the population to double from one billion to two billion? from two billion to four billion?
5. In what year do you predict the earth's population will reach eight billion?
6. What has been happening to the amount of time our population has been taking to double itself?

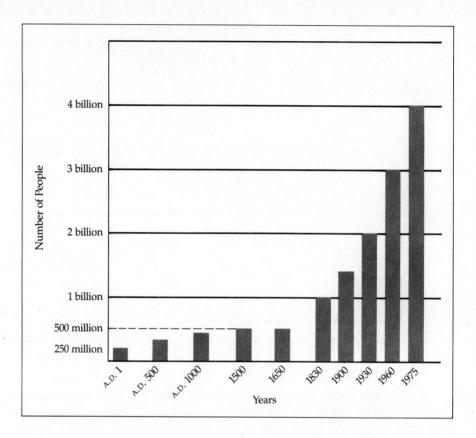

5. In the year A.D. 1, the human population of the earth was about 250 million people. It took about 1,500 years for the population to double to 500 million. By 1830, in a little over 300 years, the population had doubled again to one billion. One hundred years later, the population had doubled again to two billion, and just 45 years later, in 1975, the population was over four billion people. Our population has been taking less and less time to double itself. In only 150 years, it has grown over four times as big. Many people call this rapid growth the **population explosion**. If this present rate of growth continues, the human population will reach almost eight billion in the year 2000.

6. Can you think of any reasons why the population began to rise so fast after the year 1650? One reason is that the science of medicine began to develop at that time.

7. The population began to increase in size because people lived longer. Another reason was the development of industry. Industry produced tools to help farmers grow more food. It also provided jobs, helping more people earn enough money to buy food. This increased supply of money and food meant that more people could raise and support larger families.

8. The rapid growth of the human population may also bring some problems to the earth and its people. For example, what do you think will happen to the earth's resources if the population keeps rising so quickly? Will there be enough resources in the world for everyone to survive?

9. Some scientists say that enough food can be grown on earth to feed 40 to 50 billion people. However, most of this food cannot be grown in those places where the majority of the people in this world are located. How would you get the food to these people? What fuel would you use to transport the food? Some people believe that there are already too many people in this world who do not get enough to eat, and that more people would just make matters worse. How do you feel about the human *population explosion?*

QUESTIONS

Write your answers on a sheet of paper.

1. What term is used to describe the rapid growth of the human population?
2. When and why did the rapid increase in the human population begin?
3. What are two problems that the rapid growth of the human population may bring?

Students silently read paragraphs one to four and the graph. They complete the activity in A, following paragraph four by studying the graph and responding to each question. At this point the teacher may choose to discuss students' answers (teacher-student monitoring) or may have the students read on through paragraph five that provides an explanation of the graph and answers to the questions. Students then check their mental responses with those the author provides in paragraph five. Following either graph activity, the students complete the section through paragraph nine and continue to monitor their comprehension to determine if they are processing the content cued by the advance organizers.

Postreading Activities

Review of text information. The learners retell the text information and the teacher may probe the learners' recall to extend the retrieval of important information. If necessary, the teacher may use the structured questions the author provides following paragraph nine that restate the information cued by advance organizers in paragraph two. Also, the teacher may use questions in paragraph nine that encourage divergent thinking as a basis for expanding class discussion. The teacher may also choose to add evaluative analysis to the discussion by asking questions such as:

1. Do the topics of the questions logically follow the information you have just read?
2. Are these the kind of questions that you would think of after reading this section? Which ones? Why or why not?

Other teacher-constructed questions might focus on the graph. For example, the teacher might ask:

1. How did the graph help you understand population explosion?
2. Why is it important to "read" the graph as well as the words in the text?

Expand language/reading competence. The teacher encourages learners to write business letters to one or more of the agencies listed under the ecology heading in the appendix.

The teacher and learners discuss the first draft of letters and focus on answering questions such as the following.

1. Did I include my return address in the upper right-hand corner?
2. Did I include the correct date under the return address?
3. Is the salutation that I chose appropriate for the person I am writing to, and have I used the correct punctuation?
4. Does the body of the letter include all the information necessary to communicate my message and to receive a response?
5. Have I included an appropriate complimentary closing?
6. Have I signed my letter with my signature?

Learners may also compare the form of their business letters to a model business letter on display in the class. Students then edit the letters both for form and content and prepare a final draft for mailing.

EVALUATIVE TEACHING

The teacher thinks about student responses during a review of the text information and notes if the students have understood the major concepts, the relation of the graph to the text material, and whether student responses to questions presented to stimulate divergent thinking are logical and creative.

Because the reading material serves primarily as an introduction to the next two sections in the unit, the only written products for evaluating are the students' business letters. The teacher evaluates these letters as a final product after a process of editing and rewriting. Of course, the teacher reflects on the process as well as the product.

Summary

This chapter presents illustrative teaching/learning plans using content area textbooks in detail. Each lesson plan includes background material for the teacher, covering content and text organization, and a series of direct instructional activities to guide the teacher during interactive teaching. The lesson includes some comments to help the teacher evaluate the teaching/learning process.

PART

V

LEARNERS WITH SPECIAL NEEDS

Knowing the Exceptional Learner

I n observing learners in the classroom, the teacher becomes aware of identifiable subgroups of children whose needs in reading instruction may vary from that of the general school population. Experts refer to these learners as exceptional because they deviate from the norm. Among the most common exceptional learners in the regular classroom are children who exhibit one or more specific deficits in learning and children who are unusually talented readers. These learners have been designated learning-disabled learners and gifted learners, respectively.

For both the learning-disabled learner and the gifted learner, schools may provide a range of programming alternatives. For the learning disabled child, educational services include self-contained special classes, resource rooms within school buildings, and itinerant teachers who may serve two or more schools. For the gifted child these services include acceleration, enrichment in the regular classroom, special classes on a part-time or full-time basis, and special school-based offerings outside the school day.

This chapter speaks to the classroom teacher who may have both learning-disabled and gifted children in the classroom. We will give characteristics of each of these populations along with some guidelines to use in identifying these exceptional children. In addition, we provide some suggestions for creating a supportive classroom environment within a language-thinking approach to reading to enable these children to function maximally.

The Learning Disabled

When experts label a child as having a "learning disability," they imply some deficit in the learning process. The term itself communicates that the child is not performing in school-related activities at a level commensurate with predicted intellectual abilities. In most cases the learning problems seem to arise from some type of selective central nervous system dysfunction: some interference with the workings of the brain, in particular the cerebral cortex, the center for higher thought processes, and the spinal cord, which carries messages between the brain and parts of the body. This interference may be the result of many different factors such as prenatal or perinatal difficulties, illness or injury, biochemical factors, genetic factors, or developmental delay. Note that not all children with some type of central nervous system dysfunction have problems in learning.

The identification of specific etiology for a particular child is often obscure, because most case histories are retrospective; not until after the interferences become evident in school-related activities do professionals hear about these children. Even an in-depth evaluation may not show positive neurological evidence for some children due either to the inherent weaknesses in current evaluation procedures or to the subtle nature of the physiologically based disorders. Although determining the exact cause of a learning problem is not easy, mild to severe problems do exist. For the teacher the focus should be on understanding how these difficulties manifest themselves in classroom functioning regardless of etiology.

DEFINITION OF LEARNING DISABLED

Most definitions of the "learning disabled" are descriptive of behaviors and focus on symptoms. Most authorities accept the definition of children with learning disabilities formulated in 1968 by the National Advisory Committee on Handicapped Children and placed into law with the 1969 Children with Specific Learning Disabilities Act.

> Children with special learning disabilities exhibit a disorder in one or more of the basic psychological processes involved in understanding or using spoken or written language. These may be manifested in disorders of listening, thinking, talking, reading, writing, spelling or arithmetic. They include conditions which have been referred to as perceptual handicaps, brain injury, minimal brain dysfunction, dyslexia, developmental aphasia, etc. They do not include learning problems which are due primarily to visual, hearing, or motor handicaps, to mental retardation, emotional disturbance, or to environmental disadvantage. (p. 4)

As the broadness of the definition indicates, learning-disabled children do not constitute a homogeneous group; this group includes children with mild to severe interferences in many different school-related areas. Some children display only limited deficiencies in particular areas, whereas others experience problems in several areas. Further, the reaction of other children to their problems and the reaction of significant adults in their environment influence the functioning of these children and further differentiate the group of children labeled as "learning disabled." Thus, children's needs may be different and require individual teaching adaptations once the teacher in consultation with specialists has established patterns of strengths and weaknesses.

PL94-142 AND THE LEARNING DISABLED

The federal government in Public Law 94-142, Education of the Handicapped Act (Federal Register, 1977), has mandated that educators develop individualized educational programs for all handicapped children including the category of learning disabled. This law provides for the involvement of parents in planning for the educational programs of their children. Parents in conference with educational personnel must agree on the individual educational plan (IEP) established for each child.

Although actual IEPs vary from state to state and even district to district in specific localities, they all are mandated to include (1) a statement of the child's present levels of educational performance based on a complete psychoeducational evaluation; (2) annual goals including short term instructional objectives; (3) specific special education and related services to be provided; (4) the extent to which the child will be able to participate in regular educational programs; (5) projected dates for the initiation of services and the anticipated duration of services; and (6) objective criteria and evaluation procedures and schedules for determining if the child is achieving the instructional objectives. An important feature of the law is the concept of *least restrictive environment*. In general, this means that all children including the handicapped should receive an education that does not inhibit their interaction with peers and that offers an environment that is most conducive to helping the child learn, given the child's handicapping condition.

Mainstreaming, integrating handicapped children in regular classrooms, may be least restrictive for many children but is only one of several options that may be least restrictive depending on an individual child's needs (Meyen, 1982). For the learning-disabled child, least restrictive environment may mean full-time placement in a special class, part-time placement in a special class, placement in a regular class setting with supplementary education in a specialized setting such as a resource room or by an itinerant teacher in the regular classroom, or placement in a regular class with minimal supportive services such as the use of a consultant to aid the classroom teacher in planning for instruction. In the latter case, the classroom teacher maintains primary responsibility for the child's education (Reid & Hresko, 1981).

When educators have determined that the best environment for a learning disabled child is a part-time special class or a regular class with supportive services, the teacher must still plan and implement language and reading experiences for the child, as well as coordinate plans with the special educator.

Criticisms of PL94-142

Reid (1978), although not opposed to PL94-142, has criticized aspects of the law, particularly those that lead to a behavioral approach to special education. Her criticisms are particularly relevant for classroom teachers who are teaching reading through a language-thinking approach. She notes that for the most part IEPs have been interpreted as necessitating the spelling out of specific behavioral objectives that allow only a narrow definition of both curriculum and competence. Reid argues that those who advocate educational procedures based on the attainment of behavioral objectives view knowledge as finite, well-defined, and acquired through social transmission. This perspective is in direct conflict with what experts know about the active nature of learning and the complex process of reading. This behavioral approach to teaching ignores the personalized and active nature of learning in which learners understand they are responsible for their own learning. Since learning-disabled children tend to have problems in learning on their own, in organizing and integrating information, a fragmented skills approach to learning to read only reinforces these problems of independent learning for such children. Organizing behavioral objectives around skills hierarchies distorts the reading process.

IEPs and Meaning-Based Instruction

PL94-142, although typically interpreted by educators as a behavioral approach to teaching, does not mandate that IEPs focus on detailed skill hierarchies or that teachers must use materials such as workbooks, kits, and machines in the instructional program. Within the parameters of PL94-142, educators can evaluate learning-disabled children by observing their language, using a modification of the Reading Miscue Inventory, analyzing their silent reading behavior and responses to written material, and examining their writing samples. In the instructional program IEPs can—and should—include purposeful reading and writing experiences using real materials instead of isolated exercise materials.

For example, the following IEP illustrates a meaning-based approach to evaluation and teaching.

Charles: Age 8 years 10 months

Present level of educational performance. Interviews, observations, and evaluation based on a modified Reading Miscue Inventory indicate that Charles focuses on accuracy of decoding rather than meaning. When he reads aloud, he does not sample from print but focuses on matching sounds and symbols. He often confuses long and short vowel sounds even in context. He is able to retell specific story details but often does not distinguish relevant from irrelevant information.

Annual goal. Charles will learn to read stories and informational material and respond in a way that shows he is constructing meaning. Meaningful substitutions, deletions, and insertions that indicate attention to meaning at the sentence and passage levels will characterize his oral reading miscues.

Short-term objectives. Charles will dictate language-experience stories on topics of personal interest and share them with others.

Charles will listen to stories with predictable story events and learn to retell the important events of the story.

He will silently read story and informational material and learn to respond to questions that focus on the relevant ideas.

He will read stories from which the teacher has deleted predictable words and replace the deleted words with words or phrases that make sense.

He will learn to distinguish between vowel sounds that confuse him and read passages that contain a variety of words with these sounds. (Husselriis, 1982).

READING AND THE LEARNING DISABLED

Many learning disabled children fall into that category of children for whom learning to read is a difficult task. These children require not only intensive teacher-directed instruction including highly structured specific strategy lessons but also many opportunities to apply their learning in natural reading situations. In those cases in which a special educator is using a behavioral approach to teaching reading the classroom teacher must provide opportunities for children to apply their specific learnings in understanding real reading materials.

Experiences in the classroom should include using the language experience approach and reading stories and expository text as we describe throughout this book. For learning-disabled children who have more than the usual amount of difficulty in constructing meaning from text, understanding that reading is an enjoyable, communicative activity is especially crucial. From the start of schooling, these children, as all children, must *actively* take part in a language and print-rich environment in which they listen to stories and poems, read along as stories are read, share their ideas with others orally and through print, and read materials of interest at whatever level is comfortable. What learning-disabled children cannot decode, the teacher must read aloud to them.

These shared language and reading experiences are even more important for children having difficulty learning to read than for others. These experiences help them to develop many of the understandings about reading that most other children develop naturally as they read. They learn what reading is all about, they gain familiarity with the structure and content of stories and informational materials, and they learn to relate what they already know to what is read. Only these types of ongoing experiences can build the necessary background to help children understand how authors use language to present ideas. These experiences involving oral language and print provide children with knowledge needed to understand other stories, poems, and informational material.

When children are exposed only to a behavioral approach to learning to read, they miss these repeated experiences with different forms of written materials. These experiences are necessary to build an internal structure or schema for recognizing how writers organize stories and informational materials. Without this knowledge most children, let alone the learning disabled, have difficulty understanding what they read. To learn decoding isolated from a focus on meaning can only be detrimental for these children. Even if they become accurate decoders, their problems in organizing and integrating information will most probably still persist and interfere with reading. Further, a reading program for the learning disabled that focuses on accurate word reading to the neglect of reading and thinking about the structure and content of real materials wastes valuable time for this learner who requires more guidance, time, and effort than others in learning to be an active reader; such a reading program reinforces the misconception that reading is tedious and minimally useful.

IMPLICATIONS FOR THE TEACHER

In any regular classroom the teacher may expect to find one or two learning-disabled children who require an adapted learning program in order to function. Experts have estimated the incidence of severe cases at 1 to 3 percent of the school population (National Advisory Committee on Handicapped Children, 1968). When mildly handicapped children are included, the prevalence of learning disabilities increases to anywhere from 5 to 15 percent. However, when a school system makes a concerted effort to exclude children whose problems are not really handicapping as well as those children who are more appropriately conceptualized under other categories of handicapping conditions, the one to three percent prevalence estimate seems satisfactory (Reid & Hresko, 1981).

As you can see, this population is heterogeneous and includes children who have mild to severe learning problems. Within this population are children who can compensate for many of their learning problems and exhibit only subtle signs of learning disability. These children, usually of superior ability, adapt their classroom performance so that their problems are not readily evident. Generally, this group of children functions at age- and grade-appropriate levels rather than the advanced levels expected in terms of their academic potential. However, some of these children who have adequately compensated in the lower grades begin to exhibit some of the problems of the learning disabled when they face the increasingly complex academic tasks of the middle and upper grades. All of these children, although differing in degree of adaptation to their learning problems, share a common problem: Learning and appropriate school behavior involve excessive effort and emotional stress.

Recognizing the Learning Disabled

Part of a classroom teacher's responsibility is recognizing those children who may be learning disabled and referring them for evaluation. The first indication of a problem is that the child is not learning at the expected level given what the teacher knows and observes about the child.

This section provides some guidelines to help the teacher in observing overall classroom functioning, some guidelines specific to observing reading and writing performance, and a discussion of how problems in learning may interact with social-emotional functions.

Within a language-thinking environment that encourages active participation and communication, some general areas of importance cut across most school activities. Teachers may observe problems in some of these general areas in children who upon evaluation they classify as having learning disabilities. We suggest the following questions as a guide.

In general, does the learner

remain attentive and focused on the relevant aspects of learning situations?

construct meaning from written or spoken language across different communication situations?

organize ideas for speaking or writing?

retain and recall written material or orally presented information?

discriminate different letters, words, or numbers in written or oral form?

work for the expected amount of time without becoming unduly tense or tired?

sit for required lengths of time?

Children who are not learning disabled may have problems in these same areas due to many factors such as emotional problems, visual or hearing problems, experiential deficits, or inappropriate instruction. The purpose of a complete psychoeducational and neurological evaluation is to determine if the noted problems have a physiological basis that affects the basic psychological processes of language, attention, memory, and perception and, therefore, places these children in the category of learning disabled.

The teacher who is screening children for learning disabilities can see learning problems most clearly when the child reads and writes. The following questions can serve as a guide in observing children as they function. As we cautioned previously, only a follow-up evaluation by a specialist can determine if the nature and extent of the problem warrants the label "learning disabled" because certain children exhibit similar behaviors when reading and writing and yet are not learning disabled.

In reading, does the learner

read mechanically without expression?

frequently reverse letters, numbers, and words?

have difficulty in applying word identification skills?

have difficulty in identifying whole words by sight?

hesitate or read very slowly compared to peers?

repeat words or lose his or her place?

move his or her lips during silent reading (subvocalization)?

read aloud frequently but with limited comprehension?

exhibit a wide discrepancy between listening comprehension and reading comprehension?

focus on irrelevant ideas and have difficulty relating them to each other and prior experience?

focus on the concrete and explicit details?

lack a sense of story sequence or information order?

In writing, does the learner

write beyond the limits of the page and line?

consistently reverse letters, numbers, and words?

copy incorrectly from the chalkboard or from materials at the desk?

tend to write incomplete sentences?

present ideas in a disorganized form?

frequently use incorrect punctuation?

lack the ability to use phonic cues for correct spelling?

display written work that deteriorates when the student is under the pressure of time testing or when work is long or demanding?

avoid written work though highly verbal in class?

In any discussion of learning problems, we cannot overlook the social and emotional aspects. Social and emotional problems, to differing degrees, also frequently plague children with learning disabilities. Although learning problems and adjustment problems often appear together, no simple relationship exists between the two. Many factors influence a child's affective development and *affect* and *cognition* are closely related. All children's experiences, as well as the interpretations they give to these experiences, help form their developing personalities, affect the way they view new information, and influence behavior. If children have problems learning on their own and organizing and integrating information, these problems may not be limited to reading or writing situations or other academic areas. Understanding the requirements of social situations also involves attention, focus on relevant information, and the organization and integration of this information with prior knowledge in a way that matches the expectations of others. Some learning-disabled children can do this; a small number even do this with ease. But many children who are having problems making sense of aspects of their world and organizing themselves in their world have difficulties in interpersonal relations. These difficulties stem from problems in interpreting and acting appropriately on the many messages in their social environment—school, community, or home. Other factors also influence the social-emotional development of learning-disabled children.

As we discuss in Chapter 2, in our literate society unyielding pressures push children to learn how to read. One of the major school tasks in the elementary years is to accomplish mastery of written communications. Problems in this area make a developing child vulnerable to feelings of inadequacy and inferiority. If present, these feelings become part of the child's basic sense of self and affect the child's approach to new social and learning situations. The way in which the family, the school, and peers treat the child and the learning problem also influences the child's self perceptions and reactions. An important consideration for the educator in understanding the type and extent of any social-emotional problems for a learner is determining if the child has the observed problem behaviors in certain learning situations only or if the child has them in many different contexts. Therefore, the teacher must observe the child in a variety of academic and nonacademic settings to gain a realistic picture of overall functioning.

Providing a Supportive Environment

Because school-related activities require additional effort for learning-disabled children, creating a supportive environment geared to meet their specific educational and social-emotional needs is important. Learning-disabled children, by the very nature of their disabilities, frequently work under excessive tension and pressure that may further interfere with their academic functioning. The classroom teacher and educational specialist create an environment jointly, based on specific assessment data following learner evaluation. This environment varies from child to child because it depends on specific evaluation data. However, teachers may implement some general guidelines in working with all learning-disabled children. Among these are to:

1.   follow all referrals to both in-school and out-of-school services. This follow-up should be coordinated with guidance counselors or school psychologists if these services are available.

2.   coordinate the work of all specialists involved with the learning-disabled child. This may involve the school psychologist, learning disability resource teacher, speech/language clinician, reading specialist, and all related out-of-school services.

3.   follow and adapt the guidelines specialists suggest to allow the child to both receive and express informational content through those means most facilitative for the child. That is, provide the necessary methodology and materials to help these learners compensate for—or work around—their problems.

4.   discuss the child's problems openly with the child in an understanding and supportive manner. This will encourage the child to communicate feelings and problems to the teacher openly.

5.   accept the interruptions that result when a learning-disabled child has to move in and out of the regular classroom for specialized work.

6.   encourage classmates to understand that some children may have difficulties in learning or performing certain activities and that these difficulties are not necessarily related to effort or intellectual ability.

7.   help classmates to understand that learning-disabled children may exhibit disturbing behaviors at times and that these behaviors are not necessarily intentional nor directed at a particular individual.

8.   communicate with parents of learning-disabled children in a

planned, continuous way, including conferences and written communication. As a result, both parent and teacher can be fully aware of learning progress and needs.

The Gifted Learner

The gifted child has been notably neglected in the area of reading. Reading programs for the gifted are scarce even though experts estimate that a minimum of 3 to 5 percent of the school population may be classified as gifted (Marland, 1972). In contrast to other categories of exceptional children, at this time no federal mandates exist for school districts to provide special services for the gifted and talented. Special programs for this group of children are at the discretion of state and local school districts. As a result, at present services in the schools for these exceptional children are limited.

DEFINITION OF THE GIFTED

Congress in 1978 passed the Gifted and Talented Children's Education Act (PL95-596) that defines gifted as follows:

> . . . gifted and talented children, and whenever applicable, youth, who are identified at the preschool, elementary, or secondary level as possessing demonstrated or potential abilities that give evidence of high performance capability in areas such as intellectual, creative, specific academic, or leadership ability, or in the performing and visual arts, and who, by reason thereof, require services or activities not ordinarily provided by the school. (Federal Register, October 1978)

Children's ability in manipulating internally learned symbol systems is perhaps the *sine qua non* of giftedness. It allows children to learn on their own and to imagine and create new forms and products without waiting for direction from teachers or stimulation from the environment (Gallagher, 1977). Students can have special abilities in any one of the symbol systems in the environment. They may show special talent in areas such as language, mathematics, science, performing arts, or visual arts. More specifically, educators, comparing gifted children with their age peers, note that on the whole the former tend to have:

> a longer attention span, a persistant curiosity, a desire to learn rapidly, a good memory, an awareness and appreciation of people and things, a wide range of interests, and the ability to solve the many problems besetting society. They value independence which is task and contribution oriented, reject conformity, hold high social ideals and values, and possess individuality and originality. (Labuda, 1974, p. 4)

Further, most authorities familiar with definitions of the gifted agree that the gifted child is superior in the ability to generalize, to recognize relationships, to comprehend meanings, and to think logically. An advisory panel to the U.S. Commissioner of Education (Marland, 1972) cautioned against the use of a definition that is too specific and does not allow for flexibility. They suggested the following operational definition that focuses on evidence for determining special intellectual gifts or talents:

consistently superior scores on many appropriate standardized tests;

judgment of teacher, pupil personnel specialists, administrators, and supervisors familiar with the abilities and potentials of the individual;

demonstration of advanced skills, imaginative insight, and intense interest and involvement;

judgment of specialized teachers (including art and music), pupil personnel specialists, and experts in the arts who are qualified to evaluate the pupil's demonstrated and/or potential talent (p. 21).

In a creative thinking seminar with E. Paul Torrance (1962), 87 teachers, counselors, and school administrators drew up a set of behavioral indicators of creative talent. Most of the behaviors the group listed can be organized according to the six kinds of thinking ability Guilford and Merrifield (1960) consider part of creativity.

1. *Sensitivity to problems:* seeing defects, needs, deficiencies; seeing the odd, the unusual; and seeing what must be done.
2. *Flexibility:* ability to shift from one approach to another and from one line of thinking to another and to free oneself from a previous set.
3. *Fluency:* ability to produce many ideas.
4. *Originality:* ability to produce remote, unusual, or new ideas or solutions.
5. *Elaboration:* ability to work out the details of a plan, idea, or outline; and ability to "embroider" or elaborate.
6. *Redefinition:* ability to define or perceive in a way different from the usual, established, or intended way or use.

Although identifying gifted students seems relatively easy, not all gifted children display the overt eagerness for learning or the extraordinary academic characteristics consistent with our common perception of the gifted. Some children, although gifted, may not function at the exceptionally high level expected of a gifted learner. They tend to be either uninterested or bored, overconforming to classroom activities, or living in an environment that rarely recognizes or encourages giftedness. These children, as well as children more easily identified as gifted learners, need special programming to help them function at their optimal level.

READING AND THE GIFTED
In reading, gifted children as well as other children need a program that provides differentiation in both instruction and selection of materials. For gifted children who can read at school entrance, the teacher must provide a

variety of opportunities in which they can extend and refine their reading performance. Throughout the school years gifted learners should have many opportunities to read various materials—prose, poetry, fiction, non-fiction, drama, and essays at their level of functioning. Reading and related language activities should challenge those children to reach their highest potential levels of functioning. Torrance (1965) aptly describes the gifted reader as a person who reads creatively and is sensitive to problems and possibilities in whatever is read. This reader is aware of gaps in knowledge, unsolved problems, missing elements, and elements that are incomplete or out of focus. This reader sees new relationships, creates new combinations, synthesizes relatively unrelated elements into coherent wholes, redefines or transforms certain pieces of information to discover new uses, and builds onto the known. Thus, according to Torrance, the gifted reader is both a critical and creative reader. As a critical reader the child is aware of the biases and deficiencies in writing; as a creative reader the gifted child is able to understand the reasons behind discrepancies in writing and come to sound conclusions about what is true. In addition, the gifted reader is able to relate the content read to previous knowledge, apply content read to new situations, and relate the information to other fields.

When reading Torrance's description of the creative and critical reader, remember that his description is applicable to all children in varying degrees. As we emphasize throughout this book, the goal of reading instruction is to encourage all children to think about what they read, to integrate what they read with prior knowledge, and to apply their new knowledge to new situations. Teaching reading as a language-thinking process enables all children, including the gifted, to reach their highest level of thinking ability. A special problem in teaching the gifted is for the teacher to recognize unusual talents and not be satisfied with what may appear to be a superior performance when compared to peers but is not at the limits of the gifted student's capabilities.

IMPLICATIONS FOR THE TEACHER
The teacher needs to recognize gifted learners and provide them with an environment that facilitates their expected high levels of functioning. This section provides questions to structure teachers' observations as they screen children for giftedness and gives suggestions for expanding the language-thinking environment to meet the special needs of the gifted.

Observing the Learner
Teachers must frequently make judgments about who is gifted and in need of specialized reading experiences. To help the teacher in this process, we suggest the following questions specific to *reading* based on the work of Boston (1979), Guilford and Merrifield (1960), and Walton (1961).

Does the learner:
    acquire information readily through reading and retain this information?

exhibit a reading vocabulary superior for age and grade?

apply a high level of abstract thinking in relating ideas and recalling information?

determine underlying principles to make valid generalizations about text content and structure?

select high-level reading materials and successfully integrate the information with prior knowledge?

discuss ideas gained through reading with depth, elaboration, and fluency?

show awareness that different texts have different reading requirements and adjust to meet the specific requirements?

exhibit curiosity about topics read and spontaneously follow up with additional reading or experiences?

respond to questions based on written material with multiple and unique answers?

show insight into author inconsistencies and spontaneously read other source material to prove or disprove points?

show sensitivity to unanswered questions and methodically search for answers by applying appropriate problem-solving strategies?

In examining this list of questions typically used to identify gifted readers, you can see that these are children who are thinking logically and creatively and are independently applying their high-level cognitive abilities to written materials. These learners tend to fall into the group described in Chapter 1 as learners for whom learning to read is an easy process and who achieve high levels of reading proficiency with minimal teacher-directed instruction.

However, there is another group of children or youth who have the potential for being gifted readers but do not exhibit behaviors that make them easily identifiable. "It seems probable that our society discovers and develops no more than perhaps half its potential intellectual talent" (Havighurst, 1961, p. 524). These learners exhibit unusual amounts of curiosity on school-related and nonschool-related topics and are able to show sustained interest in these topics. Like other gifted learners, they respond to information by frequently asking how or why but do not necessarily pursue a topic, particularly in those areas schools value. In day-to-day functioning these learners may often appear uninterested and resist routine activities and/or conformity to classroom procedures but are able to display knowledge when specifically questioned and are able to pursue areas of self-interest. Often these learners exhibit significantly greater skill in listening or responding to oral language than written language and exhibit talents in areas not language related such as art, music, and drama.

Whenever the teacher thinks that a child may be gifted, the teacher should make a referral to a specialist for individual psychoeducational evaluation. If results indicate giftedness, the child can obtain special placement or receive an enriched curriculum within the regular class setting. Even those children who do not meet a school or district-wide criteria for giftedness may need special consideration to enrich their program within the classroom.

Providing a Supportive Environment

> Certainly no classroom teacher could exist very long with a group of gifted children if he pretended to be the fount of all knowledge. The ability to say "I don't know," coupled with the ability to direct the child to proper references would be a characteristic expected of a teacher of gifted children. A broad background of experience helps to make the children's learning more alive and personal. (Gallagher, 1977, p. 137)

In keeping with this statement, obviously the teacher is central in establishing the optimal environment for encouraging and developing gifted readers. Among the things that the teacher can do are to:

1. accept and value creativity by being open to novel or even preposterous ideas and a variety of opinions and viewpoints;
2. provide sufficient structure to give the gifted child a feeling of security while providing opportunities for self-direction and cognitive risk taking;
3. accept the strong interests of these children in specific areas and encourage them to pursue these interests in depth;
4. provide opportunities for gifted readers to meet across age and grade levels;
5. exempt gifted readers from routine classroom and library assignments to allow time for self-directed reading and research projects;
6. allow gifted readers to proceed at their own paces and to work independently for long periods;
7. recognize that teachers should assess gifted readers on the basis of their potential as opposed to assessing them with regard to age and grade expectations;
8. accept reader interests in areas that are not curriculum or age related;
9. provide nonlanguage activities in diverse areas (art, music, mime) to build interest in reading for those learners who may be gifted but are not performing at the expected level in language activities;
10. coordinate interests in nonschool or nonlanguage areas with appropriate reading materials to foster interest in reading as well as broadening knowledge in the area of interest.

Gifted children and youth, as all learners, need an environment and instructional procedures that foster self-acceptance, respect for individual ideas and interests, and allow all children to develop in reading to their maximum potential. For the gifted, reading experiences should foster creative reading at the highest level of thinking. This goal for the gifted should be the long-range goal for all readers.

Summary

This chapter presents definitions of learning-disabled and gifted children and discusses the implications of legislation on instructional policies. We address how to meet the reading needs of these exceptional children within the framework of meaning-based instruction. The chapter provides some guidelines for screening children for special needs and some suggestions for creating a supportive classroom environment.

Bilingual and Bidialectal Learners

Overwhelming evidence shows that when both middle-class and non-middle-class children—no matter what their native language, dialect, or ethnic background—come to school at the age of five or six, they have control of their language system. The fact that their system is distinct from that of the teacher or school does not mean that their speech is not rule-governed (Gumperz & Chavez, 1972). This well-formed system has been their means of communicating up to this time. And this language system is rooted in the family, peer group, and subculture. For children whose native language is not English and for those children who speak a dialect of American English that is not the same as that of the school environment, the school's responsibility is to accept the language of the child and expand it to include the language of the general culture. The child should give up only that part of the language no longer needed and must add language to meet new needs (Smith, Goodman, & Meredith, 1976). The bilingual learner retains the native language while adding the English language. The bidialectal learner retains those aspects of the dialect needed in the subculture while adding Standard English to meet new needs. This expansion of language allows the learner flexibility and choice in language usage. This chapter will describe bilingual and bidialectal learners and some implications of their presence in the classroom for the teacher.

The Bilingual Learner

> Bilingualism—recognized whenever a native speaker of a language makes use of a second language, however partially or imperfectly—ranges, in terms of individual speakers, from those who seldom use anything but the native language, through speakers who make use of the second language in varying degrees, to the rarely encountered ambilingual who achieves complete mastery of both languages and uses both in all communication situations. (Laosa, 1975, p. 617)

Thus, the term bilingual learner as currently used encompasses any learner who functions in a dual language environment regardless of the proficiency of that learner in either the native (first language) or the second language.

As the term encompasses such a varied population, viewing bilingual learners descriptively is helpful. Del Prado (1975) lists the following characteristics of bilingual learners: They can be:

1. English-dominant, able to think and speak in the conventional structures of English only;
2. native-language (other than English) dominant, able to think and speak in the conventional structures of their native language only;
3. fully bilingual, able to think and speak in two languages;
4. inadequate in any language development; they may be inadequate in English, or their native language, or both (if environmentally exposed

to both). They lack a conventional language since idioms and incomplete language structures are used in oral communication (pp. 102–103).

In regard to reading, bilingual children can be distinguished as being preliterate or functionally illiterate. A preliterate learner can be either a young child or even an older child who has never been in a reading program in any language. These two groups of preliterate children bring to the learning environment different levels of maturity and thus different levels of experience and language. The functionally illiterate child, on the other hand, has been exposed to print in both the native language and English and is having difficulty reading either one or both languages (Thonis, 1976).

For these children whose native language and cultural background do not reflect the school environment, several conditions can contribute to failure and confusion:

1. a lack of experiences in the dominant culture from which concepts specific to the English speaking community have to be acquired;
2. an inadequate oral command of the English language that is the language of the instructional program;
3. a lowered sense of self-esteem resulting from repeated feelings of inadequacy; and
4. an unrealistic curriculum that imposes reading and writing English before listening comprehension and speaking fluency have been established. (Thonis, 1976, p. 1)

SPECIAL NEEDS OF BILINGUAL LEARNERS

These conditions, which may lead to various learning problems, highlight the special needs of the bilingual learner. The teacher must be aware of the cultural values of the bilingual child and accept the child's culture and language in order to minimize learning problems. An integral part of this acceptance is the building of a program of instruction based on the experiential-conceptual background of the learner (Ching, 1976). This bilingual-bicultural program should include the following components:

1. concept acquisition and development in the learner's native language;
2. native language maintenance: both development and literacy;
3. second language acquisition, for instance, English as a Second Language (ESL); and
4. study of cultures and contributions of minority groups to develop a positive self-concept (del Prado, 1975).

A bilingual program involves providing for classroom learning experiences in the native language and using such experiences and associated language as the basis for beginning reading instruction. There is considerable support in the literature for special bilingual programs and for teaching reading to bilingual children in their native language first (del Prado, 1975; Nava & Sancho, 1975; Thonis, 1976).

As La Fontaine (1977) has stated:

> There is absolutely no logical argument supporting the concept that one must suppress or even eliminate the skills a student possesses in one language in order to have that student learn a second language. On the contrary, the potential psychological and emotional damage that may result from such an approach is of such great impact that it could negate all other efforts to assist the student in successfully pursuing his studies.
>
> This concern for the student's overall cognitive and affective development also underlines our insistence that the cultural background of the student be not only recognized but utilized appropriately in the curriculum as a means for helping the students to develop self-confidence based on positive self image. (p. 2)

There are many children in the schools who need bilingual programs. The U.S. Office of Education estimates that at least 5 million children in the nation's schools may be classified as bilingual. Since bilingual programs are not available for all children who need them, many bilingual children are in regular classrooms where English is the language of instruction. Therefore, the classroom teacher's role is to gain familiarity with the culture and language of these bilingual learners and to foster acceptance of the culture on the part of children from the dominant culture and the bilingual children themselves.

Cultural acceptance involves recognizing and understanding the children's ideas, values, and practices that may be different from those of the teacher and school culture. Accepting the child involves accepting the child's language and understanding the similarities and differences between the native and second language systems, so that language/reading instruction can build on these similarities and avoid unnecessary difficulties due to the differences. Teachers, therefore, should have some familiarity with the language their children speak so they will understand their children's oral language and can differentiate between miscues in oral reading that are the result of being a speaker of two languages or miscues that are related to the reading process. Teachers need to be aware that the sounds and patterns of children's native speech have been overlearned and practiced to the point of automatic response. These well-ingrained native language habits may get in the way of the children's acquisition of new language responses (Thonis, 1976).

LANGUAGE VARIATIONS

Since the largest group of bilingual children in the United States are native speakers of Spanish, a comparison of English-Spanish language variations illustrates the type of information that some teachers may need. Table 15.1 indicates some of the differences between the sound systems of English and

Table 15.1 Some Differences Between the English and Spanish Sound Systems

English Form	Spanish Equivalent	For the Spanish-English Pronunciation of: _____ the Child May Say _____ or To the English Speaker _____ Sounds Like _____	
/i/	/iy/	bit	beet
		pit	peat
/æ/	/e/ or /a/	bat	bet
		hat	hot
/a/	/e/ or /a/	but	bet
		fun	fawn
		shut	shot
/ey/	/e/	late	let
		mate	met
/u/	/uw/	full	fool
/b/	/p/	bar	par
		cab	cap
/b/ (between vowels)	/v/[β]	babies	bavies
/v/	/b/ [b]	vote	boat
/š/	/č/	shoe	chew
/g/	/k/	goat	coat
		dug	duck
/ǰ/	/č/	jump	chump
	/y/		yump
/m/ (final)	/n/	comb	cone
		dime	dine
/θ/ (voiceless)	/s, t, or f/	thank	sank
		path	pass
/ḏ/ (voiced)	/d/	this	dis
		though	dough
/w/	/gw/	way	guay
/z/	/s/	zoo	sue
		buzz	bus
/ž/	/č/	measure	meachure
	/š/		meashure

Source: From an adaptation by Ruddell in *Reading-language instruction: Innovative practices*, pp. 273–74. Copyright © 1974 by Prentice-Hall, Inc. Reprinted with permission.

Spanish. Table 15.2 describes some differences in the syntactic systems between the two languages.

These lists focus on the major differences between English and language forms used by Puerto Rican and Mexican-American children. The lists, however, are not able to take into account the various differences in language performance found among these native Spanish-speaking children. Although these children share the same native language, as with all children, their oral language communications reflect the totality of their prior personal language experiences and environments.

Table 15.2 Some Differences Between the English and Spanish Syntactic Systems

Description	Example	
	English Speaker	**Spanish-English Speaker**
A. Use of verb forms		
1. Subject-predicate agreement	The cars run.	The cars runs.
	The car runs.	The car run.
2. Tense	Joe said that he was ready.	Joe said that he is ready.
	I needed help yesterday.	I need help yesterday.
3. Use of *be*	I am five years old.	I have five years.
4. Negative	Joe isn't here.	Joe is no here.
	He didn't go home.	He no go home, *or*
		He didn't went home.
	Don't come.	No come.
B. Use of noun and determiner forms		
1. Plural form	The two cars are big.	The two car are big.
2. Omission of determiner with noun in certain contexts	He is a farmer.	He is farmer.
C. Use of pronoun forms		
1. Omission in question	Is he a farmer?	Is farmer?
2. Omission in statement	It is ready.	Is ready.
D. Use of adjectives		
1. Order	The red cap is pretty.	The cap red is pretty.
2. Ending	The red caps are fine.	The caps red are fine.
3. Comparison	It is bigger.	Is more big.
	It's bigger.	
	It is the biggest.	Is most big.
	It's the biggest.	

Source: From an adaptation by Ruddell in *Reading-language instruction: Innovative practices*, pp. 274–75. Copyright © 1974 by Prentice-Hall, Inc. Reprinted with permission.

IMPLICATIONS FOR THE CLASSROOM

The teacher enhances the educational experiences of the bilingual learner by being aware of the needs and characteristics of this learner, understanding the learner's language functioning, and incorporating this knowledge into actual classroom practice. This necessitates observing bilingual learners as they function and providing an environment that will maintain and encourage growth of the native language while developing proficiency in the English language.

Observation of the Learner

We suggest the following questions as a guide to the teacher in understanding the language functioning of bilingual children:

In listening is
> information in the native language processed better than information in English (the second language)?[1]

> information in English processed better than information in the native language?

> information processed better than through reading, in English and/or the native language?

> comprehension better than would be expected from the learner's spoken language in both English and/or the native language?

In speaking, is (are)
> communication better in the native language than in English (thoughts expressed)?

> communication better in English than in the native language (thoughts expressed)?

> vocabulary and syntax appropriate for age and grade in English and in the native language?

In reading, is
> information processed better in the native language than in English?

> information processed better in English than in the native language?

> more information gained than through listening in English and/or the native language?

In writing, are
> thoughts expressed better in the native language than in English?

> thoughts expressed better in English than in the native language?

> vocabulary and sentence structure age- and grade-appropriate in English and/or the native language?

The Classroom Environment

The bilingual child, as all other children, must learn school behavior but in addition frequently must learn to respond within the school situation by using the language that is not the dominant one (Kaminsky, 1976). Teachers need to accept and use children's language and cultural experiences as a base for teaching reading. A supportive classroom environment is most important for bilingual learners to ensure that their self-concept as learners is a positive one and that they feel comfortable in taking risks as they learn the dominant language. The teacher as the creator of the environment should:

---

[1] The classroom teacher may need to use resource personnel who are fluent in the child's native language to answer questions such as this one.

1. understand the cultural background and language of the bilingual child and communicate the importance of this culture and language to the bilingual child and other children/adults in the school environment;
2. know the phonological and syntactic variations between the native language and English so that the language functioning of the learner is understood and accepted;
3. recognize differences in skill and level of usage among bilingual learners in both the native language and English;
4. accept the language of the child when both vocabulary and syntax from the native language are interspersed with English to foster oral communication;
5. understand that generally bilingual children comprehend more English language than they can express;
6. encourage the use of English in everyday social situations through peer and adult interactions;
7. understand that competence in oral language precedes reading, important for both the native language and English;
8. use the bilingual child's interests and culture as the basis for extending reading ability in both the native language and English;
9. emphasize comprehension, in both oral language and reading, so that meaning is always dominant in all activities.

The Bidialectal Learner

> Sociolinguists have been careful to point up that dialect variation is more a continuum than a polarity and that speakers of one dialect may differ from those of another in such minute matters as the frequency of occurrence of a particular feature more than its categorical presence or absence. (Shuy, 1980, p. 4)

Regional and socioeconomic factors influence the particular dialect that language learners develop as they learn the phonological, syntactic, and semantic patterns of their surrounding speech communities. All children bring to the school five or six years of language and experience. Their language is closely intertwined with the culture of their community embodying the cultural values and structures, the way they perceive the world, and the way they communicate reactions (Goodman, 1969b). They have developed language at school entrance so well that it is deeply internalized, and they require no conscious effort to use it. Children are able to detect fine differences in sounds that are important in the dialect and have mastered the syntax of the dialect so that they can create novel sentences that are grammatical within the dialect. In all respects the process of language acquisition is the same in learning any one of the many English dialect varieties (Smith and others, 1976).

Even though in any language all of its native speakers speak it somewhat differently, the "dialect" that in our society most people use habitually and, therefore, is most socially acceptable, is Standard American English. This is the dialect with some regional variations children hear, read, and are expected to use in most school settings. Children who develop language in communities in which Standard American English is the dominant language find a close match between the familiar communication environment of home and neighborhood and that of the school. Children who develop language in communities in which a dialect of Standard American English is the dominant form of communication may not find this familiar language environment on school entry. Some children will use more dialect features than others and, therefore, the amount of disparity will depend on the particular child's cultural group and specific language experiences. These language experiences are most influenced by the home environment, and are further expanded by peers, and adults in the child's community.

READING AND THE BIDIALECTAL CHILD

In the United States much of the interest and research on the influence of dialect on learning has focused on children who speak black dialect and the possibility that these children may have special difficulties in learning due to differences between their language systems and that of the school environment. Goodman (1969b) has referred to these speakers as divergent speakers to avoid labeling their language system as less correct than Standard American English. It gives recognition to the sophisticated and systematic use of language for effective communication by these speakers.

Of course, not all black children speak black dialect. The speech of many black children is indistinguishable from the speech of other children from the same region or social class, and many other children's speech can be identified as black only through a few slight differences in pronunciation and vocal quality (Fasold & Wolfram, 1970). Still other children in this country who are not black speak a dialect much like black dialect; most of them come from economically poor homes primarily in the southern regions of the United States.

Cazden (1972) has indicated that, with the exception of a few features such as the special use of *to be*, the differences between black dialect and Standard American English are primarily matters of surface structure and do not affect meaning at all. Further, when experts examine dialects of English from the point of view of language functions, the differences are largely superficial, rather low-level processes that have little effect on meaning (Labov, 1970). Therefore, a child who is a speaker of black dialect should be able to express any and all ideas in the dialect. In regard to language reception, linguists have found that the use of dialect has no significant effect on the understanding of Standard American English (Anastasiow, 1973). As Shuy (1972) has noted, "We all have a 'use' vocabulary and a 'recognition' vocabulary. We can input through either set but we usually output only through the former" (p. 68).

Reading research indicates that comprehension of materials written in Standard American English is not related to whether a reader speaks

Standard English or black dialect (Goodman & Buck, 1973; Melmed, 1973; Venesky & Chapman, 1973; Simons & Johnson, 1974; Sims, 1976, 1982). Goodman and Buck (1973) concluded that dialect-involved miscues do not interfere with the reading process or the construction of meaning. In fact, rejection or correction by the teacher of any dialect-based miscues moves readers away from using their own language competence to get to meaning toward a closer correspondence to the teacher's expected response to the text. This word-for-word accuracy becomes the goal of reading rather than the acquisition of meaning.

Just as all readers, speakers of black dialect process text with comprehension provided that they can relate the information to their experiential and conceptual background. When these readers read silently, the teacher is unaware of any reader variations from the printed text. Only when they read text orally are phonological, syntactic, and vocabulary variations evident. In oral reading, phonological level variations comprise by far the greatest percentage of dialect related miscues and are the ones the teacher perceives most immediately. These phonological variations involve alternations, simplifications, or omissions of phonemes but do not interfere with the construction of meaning. Syntactic variations tend to be limited and highly predictable variations of the inflectional and marker systems of English. They are only simple alterations of the surface level structures (Burke, 1973b). Although these miscues relate directly to the oral language of the reader, this type of dialect usage occurs less in oral reading than in the more natural speech of the reader when retelling what has been read (Goodman and others, 1973).

Although teachers should not consider dialect-related miscues reading errors, other miscues may not reflect the oral language patterns of the child and may interfere with constructing meaning. Clearly the teacher is concerned about these miscues and should treat them just like miscues of other children because such miscues are part of the ongoing diagnostic information the teacher uses to plan specific teaching strategies. The teacher, therefore, although recognizing language variations specific to black dialect, should not interfere with dialect usage if meaning is properly constructed and should recognize errors unrelated to dialect. As Cazden (1972) has stated, "Once reading has begun, comprehension and not pronunciation must be the critical test" (p. 161) of reading competency.

Although experts have shown that dialect speakers readily comprehend spoken and written Standard American English, more of these speakers have reading problems than speakers of Standard dialects. Research suggests that teacher rejection of the learner's language, culture, and experiential background, not the language itself, is a major handicap to the learner's reading success (Goodman & Buck, 1973; Simons & Johnson, 1974; Smith, 1975; Cunningham, 1977).

Goodman and Buck assert that a

special disadvantage which speakers of low-status dialects suffer in learning to read is one imposed by teachers and schools. Rejection of their dialects and educators' confusion of linguistic difference with linguistic deficiency interferes with the natural process by which reading is acquired and undermines the linguistic self-confidence of divergent speakers. Simply speaking, the disadvantage of the divergent speaker, Black or White, comes from linguistic discrimination. Instruction based on rejection of linguistic difference is the core of the problem. (1973, pp. 6–7)

This rejection is a rejection not only of the child's language but of the specific culture in which the child learned the language and the related experiences of the child. To avoid this rejection, the teacher should use the child's culture, experience, and language as a base for language and reading instruction. This does not mean, however, that teachers should not provide opportunities for children to expand their language usage to include Standard American English. Knowing Standard American English, in addition to the dialect, affords people a choice as to the use of Standard American English or a particular dialect. In our society this ability "to choose" has important implications for educational and career opportunities.

FEATURES OF BLACK ENGLISH

Acceptance and expansion of learner language requires teachers to be knowledgeable about the dialects and cultures of the children they teach. The Ann Arbor Decision (Joiner, 1979), in which the court has mandated that teachers in the Ann Arbor School District take into account children's language in teaching them to read Standard American English, upheld the concept of teacher knowledgeability.

In working with children who are bidialectal, the teacher should recognize the features of their particular dialect. The teacher needs to listen to the children's oral language in different communication situations to develop "an ear" for the children's language. Knowing the features of black English is useful as teachers listen to the oral language of their children. This knowledge provides familiarity with some aspects of black dialect that some children use at times. A number of researchers have described the features of black English dialects. Although many characteristic features of these dialects exist, we present only some of the principal ones. Table 15.3 indicates some structure patterns of black English and Table 15.4 indicates some sound patterns of black English. We have adapted the categories of patterns and examples from the work of Smitherman (1977).

In reviewing these tables, we need to restate certain cautions. Not all black children speak black dialect, and those who do will vary greatly in their use of dialect features. Also, some white children, particularly in the southern regions of the United States, will use some of the same language features used by black dialect speakers.

Other aspects of language including specific vocabulary and the use of language to accomplish specific goals (the functions of language) are also important. As teachers listen to their children's oral language, they become

Table 15.3   Structure Patterns of Black English

Pattern	Black English
Repetition of noun subject with pronoun	My father, he work there.
Question patterns without *to do*	What it come to?
Possession not marked by apostrophe *s*	Mr. Johnson store got burned down.
Same form of noun for singular and plural	one boy; five boy
Same form of verb for singular and plural	He do the same thing they do.
Hypercorrection of plurals	five womens; these mens
No tense indicated in verb; emphasis on manner or character of action	I know it good when he ask me.
Same verb form for all subjects	I know; you know; he know; we know; they know
No -s on verb *to do*	My momma do that all the time.
No form of verb *to be* (zero copula) meaning the event does not recur	They rowdy.
Use of verb *to be* as *bees* or *be's,* meaning that the condition or event occurs habitually	The coffee *bees* cold.
Use of the verb *to be* to convey future time	The family be gone Friday.
Use of the verb *to be* in tag questions	You ain't sick, is you?
Use of *been* to express past action that has recently been completed	He *been* there before.
For Negation	
1. if the statement consists of only one sentence, every item is negated.	*Don't nobody ever help me do my work.* (No one ever helps me do my work.)
2. if the statement consists of two or more sentences combined as one,	
A. the use of all negatives indicates a positive statement.	*Don't nobody pay no attention to nobody that ain crazy.* (If you are crazy, you will get attention.)
B. the use of all negatives plus one positive indicates a negative statement.	*Don't nobody pay no attention to nobody that's crazy.* (If you are crazy, you will not get any attention.)

Source: Adapted from *Talkin and testafyin: The language of black America* by Geneva Smitherman, pp. 6–9, 19–22, 28, 30. Copyright © 1977 by Geneva Smitherman. Used with permission of Houghton Mifflin Company.

familiar with the particular vocabulary used by the children and the ways children use language to accomplish their goals. This information is an important addition to the teacher's knowledge base.

Table 15.4   Sound Patterns of Black English

Pattern	Black English
1. No consonant pairs in final positions	*jus* (for just) *men* (for *mend*)
2. Deletion of most final consonants	*hoo* (for *hood*) *be* (for *bed*)
Pluralized forms ending in double consonants add *es*	*tesses* (for *tests*)
3. Few long vowels or two-part vowels (diphthongs)	*rat* or *raht* (for *right*) *tahm* (for *time*)
4. Deletion of middle and final /r/ sound	*doing* (for *during*) *mow* (for *more*)
5. Deletion of middle and final /l/ sound	*hep* (for *help*) *wi* (for *will*)
6. Initial /th/ = /d/	*dis* (for *this*)
7. Final /th/ = /f/	*souf* (for *south*)

Source: Adapted from *Talkin and testafyin: The language of black America* by Geneva Smitherman, pp. 7, 17. Copyright © 1977 by Geneva Smitherman. Used with permission of Houghton Mifflin Company.

IMPLICATIONS FOR THE CLASSROOM

In teaching children with dialect variations, teachers should use a language experience approach along with the reading of many stories and informational materials. These activities should form the basis for the reading program for such students just as they should be the basis of reading programs for all other children. Unfortunately, all too often, programs for black children have focused on fragmented skills on the assumption that these children needed more structure and more concrete experiences than other children. As a result, teachers have sacrificed attention to whole language and reading comprehension (Sims, 1982).

Observation of the Learner

In using a language-thinking approach to reading with bidialectal children, the teacher will find the following questions useful in understanding the oral and written language of their children:

In listening, does the learner
  indicate adequate interpretation of the oral message?

  accurately interpret Standard American English subtleties of meaning transmitted through intonation patterns (stress, pitch, pause)?

  understand those vocabulary words that for the dialect speaker become homophones due to phonological variations?

In speaking, does the learner

use phonological variations particular to a dialect and if so, which phonological variations?

use syntactic variations particular to a dialect and if so, which syntactic variations?

use vocabulary specific to a dialect?

alternate between Standard American English and dialect in a consistent way?

In reading, does the learner

indicate adequate understanding of the material?

produce miscues in oral reading related to systematic phonological variations of the dialect?

produce synonyms particular to the dialect as substitutes for Standard American English vocabulary?

In writing, does the learner

spell words according to phonological variations of the dialect?

construct sentences that reflect syntactic variations of the dialect?

use synonyms that are particular to the dialect?

The Classroom Environment

The bidialectal child needs an environment that accepts the child's language and culture and uses this background to facilitate and expand the child's use of Standard American English in a variety of communicative situations. In this context the teacher should:

1. understand the cultural background of the child and communicate the importance of this culture to children and adults in the school environment;
2. use the culture and experiential background of the child as a base for expanding language and reading;
3. encourage the child to communicate with peers and adults in the school environment even though there may be language differences between the child and the school environment;
4. understand that children who speak a dialect of English understand Standard American English;
5. accept the dialect of the child as a complete and effective language system;
6. emphasize comprehension in both oral language and reading so that meaning rather than pronunciation is dominant in all activities;
7. accept responses that may use a combination of dialect and Standard American English to foster overall communication;

8. recognize the phonological, syntactic, and semantic variations in the child's use of dialect in order to differentiate between those miscues that are "reading errors" and those miscues that are consistent with the child's use of the dialect during oral reading;

9. expand children's ability to communicate in Standard American English so that they have the opportunity for choice in their language usage.

Summary

This chapter focuses on learners with diverse language and culture—the bilingual learner and the bidialectal learner. We describe the language of both groups of children, suggest a series of questions for the teacher to use in observing learners, and give some ideas for creating a supportive classroom environment. Teaching bilingual and bidialectal children requires extensive knowledge on the part of teachers because they are expected to teach children from many diverse cultures and language backgrounds. We emphasize that this chapter serves as an introduction to the topic, and we suggest that teachers refer to additional sources of information in order to better understand the culture, language functioning, and needs of their particular children. Although the chapter treats bilingual and bidialectal children separately from learning disabled or gifted learners, a learner may, of course, belong to more than one group.

PART
VI

READING AND . . .

A Final Word

16

Reading and Writing

Researchers studying the relationship between reading and writing are beginning to document similarities between the two processes. Both reading and writing are language-thinking processes that require the learner to participate actively. Both require a background of varied experiences or content and the sharing of these experiences through listening and speaking. As children listen to stories and learn to read, they become aware of the writer as a communicator and the ways that writers use language to present ideas. As learners increase their proficiency in reading, they expand their knowledge of content and form in writing. Children who write at the same time they are learning to read gain understanding of both sides of the written communication process. What they learn from one encounter with language becomes the anticipatory data available for subsequent encounters. For example, what children learn about language from reading becomes available linguistic data for output in another expression of language like writing. Similarly, using language to construct messages in writing enhances the readers' ability to understand what others write. The process is cyclical (Harste, Burke, & Woodward, 1982). Research on the relationship of reading and writing is in its infancy and further investigations are needed with children of different ages and abilities as they read and write in a variety of contexts (Birnbaum, 1982).

Although the content of this book focuses primarily on reading, we have integrated writing activities throughout the teaching/learning plans. The complementary nature of the reading and writing processes demands this type of integration. In this chapter we will highlight writing because of its importance in the development of communication abilities. The chapter will include an overview of writing as communication, a description of the writing process, and a discussion of the evaluation of children's writing.

Writing as Communication

Children's ability to relate scribbles to words and pictures to stories grows out of their early experiences at story time and their experiences with print in the environment. Children's interactions with adults build an awareness that the source of stories is in the pages of a book and that these pages are covered with little lines and shapes. When children recognize that these squiggles represent language and that people can write down language, they begin to connect their natural physical explorations with crayons or paint and paper to writing, and their squiggles become more purposeful and take on meaning. Children begin to ask about words and letters and to draw individual letters. Some children even begin to write in different rudimentary ways: They arrange letters, invented letters, and numbers in various ways on the page. When children start inventing spellings, they make significant advancement. When a five-year-old boy wrote the message "R U DF," to his mother who was ignoring him (Bissex, 1980), two individuals shared a legible and purposeful communication.

When children listen to stories, they begin to internalize a sense of story structure that provides a model for their own writing. Characters and their actions, story events, times and places, and different story themes become familiar components of stories for children: They learn to anticipate story elements and often to predict them. Children's enjoyment in listening to stories sparks their imagination, stimulates their thinking about different experiences and feelings, and leads to a sharing of their own ideas and stories. At first children tell their stories orally to others. This shared experience provides an important link to writing. Even those children who may be able to tell about their experiences fluently may not yet be able to write their stories independently. Recording the child's stories for them provides the bridge between the child's oral language fluency and the child's writing. This shared activity of telling and recording introduces them to the idea that they too can be authors. In classrooms in which teachers encourage writing, young children gradually begin to write their own stories and record their feelings and experiences for others to read. This personal type of writing in which children communicate whatever is on their minds is a way of exploring ideas and sharing them with others. Children take for granted that the reader is interested in what they as writers have to say.

With increased exposure to the environment, different subject matter, other people, and ongoing experiences in writing, children's writing expands to include the communication of different types of factual information. Learners begin to record what is happening around them, they describe what they experience, they organize information to report their ideas, they attempt to persuade or advise others, and at times they may speculate or theorize about what can happen.

What is important in this type of writing is that the writer integrates factual information with personal experiences, thoughts, feelings, or observations that the teacher or other audiences for whom the writer writes do not necessarily know. If the learner-writer limits informational writing to facts the audience already knows, the writer may view writing as a school chore rather than a communicative experience. In such cases learners view the purpose for writing as evaluation rather than communication because readers already know the informational content. In contrast, when the teacher encourages the neophyte writers to integrate factual information with their own ideas or experiences, writing becomes a real message to share.

As children grow in their experience with writing and language, some become increasingly aware of the form of writing. They expand their use of written language to allow for play with language. They attend to word sounds, rhythms, and patterns that words can make when strung together. They daydream, reflect, and contemplate about their own feelings and thoughts, the experiences of others they have observed, and other writing they have read. They begin to communicate their personal ideas through creative writing in the form of stories and poems. These writings appeal to the senses and emotions of the reader through the use of vivid descriptions, both literal and figurative (Martin and others, 1976).

Children's personal writing, factual writing, and creative writing are labeled the expressive, transactional, and poetic functions of writing, respectively (Britton and others, 1975). Expressive writing is very much like written speech. People communicate with each other this way most of the time. Experts think that this type of writing forms the base from which other more specialized and differentiated writing—transactional and poetic—grows. Transactional writing is the writing of science and intellectual disciplines and thus common to school texts and materials. Although this writing is generally depersonalized exposition, sometimes writers integrate factual information with personalized responses to the information. At all times readers take for granted that writers mean what they say and that readers can challenge the truthfulness and the logic of the writing. In poetic writing truth is not the issue. Such writers share feelings and ideas through their heightened awareness using symbols and sensory descriptions.

Much writing appears to be somewhere on the continuum between expressive and transactional or expressive and poetic functions (Britton, 1978).

> The move out of an expressive use of language in either direction, towards the poetic or toward the transactional, involves a heightened degree of organizing thought and shaping it. But the direction taken will deeply affect the nature of that organization. In the transactional function the emphasis is toward a linear, logical set of connections—an inductive or deductive hierarchy of points. In the poetic function . . . the patterning is non discursive; the connections are implicit and themselves provide the structure which renders the whole inseparable from the parts. (Martin and others, 1976, p. 12)

As children move from expressive writing to other forms, they demonstrate growth in the ability to understand and address themselves to the needs of varied audiences. They answer the question "Why am I writing this?" by understanding the three general functions that writing serves, and they answer the question, "Who will read what I write?" by learning to adjust their writing to different audiences. They have to understand that different viewpoints exist and that people may have different background experiences and feelings. They also have to make inferences about other people's cognitive activity (Barritt & Kroll, 1978).

As we know, the ability to communicate to different audiences depends on both developmental factors and experiences with language. As children progress through school, they need to write to many different audiences. The teacher should structure writing experiences so that the child recognizes the audience and so that the audience is real for the child.

Children may be their own audience when they write diaries, notes, and first drafts of written materials. In these cases the writer does not have to recognize the needs of any other readers.

Children's audiences may expand to include a trusted adult with whom they share writing about personal matters and from whom they expect sympathetic responses. A teacher may serve in the role of trusted adult, but generally a learner sees the teacher as a partner in writing or as an evaluator of writing. When learners view the teacher as a partner, writing is generally concerned with the subject matter of school and sometimes with personal feelings. In this audience situation the writer assumes that the teacher is interested and will respond in a helpful way. In the teacher-as-evaluator situation, children produce writing to satisfy the teacher's demands, and they expect the teacher to judge their writing either for content or structure or both. Thus, teachers are either partners in creating dialogue, responding to the written material in a way that is helpful to the child, or they are evaluators judging how well students write or how much knowledge is illustrated in a particular writing assignment.

Writing for peers presents another type of audience situation. Children may write for peers and assume such roles as expert, co-worker, or friend. Of course, the teacher may be part of this group, but the focus is on communicating with peers.

Finally, writers communicate with remote individuals, unknown people, or public audiences. Writers express what they think is of value although they are not addressing any particular audience. Published materials such as textbooks, novels, and poetry are typically written for unknown audiences as are some school writings that may include poems, stories, or articles for school magazines or newspapers. As children expand their understanding that writing has different functions and that they may direct their own writing to different audiences, they increase their competence as writers (Britton, 1978).

The Writing Process

Just as reading is an active process of constructing meaning, so is writing an active process. The writer, very much like the reader, ponders, understands, and integrates ideas during the process of writing. Current research on writing, similar to research on reading, has moved from emphasis on the product to emphasis on the writer and the process (Perl, 1979; Hayes & Flower, 1980). The process-oriented research reveals that learners bring their background knowledge, experiences, and feelings to the task as they construct meaning. This includes information about the topic (the content), knowledge about writing (the structure), and knowledge about the abilities and needs of the projected audience. This knowledge of the writer interacts with the writing task and forms the context for writing—"everything outside the writer's skin" (Hayes & Flower, 1980, p. 12) that influences writing. This "everything" includes the writing assignment or topic, the audience, the motivational factors, and the writing itself as generated. Writing referred to as composing is a continuous process: As it progresses, it helps shape what follows.

In writing, as in reading, learners move through three phases: They participate in activities prior to the actual reading and writing, they self-monitor as they are reading and writing, and they review what they have read or written. Writing researchers describe these three phases of the writing process as prewriting, writing, and revision. These three phases, however, do not occur in linear progression. Research indicates that the writer moves between planning, composing, and revising, and rereading and digesting (Perl, 1979). A description of the three phases appears below.

PREWRITING
In the prewriting or planning phase, writers ready themselves for writing by clarifying purpose and audience. Many times the purpose for writing grows out of previous learning activities and interests of children. Of course, at times, the teacher will identify a specific purpose for writing, but in both cases learners will be aware of a "real world" or practical communication need. Because writing is a form of thinking, obviously writing about familiar content is easier. And writing on a topic of personal interest rather than on an assigned topic seems to produce compositions of greater length and range (Graves, 1975).

Frequently the incentive for writing comes from a group discussion following a specific classroom activity or after the teacher schedules a discussion specifically to motivate writing. Such discussions give children an opportunity to talk about their experiences, share ideas and opinions, and expand vocabulary and concepts. Other strategies for stimulating ideas include brainstorming with a small group, asking others for suggestions, trying ideas on someone else, keeping a journal of interesting ideas and events, and looking through source materials such as books or peer writing.

Reading itself provides a natural stimulus for writing. When learners read stories and think about and discuss the plot, events, and characters, they may react to the story in a variety of ways. They may write about their feelings and ideas as they relate directly to the story or about their own experiences or feelings in situations similar to those in the story. They may create variations of the story or write original stories triggered by something in their reading.

Reading expository text for information may stimulate several additional types of writing activities. Learners may react to informational text by writing a report, an essay, or a business letter, or may express feelings and ideas about the content by writing exposition, poems, or stories.

Reading can stimulate writing in countless ways and provide children with a way to explore and express their many thoughts as they move along the continuum between the expressive and transactional and the expressive and poetic functions of writing. For examples of specific writing activities stories and textbook reading can stimulate, see teaching plans for "Su An" (Chapter 9), "The Story of Money" (Chapter 13), and "Harriet Tubman" (Chapter 13).

Learners should record or jot down ideas generated during the prewriting phase in a nonstructured way. Writing down ideas at the time the writer generates them allows the writer to manipulate these ideas which can in turn result in the writer generating more new ideas (Collins & Gentner, 1980). Thus, in preparing to write, writers draw on their experiences, seek additional information, ponder ideas, and make mental outlines or written notes.

COMPOSING

Composing begins with the writing of a first draft. The conventions of English (spelling, punctuation, syntax, and so on) should not be a primary concern at this point; writers can correct any inaccuracies during the revision phase. Writers move between composing and reading—evaluating their work for meaning. In this process they often discover new ideas and clarify all their ideas. When children compose, the teacher should respond to their questions and should circulate the room offering help—encouraging writers who are having problems, giving missing words, sharing an idea, or, if invited, reading a first draft. During this phase the writer should be particularly concerned with making the text comprehensible, convincing, enticing, and memorable. Some teachers find they can help students by collecting first drafts and keeping them a day or two to provide distance between the composing and revising phases. In this case, teachers may read the drafts to see how the writing is progressing but should not make corrections or comments on the papers at this point.

REVISION

Children can learn to revise their first drafts if they participate in a variety of activities. Writers usually reread first drafts prior to sharing them with others. This reading of completed first drafts allows writers to see what they have written and determine if the written message presents their intended meaning. After this private reading of the draft, feedback from other individuals becomes an important part of revision. This feedback focuses first on the content and the clarity of the writing and on its organization and coherence. Peer conferencing accomplishes this step in the revision process most successfully. The children read their products to each other in small groups. This exchange provides both an audience and a way of finding out if listeners hear what the author intends. These small peer group sessions generally use questions to examine the writing. Learners may ask each other questions such as:

What am I saying?

Is there a part that you particularly like?

Do the ideas fit together?

Do the ideas follow in a logical order?

Is there a part that you would like to hear more about?

Is there a part that you would leave out?

These questions may form the basis for a general group discussion, or specific students may be responsible for asking particular questions. This question and answer session helps the writer clarify any ideas not readily communicated to the group.

After peer conferencing, writers make needed content changes such as elaborating ideas through added details, deleting, rephrasing to narrow focus, rewording to create stronger openings, providing transitions or summaries, and changing language choices. Some techniques teachers have found helpful in this stage of the revision process are slotting, sentence expansion, and sentence combining. *Slotting* requires children to replace words that are too general, boring, or repetitious with other words or phrases that are more appropriate. *Sentence expansion* involves adding details to clarify ideas or enhance descriptions. Writers make sentences longer when teacher or peers ask them to describe an event or to tell when or where it occurred. As they lengthen sentences, writers may have to delete extraneous information. In this reduction process, the student also reviews the additions to determine which are unnecessary.

Sentence combining encourages children to vary the structure of their sentences by combining some simple sentences through the use of appropriate connectives to form complex or compound sentences. This technique provides variety in style and frequently clarifies the meaning through careful selection of transitional words and the combining of ideas. Learners may acquire these techniques individually as they reread their writing or during peer conferencing as other learners suggest alternative words, sentences that they can expand, and sentences that they can combine. If these techniques are not familiar, the teacher should introduce and teach them in a structured setting. The children's and teacher's writings should serve as the content for these sessions that take place separately from revision activities.

The last activity in the revision process is *editing*, correcting mechanical problems including syntax, spelling, punctuation, and capitalization. Children learn to become their own editors over the years as they internalize the conventions of writing.

GOING PUBLIC

The final phase in the writing process, although not actually a writing step, is "going public" (Yatvin, 1981). This phase brings the writing from the writer to the audience and may include such activities as book binding, making envelopes, setting up public displays. Activity of this type validates the writing process and demonstrates to students that they have written for an audience.

Evaluating Writing

Teacher evaluation of children's writing involves the assessment of both the writing process and written products. Assessing the writing process requires observing children's behavior during prewriting, composing, and revising. In order to understand children's writing performance, the teacher needs information about the children's background and writing experience.

In prewriting, teacher observations focus on noting the ways in which children prepare for writing. This includes noting the amount of time children take to analyze the task, the amount and quality of their interactions during group discussions, the ways in which children organize their ideas for writing, and the amount of time they spend in actual preparation for writing.

During composing, the teacher observes children's ability to alternate behavior between writing and reading their compositions. The teacher observes pauses in the composing process and tries to determine if these pauses are signs of thinking and rereading or the result of confusion or frustration. If the latter is the case, the teacher notes if this confusion or frustration leads the child to seek help in the form of outside resources including the teacher and other children.

In the revision stage, the teacher checks to see if the child has reread the first draft prior to sharing it with others. Also, the teacher notes the amount and quality of the child's participation with peers during peer conferencing when drafts are read and critiqued. The teacher is alert to whether the child incorporates changes that the group suggests into the next draft.

Children's final versions indicate how successful the writing process is. The teacher has general criteria in mind to evaluate writing. Questions such as the following focus on the purpose for writing and the intended audience rather than on setting a grade for the child:

Did the child communicate the intended message?

Did the child communicate in a way that appealed to the reader?

Did the child communicate in a way appropriate for the intended audience?

When teachers and children read and talk about writing, these general criteria become a framework for children to evaluate their own work and that of others. In this type of evaluation, children learn to improve their writing by writing and by receiving feedback relevant to the content of the specific piece of writing. The type and extent of the feedback varies depending on the developmental level and writing experience of the child.

Unfortunately, teacher responses to writing all too often tend to focus primarily on form (structure and mechanics) rather than content. Learning the structure and mechanics of writing is a developmental process that occurs as a continuing refinement of the whole process of composing and that should occur as part of an environment focused on meaning. The teacher's initial response to children's writing should center on the purpose for which learners are using language and the message that the language conveys and not on the language itself (Searle & Dillon, 1980).

Teachers may respond to the content of student writing while students are composing, during student-teacher conferences, or after projects are complete either by responding orally or by writing their comments for students to read. During the composing stage, teachers should always make themselves available and may comment or question students as their writing progresses. Individual teacher-student conferences are an excellent opportunity to react to the message that the writer has conveyed, either after a first draft or after revision. Comments such as "Something like that happened to me recently," or "I think John would enjoy reading this," focus on content in contrast to comments like, "I see you are beginning to use quotation marks," or "You should look up these words and spell them correctly," which emphasize form. Teachers who respond to children's work by writing their comments have an opportunity to model good writing—both in content and form. Teachers should write on a page separate from the student's writing so as not to interfere with other audiences who may read the composition. In their comments, teachers may write a personal reaction to the ideas, they may relate an experience similar to the one described, they may suggest that the writing be submitted to a class or school publication, or they may request more information about or clarification of a particular aspect of the paper. Teachers should not note children's errors in the structure and mechanics of writing (grammar, punctuation, capitalization, spelling) on the children's writing. The teacher notes such information separately and uses it to help in planning strategy lessons on these aspects of writing.

Individual writing folders should be a part of every writing program and are a necessary component of carrying out evaluation within the framework described. These folders contain all of a child's writing and teacher's written responses to writing. They may include notes and ideas for future writing. Maintaining folders allows teachers and children to look at work over time to determine growth and specific needs. Both can choose to trace the growth of writing over time by examining a series of writings, or they may choose to compare two samples of writing from different points in time. The folders also provide a way for children to reread their writings as a form of self-evaluation, or children may read each other's folders as a form of peer evaluation.

When teachers plan for writing experiences and evaluate children's writing, they always keep in mind the background and experiences of the child and the requirements of the specific writing situation. At the same time they need to be aware of the criteria by which the work of proficient

Table 16.1 Standards for Judging Proficient Writing

Narrative Writing

Story Structure	Story Setting	Story Characters	Story Conversation	Story Idea
Identifiable beginning, middle, and end. Characters introduced and problem presented. Characters and problem well-developed with appropriate conversational or descriptive detail. Story ends with believable resolution of problem.	Time and place of story clearly set. Specific details related to setting given in appropriate context. Setting consistent throughout.	Characters believable. Descriptive or conversational detail develops character personality. Action of characters relates to problem. Major characters more fully developed than minor ones.	Conversation appropriate to story circumstances and to personality of each character. Conversation used to reveal character and develop inter-relationships among characters. Conversation clearly relates to story.	Story idea is fresh or imaginative. Story plot is well-developed, is consistent, and comes to a satisfying, surprising, or otherwise highly effective ending.

Expository Writing

Quality of Ideas	Quality of Organization	Selection of Words	Structure of Sentences	Structure of Paragraph
Ideas relevant to the topic, fully developed, rich in thought and imagination, and clearly presented.	Introduction, development, and conclusion well-structured, complete, and easily identified. Emphasis of major and minor points well-balanced. Sentences and paragraphs clearly related by transitions. Logical forward movement.	Facility and flair in word selection. Writer experiments with words in unusual and pleasing ways. Figurative language used, often in interesting and imaginative ways.	Sentence length and structure varied. Sentences consistently well-formed. Smooth flow from sentence to sentence. Run-on sentences and sentence fragments rarely appear.	Topic sentences stated and supported with relevant details. Appropriate variety used in ordering details (chronological, spatial, climactic). Four types of paragraphs used when appropriate (narrative, explanatory, descriptive, persuasive).

Mechanics of Writing

Grammar and Usage	Punctuation	Capitalization	Spelling
Grammatical conventions of inflections, functions, modifiers, nouns, pronouns, and verbs observed. Grammatical errors infrequent.	Sentences consistently end with appropriate punctuation. Internal punctuation and other less common punctuation usually correctly used.	First word of a sentence and the pronoun *I* always capitalized. Well-known proper nouns nearly always capitalized. Good command of other capitalization rules regarding titles, languages, religions, and so on.	Nearly all words spelled correctly. Shows an independent spelling level (90%). Approaches 100% accuracy in edited work. Misspellings close to correct spellings.

Source: Adapted from *Language structure and use.* Teacher's Edition Grade 8 by Ronald L. Cramer and others. Copyright © 1981 by Scott, Foresman and Company. Reprinted by permission.

writers is judged. As children develop in writing and begin to become proficient writers, teachers use these criteria along with knowledge about their children in planning for writing experiences and determining areas for specific instruction. Figure 16.1 describes the standards for judging proficient writing within the categories of narrative and expository writing. The mechanics of writing are essentially the same for both types of writing.

In looking at this table you will notice that the relationship between reading and writing stands out. The writer must include the same characteristics highlighted as important in constructing meaning from print. As children increase their proficiency as writers, they become better readers and, conversely, as they increase their understanding of the reading process, this knowledge helps them to develop their proficiency as writers (Cramer, 1982).

Summary
This chapter discusses writing as part of the communication process. We describe the different functions of writing and discuss various audiences for student writing. The chapter discusses the writing process including prewriting, composing, and revising activities and the evaluation of children's writing, with an emphasis on improving children's writing as the goal.

17

Parents
and Reading

Parents and Schools

The Role of the School
IMPROVING COMMUNICATION
EXPANDING PARENTS' KNOWLEDGE
UTILIZING PARENTS IN THE SCHOOL

Community-Based Parent Programs

Summary

We cannot conclude a book about teaching reading from a language-thinking approach without highlighting the importance of parents and the home environment. Learning, feelings about learning, and using language in learning are rooted in early experiences at home. Parents, siblings, other family members, and caretakers influence a child's cognitive development, language development, and affective development. All experiences and particularly experiences with language and print are important in children's development as language users and readers. Since parents have actively participated in their children's learning for at least five years, the role of parent as partner in the child's education should continue as children enter and progress through school.

This chapter will discuss the relation of parents and schools, the role of the school in fostering parent-school relations, and the role of community-based programs in supporting parental involvement in the language and reading activities of their children.

Parents and Schools

In considering parents' relations with the school, we must recognize that parents are not a cohesive group. Parents have their own backgrounds of experiences, their own needs, and their own interests that will affect the ways in which they relate to schools.

For some parents, school is a familiar and comfortable environment. They have positive attitudes toward schooling and consider their role in the education of their children as a natural extension of their role at home. These parents expect to be involved in school activities and anticipate close working relationships with their children's teachers. Their attitudes and understandings enable them to be active participants in their children's education in a way that complements the school's learning program. Other parents fully support the goals of the school but feel culturally distanced from the school and, therefore, may be uninvolved. Many of these parents see schools as fulfilling their aspirations for their children, but these parents are personally unable to participate in the formal education of their children. They may not understand how schools work, they may view the schools as the authority, they may believe that they are unable to influence the school, and in some cases they may be unaware that they should be involved in school policies and planning. Some other parents view schools as an institution over which they can exercise their authority. Although these parents may believe that involvement in the education of their children is their main concern, their personal needs tend to influence them more than the educational needs of their children. These personal needs will be different for different people and may include the need to have a public forum, the need to have status in the community, the need to show power over authority, and the need to control others. These parents may try to dominate school decision-making and, despite good intentions, may often be in conflict with some of the goals of their children's teachers.

These descriptions of parents' behaviors and attitudes only sample the many different ways that parents may behave in their relations with schools. Teachers will meet parents ranging from those who find it easy to work in concert with the schools to those who do not see themselves as having any role in their children's formal education.

Just as parents have attitudes and understandings about teachers and schools, teachers also have feelings and beliefs about their children's parents. Some teachers view parents as partners in children's learning and encourage parents' active participation in ongoing classroom and school activities. At the other end of the continuum, some teachers view parents as difficult and interfering, and tend to want to restrict parents' involvement in the school. In cases where parents feel culturally distant from the school, some teachers will accept this feeling and do little to encourage parent participation, whereas others will attempt to improve relations between these parents and the school.

Teachers will vary in their attitudes and behavior toward parents, and relationships with parents will reflect the wide range of feelings and beliefs that both teachers and parents bring to their school interactions. Teachers, parents, and children all gain from a cooperative relationship between parents and school. Parents are valuable resources for the teacher in sharing information about children that affects the learning situation. Parents are the best source of information in helping a teacher learn about a child's experiences, interests, culture, and specific needs. Also, parents are important educational resources when they provide out-of-school experiences for their children that support the learning program and when they participate in ongoing in-school activities that broaden the learning experiences for all children.

At the same time that parents are helping teachers, the parents themselves benefit. The school is a valuable resource for parents. They learn more about their children by observing them in learning situations, they increase their understanding of the educational program and how they can best support it with out-of-school activities, and they expand their own growth as they interact with teachers, administrators, specialists, other parents, and children. Through ongoing interactions teachers and parents increase their trust and respect for each other and learn to serve as resources for each other in the education of their children.

The Role of the School

Extending parent-school relations involves the coordinated efforts of administrators, teachers, and parents. Joint planning is the first step. A planning group consisting of interested parents and school personnel begins by exploring the needs, attitudes, and interests of parents and teachers as they relate to the school reading program. Some important questions for the group to answer include the following:

How do teachers feel about parent involvement in the schools?

How do parents perceive their roles in the school?

What knowledge do parents have about the development of children's language and reading?

What additional information would be helpful to parents?

What are some ways of disseminating this information?

How can parents serve as a resource for the school and teachers?

Questions like these help the planning group focus on the background, needs, attitudes, and interests of both teachers and parents. A challenge for this group is to involve those who at present do not participate in school activities. Another challenge is to keep those parents who are involved but may be working at cross-purposes to the group. The group's efforts should be to redirect these parents' energies toward working cooperatively in areas that the planning group has set as goals.

Although schools differ in their need to expand parent-school relations, some common goals all schools should attempt to implement are

1. to improve communication between school and home;
2. to expand parents' knowledge of language and reading development;
3. to utilize parents as supportive of school programs.

We will briefly describe some ways to implement each of these goals.

IMPROVING COMMUNICATION
A major concern of the school and the parents is the quality of communication between home and school. In establishing a communication network between parents and schools, realizing that neither parent may be available during the day is important. Therefore, a communication network should include written communications, telephone communications, evening group meetings, individual conferences, daytime parent-teacher conferences, and a school resource room for parents. Written communications range from personal notes between parents and teachers to regular newsletters. Teachers and parents too often limit personal notes to times when there is a problem. The use of personal notes from the teacher to the home should include information about the child that a parent might want to know, a suggestion for a particular out-of-school experience that would support school learning, positive comments about school performance, or the titles of two or three books that the parent might borrow from the library for oral reading. Class or school newsletters are an excellent way of disseminating information regularly. The content of these newsletters varies but may include descriptions of home activities that would expand children's use of language; an annotated bibliography of books children

enjoy reading; children's writing such as poems, short stories, riddles, and jokes; and a listing of community activities of interest to parents.

An important opportunity for communicating with parents is the individual parent-teacher conference. A major factor in having parents attend is scheduling conferences at a time that is convenient for parents. Time must be available both early and late in the day for parents who cannot come to school during regular school hours. Teachers should schedule conferences well in advance and parents should confirm appointments. Teachers need to be well-prepared for these conferences so they can discuss the class program, describe children's progress, make suggestions for parent support, be ready to answer any questions that may arise, and, when necessary, refer parents to outside resources.

Telephone communication is another way of reaching parents to relay important information or on occasion to take the place of a parent-teacher conference. Parents can use the telephone to establish their own communication network and may set up a system to relay messages.

Another way to communicate with parents and help parents share ideas is to set up a parent resource room. This room should be in a comfortable space within the school building and should have informational material from library and education sources.[1] This room provides a place for parents to meet informally, to read and discuss materials, to discuss problems or concerns, and to post messages of information about school or community events. Some parents may use this setting for ongoing parent groups concerned with different topics and issues.

Some communities are exploring the use of closed circuit or cable television as another means of reaching parents. Television can broaden parents' background on various topics, highlight events in the local school, present children's work, and announce important school and community information.

EXPANDING PARENTS' KNOWLEDGE

In conjunction with ongoing communications, some specific activities can increase parents' knowledge of children's language and reading. Parent workshops, parent visits to classrooms, reading conferences, and book fairs are examples of such activities. The school holds workshops periodically, planned around topics of interest to parents. In planning a workshop, the school should consider an accessible location for the meeting, a convenient time for parents, interesting speakers, adequate publicity, and provisions for child care. All of these factors encourage attendance. General topics of concern for all parents include establishing a home environment that encourages reading, developing oral and written language competence, supporting specific school language and reading activities, and

---

[1]Some good materials for parent resource rooms are available from The Children's Book Council, 67 Irving Place, New York, NY; The National Council of Teachers of English, 1111 Kenyon Road, Urbana, Ill.; and The International Reading Association, 800 Barksdale Road, P.O. Box 8139, Newark, Del.

implementing activities that use reading in day-to-day experiences. Seminars or workshops can generate specific topics from among these and related areas based on the interests and needs of the school's parents. The planning group may also refer to references directed to parents to aid in topic selection. Some publications also provide lists of activities to encourage parent involvement (see appendix for references).

In addition to these resources, the International Reading Association publishes brochures for parents on specific topics ranging from the preschooler to the adolescent. Schools can order these brochures in quantity for distribution at parent workshops.

Once parents show interest in the language and reading program of their school-age children, workshops and related activities can also focus on the needs of their preschool-age children. All activities highlight the importance of family involvement in preparing even very young children for school experiences. The emphasis is on talking with and listening to children, the value of early storytime experiences, and the importance of using books and toys specifically created to encourage infants and toddlers to explore their environment through the different senses.

Another component of a coordinated school-home effort includes parent observations of the class so they can increase their familiarity with the classroom reading program. These visits enable parents to become familiar with the day-to-day classroom requirements and routines and the language-and-reading program and to see how their children function in school. To avoid any unnecessary misunderstandings, preparations for visits should include discussions of the feelings and attitudes of teachers and parents about having parent observers in the classroom. Visits can be scheduled or flexible depending on school and individual teacher preferences. For these visits to be effective, planned periods for follow-up discussions of what parents have observed must take place with teachers and administrators. These discussions should focus on questions that parents may have about the classroom reading program as well as how the home can support the program. Repeated visits at different points in the school year enable parents to see their children's progress and how teachers are implementing long-range goals.

Schools also hold school- or district-wide reading conferences for parents. Conferences are another way to expand parents' knowledge of the reading process, to stimulate them to support school reading programs, and to provide them with specific activities that they can use with their children in the home and community. Conferences give parents an opportunity to increase their background knowledge by hearing experts in the field and speakers from community institutions. Specialists in language and reading, children's book authors, and individuals from local universities, museums, libraries, and other community agencies may also share their knowledge. And programs can include workshops and demonstrations by teachers, students, and parents. These meetings are a way for parents to meet people from different schools and districts. These interactions provide parents with opportunities to learn and to share ideas. A book fair is an important addition to any conference because it gives parents an opportunity to buy books for their children as well as for themselves. Parents' modeling of interest in books and reading behaviors is an important part of a child's reading growth.

UTILIZING PARENTS IN THE SCHOOL
Parents can enhance the classroom language-reading program by serving as resource people for special purposes, by contributing their time to assist the classroom teacher on an ongoing basis, and by supplying classes with special books or materials related to a topic of study.

In order for parents to serve effectively as resources in the classroom, teachers need to know parents' interests, backgrounds, and areas of expertise. With this knowledge teachers can invite specific parents to participate in special classroom activities. Parents can share their knowledge by describing their jobs, their hobbies, their travels, and other experiences. Parents with special expertise or talent can perform or demonstrate skills relevant to particular content areas. In some cases parents may invite children to visit places of business and serve as guides for the visit.

Parents who can assist the teacher on an ongoing basis are particularly valuable because they can become part of the regular program. Important ways they can assist in language and reading activities include speaking and listening to children, recording their language experiences, and reading aloud to individuals and small groups. Having parents in the classroom serves as a bridge between the school and the community. Parents reflect the culture of the community and provide important models for the community's children.

When there is ongoing communication between parents and teachers, parents often become important sources of materials relevant to the classroom program. Teachers can notify parents of their needs, and parents have an opportunity to expand the resources of the classroom.

Community-Based Parent Programs
In planning for parent involvement, the teacher should be alert to community-based projects that can support the school program. Local libraries and universities may sponsor special programs for parents that can supplement school-based programs. For example, in the late 1970s the Children's Book Council (1980) funded a series of programs developed to increase parents' participation in their children's reading. Some of these programs illustrate the diversity of experiences that can help parents.

Three programs involve local libraries. In Los Angeles, California, the public library offered a series of 10 half-hour sessions focusing on integrating children's books into family life in the children's library room. The sessions took place at noontime so that persons employed in the area could spend their lunch hour hearing specialists talk on topics such as, "The Rewards When Parents and Grandparents Share Books with Children,"

"How to Develop Reading Habits in the Home," "How TV Can Help Your Child's Reading," and "Getting to Know Your Child's School Library." Local newspapers ran weekly announcements of the events. Each session was independent of the others, and the library staff prepared and distributed book lists relating to each topic. Books were available for purchase as well as circulation. The slogan of the program was "Books and Kids Need Each Other." Out of this series a core group of participants evolved who continued monthly meetings to discuss children's books.

In Boise, Idaho, the public library, the Children's Reading Roundtable, and a local bookshop cooperatively developed a program specifically directed at fathers. They sponsored a series of monthly meetings to discuss books that participating fathers had read to their children. Discussions centered on the children's and fathers' reactions to the shared story experience. A total of 46 fathers, approximately 12 per session, from diverse backgrounds participated. As part of the project fathers received two free books that they selected from 81 available titles; the fathers could obtain all titles from the library or could purchase them at a local bookstore. At the conclusion of the year-long project after an evaluation, a committee of three fathers organized to improve the program. They developed a new format to allow the fathers themselves to administer the program.

The Orlando, Florida, public library developed a program aimed at new mothers in cooperation with eight area hospitals. They developed a booklet entitled, "Catch 'em in the Cradle," which new mothers received in hospital maternity wards. The booklet consisted of a cover letter emphasizing the importance of talking, singing, and reading to infants and young children; a list of books for very young children, a list of books for parents on parenting, child care, and children's reading; descriptions of finger games; directions for making simple puppets to represent story characters; and descriptive information about the library and its services. The library supplemented this information by offering a program at the library entitled, "You, Your New Baby, and the Library." In addition, this library had a short film, "What's So Great About Books," available nationally for parent programs.

"The Book Bag," a literature program for young children through teenagers in Galveston, Texas, took a different approach. Its focus was on bringing books and book talks into the home. The organizers of this program arranged to visit homes in the community, sharing information, and making books available for purchase. In addition, the group hosted a three-day book fair at a local school.

A cooperative effort between Wright State University in Celina, Ohio, and a local television station resulted in the development of four short television programs. These programs examined the value of reading to and with children, book selection, reading techniques, and follow-up activities. The producers designed these programs for local showings on cable TV and at PTA and Headstart meetings. Currently two commercial television stations are considering broadcasting the programs. In addition, the university invited parents to attend workshops and distributed packets of materials on reading and children's books.

The funded projects we have described exemplify how community-based programs can support home and school activities. Teachers, administrators, and parents can use community-based projects to supplement their own efforts and adapt ideas for use in the schools. Children's interests in books and competence in reading will expand as adults in their environment share a common concern for children's language-reading development. Adults working cooperatively to make books an important part of children's lives help children to understand that reading is an important lifetime activity.

Summary
The chapter emphasizes the importance of parent participation in the schools. We discuss the role of the school in expanding parent involvement in schools and focus on improving communication between home and school, increasing parents' background knowledge about language and reading, and present ways to involve parents in the ongoing school program. The chapter also discusses community-based programs that support school language and reading programs to alert teachers to resources that may be available in their communities.

A Final Word

In the last decade, research has provided us with a model of reading based on language-thinking processes in which children construct meaning from print. Our expectation is that educators will continue this line of research and maintain the basic model. We believe that the information in this text will serve as a foundation from which you will be able to build new knowledge from findings in the field. Our hope is that you will then adjust and expand your theory of communication as you continue to teach language and reading.

Because learning is a dynamic process, rethinking what you know and applying knowledge consciously are continual processes. Applying the information that we have presented, therefore, is only a beginning. Only you, the classroom teacher, using a hypothesis-testing framework can decide what works for you and your children. What is important is that your theory and practice are congruent with each other and consistent with your children's ideas about reading and learning.

Some of the children you teach or will teach may already understand that reading is communication and that they are active participants in the process. Others may not have arrived at this view of reading. These children may think of reading as deciphering individual letters and words; and they expect that if they can break the code, understanding the ideas will follow automatically. They do not yet understand that their task as active participants in the process is to construct meaning by relating what they know to the ideas the author wishes to communicate, by relating ideas in the text to each other, and by reacting critically to ideas. Children's reading behavior will reveal their implicit theories of reading.

As teachers who understand your children's reading behavior, you will decide which reading instruction is appropriate for moving your children toward a language-thinking concept of reading. The decisions you make every day reflect what you know about children's cognitive and affective development, the process of reading, and the specific needs of your students. Our goal in writing this book was to provide you with information that will help you in your decision-making process and stimulate you to read and explore additional resources in the field.

Among the resources available to you are reading education textbooks and journals and publications from professional organizations. The International Reading Association (IRA), the National Council of Teachers of English (NCTE), the National Reading Conference (NRC), and the National Conference for Research in English (NCRE) are among the groups that publish timely journals, monographs, and books. They also sponsor local, regional, and national meetings for professionals in the field. Sharing ideas and materials with colleagues is an invaluable resource: You have the opportunity to explore new ideas, discuss problems, and share successful language/reading activities. Other interactions, more local in nature, with school-based personnel, parents, and community leaders provide excellent opportunities for expanding your understanding of children's language and learning needs.

You, too, may become a valuable resource. Applying current research and reading theories in your classroom yields important information to those professionals who are not in the classroom on a regular basis. You should share with others information about how different children respond to specific reading practices. By assessing your children's learning and adjusting your teaching to their needs, you generate important information. Your value will depend on your ability to record and disseminate this information. Researchers and teacher educators want feedback from the classroom to enable them to modify their theories and to suggest improved classroom practices. Your participation in professional meetings and publications in teacher magazines and journals will enrich the field. In this way, you will join with others to enlarge the community of professionals who are concerned with children's reading and learning growth. We welcome your active involvement.

Appendix:
Sources of Information

Ecology Unit

Animal Research
Conservation Center
Bronx Zoo
Bronx, New York 10460

Canadian Wildlife Federation
1673 Carling Avenue
Ottawa, Ontario
Canada K2A 1C4

National Audubon Society
950 Third Avenue
New York, New York 10022

National Wildlife Federation
1412 16th Street N.W.
Washington, D.C. 20036

New York Zoological Society
Southern Boulevard
Bronx, New York 10460

The Defenders of Wildlife
1244 19th Street N.W.
Washington, D.C. 20036

Zoological Society of San Diego
Balboa Park
San Diego, California 92101

Parents and Reading

Butler, D. & Clay, M. *Reading begins at home.*
Exeter, N.H.: Heinemann Educational
Books, 1982.

Ervin, J. *How to have a successful parents and
reading program.* Newton, Mass.: Allyn &
Bacon, 1982.

Gordon, I.J., & Breivogal, W.F. (Eds.). *Building effective home-school relationships.* Boston:
Allyn & Bacon, 1976.

Larrick, N. *A parents' guide to children's reading.* Garden City, N.Y.: Doubleday, 1980.

Sartain, H.E. (Ed.). *Mobilizing family forces for
world- wide reading success.* Newark, Del.:
International Reading Association, 1981.

Smith, C.B. *Parents and reading.* Newark, Del.:
International Reading Association, 1971.

Professional Organizations

International Reading Association
800 Barksdale Road
P.O. Box 8139
Newark, Delaware 19711
(302) 731-1600

National Conference on Research in English
ERIC Clearinghouse
1111 Kenyon Road
Urbana, Illinois 61801
(217) 328-3870

National Council of Teachers of English
1111 Kenyon Road
Urbana, Illinois 61801
(217) 328-3870

National Reading Conference
1070 Sibley Tower
Rochester, New York 14604
(716) 546-7241

Selected Readings

The Reading Process: Theory and Application

Allen, P.D., & Watson, D.J., (Eds.). *Findings of research in miscue analysis: Classroom implications.* Urbana, Ill.: ERIC Clearinghouse on Reading and Communication Skills and National Council of Teachers of English, 1976.

Presents the concepts and assumptions underlying the oral reading miscue research and discusses implications for instruction. The contributors to this volume were all involved directly in the research that led to the development of the miscue analysis technique.

Anderson, R.C., Spiro, R.J., & Montague, W.E. (Eds.). *Schooling and the acquisition of knowledge.* Hillsdale, N.J.: Lawrence Erlbaum Associates, 1977.

Proceedings of a conference that focused on the influence of prior knowledge on learning from educational experiences. The questions addressed included: How is knowledge organized? How does knowledge develop? How is knowledge retrieved and used? What instructional techniques promise to facilitate the acquisition of new knowledge?

Halliday, M.A.K., & Hansan, R. *Cohesion in English.* London, Eng.: Longman, 1976.

A theoretical presentation of those elements that the authors have identified as distinguishing text from a disconnected sequence of sentences. Understanding the concept of cohesion and the specific elements that unify a text is important background information for teachers as they plan specific teaching strategies to help their students relate the ideas in a text.

Langer, J.A., & Smith-Burke, M.T. (Eds.). *Reader meets author/bridging the gap: A psycholinguistic and sociolinguistic perspective.* Newark, Del.: International Reading Association, 1982.

A series of articles that examines how comprehension is affected by what the reader brings to text, the manner in which text is structured, and the contextual variables that shape the meaning a reader derives from text. Theory and research are presented as well as implications for practice.

Resnick, L.B., & Weaver, P.A. (Eds.). *Theory and practice of early reading,* Volumes I, II, III, Hillsdale, N.J.: Lawrence Erlbaum Associates, 1979.

A collection of readings that explores important theoretical and practical information about current issues in early reading instruction. Topics included are the nature of skilled reading performance, the acquisition of reading skill, and suggestions for reading instruction.

Singer, H., & Ruddell, R.B. (Eds.). *Theoretical models and processes of reading.* Newark, Del.: International Reading Association, 1976.

A comprehensive collection of research papers focusing on the reading process from a variety of perspectives. Articles are organized and grouped into three areas: processes of reading, models, and teaching and research. The volume is designed to stimulate theory formulation and further research in each of these areas.

Spiro, R.J., Bruce, B.C., & Brewer, W.F. (Eds.). *Theoretical issues in reading comprehension.* Hillsdale, N.J.: Lawrence Erlbaum Associates, 1980.

A collection of papers that brings recent developments in several disciplines to the study of reading comprehension. The focus is on cognitive processes involved in reading comprehension from the perspective of linguistics, artificial intelligence, cognitive psychology, and reading education.

Cognitive and Affective Development

Anglin, J.M. (Ed.). *Jerome S. Bruner: Beyond the information given.* New York: W.W. Norton, 1973.

A collection of Jerome S. Bruner's major ideas on the psychology of knowing. The papers represent his work in the areas of cognition, development, and education. The most fundamental theme is Bruner's concern with the process of knowing, with what we do with the information, and how we go beyond it to achieve insight, understanding, and competence.

Clark, M.S., & Fiske, S.T. (Eds.). *Affect and cognition.* Hillsdale, N.J.: Lawrence Erlbaum Associates, 1982.

A series of papers stemming from the Carnegie Symposium on Cognition that brought cognitive and social psychologists together. These theoretical papers include research on the cognitive underpinnings of affect, the interaction of affect and cognition, and the emotional influences on cognition. The contributors to this book emphasize the important interactions between affect and thought and discuss the need for increasing our understanding of the relation of these factors.

Flavell, J.H. *Cognitive development.* Englewood Cliffs, N.J.: Prentice-Hall, 1977.

An introductory textbook about human cognitive development with an emphasis on Piaget's work. The major landmarks of general mental growth from birth to adulthood are described including the child's growing intellectual mastery of the social and nonsocial environment. Included are the areas of perception, communication, and memory that reflect the book's emphasis on a broader rather than a narrower view of cognition.

Hetherington, E.M., & Parke, R.D. (Eds.). *Contemporary readings in child psychology.* New York: McGraw-Hill, 1981.

A series of articles focusing on recent findings, methods, and theories of child psychology. Infants and children are viewed as competent, active, and influential in their own development. The important relationship between cognitive and social development is recognized. In general, the articles aim to describe the nature of the child's development and to explain the processes that account for the developmental progression.

Sigel, I.E., & Cocking, R.R. *Cognitive development from childhood to adolescence: A con-* ·

structivist perspective. New York: Holt, Rinehart and Winston, 1977.

This book provies a review of Piagetian theory and the author's interpretation of how it is relevant to education. The growth patterns presented by Piaget are described in detail. There is a focus on the interrelationship of language and cognitive growth as well as the social and communication aspects that stimulate cognitive development. The authors conclude with a discussion of some aspects of the Piagetian framework that need elaboration, revision, or further explication.

Language

Language and learning: Investigations and interpretations. *Harvard Education Review,* Reprint Series No. 7, 1972. Cambridge, Mass.: Harvard University.

A collection of essays that focuses on the relationship between language and pyschology. Theoretical viewpoints and research on children's acquisition and use of language are presented.

Lindfors, J.W. *Children's language and learning.* Englewood Cliffs, N.J.: Prentice-Hall, 1980.

Introductory material about fundamental concepts and questions about language are presented and related directly to the concerns of the classroom teacher. Because the theoretical framework is linked to real classroom situations the book is useful in planning for language instruction.

Reading, language and learning. *Harvard Education Review.* August 1977, 47 (3), Cambridge, Mass.: Harvard University.

A special issue devoted to the interrelationships of reading, language, and learning and their implication for educational practices. Considers all levels of reading from a variety of theoretical viewpoints.

Smith, B.E., Goodman, K.S., & Meredith, R. *Language and thinking in school* (2nd. ed.). New York: Holt, Rinehart & Winston, 1976.

Explores the relationships among language, thought processes, and education. Both theoretical positions and practical applications appear within the framework of a language-thinking view of teaching and learning.

Trough, J. *Talking, thinking, growing*. New York.: Schocken Books, 1974.

Demonstrates the importance of child-adult communication to build language resources for the child and to develop strategies for learning. Illustrates concepts with many examples of children communicating with family members, teachers, and other children.

Learning and Teaching

Aulls, M.W. *Developing readers in today's elementary school*. Boston: Allyn & Bacon, 1982.

An introductory text presenting both traditional and recent views of the reading process and reading instructional practices. Provides in-depth coverage for teaching reading in the primary and intermediate grades with an emphasis on having teachers develop their own reasoned view of reading instruction.

Braun, C., & Froese, V. (Eds.). *An experience-based approach to language and reading*. Baltimore, Md.: University Park Press, 1977.

Presents language experience approach within a diagnostic teaching framework and relates it to content area teaching. Many practical examples, sources of information, and samples of children's work are included.

Clendening, C.P., & Davies, R.A. *Creating programs for the gifted*. New York: R.R. Bowker, 1980.

Describes gifted and talented children, administrative arrangements for special programs, and a number of model programs. Teaching activities are described in detail so that teachers may adapt some of the ideas for use in their classrooms.

Duffy, G.G., Roehler, L.R., and Mason, J. *Comprehension instruction: Perspectives and suggestions*. New York: Longman, 1983.

A series of papers that brings together new developments on both reading comprehension and instruction. The underlying philosophy is that reading is an interactive process and instruction involves teacher planning, judgment, and decision-making. Teaching is viewed as a complex cognitive process. The papers focus on what to teach in comprehension and how to teach it. The authors provide suggestions for improving instruction in reading comprehension within the framework of the realities of schools.

Goodman, Y.M., & Burke, C. *Reading strategies: Focus on comprehension*. New York: Holt, Rinehart and Winston, 1980.

A practical book applying psycholinguistic concepts to reading with specific lesson plans. Reading is placed within a language framework and the authors integrate reading instruction with listening, speaking, and writing. The specific strategy lessons provide background information for the teacher and the materials for instruction.

Hall, M.A. *Teaching reading as a language experience*. Columbus, Oh.: Charles E. Merrill, 1976.

Describes the language experience approach and identifies instructional practices that can be followed in teaching reading within this framework. The theoretical background of the language experience approach is presented briefly and is followed by practical implementation in the classroom.

Johnson, D.D., & Pearson, P.D. *Teaching reading vocabulary*. New York: Holt, Rinehart and Winston, 1978.

Provides a theoretical base for the teaching of vocabulary. Teaching suggestions are presented in the areas of basic sight vocabulary, meaning vocabulary, phonic analysis, structural analysis, contextual analysis, and the use of the dictionary and the thesaurus.

Pearson, P.D., & Johnson, D.D. *Teaching reading comprehension*. New York: Holt, Rinehart and Winston, 1978.

Presents theory and practice in the area of reading comprehension. General principles and instructional techniques can be adapted for use with either narrative or expository text. A particularly important contribution to the field is the authors' detailed discussion on the use of questioning.

Pikulski, J.J., & Shanahan, T. (Eds.). *Approaches to the informal evaluation of reading*.

Newark, Del.: International Reading Association, 1982.

A series of papers that describes in detail a considerable range of informal reading evaluation procedures. The information presented supplements the teachers' resources in the area of informal diagnosis.

Reid, D.K., & Hresko, W.P. *A cognitive approach to learning disabilities.* New York: McGraw-Hill, 1981.

Discusses implications of current research and theory on instruction of learning disabled children, including issues related to assessment and instructional planning. The book presents a discussion of content to be learned and descriptions of traditional and cognitive approaches to teaching learning disabled children. The authors advocate trying new instructional approaches in which teaching is viewed as problem solving, and learners are active and self-directed.

Smith, F. *Comprehension and learning: A conceptual framework for teachers.* New York: Holt, Rinehart and Winston, 1975.

Examines the fundamental aspects of comprehension and learning from the perspective of a cognitive psychologist. The author's basic premise is that the only effective and meaningful way in which anyone can learn is by attempting to relate new experiences to what is already known. He emphasizes that all children know how to learn and the task of teachers is to understand and build upon children's ways of learning.

Bilingualism and Bidialectalism

Simões Jr., A. (Ed.). *The bilingual child.* New York: Academic Press, 1976.

Presents theories, principles, and practical applications in the area of bilingual-bicultural education. Of particular interest is the chapter on bilingualism and learning to read that approaches the subject from a psycholinguistic perspective.

Smitherman, G. *Talkin and testifyin: The language of black America.* Boston: Houghton Mifflin, 1977.

Defines black English as comprising a set of grammatical and phonetic rules, a special lexicon, and a particular rhetorical style. When analyzing these elements, the author includes discussion about attitudes toward language. The number and variety of language examples makes this book highly readable.

Thonis, E.W. *Literacy for America's Spanish speaking children.* Newark, Del.: International Reading Association, 1976.

Describes the background of strengths and needs of Spanish speaking children in relation to language and reading programs, and alternatives for these children. Some special problems for speakers of two languages are discussed from a developmental perspective.

Williams, R.L., (Ed.). *Ebonics: The true language of black folks.* St. Louis, Mo.: The Institute of Black Studies, 1975.

This group of papers emerged from a national conference that dealt with cognitive and language development of black children. The papers include a broad range of topics of value to teachers. Articles present information such as a historical evaluation of the development of black English curriculum, formal testing for students who speak black English, and attitudes toward black English within the black community.

Wolfram, W. & Christian, D. *Dialogue on dialects.* Arlington, Va.: Center for Applied Linguistics, 1979;

Christian, D. & Wolfram, W. *Exploring dialects.* Arlington, Va.: Center for Applied Linguistics, 1979;

Wolfram, W. *Speech pathology and dialect differences.* Arlington, Va.: Center for Applied Linguistics, 1979;

Wolfram, W., Potter, L., Yanofsky, A.M. & Shuy, R.W. *Reading and dialect differences.* Arlington, Va.: Center for Applied Linguistics, 1979;

Christian, D. *Language arts and dialect differences.* Arlington, Va.: Center for Applied Linguistics, 1979.

A series of booklets covering dialect differences and specialized educational issues related to dialect. A question and answer format appears with questions representing the concerns of practitioners. Answers are based on current research information.

Writing

Bissex, G.L. *GNYS AT WRK: A child learns to write and read.* Cambridge, Mass.: Harvard Univ. Press, 1980.

A detailed case study of one child's learning to read and write, from the beginnings of literacy at age five to age eleven. The author's observations support that learning to write and read are processes shaped by more comprehensive patterns of human growth and learning: the acquisition of universals before culture-specifics, development from global to differentiated and integrated functioning, and movement outward beyond the immediate in time and space and beyond a personal perspective. The tracing of these processes provides teachers with insights about children's development.

Graves, D.H. *Writing: Teachers and children at work.* Exter, N.H.: Heinemann Educational Books, 1982.

Presents the results of the author's experiences with children as writers. Among the subjects covered are how children deal with spelling, handwriting, and revision; how they use writing conferences; and how they choose and organize topics. Includes helpful suggestions for teachers.

Gregg, L.W., & Steinberg, E.R. (Eds.). *Cognitive processes in writing.* Hillsdale, N.J.: Lawrence Erlbaum Associates, 1980.

A series of papers based on an interdisciplinary symposium on writing. The book presents theoretical approaches to the writing process, discusses current research on how people write, and describes some applications for teaching writing. The focus on process parallels in many ways current research in the field of reading comprehension. The papers also address areas for additional research in writing.

Mayher, J.S., Lester, N.B., & Pradl G.M. *Learning to write/writing to learn.* Montclair, N.J.: Boynton/Cook, 1983.

This book explains how children and adolescents learn to write and can use writing as a means of learning content in all subjects. The book is based on a process approach to writing and a developmental model of the emergence of writing abilities. Combining theory and practice, this text explains why writing should be approached developmentally and provides practical avenues for implementing this approach in the classroom, from elementary school through the freshman year of college.

Sealey, L., Sealey, N., & Millmore, M. *Children's writing: An approach for the primary grades.* Newark, Del.: International Reading Association, 1979.

Presents a brief rationale for writing along with a description of the different kinds of writing that can be expected in the elementary grades. Describes a structured approach to writing for young children in detail, presents some practical aspects for organizing writing activities, and describes a number of specific writing activities.

Smith, F. *Writing and the writer.* New York: Holt, Rinehart and Winston, 1982.

The author offers a framework for thinking about the act of writing in both theoretical and practical ways. He explores the writing act, the manner in which individuals develop and perform the various skills that enable them to write. He considers the consequences that learning to write and writing have on those who write. The creative and productive aspects of writing are a focus, with fluent writing the primary concern. Thus, thinking and process are emphasized throughout the book.

Whiteman, M.F., (Ed.). *Writing: The nature, development, and teaching of written communication, Volumes I & II.* Hillsdale, N.J.: Lawrence Erlbaum Associates, 1981.

The papers in Volume I explore writing in its many social and cultural variations and discuss the functions of writing and the effects of oral language differences on the learning and teaching of writing. In Volume II the papers explore writing as a cognitive, linguistic, and communicative process and discuss the ways in which such processes develop and can be encouraged.

Children's Literature

Cullinan, B. *Literature and the child*. New York: Harcourt Brace Jovanovich, 1981.

Discusses outstanding books of yesterday and today and offers ways they can be introduced to readers. The approach is child-centered and is based on Piagetian developmental principles, language learning research, and reader response theory. The author provides a useful guide to story selection according to the developmental level of the child. This is accompanied by a list of books to illustrate materials appropriate for different levels.

Lukens, R.J. *A critical handbook of children's literature*. Glenview, Ill.: Scott, Foresman, 1982.

A detailed presentation of the major genre of fiction with guidelines for their evaluation.

Separate chapters describe each of the story characteristics including character, plot, setting, theme, and point of view. One chapter describes and evaluates nonfiction writing. An excellent resource for the teacher in planning for instruction and in selecting materials.

Sutherland, Z., Monson, D.L., & Arbuthnot, M.H. *Children and books*. Glenview, Ill.: Scott, Foresman, 1981.

A comprehensive text for classroom teachers interested in using children's literature as part of their reading program. Presents in-depth coverage of books with specific suggestions for teaching activities. A strong developmental and language framework forms the base for the discussion of children's books. A separate chapter is devoted to discussing story characteristics, different types of books, and criteria for evaluating children's literature.

References

Allen, R.V., & Allen, C. *Language experiences in early childhood: A teacher's resource book.* Chicago: Encyclopedia Britannica Press, 1969.

Anastasiow, W.J. Cognition and language: Some observations. In J.L. Laffey & R. Shuy (Eds.), *Language differences: Do they interfere?* Newark, Del.: International Reading Association, 1973, 17–28.

Anderson, R.C. *A proposal for a center for the study of reading.* Submitted to the National Institute of Education by the University of Illinois at Urbana-Champaign and Bolt, Beranek & Newman, Inc., June 1976.

Anderson, R.C., Reynolds, R.E., Schallert, D.L., & Goetz, E.T. Frameworks for comprehending discourse. *American Educational Research Journal,* 1977, 14 (4), 367–81.

Anderson, T.H. Study strategies and adjunct aids. In R.J. Spiro, B.C. Bruce, & W.F. Brewer (Eds.), *Theoretical issues in reading comprehension.* Hillsdale, N.J.: Lawrence Erlbaum Associates, 1980.

Anderson, T.H. Study skills and learning strategies. In H. O'Neil (Ed.), *Learning strategies.* New York: Academic Press, 1978.

Anderson, T.H., & Armbruster, B.B. Studying. In P.D. Pearson (Ed.), *Handbook of reading research.* New York: Longman, 1984.

Applebee, A. *The child's concept of story.* Chicago: Univ. of Chcago Press, 1978.

Armbruster, B.B., & Anderson, T.H. The effect of mapping on the free recall of expository text. *Technical Report No. 160* Urbana-Champaign, Ill.: Center for the Study of Reading, University of Illinois, February 1980. (ERIC No. ED 182 735)

Athey, I. (Ed.). Essential skills and skill hierarchies in reading comprehension. *Report of National Institute of Education, Panel #10.* Washington, D.C.: National Institute of Education, 1976.

Athey, I. Syntax, semantics, and reading. In J.T. Guthrie (Ed.), *Cognition, curriculum, and comprehension.* Newark, Del.: International Reading Association, 1977, 71–98.

Athey, I. *Discussion of Elkind's paper: Stages in the development of reading.* Presented at the National Reading Conference, New Orleans, Dec. 1977.

Athey, I. *Thinking and experience: The cognitive base for language experience.* Paper presented at the International Reading Association, St. Louis, Mo., May 1980.

Baker, L., & Brown, A.L. Metacognitive skills and reading. In P.D. Pearson (Ed.), *Handbook of reading research.* New York: Longman, 1984.

Barnitz, J.G. Reading comprehension of pronoun-referent structures by children in grades two, four, and six. *Technical Report No. 117.* Urbana-Champaign, Ill.: Center for the Study of Reading, University of Illinois, March 1979. (ERIC No. ED 170 731)

Barritt, L.S., Kroll, B.M. Some implications of cognitive developmental psychology for research in composing. In C.R. Cooper & L. Odell (Eds.), *Research on Composing: Points of Departure.* Urbana, Ill.: National Council of Teachers of English, 1978, 49–57.

Berry, M.F. *Language disorders of children: The basis and diagnosis.* New York: Appleton-Century-Crofts, 1969.

Birnbaum, J.C. The reading and composing behavior of selected fourth- and seventh-grade students. *Research in the Teaching of English,* 1982, 16 (3), 241–60.

Bissex, G.L. *GNYS AT WORK: A child learns to read and write.* Cambridge, Mass.: Harvard Univ. Press, 1980.

Boston, B. *Characteristics of the gifted and talented.* Washington, D.C.: U.S. Office of Gifted and Talented, 1979.

Britton, J. The composing processes and the functions of writing. In C.R. Cooper & L. Odell (Eds.), *Research on composing: Points of departure.* Urbana, Ill.: National Council of Teachers of English, 1978, 13–28.

Britton, J., Burgess, T., Martin, N., McLeod, A., & Rosen, H. *The development of writing abilities (11-18).* London, Eng.: MacMillan Educational Ltd., 1975.

Brown, A.L. Metacognitive development and reading. In R.S. Spiro, B.C. Bruce, & W.F. Brewer (Eds.), *Theoretical issues in reading comprehension*. Hillsdale, N.J.: Lawrence Erlbaum Associates, 1980, 453–481.

Brown, A.L. Metacognition: The development of selective attention strategies for learning from texts. In M.L. Kamil (Ed.), *Directions in reading: Research and instruction, Thirtieth Yearbook of the National Reading Conference*. Washington, D.C.: National Reading Conference, 1981, 21–43.

Brown, A.L., Campione, J.C., & Day, J.D. Learning to learn: On training students to learn from texts. *Educational Researcher*, 1981, *10* (2), 14–21.

Brown, A.L., & Day, J.D. *Strategies and knowledge for summarizing texts: The development of expertise*. Unpublished manuscript, University of Illinois, 1980.

Brown, R. *Psycholinguistics: Selected papers*. New York: The Free Press, 1972.

Bruner, J.S. The course of cognitive growth. *American Psychologist*, 1964, *19* 1–15.

Bruner, J.S. On cognitive growth. In J.S. Bruner, R.R. Olver, & P.M. Greenfield (Eds.), *Studies in cognitive growth*. New York: John Wiley & Sons, 1966.

Bruner, J.S. The growth of representational processes in childhood. In J.M. Anglin (Ed.), *Jerome S. Bruner: Beyond the information given*. New York: W.W. Norton, 1973, 313–323.

Bruner, J.S., Goodnow, J.J., & Austin, G.A. *A study of thinking*. New York: John Wiley & Sons, 1956.

Burke, C.L. Preparing elementary teachers to teach reading. In K.S. Goodman (Ed.), *Miscue analysis: Applications to reading instruction*. Urbana, Ill.: National Council of Teachers of English and ERIC Clearinghouse on Reading and Communication Skills, 1973a, 15–29.

Burke, C.L. Dialect and the reading process. In J.L. Laffey & R. Shuy (Eds.), *Language Differences: Do they interfere?* Newark, Del.: International Reading Association, 1973b, 91–100.

Burke, C.L. Oral reading analysis: A view of the reading process. In W.D. Page (Ed.), *Help for the reading teacher: New directions in research*. Urbana, Ill.: National Conference on Research in English and ERIC Clearinghouse on Reading and Communication Skills, 1975, 23–33.

Cameron, N. *Personality development and psychopathology*. Boston: Houghton Mifflin, 1963.

Carroll, J.B. Words, meaning, and concepts. *Harvard Educational Review*, 1964, *34*, 178–202.

Cazden, C.B. *Child language and education*. New York: Holt, Rinehart & Winston, 1972.

Children's book council parent activities committee report. New York: The Children's Book Council, 1980.

Ching, D.C. *Reading and the bilingual child*. Newark, Del.: International Reading Association, 1976.

Chomsky. C.S. *The acquisition of syntax in children from 5 to 10*. Cambridge, Mass.: MIT Press, 1969.

Clark, C.M., & Yinger, R.J. Research on teacher thinking. *Research Series No. 12*. East Lansing, Mich.: The Institute for Research on Teaching, Michigan State University, April 1978.

Clark, H.H., & Clark, E.V. *Psychology and language: An introduction to psycholinguistics*. New York: Harcourt Brace Jovanovich, 1977.

Clark, H.H., & Haviland, S.E. Comprehension and the given—new contrast. In R.O. Freedle (Ed.), *Discourse production and comprehension*. Norwood, N.J.: Ablex Publishing, 1977.

Coltins, A., & Gentner, D. A framework for a cognitive theory of writing. In L.W. Gregg & E.R. Steinberg (Eds.), *Cognitive processes in writing*. Hillsdale, N.J.: Lawrence Erlbaum Associates, 1980, 51–72.

Collins, A., & Smith, E.E. Teaching the process of reading comprehension. *Technical Report No. 182*. Urbana-Champaign, Ill.: Center for the Study of Reading, University of Illinois, September 1980. (ERIC No. ED 193 616.)

Cramer, R.L. Informal approaches to evaluating children's writing. In J.J. Pikulski & T. Shanahan (Eds.), *Approaches to the informal evaluation of reading*. Newark, Del.: International Reading Association, 1982, 80–93.

Cramer, R.L., Wellesfeder, C., Lim, L., McCarthy T., Najimy, N.C., Prejza Jr., J., & Triplett, D. *Language structure and use, grade 8 (teacher's edition)*. Glenview, Ill.: Scott, Foresman, 1981.

Crystal, D. *Child language, learning, and linguistics*. London, Eng.: Edward Arnold Publishers, 1976.

Cullinan, B.E. *Literature and the child*. New York: Harcourt Brace Jovanovich, 1981.

Cunningham, P.M. Teacher's correction responses to black-dialect miscues which are non-meaning-changing. *Reading Research Quarterly*, 1977, 12 (4), 637–653.

del Prado, Y. Bilingual-multicultural education: A definition. In M.P. Douglass (Ed.), *Claremont Reading Conference, Thirty-Ninth Yearbook*. Claremont, Ca.: The Claremont Reading Conference, Claremont Graduate School, 1975, 101–106.

Doake, D.B. *Book experience and emergent reading behavior*. Paper presented at the International Reading Association, Atlanta, Ga.: April 1979.

Durrell, D. *Speech to print phonics, manual*. New York: Harcourt Brace Jovanovich, 1972.

Earle, R.A. Reading and mathematics: Research in the classroom. In H.A. Robinson & E.L. Thomas (Eds.), *Fusing reading skills and content*. Newark, Del.: International Reading Association, 1969, 164–170.

Erikson, E.H. *Childhood and society*. New York: W.W. Norton, 1963.

ERS Report. *Procedures for textbook and instructional materials selection*. Arlington, Va.: Educational Research Services, 1976.

Escalona, S.K. Mental health, the educational process, and the schools. *American Journal of Orthopsychiatry*, 1967, 37 (1), 1–4.

Fasold, R., & Wolfram, W. Some linguistic features of Negro dialect. In R. Fasold & R. Shuy (Eds.), *Teaching Standard English in the inner city*. Washington, D.C.: Center for Applied Linguistics, 1970.

Federal Register, Gifted and Talented Children's Education Act. Washington, D.C.: October 1978.

Flavell, J.H. Concept development. In P.H. Mussen (Ed.), *Carmichael's manual of child psychology* (Vol. 1). New York: John Wiley & Sons, 1970, 983–1060.

Flavell, J.H., & Wellman, H.M. Metamemory. In R.V. Kail, Jr., & J.W. Hagen (Eds.), *Perspectives on the development of memory and cognition*. Hillsdale, N.J.: Lawrence Erlbaum Associates, 1977.

Frederiksen, C.H. Representing logical and semantic structure of knowledge acquired from discourse. *Cognitive Psychology*, 1975a, 7, 371–458.

Frederiksen, C.H. The effects of context-induced processing operations on semantic information acquired from discourse. *Cognitive Psychology*, 1975b, 7, 139–66.

Frederiksen, C.H. Discourse comprehension and early reading. In L. Resnick & P. Weaver (Eds.), *Theory and practice in early reading*. (Vol. 1). Hillsdale, N.J.: Lawrence Erlbaum Associates, 1979, 155–86.

Freud, A. *Normality and pathology in childhood: Assessments of Development*. New York: International Universities Press, 1965.

Furth, H.G. Research with the deaf: Implications for language and cognition. *Psychological Bulletin*, 1964, 62, 145–62.

Gallagher, J.J. The gifted child in elementary school. In W. Dennis & M.W. Dennis (Eds.), *The intellectually gifted: An overview*. New York: Grune & Stratton, 1977.

Genette, G. *La littérature selon Borges*. Paris, France: L'Herne, 1964, 323–27.

Gibson, E.J., Pick, A., Osser, H., & Hammond, D. The role of grapheme-phoneme correspondence in the perception of words. *American Journal of Psychology*, 1962, 75, 554–70.

Glass, G.G., The teaching of word analysis through perceptual conditioning. In J. Figural (Ed.), *Reading and inquiry*. Newark, Del.: International Reading Association, 1965.

Glass, G.G. *Glass analysis for perceptual conditioning*. Garden City, N.Y.: Adelphi Univ. Press, 1973.

Glass, G.G., & Burton, E.H. How do they decode? Verbalizations and observed behaviors of successful decoders. *Education*, 1973, 94, 58–64.

Gleitman, L.R., & Rozin, P. Teaching reading by use of a syllabary. *Reading Research Quarterly,* 1973, *8* (4), 447–83.

Good, T.L., & Brophy, J.E. *Looking in classrooms* (2nd ed.). New York: Harper & Row, 1978.

Goodman, K.S. Analysis of oral reading miscues: Applied psycholinguistics. *Reading Research Quarterly,* 1969a, *5* (1), 9–30.

Goodman, K.S. Dialect barriers to reading comprehension. In J.C. Baratz & R.W. Shuy (Eds.), *Teaching black children to read.* Washington, D.C.: Center for Applied Linguistics, 1969b, 14–28.

Goodman, K.S. Psycholinguistic universals in the reading process. In F. Smith (Ed.), *Psycholinguistics and reading.* New York: Holt, Rinehart & Winston, 1973, 21–27.

Goodman, K.S. The reading process. In S.S. Smiley, & J.C. Towner (Eds.), *Sixth western symposium on learning: Language and reading.* Bellingham, Wash.: Western Washington State College, 1975, 19–28.

Goodman, K.S. What we know about reading. In P.D. Allen & D.J. Watson (Eds.), *Findings of research in miscue analysis: Classroom implications.* Urbana, Ill.: ERIC Clearinghouse on Reading and Communication Skills and National Council of Teachers of English, 1976, 57–70.

Goodman, K.S., & Buck, C. Dialect barriers to reading comprehension revisited. *The Reading Teacher,* 1973, *27* (1), 6–12.

Goodman, K.S. & Goodman, Y.M. Learning to read is natural. In L.B. Resnick & P.A. Weaver (Eds.), *Theory and practice in early reading* (Vol. 1). Hillsdale, N.J.: Lawrence Erlbaum Associates, 1979, 137–54.

Goodman, Y.M., & Burke, C.L. *Reading miscue inventory manual.* New York: Macmillan, 1972.

Gough, P. One second of reading. In J.F. Kavanaugh & I.G. Mattingly (Eds.), *Language by ear and by eye.* Cambridge, Mass.: MIT Press, 1972, 331–58.

Graves, D. An examination of the writing processes of seven-year-old children. *Research in the Teaching of English,* 1975, *9* (3), 227–41.

Guidelines for selecting bias free textbooks and storybooks. New York: Council on Interracial Books for Children, 1980.

Guilford, J.P. Three faces of intellect. *American Psychologist,* 1959, *14,* 469–79.

Guilford, J.P., & Merrifield, P.R. The structure of intellect model: Its uses and implications. *Reports from the Psychological Laboratory.* University of Southern California, No. 24, 1960.

Gumperz, J.J. & Hernandez-Chavez, E. Bilingualism, bidialectalism, and classroom interaction. In C.B. Cazden, V.P. John, & D. Hymes (Eds.), *Functions of language in the classroom.* New York: Teachers College Press, 1972, 84–108.

Haley-James, S.M., & Hobson, C.D. Interviewing: A means of encouraging the drive to communicate. *Language Arts,* 1980, *57* (5), 497–502.

Hall, M.A. *Teaching reading as a language experience.* Columbus, Oh.: Charles E. Merrill, 1976.

Halliday, M.A.K. *Explorations in the functions of language.* London, Eng.: Edward Arnold Publishers, 1973.

Halliday. M.A.K. Learning how to mean. In E.H. Lenneberg & E. Lenneberg (Eds.), *Foundations of language development* (Vol. 1). New York: Academic Press, 1975, 239–65.

Halliday, M.A.K., & Hasan, R. *Cohesion in English.* London, Eng.: Longman, 1976.

Harste, J.C., & Burke, C.L. A new hypothesis for reading teacher research: Both the teaching and learning of reading are theoretically based. In P.D. Pearson (Ed.), *Reading: Theory, research and practice, Twenty-sixth Yearbook of the National Reading Conference.* Clemson, S.C.: The National Reading Conference, 1977, 32–40.

Harste, J.C., Burke, C., & Woodward, V.A. Children's language and world: Initial encounters with print. In J.A. Langer and M.T. Smith-Burke (Eds.), *Reader meets author/bridging the gap: A psycholinguistic and sociolinguistic perspective.* Newark, Del.: International Reading Association, 1982, 105–131.

Harvey, O.J., Hunt, D.E., & Schroder, H.M. *Conceptual systems and personality organization.* New York: John Wiley & Sons, 1961.

Havighurst, R.J. Conditions productive of superior children. *Teachers College Record,* 1961, 62, 524–31.

Hayes, D.A., & Tierney, R.J. Developing reader's knowledge through analogy. *Reading Research Quarterly,* 1982, 17 (2), 256–80.

Hayes, J.R., & Flower, L.S. Identifying the organization of writing processes. In L.W. Gregg & E.R. Steinberg (Eds.), *Cognitive processes in writing.* Hillsdale, N.J.: Lawrence Erlbaum Associates, 1980, 3–30.

Herber, H.L. *Teaching reading in content areas.* Englewood Cliffs, N.J.: Prentice-Hall, 1978.

Hittleman, D.R. *Developmental reading: A psycholinguistic perspective.* Chicago: Rand McNally, 1978.

Holland, N.N. *Poems in persons: An introduction to the psychoanalysis of literature.* New York: W.W. Norton, 1973.

Hook, J.N. *Writing creatively.* Boston: D.C. Heath, 1963.

Huey, E.B. *The psychology and pedagogy of reading.* Boston: MIT Press, 1974.

Hunter, Grudin, E. *Literacy.* New York: Harper & Row, 1979.

Husselriis, P. IEPs and a whole-language model of language arts. *Topics in Learning and Learning Disabilities: Instruction in Reading Comprehension* 1 (4), Aspen Systems Corporation, 1982, 17–21.

Hutson, B.A., & Shub, J. *Developmental study of factors involved in choice of conjunctions.* Paper presented at the annual meeting of the American Educational Research Association, Chicago, April 1974.

Ives, J.P., Bursuk, L., & Ives, S. *Word identification techniques.* Chicago: Rand McNally, 1979.

Jakobson, R. Closing statement: Linguistics and poetics. In T.A. Sebeok (Ed.), *Style in language.* Cambridge, Mass.: MIT Press, 1960.

Jakobson, R., & Halle, M. *Fundamentals of language.* The Hague: Mouton, 1956.

Johnson, D.D., & Pearson, P.D. *Teaching reading vocabulary.* New York: Holt, Rinehart & Winston, 1978.

Joiner, C.W. *The Ann Arbor Decision.* Arlington, Va.: Center for Applied Linguistics, 1979.

Jones, W.V. *Decoding and learning to read.* Portland, Ore.: Northwest Regional Educational Laboratory, 1970.

Kaminsky, S. Bilingualism and learning to read. In A. Simões, Jr. (Ed.), *The bilingual child: Research and analysis of existing educational themes.* New York: Academic Press, 1976, 155–71.

Kendler, T.S. An ontogeny of mediational deficiency. *Child Development,* 1972, 43, 1–17.

Kintsch, W. *The representation of meaning in memory.* Hillsdale, N.J.: Lawrence Erlbaum Associates, 1974.

Kintsch, W. On modeling comprehension. *Educational Psychologist,* 1979, 14, 3–14.

Kintsch W., & van Dijk, T.A. Toward a model of text comprehension and production. *Psychological Review,* 1978, 85, 363–94.

Klausmeier, H.J., Ghatala, E.S., & Frayer, D.A. *Conceptual learning and development: A cognitive view.* New York: Academic Press, 1974.

Klausmeier, H.J., & Goodwin, W. *Learning and human abilities: Educational psychology.* New York: Harper & Row, 1975.

Klausmeier, H.J., & Ripple, R.E. *Learning and human abilities: Educational Psychology.* New York: Harper & Row, 1971.

Koppenhaver, A.H. The affective domain: No afterthought. In M.P. Douglass (Ed.), *Claremont reading conference, Fortieth Yearbook.* Claremont, Ca.: The Claremont Reading Conference, Claremont Graduate School, 1976, 103–13.

Krathwohl, D.R., Bloom, B.S., & Masia, B.B. *Taxonomy of educational objectives, Handbook II: Affective domain.* New York: David McKay, 1964.

LaBerge, D., & Samuels, S.J. Toward a theory of automatic information processing in reading. *Cognitive Psychology,* 1974, 6, 293–323.

Labov, W. *The study of nonstandard English.* Champaign, Ill.: National Council of Teachers of English, 1970.

Labuda, M. *Creative reading for gifted learners: A design of excellence.* Newark, Del.: International Reading Association, 1974.

La Fontaine, H. Testimony presented in hearings on Title VII ESEA legislation held by the subcommittee on Education, Arts, and Humanities of the United States Senate Committee on Human Resources. Washington, D.C., October 20, 1977.

Langer, J.A. Facilitating text processing: The elaboration of prior knowledge. In J. Langer & M.T. Smith-Burke (Eds.), *Reader meets author/bridging the gap: A psycholinguistic and sociolinguistic perspective.* Newark, Del.: International Reading Association, 1982, 149–62.

Laosa, L.M. Bilingualism in three United States Hispanic groups: Contextual use of language by children and adults in their families. *Journal of Educational Psychology,* 1975, *67* (5), 617–27.

Lenneberg, E.H. Of language knowledge, apes, and brains. *Journal of Psycholinguistic Research,* 1971, *1,* 1–29.

Lukens, R.J. *A critical handbook of children's literature.* Glenview, Ill.: Scott, Foresman & Co., 1982.

Mackworth, J.F. Some models of the reading process: Learners and skilled readers. In F.B. Davis (Ed.), *The literature of research in reading with emphasis on models.* East Brunswick, N.J.: Iris Corporation, 1971.

Mandler, J.M. & Johnson, N.S. Remembrance of things passed: Story structure and recall. *Cognitive Psychology,* 1977. *9,* 111–51.

Marland, S.P. *Education of the gifted and talented.* Office of Education, Washington, D.C.: U.S. Government Printing Office, 1972.

Marshall, N., & Glock, M.D. Comprehension of connected discourse: A study into the relationships between the structure of text and information recalled. *Reading Research Quarterly,* 1977, *14* (1), 10–56.

Martin, N., D'arcy, P., Newton, B., & Parker, R. *Writing and learning across the curriculum, 11–16.* London, Eng.: Ward Lock Educational, 1976.

McNeill, D. *The acquisition of language.* New York: Harper & Row, 1970.

Melmed, P.J. Black English phonology: The question of reading interference. In J.L. Laffey & R. Shuy (Eds.), *Language differences: Do they interfere?* Newark, Del.: International Reading Association, 1973, 70–85.

Menzel, P. The linguistic bases of the theory of writing items for instruction stated in natural language. In J.R. Bormuth (Ed.), *On the theory of achievement test items.* Chicago: Univ. of Chicago Press, 1970.

Meyen, E.L. *Exceptional children and youth.* Denver, Col.: Love Publishing, 1982.

Meyer, B.J.F. *The organization of prose ands its effects on memory.* Amsterdam: North-Holland Publishing, 1975.

Meyer, B.J.F. The structure of prose: Effects on learning and memory and implications for educational practice. In R.C. Anderson, R. Spiro, & W.E. Montague (Eds.), *Schooling and the acquisition of knowledge.* Hillsdale, N.J.: Lawrence Erlbaum Associates, 1977, 179–200.

Meyers, R.S., Banfield, B., & Gastón-Colón, J. *EMBERS: Stories for a changing world.* New York: The Council on Interracial Books for Children, 1983.

Meyers, R.S., & Ringler, L.H. Teacher interns' conceptualization of reading theory and practice. In M.L. Kamil & A.J. Moe (Eds.), *Perspectives on reading research and instruction, Twenty-Ninth Yearbook of National Reading Conference.* Washington, D.C.: National Reading Conference, 1980, 238–42.

Minimum teaching essentials, grades K-9. New York: Board of Education of the City of New York, 1979.

Nappi, A.T., Luksetich, W., & Dawson, G.G. *Learning economics through children's stories.* New York: Joint Council on Economic Education, 1978.

Nash-Webber, B. Anaphora: A cross-disciplinary survey. *Technical Report No. 31.* Urbana-Champaign, Ill.: Center for the Study of Reading, University of Illinois, April 1977. (ERIC No. ED 144 039)

National Advisory Committee on Handicapped Children. *First annual report, special education for handicapped children.* Washington, D.C.: U.S.O.E., Department of Health, Education and Welfare, 1968.

Nava, A.R., & Sancho, A.R. Bilingual education: Una hierba buena. In M.P. Douglass (Ed.), *Claremont Reading Conference, Thirty-Ninth Yearbook*. Claremont, Ca.: The Claremont Reading Conference, Claremont Graduate School, 1975, 113–18.

Ortony, A. Some psycholinguistic aspects of metaphor. *Technical Report No. 112*, Urbana-Champaign, Ill.: Center for the Study of Reading, University of Illinois, January 1979. (ERIC No. ED 165 115)

Ortony, A., Reynolds, R.E., & Arter, J.A. Metaphor: Theoretical and empirical research. *Technical Report No. 27*, Urbana-Champaign, Ill.: Center for the Study of Reading, University of Illinois, March 1977. (ERIC No. ED 137 752)

Ortony, A., Schallert, D.L., Reynolds, R.E., & Antos, S.J. Interpreting metaphors and idioms: Some effects of context on comprehension. *Technical Report No. 93*, Urbana-Champaign, Ill.: Center for the Study of Reading, University of Illinois, July 1978. (ERIC No. ED 157 042)

Pearson, P.D. The effects of grammatical complexity on children's comprehension, recall, and conception of certain semantic relations. *Reading Research Quarterly*, 1974–1975, *10* (2), 155–92.

Pearson, P.D. *Scripts, texts, and questions*. Paper presented at the National Reading Conference, Atlanta, Ga. December 1976.

Pearson, P.D., & Johnson, D.D. *Teaching reading comprehension*. New York: Holt, Rinehart & Winston, 1978.

Pearson, P.D., Raphael, T., TePaske, Nm & Hyser, C. The function of metaphor in children's recall of expository passages. *Technical Report No. 131*, Urbana-Champaign, Ill.: Center for the Study of Reading, University of Illinois, July 1979. (ERIC No. ED 174 950)

Perl, S. The composing processes of unskilled college writers. *Research in the Teaching of English*, 1979, *13* (4).

Piaget, J. *The origins of intelligence in children.* New York: International Universities Press, 1952.

Piaget, J. *Language and thought of the child.* London, Eng.: Routledge & Kegan Paul, 1960.

Piaget, J. Development and learning. In R.E. Ripple & V.N. Rockcastle (Eds.), *Piaget rediscovered: A report of the conference on cognitive studies and curriculum development.* Cornell University, Ithaca, N.Y.: 1964.

Piaget, J. Intellectual evolution from adolescence to adulthood. *Human Development*, 1972, *15*, 1–12.

Reder, L.M. The role of elaboration in the comprehension and retention of prose: A critical review. *Review of Educational Research*, 1980, *50* (1), 5–53.

Reid, D.K. Genevan theory and the education of exceptional children. In J.M. Gallagher & J.A. Easley (Eds.), *Knowledge and Development, (Vol. 2): Piaget and Education.* New York: Plenum, 1978.

Reid, D.K., & Heresko, W.P. *A cognitive approach to learning disabilities.* New York: McGraw-Hill, 1981.

Report of the Animal Research and Conservation Center. New York Zoological Society, 1980.

Rhodes, L.K. Comprehension and predictability: An analysis of beginning reading materials. In J.C. Harste & R. Carey (Eds.), *Monographs in language and reading studies: New perspectives in comprehension.* Bloomington, Ind.: Univ. of Indiana, 1979.

Robinson, F.P. *Effective study* (Rev. ed.). New York: Harper & Row, 1961.

Ruddell, R.B. *Reading-language instruction: Innovative practices.* Englewood Cliffs, N.J.: Prentice-Hall, 1974.

Rumelhart, D.E. Notes on a schema for stories. In D.G. Bobrow & A.M. Collings (Eds.), *Representation and understanding: Studies in cognitive science.* New York: Academic Press, 1975.

Rumelhart, D.E. Toward an interactive model for reading. *Technical Report No. 56*, Center for Human Information Processing. San Diego, Ca.: University of California, 1976.

Sapir, E. *Language.* New York: Harcourt Brace Jovanovich, 1921.

Sarason, S.B. *The culture of the schools and the problem of change.* Boston: Allyn & Bacon, 1971.

Schank, R.C. The role of memory in language processing. In C.N. Cofer & R. Atkinson (Eds.), *The nature of human memory.* San Francisco: Freeman, 1975.

Searle, D., & Dillon, D. Responding to student writing. What is said or how it is said. *Language Arts,* 1980, *57* (7), 773–81.

Shapiro, T., & Perry, P. Latency revisited: The age 7 plus or minus 1. In R.S. Eissler, A. Freud, M. Kris, & A.J. Solnit (Eds.), *The Psychoanalytic Study of the Child.* New Haven, Conn.: Yale Univ. Press, 1976, 79–105.

Shavelson, R.J. Teachers' decision making. In N.L. Gage (Ed.), *The psychology of teaching methods.* The National Society for the Study of Education, Chicago: University of Chicago Press, 1976.

Shuy, R.W. Speech differences and teaching strategies: How different is enough? In R.E. Hodges & E.H. Rudorf (Eds.), *Language and learning to read.* New York: Houghton Mifflin, 1972, 55–72.

Shuy, R.W. Vernacular black English: Setting the issues in time. In M.F. Whiteman (Ed.), *Reactions to Ann Arbor: Vernacular black English and education.* Arlington, Va.: Center for Applied Linguistics, 1980.

Simons, H.P., & Johnson, K.R. Black English syntax and reading interference. *Research in the Teaching of English,* 1974, *8* (3), 339–58.

Sims, R. What we know about dialects in reading. In P.D. Allen & D.J. Watson (Eds.), *Findings of research in miscue analysis: Classroom implications.* Urbana, Ill.: ERIC Clearinghouse on Reading and Communication Skills and National Council of Teachers of English, 1976, 128–31.

Sims, R. Dialect and reading: Toward redefining the issues. In J.A. Langer, & M.T. Smith-Burke (Eds.), *Reader meets author/bridging the gap: A psycholinguistic and sociolinguistic perspective.* Newark, Del.: International Reading Association, 1982, 222–36.

Sinclair, H.J. The role of cognitive structures in language acquisition. In E.H. Lenneberg & E. Lenneberg (Eds.), *Foundations of language development* (Vol. 1). New York: Academic Press, 1975, 223–39.

Sinclair-de Zwart, H. Language acquisition and cognitive development. In T.E. Moore (Ed.), *Cognitive development and the acquisition of language.* New York: Academic Press, 1973.

Singer, H. & Donlan D. *Reading and learning from text.* Boston: Little, Brown, 1980.

Slobin, D.I. *Psycholinguistics.* Glenview, Ill.: Scott, Foresman, 1971.

Smith, E.B., Goodman, K.S., & Meredith, R. *Language and thinking in school.* New York: Holt, Rinehart & Winston, 1976.

Smith, F. *Understanding reading.* New York: Holt, Rinehart & Winston, 1971.

Smith, F. *Comprehension and learning.* New York: Holt, Rinehart & Winston, 1975.

Smith, N.B. Cultural dialects: Current problems and solutions. *The Reading Teacher,* 1975, *29,* 137–41.

Smitherman, G. *Talkin and testifyin: The language of black America.* Boston: Houghton Mifflin, 1977.

Stein, N.L., & Glenn, C.G. An analysis of story comprehension in elementary school children. In R.O. Freedle (Ed.), *New directions in discourse processing* (Vol. II). Norwood, N.J.: Ablex Publishing, 1979, 53–120.

Sutherland, Z., Monson, D.L., & Arbuthnot, M.H. *Children and books.* Glenview, Ill.: Scott, Foresman, 1981.

Taba, H. The teaching of thinking. In R.G. Stauffer (Ed.), *Language and higher thought processes.* Champaign, Ill.: National Council of Teachers of English, 1965.

Templin, M.C. *Certain language skills in children: Their development and interrelationships.* Minneapolis, Minn.: Univ. of Minnesota Press, 1957.

Thonis, E.W. *Literacy for America's Spanish speaking children.* Newark, Del.: International Reading Association, 1976.

Thorndyke, P.W. Cognitive structures in comprehension and memory of narrative discourse. *Cognitive Psychology,* 1977, *9,* 77–110.

Tierney, R.J., Bridge, C.A., & Cera, M.J. The discourse processing operations of children. *Reading Research Quarterly,* 1978–79, *14* (4), 539–73.

Torrance, E.P., Non-test ways of identifying the creatively gifted. *The Gifted Child Quarterly,* 1962, *6* (3), 71–75.

Torrance, E.P. *Gifted children in the classroom.* New York: Macmillan, 1965.

Trabasso, T. On the making of inferences during reading and their assessment. In J.T. Guthrie (Ed.), *Comprehension and teaching: Research reviews.* Newark, Del.: International Reading Association, 1981, 56–76.

Trabasso, T., & Nickolas, D.W. Memory and inferences in the comprehension of narratives. In F. Wilkening & J. Becker (Eds.), *Information integration by children.* Hillsdale, N.J.: Lawrence Erlbaum Associates, 1980.

Trough, J. *The development of meaning.* New York: Halstead Press, 1977.

van Dijk, T.A. Semantic macro-structures and knowledge frames in discourse comprehension. In M.A. Just & P.A. Carpenter (Eds.), *Cognitive processes in comprehension.* Hillsdale, N.J.: Lawrence Erlbaum Associates, 1977, 3–32.

Venezky, R.L., & Chapman, R.S. Is learning to read dialect bound? In J.L. Laffey & R. Shuy (Eds.), *Language differences: Do they interfere?* Newark, Del.: International Reading Association, 1973, 62–69.

Vygotsky, L. *Thought and learning.* Cambridge, Mass.: MIT Press, 1962.

Walton, G. *Identification of the intellectually gifted children in public school kindergarten.* Unpublished doctoral dissertation, University of California, Los Angeles, 1961.

Warren, W.H., Nickolas, D.W., & Trabasso, T. Event chains and inferences in understanding narratives. In R.O. Freedle (Ed.), *New directions in discourse processing* (Vol. II). Norwood, N.J.: Ablex Publishing, 1979, 23–52.

Weeks, T.E. *Born to talk.* Rowley, Mass.: Newbury House Publishers, 1978.

Westby, C.E. *Children's narrative development: Cognitive and linguistic aspects.* Paper presented at the American Speech-Language-Hearing Association Convention, November 1979.

Whorf, B.L. *Language, thought, and reality.* New York: John Wiley & Sons, 1956.

Yatvin, J. A functional writing program for the middle grades. In S. Haley James (Ed.), *Perspectives on writing, Grades 1-8.* Urbana, Ill.: National Council of Teachers of English, 1981.

Yinger, R.J. *A study of teacher planning: Description and a model of preactive decision making.* Paper presented at the Annual Meeting of the AERA, Toronto, Ont.: March 1978.

References of Children's Materials

Aaron, I.E., Jackson, D., Riggs, C., Smith, R.G., & Tierney, R. Too much talk. In *Calico caper*. Scott, Foresman Basics in Reading. Glenview, Ill.: Scott, Foresman, 1978.

Abruscato, J., Hassard, J., Fossaceca, J.W., & Peck, D. (Eds.). *Elementary science*. New York: Holt, Rinehart & Winston, 1980.

Baum, F.L. The cowardly lion. In Z. Sutherland (Ed.), *Burning bright*. LaSalle, Ill.: Open Court Publishing, 1979.

Black, H. *Dirt cheap: The evolution of renewable resource management*. New York: William Morrow, 1979.

Brothers Grimm. Snow White and the seven dwarfs. In M. Carus, T.G. Anderson, & H.R. Webber (Eds.), *A magic world*. LaSalle, Ill.: Open Court Publishing, 1976.

Brandwein, P.F., Bauer. N.W., Daley, D.J., Knutson, J.N., Scott, R.W., Simpson, E.L., & Wise, M.A. *The social sciences: Concepts and values*. New York: Harcourt Brace Jovanovich, 1970.

Burningham, J. *Mr. Gumpy's motor car*. New York: Harper & Row, 1951.

Childress, A. *When the rattlesnake sounds*. New York: Coward, McCann & Geoghegan, 1975.

Clark, E. At the bottom of the sea. In *Lady with a spear*. New York: Harper & Row, 1951.

Cone, M. *Mishmash and the substitute teacher*. Boston: Houghton Mifflin, 1965.

Defoe, D. Robinson Crusoe. In M. Carus, T.G. Anderson, & H.R. Webber (Eds.), *A magic world*. LaSalle, Ill.: Open Court Publishing, 1976.

Epstein, S., & Epstein, B. *Harriet Tubman: Guide to freedom*. Champaign, Ill.: Garrard Publishing, 1968.

Fay, L., & Anderson, P.S. *Twirling parallels*. Rand McNally Reading Program. Chicago: Rand McNally, 1978.

Freedman, F. *Two tickets to freedom: The true story of Ellen and William Craft, fugitive slaves*. New York: Simon & Schuster, 1971.

George, G. *All upon a stone*. New York: Thomas Crowell, 1971.

Gordon, D. The big enormous carrot. In *Highlights for Children*. Columbus, Oh.: Highlights for Children Inc., 1974.

Hanson, B.J. Darkness by the river. In *Jack and Jill Magazine*. Indianapolis, Ind.: Saturday Evening Post, 1980.

Hasinbiller, D. Happy birthday. In R.B. Ruddell, M. Shogren & A.L. Ryle (Eds.), *Moon magic*. Pathfinder–Allyn & Bacon Reading Program. Boston: Allyn & Bacon, 1978.

Johnson, D. *Su An*. Chicago: Follett, 1968.

Johnson, J. Harriet Tubman. In *A special bravery*. New York: Dodd, Mead, 1967.

Koenig, R. *The seven special cats*. New York: The World Publishing, 1961.

Lawson, R. *Ben and me*. Boston: Little, Brown, 1939.

Leach, M. Wait till Martin comes. In *The thing at the foot of the bed and other scary tales*. New York: Philomel Books, Putnam Publishing Group, 1959.

Lindstrom, A.J. *Sojourner Truth: Slave, abolitionist, fighter for women's rights*. New York: Julian Messner,0.

McCoy, J.J. *A sea of troubles*. New York: Seabury Press, 1975.

McGovern, A. *Runaway slave, the story of Harriet Tubman*. New York: Scholastic Magazines, 1965.

Petry, A. *Harriet Tubman, conductor on the underground railroad*. New York: Thomas Y. Crowell, 1955.

Pringle, L. *This is a river: Exploring an ecosystem*. New York: Macmillan, 1972.

Pringle, L. *Energy: Power for people*. New York: Macmillan, 1975.

Reel, A. *A common bond.* In *American Junior Red Cross News.* Washington, D.C.: American Red Cross, April 1961.

Risjord, N.K., & Haywoods, T.L. *People and our country.* New York: Holt, Rinehart & Winston, 1978.

Ruddell, R.B., Crews, R., & Livo, N.J. *Free rein.* Pathfinder–Allyn & Bacon Reading Program. Boston: Allyn & Bacon, 1978.

Sterling, D. *Freedom train, the story of Harriet Tubman.* New York: Doubleday, 1954.

Swenson, M. The even sea. In *New and selected things taking place.* Boston, Mass.: Little, Brown, 1958.

Swift, H.S. *The railroad to freedom.* New York: Harcourt Brace Jovanovich, 1960.

Williams, B. The Right Answer. In *The secret name.* New York: Harcourt Brace Jovanovich, 1972.

World book encyclopedia, The. (Vol. M & Vol. 22), Chicago: World Book–Childcraft International, 1982.

Credits
and Acknowledgments

Illustration Credits

Photography by Hildegard Adler, Madison, Wisconsin.

Line art by Fred Haynes, Westbury, New York.

Teacher's handprinting by Sister Kathleen Walsh, San Diego, California.

Children's handprinting by children of St. Vincent's School, San Diego, California.

Figure 2–1 A. H. Koppenhaver, "The Affective Domain: No Afterthought," in M. P. Douglass, ed., *Claremont Reading Conference, Fortieth Yearbook.* Claremont, Calif.: Claremont College, 1976, p. 112.

Figure 12–3 By courtesy of Pfeister Barter, Inc., New York.

Figure 13–1 and 13–A From *The World Book Encyclopedia,* © 1982 World Book–Childcraft International, Inc.

Figure 13–2 Adapted from art by Norbury L. Wayman–Delineator.

Copyrights and Acknowledgments

The authors are grateful to the following publishers and copyright holders for permission to use excerpts reprinted in this book:

ALLYN AND BACON, INC. D. Hasinbiller, "Happy Birthday," from *Moon Magic* by R. B. Ruddell, M. Shogren, and A. L. Ryle in Pathfinder–Allyn and Bacon Reading Program. Copyright © 1978 by Allyn and Bacon, Inc. Reprinted with permission.

CORNELL UNIVERSITY. "Development and Learning" by J. Piaget, in R. E. Ripple and V. N. Rockcastle, eds., *Piaget Rediscovered: A Report of the Conference of Cognitive Studies and Curriculum Development.* Copyright © 1964 by Cornell University. Reprinted with permission.

COUNCIL ON INTERRACIAL BOOKS FOR CHILDREN. R. S. Meyers, B. Banfield, and J. Gaston-Colon, *Embers: Stories for a Changing World.* Copyright © 1983 by the Council on Interracial Books for Children. Reprinted with permission.

DAVID B. DOAKE. "Book Experience and Emergent Reading Behavior." Unpublished paper presented at IRA Annual Convention, Atlanta, 1979. Used with the permission of the author.

DODD, MEAD & COMPANY, INC. J. Johnston, "Harriet Tubman," in *A Special Bravery.* Copyright © 1967 by Dodd, Mead & Company, Inc. Reprinted by permission of the publisher.

FOLLETT PUBLISHING COMPANY. Doris Johnson, *Su An.* Copyright © 1968 by Doris Johnson. Used with permission of Follett Publishing Company.

HARCOURT BRACE JOVANOVICH, INC. P. Brandwein et al., *The Social Sciences: Concepts and Values,* Orange; copyright © 1970 by Harcourt Brace Jovanovich, Inc. Donald Durrell et al., abridged and adapted from *Speech to Print Phonics,* Teacher's Manual; copyright © 1972 by Harcourt Brace Jovanovich, Inc. Barbara Williams, *The Secret Name;* copyright © 1972 by Harcourt Brace Jovanovich, Inc. All reprinted with permission of the publisher.

HARPER & ROW, PUBLISHERS, INC. J. Burningham, *Mr. Gumpy's Motor Car* (Thomas Y. Crowell Company); copyright © 1973 by Harper & Row, Publishers, Inc. E. Clark, "At the Bottom of the Sea," in *Lady with a Spear;* copyright © 1951, 1952, 1953, by Eugenie Clark Konstantinu. Both reprinted by permission of Harper & Row, Publishers, Inc.

HIGHLIGHTS FOR CHILDREN, INC. Gordon, "The Big Enormous Carrot." Copyright © 1974 by Highlights for Children, Inc., Columbus, Ohio.

Author Index

Page numbers in italics refer to charts, figures, or tables.

Subject Index

Page numbers in italics refer to charts, figures, or tables.

A

Activities
(*see* Language Experience Approach, Postreading activities, Prereading activities, Writing)
Activity centers, 72–73
 criteria for, 73
Affect
 cognition and, 20, 32, 33
Affective development
 definition, 20
 early experiences and, 33–35
 general socialization principles and, 31
 implications for learning, 29, 32
 in Erikson's theory, 29–31
 in Koppenhaver's taxonomy, 33
 Language Experience Approach and, 82–83
 learner development and, 21, 29–32
 school adjustment and, 21
 societal influence on, 29–31
Affective factors
 listener/speaker interaction, 43, 44
 reader/writer interaction, 42–43, 44
Anaphoric relations
 application of, 238–40, 243–48
 common, 235–36
 decisions for teaching, 236, 240
 definition, 193
 interactive teaching, 236–39, 241–48
 preactive teaching, 234–36, 240–41
 strategy plans for teaching, 233–48
 structured questions for, 239, 240, 247–48
 teacher knowledge of, 233–34, 235–36
Assessment
 definition, 146
 evaluative stage of teaching and, 72, 74
 formal, 77

group, 221–28
hearing, 14–15
informal, 75–76, 84–93, 146
overview, 74–75, 146–48
previewing stories for, 148–52
steps in, 146–48, 149, 227–28
structured, 75, 76–77, 155–56
teacher analysis of data, 182–84
types of, 74–77
using Language Experience Approach, 85–93
vision, 15–16
(*see also* Informal Observation, Structured Assessment)
Assessment activities
 free recall, 152, 217, 218, 308
 miscue analysis, 131–33, 168–80, 181, 183
 preparation for group, 227–28
 probed recall, 217, 218
 structured questions, 72, 75, 148–49, 150–53, 303–04
Attention
 factors in maintaining, 14
 focusing, 70–71, 205, 232, 301–05
Attitudes
 reading, 21, 33, 34

B

Basal readers, 186, 188, 204
Beginning reading
 language/reading competencies, 84–85, 85
 readiness for, 20–21, 33–35, 82–84
 (*see also* Language Experience Approach)
Bidialectal learners, 372, 378–79
 Black English patterns of, 381–83, 382, 383
 observing, 383–84
 protocol of Edith, 89–93, 91, 92
 reading and, 379–81
 rejection of, 380–81
 supportive environment for, 384–85
Bilingualism
 definition, 372–73

Bilingual learners
 case study, Mayra, 9–10
 characteristics of, 372–73
 cultural values and, 373–74
 functionally illiterate, 373
 language variations, 374–75, 375, 376
 learning needs of, 373–74
 observing, 376–77
 preliterate, 373
 supportive environment for, 376–78

C

Case studies
 Cindy, an ineffective reader, 7–8
 Laurie, a successful learner, 5–6
 Mayra, a bilingual learner, 9–10
 Robert, a learner with health problems, 8–9
 Steven, an emotionally troubled learner, 6–7
Categorization, 27, 47
Causal relations
 application of, 254–56, 258–60
 decisions for teaching, 250–51, 256
 definition, 248
 interactive teaching, 251–56, 256–60
 non-signaled, 256–60
 preactive teaching, 248–51, 256
 signaled, 248–56
 strategy plans for teaching, 248–60
 teacher knowledge of, 248–50, 249–50
 types of, 248–50, 249–50
Child development
 affective factors, 20, 29–32
 Bruner's theory, 24–25
 cognitive factors, 20–26
 constructing meaning and, 26–29
 effect of experiences on, 21–22, 33–35
 Erikson's theory, 29–32